The Politics of Private Property

Political Theory for Today

Series Editor: Richard Avramenko, University of Wisconsin, Madison

Political Theory for Today seeks to bring the history of political thought out of the jargon-filled world of the academy into the everyday world of social and political life. The series brings the wisdom of texts and the tradition of political philosophy to bear on salient issues of our time, especially issues pertaining to human freedom and responsibility, the relationship between individuals and the state, the moral implications of public policy, health and human flourishing, public and private virtues, and more. Great thinkers of the past have thought deeply about the human condition and their situations—books in *Political Theory for Today* build on that insight.

Titles Published

The Politics of Private Property: Contested Claims to Ownership in U.S. Cultural Discourse, by Simone Knewitz
The Political Philosophy of the European City: From Polis, through City-State, to Megalopolis, by Ferenc Hörcher
John Locke and the Uncivilized Society: Resistance and Individualism in America Today, by Scott Robinson
Welcoming the Other: Student, Stranger, and Divine, edited by N. Susan Laehn and Thomas R. Laehn
Cosmopolitanism and its Discontents: Rethinking Politics in the Age of Brexit and Trump, edited by Lee Ward
Eric Voegelin's Asian Political Thought, edited by Lee Trepanier
The Spartan Drama of Plato's Laws, by Eli Friedland
Idolizing the Idea: A Critical History of Modern Philosophy, by Wayne Cristaudo
Eric Voegelin Today: Voegelin's Political Thought in the 21st Century, edited by Scott Robinson, Lee Trepanier, and David Whitney
Walk Away: When the Political Left Turns Right, edited by Lee Trepanier and Grant Havers
Plato's Mythoi: The Political Soul's Drama Beyond, by Donald H. Roy
Democracy and Its Enemies: The American Struggle for the Enlightenment, by Paul N. Goldstene
Tradition v. Rationalism: Voegelin, Oakeshott, Hayek, and Others, edited by Gene Callahan and Lee Trepanier
Aristocratic Souls in Democratic Times, edited by Richard Avramenko and Ethan Alexander-Davey

The Politics of Private Property

Contested Claims to Ownership in U.S. Cultural Discourse

Simone Knewitz

LEXINGTON BOOKS
Lanham • Boulder • New York • London

Published by Lexington Books
An imprint of The Rowman & Littlefield Publishing Group, Inc.
4501 Forbes Boulevard, Suite 200, Lanham, Maryland 20706
www.rowman.com

6 Tinworth Street, London SE11 5AL, United Kingdom

British Library Cataloguing in Publication Information Available

Library of Congress Cataloging-in-Publication Data Available

Names: Knewitz, Simone, 1979- author.
Title: The politics of private property : contested claims to ownership in U.S. cultural discourse / Simone Knewitz.
Description: Lanham, Maryland : Lexington Books, [2021] | Series: Political theory for today | Includes bibliographical references and index. | Summary: "The Politics of Private Property investigates the functions of private property within U.S. cultural discourse. It mobilizes property as an analytical category and examines how social and political debates from the early nineteenth to the twenty-first century have generated competing and contested claims to ownership"—Provided by publisher.
Identifiers: LCCN 2021007190 (print) | LCCN 2021007191 (ebook) | ISBN 9781793623751 (cloth) | ISBN 9781793623768 (epub)
Subjects: LCSH: Right of property—Social aspects—United States. | Right of property—Political aspects—United States.
Classification: LCC KF562 .K54 2021 (print) | LCC KF562 (ebook) | DDC 346.7304—dc23
LC record available at https://lccn.loc.gov/2021007190
LC ebook record available at https://lccn.loc.gov/2021007191

Contents

List of Figures

Acknowledgments

While working on this project, I have been very lucky to be able to count on the support of family, friends, colleagues, and institutions, without whom this study's completion would have been near impossible, and working on it certainly much less agreeable.

For institutional support, I thank the German-American Fulbright Commission and the German Association for American Studies for granting me the Fulbright American Studies Award in 2011, which enabled me to conduct research at George Mason University in Fairfax, VA, and at the Library of Congress during the early stages of this project. I am also grateful to the German Academic Exchange Service for a fellowship that brought me to George Washington University in Washington, D.C., and allowed me to spend a long block of research and writing time away from other obligations in an inspiring academic environment. I thank Richard Avramenko for including my book in his series at Lexington, and Joseph Parry and Alison Keefner for their editorial support.

At the University of Bonn, my deepest gratitude goes to my colleague and advisor Sabine Sielke, whose unwavering support, encouragement, and steadfast belief in my work continue to touch and inspire me. More than anybody else, she has stimulated and shaped my development as a scholar over the past now almost twenty years, and I am looking forward to many future years of collaboration. My dear (former) colleague Christian Klöckner has been this study's most constructive critic. I owe to him some of my best insights, and his thoughtful comments on and perceptive challenges of my arguments have certainly made this a more interesting book. Elisabeth Schäfer-Wünsche and I shared many interesting conversations on property and related topics. Katrin Dauenhauer has been a close friend since the very beginning of our student days in the North American Studies Program, now more than two decades ago. During the final stages of revising the manuscript, I have deeply enjoyed the conversations and close collaborations with Katharina Fackler. In addition to Sabine, Christian, Elisabeth, Katrin, and Katharina, my present and former colleagues at the North American Studies Program and the Department of English, American and Celtic Studies have provided not only a creative environment for academic work but also given me the privilege of working among friends: Sine Kontbay Busun, Birgit Capelle, Nils Hoffmann, Patrick Horst, Holger Janusch, Imke Lichterfeld, Nicole Meier, Andrew Pendakis, Ian Robinson, Peter Schniering, Matt Sheedy, Birgit Spengler, Klaas Staal, Justin Sully, and Henrike Viehrig. Edmunda Ferreira, Ilona Krupp, and Cornelia Commer in the office of the North American Studies Program have provided both administrative and emotional support, as did Mathilde Hüskes, Bettina Nakath, and Ulrike Rasanis in the department's main office.

In D.C. and northern Virginia, I thank Alison Landsberg, Paul Smith, and Tim Kaposy for hosting me at George Mason University, and Suleiman Osman and Melani MacAllister for their hospitality at George Washington University. I am happy to have made new friends during my stay in the D.C. area, among them Sandra Bruce, my wonderful landlady and roommate, as well as Mary and Ken Curtin, Elizabeth Hageman, Nan Raphael, Steve Sowers, and Bob Paul.

My research has benefited significantly from exchanges with other colleagues in American studies. Peter Schneck has been very supportive of this project from the beginning, and his invitation to the Osnabrück Summer School on the Cultural Study of the Law in 2011 decisively influenced the research framework of this study. I have also enjoyed the exchanges and collaborations with Stefanie Müller, Regina Schober, James Dorson, Sabine Meyer, Birte Christ, Eric Erbacher, Nicole Maruo-Schröder, Adam Hjortén, and Mai-Linh Hong. As this book started out as a thesis project for my postdoctoral lecturer qualification (*Habilitation*) at the University of Bonn, I am very grateful for the support of the colleagues who agreed to serve on my thesis committee, and for their feedback on the manuscript: Sabine Sielke, Ulfried Reichardt, Peter Schneck, Marion Gymnich, and Barbara Schmidt-Haberkamp. While finalizing the book, I had the opportunity to serve as Deputy Chair of American Studies at the University of Münster, and was very lucky to have Chris Wahlig as my extremely competent administrative assistant. Starting at a new institution—during a pandemic, no less—would have worked out much less smoothly without her guidance. Both Chris and Björn Bosserhoff provided invaluable support by diligently editing and carefully proofreading the final manuscript.

In my life beyond academia, I treasure the continued, decades-long friendship of Angela Porth, Sonja Gros, Eva Rudert, Alice Jacoby, Ina Jacoby, Myriam Krämer, and Silke Sczesny, as well as that of Olga and Sascha

Hottes. I am also very grateful that my parents, Gertrude and Rainer Knewitz, have always supported my chosen path, as well as Tobias Knewitz, Julia Gust, and Gisela Herrmann. My late grandmother, Gretel Knewitz, inspired me to take up her hobby and taught me most of what I know in the field of knitting, and much more. Finally, and most importantly, this book would not exist without my wife and partner, Ulrike Pfrengle. As all my work, I dedicate this study to her.

Introduction

In a series of images originally entitled "Just a Dream," American photographer John Francis Peters (2010) documents foreclosed homes in the state of New York in the aftermath of the 2008 financial crisis (figure 0.1). In these photographs, we see no people and we are not told any stories—the pictures depict almost completely empty spaces with inconspicuous traces of previous inhabitants, clutter left behind. Referencing the American dream of homeownership, Peters's color images focus on the forlorn spaces of forsaken homes and abandoned personal belongings, registering details of the previous owners' lives. The images mourn a loss that transcends the mere ownership of property: the empty spaces stand in for, pars pro toto, a perceived corruption of the American dream. Peters was not the only photographer who tried to make sense of the crisis this way; photojournalists and artists, including Bruce Gilden, Todd Hido, T. J. Proechel, Anthony Suau, John Moore, and many others, participated in the genre of "foreclosure photography" (Reyes 2010), zooming in with their lenses on family homes all over the country and taking stock of the social and economic consequences of the financial crisis.

Accompanied by a voiceover of original recordings of people who lost their homes, Bruce Gilden's photographic work of the time aim at giving what he calls "the common people" a voice (Gilden 2011). Unlike the quiet mournfulness of Peters's images, Gilden's photo essays, which focus on Fort Myers, Detroit, Fresno, and Las Vegas, are characterized by the anger and rage transported in the voices of the people Gilden had interviewed. In the project on Fort Myers, a woman, who had just become unemployed, relates, in tears, her fear that she will be evicted from her home and soon homeless (Gilden 2008). The images themselves are sometimes reminiscent of a war zone, featuring ruins instead of merely rundown houses. The black and

Figure 0.1 Foreclosed Home Photographed in Upstate New York: Image from John Francis Peters's Series *Foreclosed 2008–2010*. *Source*: © John Francis Peters.

white aesthetics here underlines the association with wartime destruction (figure 0.2). In the "Detroit" essay, we hear a man saying: "The American dream? This is a nightmare, this is a fucking nightmare." The dream of homeownership has apparently gone awry and reverted into its opposite. In a later instance, another agitated woman shouts: "Foreclosure and eviction is spiritually wrong. People deserve, through their constitutional right, to have a home" (Gilden 2009).

Some commentators, including Gilden himself, have compared these images to those of Depression-era photographers such as Dorothea Lange or Walker Evans (Reyes 2010; McClanahan 2017, 114–16), just as the financial crisis has been dubbed the "Great Recession," echoing the "Great Depression" of the 1930s. Gilden's black and white, documentary photo essays are certainly reminiscent of these previous works. Though some of Evans's best-known photographs in *Let Us Now Praise Famous Men* (1941) depict impoverished interior spaces of a sharecropper family's home, or a pair of well-worn boots, many of his images are portraits of the men, women, and children who lived in these spaces. Gilden's photos, which sometimes include owners in front of their foreclosed houses, perhaps most closely resemble Evans's work. Most foreclosure photographers, however, center on the materiality of the house itself. This is significant, as these images thereby direct our attention not toward the

Figure 0.2 Image from Bruce Gilden's Series *Detroit the Troubled City* (2009). *Source*: © Bruce Gilden/Magnum Photos/Agentur Focus.

plight or struggles of the people who lost their homes but to the objects they formerly owned.

Gilden employs these people's stories to create a narrative of the crisis that sharply distinguishes between profit-greedy capitalists and powerless foreclosure victims. The loss of one's home certainly constitutes a catastrophe for the individual person—the way Gilden dramatizes these foreclosures in his art, however, also assumes a larger cultural significance. For one thing, the feeling of the impotent anger evoked by his work is based on the assumption that the people were wronged and are now being denied the right to live in their own homes. Gilden does not raise the questions of whether homeownership for everybody is feasible or how the dominant U.S. self-conception of citizens as homeowners contributed to the housing bubble. While he thus does not address underlying structural problems, by turning homes and their dispossessed owners into symbols of a national crisis, he does reinforce the meaningfulness of property ownership for an American identity. Similarly, Peters's images of empty spaces nostalgically mourn the failed promise of the American dream.

As Annie McClanahan argues in her analysis of foreclosure photography, the images provide us with a complex negotiation of financialization and credit culture that goes beyond nostalgia (2017, 102–3). I am primarily interested in these representations because of how they stage and aestheticize the cultural investment in property ownership. Over the course of the twentieth century, the owner-occupied home became the quintessential form of private property in the American imagination. Single-family homes are still being glorified as spaces of personal and familial self-realization, while at the same time functioning as objects of conspicuous consumption, financial investment, and speculation. As McClanahan notes, during the period of appreciating house prices, prior to the crisis, homes were even endowed with an aura of erotic desirability, offered by design magazines and real estate TV channels as "real estate porn" (99; see also Botterill 2013, 327).

To many Americans, the ownership of a home appears as the epitome of being middle class; it augurs the civic and economic participation in a society of equal opportunity. Meanwhile, government policies and institutions provide residential real estate with a privileged status, for example through tax exemptions and subsidies. Such preferential treatment commonly relies on the argument that homeowners are better citizens—though little empirical evidence exists to support this claim (see, e.g., McCabe 2013; Glaeser 2011; S. M. Stern 2009). Prior to the bursting of the housing bubble, aspirational qualities were also intensely fueled by the government's promotion of homeownership, for example, through President George W. Bush's rhetoric of the United States being an "ownership society," which explicitly equaled property ownership with democratic participation. "If you own something in America, you own a stake in America's future," Bush proclaimed in 2002 (2005b, 311).

Viewed in terms of its economic impact on the population, the visual representation of the Great Recession as a crisis of the American dream hardly appears as an exaggeration. The foreclosure images reflect not only the cultural myth of home but also the fact that houses are the most significant economic asset for average Americans. In the aftermath of the foreclosure crisis, the median worth of households fell to the lowest level in 40 years, and "middle class wealth virtually evaporated" (Weissmann 2012). Between 2007 and 2010, median wealth in the United States dropped by 47 percent, and this decline disproportionately hit the middle 60 percent of wealth classes, due to the fact that they had invested two-thirds of their assets in their homes. For a large fraction of American families, houses are their most significant possession, yet their ownership is also rather precarious, due to high mortgage debt, which amounted to over half of home values in 2010. In comparison, the wealthiest 1 percent of Americans invested more than three-quarters of their savings in financial assets and only 9 percent in housing in that year; the next 19 percent of the wealthiest Americans invested 30 percent of their savings in housing and 41 percent in investment assets (Wolff 2013, 337–39). In relation to the upper quintile, the middle classes showed a much higher debt-equity ratio. The portfolio differences and the middle classes' larger relative indebtedness triggered a spike in wealth inequality after the financial crisis. Lower-income families were hit hardest by the crisis, not least because their investments were less diversified than those of the upper middle class (Reeves 2017, 26). As a result, in the last decades, the home as the guarantor of middle-class prosperity has become increasingly leveraged.

While homes are glorified in mythic ways within cultural discourse and constitute the most important form of property ownership for many members of American society, albeit in increasingly precarious ways, it is hardly surprising that the concepts of home and property have become closely associated in the popular imagination. Though by far the largest proportion of aggregate wealth exists in intangible forms of property, such as financial assets, property ownership, in its aspirational dimension, centers on physical objects and is associated with a host of moral qualities, such as independence, self-realization, agency, and citizenship. This raises fundamental questions about the relationship between the property in the cultural imaginary and the material distribution of wealth in the United States.

PRIVATE PROPERTY IN THE U.S. CULTURAL IMAGINARY

The Politics of Private Property addresses the gap between the pervasive U.S. self-conception as a universal middle-class society, characterized by a wide diffusion of property ownership, and the actual social reality, which is defined by unequal dissemination of wealth and race-based structures of exclusion. It investigates the role of property within the cultural imaginary, arguing that discourses and narratives about property ownership have helped legitimize, naturalize, and prolong social and economic inequality in the United States as well as promote structures of white domination. In making this argument, I depart from the established view that associates the commitment to property in the United States with cultural consensus and assigns it a merely conservative function. Instead, I mobilize property as an analytical category, to examine how social and political debates generate competing and contested claims to ownership. The property narratives arising out of political conflicts, I argue, serve the purpose of establishing and maintaining a hegemonic order, which keeps shifting and is subject to challenges.

If the home and homeownership figure centrally in the cultural understanding of property in the more recent history of the United States, this study projects a more expansive view of property discourses that reaches back into the early nineteenth century, as a way to historicize current public and political debates and to trace the trajectory of the cultural concept of private property. As I will explain in more detail below, the cultural meaning of property needs to be carefully carved out against the legal understanding of property, which, over the course of American history, transformed profoundly and has meanwhile become highly technical and specialized. While my investigation recognizes the significance of legal debates on property, its main focus is on the way the concept is mobilized by public and political discourses at specific historical moments. Within American political and cultural rhetoric, property functions as a central signifier in debates that negotiate social and institutional structures, the boundaries between the private and the public realms, and the relations between different social groups.

The finding that property holds a central place in the American cultural imagination certainly seems like a truism: generations of historians and cultural scholars of the United States have argued that American culture is animated by property ownership. For some, the commitment to property served as an explanation for the lack of any mass socialist movement in the United States and for the unique ideological coherence. In *Democracy in America*, Alexis de Tocqueville famously attributed the American devotion to property to the absence of a proletariat comparable to that in Europe, insisting: "In no other country in the world is the love of property keener or more alert than in the United States and nowhere else does the majority display less inclination toward doctrines which in any way threaten the way property is owned" ([1835] 1969, 638–39). In the Cold War America of the 1950s, Richard Hofstadter (1948), Louis Hartz (1955) and the consensus school of historians built on de Tocqueville, emphasizing that the commitment to property rights and individualism were quintessential American virtues.

In less celebratory ways, scholars situated on the political left have sought to expose the American ideology of property ownership with its notion of egalitarianism, as a fraught scheme and a hindrance to true social equality. Thus, the progressive historian Charles Beard, in his 1913 *Economic Interpretation of the Constitution of the United States*, in an almost conspiratorial tone, reproached the founders for allegedly pursuing their own economic interests at the expense of the majority of citizens—downplaying that the public rhetoric during the American Revolution was in fact quite explicit about the colonists' aim to protect their property rights (see also Condit and Lucaites 1993, 20; Ely 2008, 27). While the optimistic views of the consensus school may seem somewhat dated today, Beard's progressivism actually has more traction with contemporary scholars. Legal scholar Jennifer Nedelsky's landmark study, *Private Property and the Limits of American Constitutionalism*, has expanded in more nuanced ways on Beard's views, arguing that the founders' preoccupation with property "placed inequality at the center of American constitutionalism" (1990, 2). More recently, cultural studies scholar Paul Smith pronounced that, in the United States, "all social and cultural phenomena are dedicated to one central process, the process of capital accumulation" (2007, 42).

Sweeping statements such as the latter, however, may occlude rather than elucidate the processes and practices that drive U.S. culture. While these and many other scholars have forcefully underlined the American commitment to property, most have stopped short of explaining how, specifically, property has functioned as a mediator in the construction of social relationships and institutions in the United States. This book therefore explores how property discourses have, historically, served to naturalize and challenge specific forms of wealth distribution, social inclusions and exclusions, as well as the relationship between the state, the market, and the individual.

Developing property as an analytical category, *The Politics of Private Property* distinguishes itself from previous assessments of the meaning of property for U.S. cultural discourse by emphasizing the conflicts rather than the consensus surrounding the topic: I view property not simply as a category which serves to legitimize or cement social and economic inequalities. Instead, I investigate debates on property as a site of ongoing political contest and competing claims—the latter of which in the sense of declaring a material interest in a resource and asserting a specific discursive position. The category of property is instrumental not only for constant negotiations of the distribution of wealth but also for hegemonic interpretations of social and political structures. As the editors of a recent anthology note: "Contested property claims are [. . .] a window onto the politics of property at a given moment in a given social context, showing how social actors reason about and perform property when challenged to do so and what social justices and injustices are produced through property relations" (Bruun et al. 2017, 3).

My project ties in with current interrogations into the history of American capitalism and a renewed interest within American Studies in coming to terms with questions of economic inequality and its related structural conditions. Joyce Appleby (2010), Giovanni Arrighi (2010), and David Harvey (2005), among others, have critically interrogated capitalism as a long-arched historical phenomenon. Economic historians, geographers, sociologists, literary, and cultural scholars are presently engaged in providing nuanced understandings of slavery's crucial significance for the development of American capitalism (see, e.g., Beckert 2015; Beckert and Rockman 2016; Baptist 2016; Gavin Wright 2006; Schermerhorn 2015), the corporate revolution at the turn of the twentieth century (Zakim and Kornblith 2012; Lipartito and Sicilia 2004; Roy 1997), as well as the rise of modern consumer culture and the financialization of society during the twentieth century (Hyman 2011a; Calder 1999; McClanahan 2017; Quinn 2019). In addition, under the rubric of "new economic criticism" (Woodmansee and Osteen 1999), scholarship at the intersection of economics and literary and cultural studies has illuminated both the rhetorical and aesthetic dimensions of economic processes and the economies of literature and culture.

Investigating discourses of contested property claims in a historical perspective provides us with an opportunity to denaturalize established narratives about social processes at work in the United States, particularly with regard to issues of class. "'Property' and 'lack of property' are [. . .] the basic categories of all class situations," German sociologist Max Weber wrote in *Economy and Society* ([1922] 1978, 927). Yet, as Weber was very much aware, if property ownership directly relates to the distribution of wealth and resources in society, the meaning of property goes far beyond the category of a commodity. Property cannot be reduced to merely economic or legal aspects, but it is always connected to moral values and normative ideas, and it is instrumental for the construction of (racialized and gendered) identities and social relationships. Property thus interweaves economic and legal dimensions with questions of social justice, morality, and identity.

Property issues have been studied in a multitude of disciplinary contexts, ranging from law to economics, political science, sociology, geography, anthropology, history, philosophy, and literary and cultural studies. Yet, the property concepts employed in different fields are not necessarily compatible (Benda-Beckmann, Benda-Beckmann, and Wiber 2006, 4–10). Economics, for instance, understands property as referring to objects that function as commodities, whereas contemporary legal scholars think of property as an abstract set of rights. My work particularly draws on scholarship that has focused on the intersection between law and culture. As a highly interdisciplinary endeavor, cultural studies of the law engage in diverse approaches that reject "reified concepts of law and culture" (Coombe 1998, 21) and which conceptualize culture as a "set of shared signifying practices" that are both processual and contested; the law is recognized as one of these signifying practices and thus constitutes a part of culture (Mezey 2003, 39). This does not mean that the law becomes indistinguishable from other cultural practices—but describing legal meanings as cultural acts "emphasiz[es] the pervasive power of law and exclud[es] the possibility that there is an autonomous cultural realm that could be articulated without recourse to law" (47). Scholars working in the field have been particularly attentive to the textuality of law, focusing on narrative and rhetoric (see, e.g., Brooks and Gewirtz 1996; Sarat and Kearns 1994; Tait and Norris 2011). As Carol Rose's influential works in particular show, property regimes are enacted in a society's discursive and material practices. She highlights the legitimation of property as a communicative claim, or "persuasion" (1994, 5). These claims often take the narrative form; as a social institution, property relies on social symbols, stories, and meanings that help normalize legal and political arrangements. Taking my cue from Rose's work, my own investigation is interested in the kinds of property stories that the U.S. culture tells about itself.

CONTESTED CONCEPTIONS OF PROPERTY

The Politics of Private Property carves out how political actors have mobilized property narratives over the course of U.S. history to preserve and to challenge the status quo within social and economic power relations. It builds on the premise that property is a culturally constructed and essentially contested concept (Diamond 2011, 37). Property is protean in nature, a seemingly stable idea, but highly malleable, according to context. In the following, I will sketch the major fault lines, along which property has been conceptualized by philosophers, cultural, and legal scholars. Introducing two competing approaches—the rights-based and the utilitarian approach of justifying property arrangements—I will advance the idea that property claims in the United States bring into play the competing models of property as a natural right vs. property as a "bundle of rights," in order to defend or establish a particular social and economic order.

In a most basic understanding, the term private property "refers to a kind of system that allocates particular objects like pieces of land to particular individuals to use and manage as they please, to the exclusion of others [. . .] and to the exclusion also of any detailed control by society" (Waldron 2012). Importantly, as C. B. Macpherson has noted, "what distinguishes property from mere momentary possession is that property is a claim that will be enforced by society or the state, by custom or convention or law" (1978, 3). In this sense, to own property means to have an enforceable claim to some resource. The term "property," then, does not denote an object of possession, as a common-sense understanding presumes, but a *right to* that object. Moreover, to make a claim enforceable requires an institutional arrangement such as, in modern societies, the political constitution of the state. Therefore, property must be understood as a political phenomenon, or, more precisely, as a political relationship between persons, as "any given system of property is a system of rights of each person in relation to other persons" (4). Which specific sets of claims a society chooses to enforce is a matter of political negotiation. "Property is a form of power," Joseph Singer notes, "and the distribution of power is a political problem of the highest order" (2000, 9).

Its political nature implicates that property cannot be conceptualized merely as a legal institution, as claims become enforceable only if they correspond to a society's values. Property as an institution thus always requires a theory of justification: "The legal right must be grounded in a public belief that it is morally right" (Macpherson 1978, 11). The concept of property is therefore "strongly influenced by a metaphor and the metaphysics of the proper" (M. Davies 2007, 36). Rose and others have thus emphasized the close connection between property and propriety, that is, the social order deemed appropriate in a body politic (Rose 1994, 58; see also Alexander 1997; Blomley 2005). Accordingly, legal understandings of property, technical and specialized as they may be, are always deeply intertwined with ideas about property in the cultural imagination, though the relationship between both realms is not necessarily free of contradictions and tensions. Indeed, since specific property arrangements are always contested and subject to negotiation, property debates are also always conflicted. One of the aims of this study is to highlight precisely these conflicts in U.S. cultural discourses at paradigmatic historical moments.

Emphasizing property as the right to exclude, the discourse on property has assumed a key role in the social structure of the United States; and, in American cultural and political debates, the right to private property—as opposed to common or public property systems[1]—often appears as particularly naturalized and universalized. In this context, I am interested in the justifying theories of particular property arrangements articulated over the course of U.S. history. Both Jeremy Waldron and Joseph Singer have pointed to a general distinction between rights-based and consequentialist arguments to legitimate property regimes (Waldron 1988, 3; Singer 2014, 12–18). In rights-based schemes, property is considered an end in itself, mandated by a moral entitlement. In the consequentialist or utilitarian conception, property functions as a means for the achievement of a more basic good, such as social welfare.

The notion of a (natural) right to private property is rooted in liberal philosophy; it raises the question of whether property exists before the law or if it is a function of the law. For classical liberalism, property is central to the constitution of the citizen as a political actor and coextensive with the ideas of liberty and democracy. Indebted to the liberal tradition, not least to John Locke's arguments in his *Two Treatises of Government* (1689), property in the Anglo-American tradition has been conceptualized foremost as an individual right, often existing in a pre-social "state of nature." While both Thomas Hobbes and David Hume hold that private property comes only into being with the formation of civil society, Locke and his successor, the English legal theorist William Blackstone, argue that private property already exists prior to the introduction of civil society. For all these authors, however, the emergence of the sovereign state is intimately bound up with the question of property rights: in liberal theories, either private property becomes possible only through state institutions, or the state ultimately serves to protect private property interests, which had already existed in the prior natural state, but which can only be properly secured by the state. The institution of individual proprietary rights thus becomes a primary reason for state sovereignty. Macpherson (1962) has therefore famously described liberal-democratic theory as "possessive individualism."

Locke's theory derives private property from the premise that an individual exists in a state of nature, thereby presupposing a subject who is already constituted as an owner, and hence views private property as an integral part of subjectivity. For Locke every individual owns his own person and his own labor ([1689] 1988, Second Treatise, §27). In his narrative, the earth and all natural resources originally had to be considered common property, which all people received from God for their subsistence and enjoyment. Yet, as God also gave men "reason to make use of it [the world] to the best advantage of Life, and convenience" (Second Treatise, §26), they began to appropriate the land by mixing it with their labor, thereby adding value to the land. Blackstone's *Commentaries on the Laws of England* (1765–1770), which were instrumental in the justification of common law and the standard legal reference in the America of the late colonial and revolutionary eras (Banner 2011, 4), follow Locke by theorizing property as being one of the absolute rights of the individual (the other ones being the rights to personal security and liberty) (Blackstone [1765–1770] 1915, 1:129). These absolute rights, however, become subject to regulations that come with civil society. Blackstone does see a tension between private rights and public interests but stresses that private property rights can never be overridden for the public good. Private property rights always trump the public good; though it is possible to expropriate an owner in rare cases of public interest, by providing compensation for the loss of property (2:1–15).

In liberal theory, the natural right to private property thus marks the boundary of legitimate state action; it is based on a negative conception of individual liberty.[2] In contrast, an alternative rights-based conception in the tradition of Hegel—much less influential in the Anglo-American context—focuses on property in relation to personhood. In Hegel's *Philosophy of Right* (1820), property ownership appears as being instrumental for the individual to realize him- or herself in the world, for translating universal freedom into actual freedom. The individual becomes an objective feature of the external world by means of possessing, controlling, and owning material goods. Hegel's concept of property is all about our need to identify with and express ourselves in things that we make, control, and use. Since property, thus understood, is the very foundation of social relationships, Hegel here establishes a link between private property, personal identity, and community ([1820] 1967, §§ 41–70).[3]

The rights-based theories of property, both in the Lockean and Hegelian versions, conceive of private property ownership as an integral part of human subjectivity and personhood. Karl Marx, in comparison, while responding to both traditions, comes to very different conclusions. Marx accepts the premise that labor is the source of property, but he differentiates between private property under capitalism and a form of "truly human and social property," which would be achieved once capitalism was superseded by communism (Marx [1844] 2005, 281). Though the meaning of "true property" for Marx remains sketchy in his writings (Chitty 2013, 692), we may understand it in a sense similar to Hegel's idea of self-realization and of connecting with others. Property, for Marx, has positive connotations if it relates to use value, to "objects of enjoyment" and "objects of activity," which meet human and social needs (Marx [1844] 2005, 322). He characterized private property as "the product of alienated labor" (280), since capitalist property is meaningful only in terms of its exchange value, not its use value (Brenkert 1979, 125). In a private property system, human relationships become estranged because they are being replaced by relationships between objects. Private property reduces economic activity to individual, private needs instead of the needs of the community.

In his economic analysis, Marx built on Adam Smith's and David Ricardo's insights into political economy, as he argued that the commodified relationships under capitalism inevitably resulted in antagonistic class relationships between the owners of capital and the owners of labor, with the price of labor naturally gravitating to subsistence levels. These classes were necessarily opposed in their interests, since the logic of capitalism required the accumulation of capital, by reaping the surplus value of production, and the capitalist's increase in profits directly resulted from the increase in the worker's productivity. "The worker," Marx held, "becomes all the poorer the more wealth he produces" and "the devaluation of the world of men is in direct proportion to the increasing value of the world of things" ([1844] 2005, 271–72).

Marx called for the abolition of private property because he saw it as the source of social divisions and of people's estrangement from their human and social needs. As I will discuss in more detail in chapter 1, American socialist contemporaries to Marx, for the most part, rejected these radical implications. Instead, reformers such as Horace Greeley, the influential newspaper editor of the *New-York Tribune*, aimed to democratize private property ownership, and he believed in the possibility of harmony between the social classes. Though no large-scale socialist movement managed to take hold in the United States, the specter of socialism nevertheless has informed American debates on property rights. Significantly, the first red scare in the United States, in the early twentieth century, coincided with a major shift in the legal conceptualization of property in utilitarian terms, which may be read as a response to what was perceived as a communist threat to private property.

Rights-based justifications of property center on individual moral entitlements to economic resources; in distinction, utilitarian approaches are concerned with the maximization of welfare in a given society. Utilitarian theories insist that the institutions that regulate property in a society should be shaped to maximize society's net wealth. While this implies the possibility of wealth redistribution, utilitarians tend to eschew the abolition of private property. In fact, utilitarian arguments are often employed in defense of private property against common property regimes (Waldron 1988, 6). In a utilitarian perspective, private property is superior to other forms of property organization because it avoids what has been termed the "tragedy of the commons": according to theorists like Harold Demsetz (1967) and Garrett Hardin (1968), the main problem of a common property system is that it will lead to the overuse of commonly owned resources; if every individual has access to a resource that belongs to all at no cost, they will most likely try to achieve the largest possible private gain, while the costs will be borne by the community as a whole.

Historically, during the nineteenth century, the utilitarian conception gradually emerged from a positivist understanding of the law, most succinctly represented by the English philosopher Jeremy Bentham. Refuting the natural rights tradition, Bentham claimed that "no such thing as natural property" existed and instead stressed that property regimes were instituted and upheld by governments, which made property a legal creation ([1802] 1864, 111). In the early twentieth century, legal realists and progressives applied Bentham's premise in a more systematic formulation of property's social character. In two articles published in the *Yale Law Journal* in 1913 and 1917, legal scholar Wesley Newcomb Hohfeld formalized property as a complex web of legal rights, duties, and privileges between individuals. Using highly technical language, Hohfeld aimed to replace the thing-centered language of property discourse with one that emphasized legal relationships.

Utilitarian property theory thus considers property not as a single right but, more adequately, as a "bundle of rights,"[4] a flexible set of different entitlements whose distribution is subject to constant social and political reevaluation. If the social situation changes and a different distribution of resources becomes more desirable (i.e., promises greater social wealth), the legal property regime may change. With its focus on the well-being of society as a whole, this property theory is less interested in the individual's (affective) relationship to his or her possessions but instead assumes that all goods are, in principle, substitutable and commodifiable; moreover, it conceives of property not as things but as relations between people who are interconnected through the rights and obligations they hold. In effect, this legal understanding disintegrates the concept of property as such.

Though these different ways of justifying property rights are not logically associated with specific political positions, they have been historically related to particular policy preferences. The concept of property advanced by classical liberalism must be conceived as part of the attack on feudalism, thus serving important ideological functions in the emergence of the capitalist market system (Grey 1980, 75–76). Today, the liberal position on property is most directly advanced by political conservatives and libertarians, who tend to emphasize the economic and political freedom of the individual and who seek to limit the involvement of governments in what are conceived to be private affairs. Though from the political left attempts have been made to harness the power of individual rights—for instance, by Charles Reich's seminal attempt to define welfare entitlements as a "new property" in 1964, thereby using the individualist conception of property for egalitarian ends[5]—their success tends to be severely curtailed by the underlying assumption of property being a negative liberty. In distinction, the utilitarian conception of property as a bundle of rights was shaped during the progressive era, as a justification for stronger government regulation of economic activity, with the state playing an active role in the creation of public welfare.

The two different approaches to justifying property rights underlie two competing ways of conceptualizing property: the "ownership model" and the "bundle of rights model" (Singer 2000, 3, 10). Bruce Ackerman has suggested that the ownership model corresponds to a lay understanding of property—property as a thing—whereas the bundle of rights approach refers to the specialized idea of property in legal discourse (1977, 27). Yet, such a clear-cut distinction between the different discourses is misleading: instead, in recent court decisions—particularly Supreme Court decisions, as I will demonstrate more extensively in chapter 5—and in the larger cultural discourse, both ideas coexist and intersect (see also Nedelsky 1990, 234–35). The bundle of rights model provides the basis for the regulatory state as it has evolved over the course of the twentieth century; it constitutes the foundation for all legal property relationships. The ownership model is most pervasive in the political discourse on property, framing public debates around the question of how much government regulation is desirable or justified. "The ownership model," Singer explains, "is premised on the view that the meaning of property is clear and is not a matter of controversial political or moral judgment" (2000, 7). It is a flawed model because it posits a specific social and economic order as being natural and immutable and "misdescribes the ideals that underlie the institution of private property, as well as the legal rules that define the basic structure of property rights" (6–7). The bundle of rights model, in comparison, more adequately describes how property functions in practice, but it is similarly based on the ideal of a particular social structure that presupposes a balance between different social interests (13).

These observations underline that any attempt to define property is structured by political considerations and tends to naturalize a particular conception of the social world.

PRIVATE PROPERTY AND RACE-BASED EXCLUSION

Both the ownership model and the bundle of rights model of property envision a just social order built around individual property rights. Yet, neither approach adequately accounts for the social hierarchies, structural exclusions, and violence inherent in the concept of property. According to Nicholas Blomley, "violence plays an integral role in the legitimation, foundation, and operation of a regime of private property" (2003, 121). At the same time, "access to property [. . .] is an important predictor of one's position within a social hierarchy, affecting class, race, and gender relations" (122).[6] We thus need to clarify the ways in which property theories have served to exclude specific populations and even incorporated racialized exclusions in their core assumptions. As delineated above, the enlightenment philosophers and lawyers justified the existence of the liberal state with narratives of a social contract whose rationale was the protection of property rights. These narratives are, however, implicitly premised on and arise out of concrete, historically specific forms of exclusion of both indigenous populations and people of color.

Drawing on critical race and settler colonial theoretical investigations of property regimes helps us account for these exclusions and historicize seemingly abstract property theories. The philosopher Charles W. Mills has forcefully argued that the social contract must be recognized as a racial one, "an agreement among white contractors to subordinate and exploit non-white noncontractors for white benefit" (2008, 1381). A metaphor rather than an actual historical explanation, the idea of the social contract transports the vision of a polity built on the assumption of all people's moral equality, demanding equality of treatment in the legal, political, and economic realms. Yet, this vision denies factual systematic and structural exclusions; historically, the personhood and the rights of some persons have been disregarded (1381). If the social contract is a metaphor and a philosophical construct, Mills's racial contract refers to the actual social practices that the construct serves to legitimate.

Viewed through the lens of racialized exclusion, the concept of a "state of nature," assumed in contractual property narratives, appears less like a pre-political condition, overcome by the formation of the state, but rather like the permanent state of nonwhites. In the stories told by Hobbes, Locke, Blackstone, and others, the law enters as a force, promising order in a world determined by chaos, violence, and savagery. Law's own violence[7] becomes legitimized as the imposition of discipline and constraint and creates a frontier between the secure and stable space of the community and an uncertain outside realm. Thus, "the establishment of society [. . .] implies the denial that a society already existed; the creation of society requires the intervention of white men, who are thereby positioned as *already* sociopolitical beings" (Mills 1997, 13). The division between a pre-political state of nature and the state formed in a social contract is deeply racialized and invested in a colonial mythology that centrally depends on the figure of the savage, which mythically embodies the want of order, "untamed nature or barely contained human passion against which an ordering law is intrinsically set" (Fitzpatrick 1992, 81).

Property theories like Locke's did not come into being in a historical vacuum but arose in the context of the Anglo settler colonial world, which operated as a distinct mode of domination (Veracini 2017, 3) and premised the establishment of a new society on the systematic dispossession and elimination of the indigenous population (Wolfe 2006, 388). As Robert Nichols notes, this was "a space where state formation and market formation not only took place simultaneously [. . .] but also [. . .] in explicit opposition to Indigenous forms of life that presented radically distinct and divergent visions of the relationship between human societies and the lands on which they lived" (2020, 35). Locke famously conflated the symbolic state of nature and the geopolitical space of the New World, by claiming that "in the beginning all the World was *America*" ([1689] 1988, Second Treatise, §49), thereby helping to establish a persistent definition of that space as being virgin or empty land (Elkins and Pedersen 2005, 2). This myth of emptiness enabled settlers to construct a new society that sought to dispossess and replace existing Native American communities. In the Lockean framework, the indigenous population did not hold property rights to the land, since they had allegedly failed to appropriate it through labor and improvement. As a people, seemingly without property interests, native populations lacked the prerequisite of self-ownership and were therefore excluded from the contract formed to protect those interests, though in actuality white settlers had to acquire the land by force, in "a lengthy, diverse, and contested project of national state formation" (Frymer 2017, 2). Singer thus draws our attention to the fact that "the title of every single parcel of property in the United States can be traced to a system of racial violence. For non-Indians to claim an inalienable right to the current distribution of property rights is to claim a right to the benefits of a system of racial supremacy" (1991, 102).

A racialized conception of property provided not only the ideological basis for conquest, that is the appropriation of land from Native Americans, but also for the seizure of labor from enslaved people. Locke, who invested in African slavery and contributed to the 1669 Carolina Constitution, which granted slave owners absolute power over their human property (Mills 2008, 1382), defined slaves as "Captives taken in a just War" (Locke ([1689] 1988, Second Treatise, §85). As such, they had lost the right to their own lives and property and, hence, their status as a member of society. Following up on these claims, legal scholar Cheryl Harris has argued that not only are the concepts of property and race intrinsically intertwined but that whiteness has assumed the function of a form of property. Whiteness and property, Harris elaborates, share "a common premise—a conceptual nucleus—of a right to exclude" (1993, 1714) and they have historically interacted to establish and maintain a system of racial and economic oppression (1716). Blackness raised the presumption of slavery, whereas whiteness acted as a shield from slavery. With whiteness itself being turned into property, while black people were situated as objects that could be owned, property's racialized nature became enshrined in the legal and political structures of the United States.

The racialized nature of property in the United States is not merely the result of a system of oppression located in past race relationships, but it continues to be (re)produced and maintained. George Lipsitz (1998) thus speaks of a continuing "possessive investment in whiteness." Persistent social and institutional structures allow whites to profit socially and financially from advantages created by racism, thereby encouraging them to treat their whiteness as a form of property (Lipsitz 1998, vii). And this is perhaps nowhere more the case as in the area of housing and homeownership over the past hundred years. Chapters 3 and 4 will discuss in more depth the racialized housing policies implemented during the New Deal era. The material practices relating to real estate markets have resulted in a persistent segregation along the lines of race and ethnicity, and they continue to perpetuate racist structures (see, e.g., Massey and Denton 1993). Though practices of racial discrimination have changed since the 1930s, when so-called "redlining" determined the credit worthiness of neighborhoods according to their racial structure, minorities were also disproportionately hit by the 2008 foreclosure crisis: as the financial instrument of the securitized mortgage created a demand for the expansion of the pool of borrowers, banks and financial institutions turned to "subprime" customers that the markets had previously shunned. They systematically marketed predatory loans to African American and Hispanic households, "reinforc[ing] existing patterns of racial segregation and deepen[ing] the black-white wealth gap" (Rugh and Massey 2010, 632; see also Wyly et al. 2012). After the bursting of the housing bubble, foreclosures were concentrated in the minority neighborhoods that had been targeted for subprime lending. Thus, "the housing boom and the immense profits it generated frequently came at the expense of poor minorities living in central cities and inner suburbs" (Rugh and Massey 2010, 634). The continuing patterns of racial discrimination in the dissemination of property in the United States raise the question of how racial categories help produce, maintain, and transform economic practices and vice versa.

AMERICAN PROPERTY NARRATIVES

The Politics of Private Property attempts to unpack the meaning of the term "property" within U.S. public rhetoric and cultural discourse; the book sets out to investigate how property has functioned as a foundational term which structures social relationships and institutions in the United States. My study builds in particular on Ernesto Laclau's understanding of discourse, which he first advanced in his collaborative work with Chantal Mouffe in *Hegemony and Socialist Strategy* (1985) and refined in his later works, *On Populist Reason* (2005) and *The Rhetorical Foundations of Society* (2014). Laclau and Mouffe suggest that a political community emerges when "a *particular* social force assumes the representation of a *totality* that is radically incommensurable with it" ([1985] 2014, x), what they call a "hegemonic relation" (xiii). In their conception, "society" does not exist prior to discourse; the structure of a society is not predetermined to exist in a certain arrangement, but it is ordered in a specific way through the contingent articulation of interests which also determine the social identity of its elements. Social actors, occupying differential positions within discourse, establish "relations of equivalence" among themselves (xiii). Political interests are being voiced, as their particularity is structured into political antagonisms of different interests struggling for hegemony. There is no politically neutral terrain, nor is it possible to represent and reconcile all political interests or to think of society as a totality. In Laclau and Mouffe's model, all social structures are, by necessity, contingent and negotiated within the discursive field. At the same time, identities constructed in discourse are never completely fixed: while any discourse is the attempt to fixate a particular structure by excluding excessive meanings, it remains situated within a field of discursivity that acts as a repository of these additional meanings, which can enter and subvert the discourse; that is, the elements of discourse are overdetermined with a surplus of meaning. Laclau and Mouffe invoke the Lacanian notion of the *point de capiton*, what they call "nodal point" or "master-signifier," to denote "the notion of a particular element assuming a 'universal' structuring function within a certain discursive field" (xi).

Drawing on these insights, I suggest that the term "private property" is exactly such a master-signifier or nodal point: within American political and public debates the concept of property assumes a crucial structuring function for the social realm. "Property" is able to assume such a privileged function in discourse because it is a term associated with a concrete meaning—the conventional notion of "ownership of a thing"—while, at the same time, it is attributed with more abstract meanings which relate to its larger moral connotations. Property assumes meaning, synchronically, in relationship to other abstract terms, such as "freedom," "democracy," "equality," or "privacy," through its use in specific rhetorical situations. Moreover, its meaning is also circumscribed diachronically through the history of its previous uses.

In political discourse, Laclau describes abstract terms like "property" as having either "empty" or "floating" signifiers: "Empty" suggests that there is a signifier without there being something signified, while "floating" implies a surplus or overflowing of meaning (2014, 20). A signifier like "democracy" or "property" will take on floating meanings in different discourses, but these different meanings depend on a loose connection between the signifier and the signified. In a discourse on private property in the American context, "property" may be linked to "democracy," "individual rights," "freedom," and "limited government," and, as property assumes the role of a crucial component of this discourse, its meaning is determined by establishing a homology with each of the other terms associated with it. By thus creating a chain of equivalence in a web of related terms, a hegemonic formation that aims to represent a social totality is established. At various historical moments, different discursive formations are articulated to define the political field, thereby struggling for hegemony.

As I will show over the course of this study, central political and public conflicts throughout American history have been structured by the concept of property. "Private property" functions as an abstract yet enduring concept that helps negotiate, maintain, and question social and political relationships, hierarchies, and institutions, with substantial material consequences. Thus, property has been instrumental in the negotiation of significant economic, political, and cultural transformations. Studying how Americans speak about property helps us understand how specific ideas about the right social order and wealth distribution are naturalized within the society of the United States and indeed how "the social" constitutes itself.

As this book argues throughout, property narratives form a crucial part of the U.S. self-conception, and they rely on specific rhetorical strategies to normalize social and economic stratifications. Political rhetoric employs and exploits a number of culturally charged abstract terms closely associated with the idea of property. Concomitantly, political debates on property tend to reference the myths of the nation's founding, harking back to the ideals of the American Revolution and the origins of the United States, as well as to the perceived ideas of the founders and the foundational documents: the Declaration of Independence,[8] the Constitution, and the Bill of Rights.

It is therefore tempting to see the revolutionary era as the origin of the American discourse on property rights. Yet, this is a constructed beginning. Debates on property did not begin with the American Revolution, nor did the foundational documents put unchanging or unchangeable structures into place. Private property relations in the United States built upon legal institutions already erected during the colonial period and on ideas derived from Scottish political philosophy and English common law (Ely 2008, 10).[9] At the same time, U.S. property law underwent profound transformations, as the country evolved into an industrial capitalist economy over the course of the nineteenth century. The Virginia lawyer St. George Tucker, editor of the 1803 edition of Blackstone's *Commentaries*, spoke of an almost complete change in property laws in the United States during the Early Republic (see Luck 2014, 10). Contemporary legal historians have similarly stressed the significant shifts that took place at the time and characterized the development of the legal concept of property as one of increasing abstraction (Horwitz 1992a, 30). Reviewing the scholarship on property during the founding of the United States, David Schultz has pointed out that, on the level of legal institutions and judicial practice, property occupied a far less absolutist position than the rhetoric of revolution suggested and was instead subject to intense economic regulation (1993, 489).

The founding of the American nation provides a discourse on property with a central rhetorical reference point; property debates in the United States regularly invoke these beginnings in public and political contexts and in the legal system, which builds current decisions based on precedents. Thus, the political and cultural discourses on property have retained some of the thing-like qualities of property, derived from the Enlightenment ideas inscribed into the foundational documents, as well as the high significance attributed to landownership, as a principle of republicanism. In the American cultural imagination, the right to property contains an aspirational dimension that identifies property with real estate, embodied in the Declaration of Independence's famous phrase of an inalienable right to "life, liberty, and the pursuit of happiness," a variation of Locke's "life, liberty, and estates" ([1689] 1988, Second Treatise, §123). For Thomas Jefferson, the Declaration's principal author, as well as many other revolutionaries, property ownership was not an end in itself but the basis of republican government. Property equaled land for Jefferson, and the ownership of land endowed citizens with personal independence, moral virtue, and the opportunity of democratic participation (Katz 1976, 470–84).

The democratic ideal of widespread property ownership stood in tension, however, with the political and economic elite's desire to preserve established property rights. For the framers of the Constitution, the protection of property was closely associated with individual liberty and freedom from governmental coercion (Ely 2008, 43). James Madison, the principal author of the Constitution, famously wrote in *Federalist* No. 10 that "the first object of government" was "the protection of different and unequal faculties of acquiring property" (Hamilton, Madison, and Jay [1788] 2009, 48). Yet, in another place, he suggested that there were actually two "cardinal objects of government: the rights of persons, and the rights of property" (qtd. in Nedelsky 1990, 17). Madison saw an inherent tension between the rights of persons and property, as he believed that American society was divided between those with property and those without: "Property would always be at risk in a republic because it would always be vulnerable to the dissatisfaction of the (inevitable) propertyless majority; and the vulnerability of property rights revealed the nature of the republican threat to individual rights, oppression by the majority." For Madison, "the protection of property rights was essential to the stability of society and government, and stability, in turn, was necessary if republican government was to endure" (Nedelsky 1990, 25).

Recognizing the conflict between property rights and democratic participation, John Adams, in his *Defense of the Constitutions of Government*, justified the institution of a strong executive power in the new nation by pointing to the class conflict between the rich and the poor. "It must be remembered that the rich are *people* as well as the poor; [. . .] that they have as clear and as *sacred* a right to their large property as others have to theirs which is smaller," Adams warned ([1787] 1851, 65). While the legislative branch's task was to secure the rights of the people, the executive branch should shield the wealthy elite from oppression by majority rule and robbery. Emphasizing that the rich were "*people* as well as the poor," Adams rhetorically leveled the distance between the social classes, by framing their relationship in egalitarian language. Adams here exploited the polysemy of "people" with its two meanings of "persons" and "citizens" (the people): the rich, as persons, were equal to the poor and deserved, as citizens, equal political representation. The rich and the poor therefore shared the same "sacred right[s]," which included the right to own property—the difference being the size of the property they owned. Adams thus justified economic inequality by emphasizing political equality. The paradox of egalitarianism, then, is the fact that it lends itself to justifications for social inequalities and hierarchies.

Since historians and legal scholars have studied the thought and theories of the framers of the Constitution in depth,[10] it suffices here to sketch the rationales guiding the Constitutional Convention with respect to property and economic issues. The protection of property rights in the federal Constitution and the Bill of Rights built upon and reworked principles already instituted in the

Articles of Confederation as well as the state constitutions of the individual states. For all, the importance that the founders placed on property, however, in devising the federal Constitution, they did not rely on specific declarations of a natural right to property but on institutional and political arrangements, which were to limit governmental discretion in interfering with private economic rights, and on a system of checks and balances. They also did not put property qualifications for voting into place, thus allowing the individual states to impose criteria for such participation (see chapter 1). Provisions relating to property interests mainly related to the federal government's powers with regard to economic activities. Thus, the Constitution strengthened the national government by granting Congress powers of taxation, of imposing protective tariffs, and of regulating interstate and foreign commerce. At the same time, the powers of the individual states were restricted: States were no longer allowed to tax imports and exports, and they were also "prohibited from issuing bills of credit or making anything but gold or silver coin legal tender for the payment of debts" (Ely 2008, 43–45).

The protection of property in slaves constituted the Constitutional Convention's most controversial issue. With most wealth in the Southern states resting in slave property, the Southern delegates attempted to put safeguards into place that would prevent the national government from abolishing slavery. Three provisions were eventually established: Congress was prohibited to end the transatlantic slave trade until 1808; a fugitive slave clause obligated the federal government to aid the return of escaped slaves to their legal owners; and the slave states were apportioned seats in the House of Representatives for three-fifths of their slave population, guaranteeing them additional weight in the federal government (Ely 2008, 46). As chapter 2 will discuss in more detail, these provisions represented only a tenuous compromise between the so-called slave states and free states, circumventing the issue of whether the federal government, in effect, recognized slaves as a form of property. In the decades leading to the Civil War, this question became a crucial issue in political debates and structured the antagonism between the North and the South.

The Constitution's Fifth Amendment provides the only explicit reference to property rights: it includes the phrase "nor shall any person [. . .] be deprived of life, liberty, or property, without due process of law; nor shall private property be taken for public use, without just compensation." As this study will demonstrate, the Fifth Amendment constitutes the most crucial reference point for debates on property in the United States because it postulates that private property ownership marks the boundary of legitimate government action, but it simultaneously raises the question under which circumstances individual rights may be overridden: in which situations does a public benefit take precedent over private entitlements? In many instances, over the course of American history, redistributions of property were discussed through the prism of the Fifth Amendment—in relation to diverse issues such as antebellum landownership, the emancipation of slaves, or the dispossession of homeowners for private economic development. Thus, even though the American Revolution and the founding of the United States did not predetermine all subsequent property debates, the time period and its legal documents established a rhetorical framework within which property issues have been negotiated.

Establishing a long historical arch from the early nineteenth to the twenty-first century, the following chapters provide a fresh perspective on the functions of private property within U.S. cultural discourse. I will conduct rhetorical analyses of a variety of sources, which include political pamphlets and congressional speeches, newspaper and magazine articles, advertisements, Supreme Court cases, fictional and nonfictional works, as well as media representations. The selected debates highlight important developments and changes in the legal definition of property, in competition with and through the intersection of ideas on property in public and political discourses. Though *The Politics of Private Property* does not focus on real estate exclusively, debates on land- and homeownership are featured rather prominently throughout this study. One reason for this focus is that physical objects of property particularly animate the cultural imaginary. Despite—and also in reaction to—the increasing abstractness of the property concept in the legal realm, cultural debates on property tend to revolve around tangible forms of property, to which people can relate affectively. Moreover, due to the limitations of physical space, material forms of property always touch on the key problem of resource distribution. Land and homes as objects of property thus raise very different questions than, for instance, intellectual property and specifically allow us to investigate social inclusions and exclusions.

By mobilizing ideas and narratives about property, this study primarily aims to investigate how dominant political actors and discourses throughout U.S. history have managed to not only maintain hegemonic social and economic power but also ward off challenges to the status quo. The book deliberately puts a focus on the United States and does not include systematic comparisons with other nations. Nevertheless, the knowledge about the cultural meanings of property it generates may be useful to other scholars who may be making such comparisons. The contribution I seek to make is in tracing the evolution of American ideas about property over a long time span, thereby crafting a narrative about the meaning of property in U.S. life.

The Politics of Private Property shows that even though property relations have always been subject to competing claims, the particular property stories that are at the heart of U.S. cultural debates tend to appropriate and incorporate critique instead of remaining static. Private property in the United States acts as a floating signifier that serves not only those actors who seek to defend existing property relations but also those who aspire to change them, thereby oscillating between different interests. Due to the book's broad historical scope and the attention it pays to hegemonic power relations, it concentrates more on the mechanisms of exclusion inherent in dominant discourses than on giving space to the voices marginalized by these discourses. While it is highly worthwhile to explore the challenges and alternatives to the private property system of the U.S. settler colonial society, this is not the project that this book pursues. Yet, I believe that it makes a contribution that is highly compatible with such inquiries in its investigation of the structures of power and dominance.[11]

OVERVIEW

The Politics of Private Property proceeds in five chapters, spanning the time period from the early decades of the nineteenth century until the early twenty-first century, and in conclusion briefly scrutinizes the property issues of our contemporary moment. Chapter 1, "Agrarian Justice: Land, Labor, and Early Nineteenth-Century Property Discourse," establishes the foundation of this study by investigating the central representational figure of the small producer within the American cultural imaginary of the antebellum period. Here, I analyze three interrelated protest movements of wage laborers, factory workers, and tenant farmers in the northern United States, who pressed for the realization of the country's promise of egalitarian access to property. They invoked the yeoman farmer as the moral backbone of American society, while they challenged their subordinate economic positions. As the United States transitioned from a mostly agrarian into an industrial capitalist economy, with concomitant financial depressions, the workers' rhetoric notably emphasized material forms of property, which stood in tension with the development of a legal concept that redefined property in more abstract and commoditarian terms. The movement's aspirational and populist invocation of a natural right to property also significantly clashed with the request of the already propertied classes that their existing property rights receive special protection. As the chapter's final section elucidates, the rhetoric of producerism, which especially libertarians and populists continue to call up until this very day, ultimately helped to resolve—or at least mitigate—the conflict between rivaling property interests, by making public land in the West available for settlers. The workers' originally radical demands for egalitarian access to land were mainstreamed as a white middle-class endeavor that resulted in the Homestead Act of 1862.

The property conflicts in the antebellum North, discussed in chapter 1, shaped a cultural understanding of property which revolved around the right to the fruits of one's own labor—a conception that was directly at odds with the system of slavery in the South, which relied on the exploitation of unfree, involuntary labor through slaves, as a form of wealth and investment. This led to a cultural conflict which intensified during the country's westward expansion, giving rise to the question of whether new states should allow slavery or not. Chapter 2 of this study, "'That Is Property Which the Law Declares to Be Property': Debating Slavery in Antebellum America," interprets the sectional dispute over slavery, before the Civil War, as an ultimately economic question which played out in a rhetorical and legal conflict over the very definition of property and the interpretation of the Constitution. While Southerners claimed a constitutional right to own slaves, Northerners adhered to a natural rights conception, aimed primarily at preserving the rights of self-sustaining farmers. I analyze paradigmatic rhetorical battles in legislative bodies, the chambers of Congress and the Virginia legislature, between 1828 and 1850. Property in these debates appears as a political, contested concept, and a fundamentally violent one, as it depended on the dispossession of people of color. The chapter proposes that these debates were crucial for the definition of the legal and cultural concept of property as such, as well as for the American self-conception and its social exclusions and inclusions. The investigation demonstrates that the question of property rights ultimately involves collective decisions about what can or cannot be property, decisions which are, by necessity, political, since they negotiate power relations.

During the antebellum period, ideas about property in the cultural imaginary revolved around the concept of a producer economy: in a dominant understanding, property figured as the fruits of one's labor and thus bestowed upon its owner a certain form of agency, as long as one was able to control the ownership of one's body within a contractually negotiated wage relationship. Chapter 3, "A Nation of Homeowners: The Transformation of Property in the Emerging Consumer Economy," carves out a paradigmatic shift, as a culture of mass consumption emerged at the turn of the twentieth century: during this time, the figure of the homeowner began to replace the mythic ideal of the yeoman farmer as the quintessential American property owner. This shift was predicated on a larger structural transformation of the legal meanings of property being an abstract set of multiple rights, concomitant to the emergence of corporate capitalism—a legal reconceptualization that was decidedly positivist and utilitarian and which squarely contrasted with the natural rights-based conception of classical liberalism.

Chapter 3 investigates two interlinked property debates between the 1890 and the 1920s: the first of these focused on the role, responsibility, and proper social place of corporations in the "Gilded Age," that is, during a time of profound economic upheaval and economic inequality. Bringing together contributions by politicians, lawyers, activists, public intellectuals, and scholars, the chapter's analysis reconstructs the discursive lines along which the idea and institution of property was being publicly negotiated in the corporate age. The chapter interprets the second cultural debate, which centered on the functions ascribed to homeownership, as the attempt to reemphasize the affective relations between owners and their property, in reaction to the more abstract dimensions of legal property as well as to populist and socialist challenges to the institution. Scrutinizing government-sponsored homeownership and home improvement campaigns, the chapter suggests that the promotion of the owner-occupied home aimed at the continued legitimation of private property. At the same time, it shows that the government and its allies in the private sector predicated this effort on the construction of white middle-class subjectivity, as its campaigns promoted homeownership for white working-class Americans only, at the exclusion of racial minorities. The practices of the era set into motion new and long-lasting patterns of racial discrimination and segregation, which were exacerbated by the policies put into place during the New Deal era.

As the analyses in chapter 3 foreground, the home as private property moved to the center of the American cultural imagination in the early twentieth century. The two final chapters of this study therefore scrutinize how this close association of property and home has been further instrumentalized politically. Chapter 4, "Challenging the 'Possessive Investment in Whiteness': Black Power and Property Discourse in the 1960s," investigates the ways in which ownership claims structured the backlash against the expanding black liberation movements of the mid- and late 1960s. Concentrating on debates around open housing laws, the first part of this chapter analyzes the rhetoric advanced by supporters and critics of the 1964 California ballot initiative Proposition 14, which attempted to strike down the state's fair housing law. White homeowners, supported by real estate organizations, fought antidiscrimination legislation, by insisting on a constitutional right to property ownership, which, for them, included a private right to discriminate against minority homebuyers. The issue of fair housing provides the background for my subsequent analysis in the second half of the chapter, which addresses how black power activists challenged the social and economic structures of racism. Reacting to the shortcomings of the civil rights movement, the black power movement exposed the ways in which whiteness had become a form of property, while seeking to ameliorate the economic position of black communities. However, as a malleable floating signifier, "black power" was instrumental both for a radical socialist critique of the property relations between blacks and whites, and for more conservative actors who championed "black capitalism" as a form of black economic empowerment. The concept of "black power" thus helped to normalize and reintegrate black activism into the mainstream of possessive individualism. The chapter's explorations also suggest that, read through the prism of property discourse, the political upheavals of the 1960s appear very much interrelated with a (re) negotiation of the concept of property and the attempt to alter hegemonic property narratives.

The conservative appropriation of the language of constitutional property rights in the 1960s anticipated similar rhetorical strategies that conservatives would employ in the following decades. Chapter 5, "Creating an 'Ownership Society'? The Rise of the Property Rights Movement," examines the virulence of property debates during the presidency of George W. Bush. It looks at property conflicts through the prism of the government power of eminent domain. Eminent domain cases raise questions about the relative importance of individual property rights and prospective public welfare; more crucially, in political discourse, the fight against eminent domain has proven to be a very effective way for conservative advocates of limited government to call out the alleged excesses of state intervention. In the last decades, eminent domain was invoked for a number of spectacular projects, which, however, often failed to deliver the promised public benefits, for example, more jobs or increased tax revenue. Focusing, in particular, on the highly publicized Supreme Court case *Kelo v. City of New London* (2005), the chapter therefore reads the public debates on eminent domain in the 2000s in the context of the rise of a libertarian property rights movement since the late 1970s, whose main targets have been government regulation and the institutions of the welfare state. Conservative advocacy groups have thereby been contributing to an increasingly absolutist understanding of property rights. This conception can also be seen at work in President Bush's rhetoric of the ownership society, which he employed during his two terms, not only to advocate homeownership but also (though ultimately unsuccessfully) to privatize Social Security. Chapter 5 therefore concludes with an analysis of Bush's vision of a society organized around private property ownership.

Overall, this study proposes that we need to understand the commitment to private property in the United States not as a cultural consensus but as a history of political conflicts and contested claims. Property debates mirror competing interpretations of what constitutes the right social order of who should be included or excluded, as well as the material distribution of resources and wealth. At the same time, as the long-term historical trajectory established in this study reveals, the discursive lines along which property issues have been debated have proven remarkably resilient, even in the face of large social and economic transformations. The conclusion, "Contested

Property Claims," reevaluates the American discursive investment in property by shifting our view to how the history of U.S. property narratives informs current cultural debates. Contextualizing the rise of contemporary populist movements as well as Donald Trump's presidency within the established property discourse, I argue that these recent developments also constitute continuity, not an aberration. Currently, the political right reaffirms originalist interpretations of the Constitution and classical liberal narratives of individual property rights. On the political left, a progressive movement advocates stronger welfare state institutions. Meanwhile, critical intellectuals raise questions about the sustainability of capitalism in the digital age and advance postcapitalist utopias that envision the transcendence of private property. These current debates underline the book's claim that the rhetoric of property continues to remain central to political discourse in the early twenty-first century and will most likely continue to inform competing and conflicted narratives.

NOTES

1. Private property is one of three possible property systems, the other two being common and collective/public property. A common property system is guided by rules that make resources available to all members of society, introducing restrictions only insofar as to guarantee fair access for all. In a collective property system, in contrast, the community as a whole decides on how resources are to be used. In practice, these property regimes coexist and intersect in a society; even in a private property system, some resources will usually be held publicly and some can be common property (Waldron 2012). Macpherson distinguishes as follows: "Common property is created by the guarantee to each individual that he will not be excluded from the use or benefit of something; private property is created by the guarantee that an individual can exclude others from the use or benefit of something. Both kinds of property, being guarantees to individual persons, are individual rights" (1978, 5). Public property, in distinction, functions like a corporate right to exclude; public property is like privately owned property but is held by the state, not guaranteeing any rights to individuals (5).

2. The distinction between positive and negative liberty is derived from Isaiah Berlin (1969, 121–22). David Abraham emphasizes that the American legal tradition is foremost based on a negative-liberty approach: "It appears that only *negative* liberties exist as *rights*, whereas affirmative or *positive* entitlements (or whatever we might call them) exist only as discretionary or revocable *privileges*" (1996, 39–40).

3. Building on Hegel, legal philosopher Margaret Radin has further developed the connection between property and personhood by suggesting that "to achieve proper self-development—to be a person—an individual needs some control over resources in the external environment" (1993, 35). Radin distinguishes between "personal property" and "fungible property," the latter being substitutable by other goods. Personal property, however, is property to which a person connects

affectively; objects like a wedding ring or a home cannot be fully compensated or substituted, for example, by money. These objects of property are necessary for what Radin calls "human flourishing"; therefore, she argues, such "personal property" should receive greater protection by law: "Once we admit that a person can be bound up with an external 'thing' in some constitutive sense, we can argue that by virtue of this connection the person should be accorded broad liberty with respect to control over that 'thing'" (37).

4. The term "bundle of rights" is often associated with Hohfeld, who, however, appears to never have used it himself. Alexander traces the earliest use to John Lewis's *Treatise on the Law of Eminent Domain* of 1888 (1997, 455). Lewis here stated: "The dullest individual among the people knows and understands that his property in anything is a bundle of rights" ([1888] 1900, 57).

5. In "The New Property," Reich set out to reconsider the relationship between the state and the individual from the perspective of the emerging welfare state. In modern society, he argued, the role of government had changed fundamentally, giving rise to a new society in which the wealth of an increasing number of Americans depended on "government largess" (1964, 733). Reich saw this development as "the inevitable outgrowth of an interdependent world" (778). Nevertheless, he was concerned that the expansion of government came at the expense of individual rights, thereby leading to an increase of government power to regulate the lives of citizens. The wealth provided in the form of benefits, subsidies, and privileges, he suggested, was generally seen as "'gifts' to be given on conditions" and therefore easily revokable for political reasons (749). With his article, Reich argued for the recognition of benefits and entitlements as individual rights, guaranteed under the Constitution. Yet, the effectiveness of Reich's strategy to use the property concept for reform, as many critics have pointed out, was severely curtailed and eventually backfired (see, e.g., Nedelsky 1990, 243). David Abraham observes that "Reich fully adopted the classical natural-rights, property basis of personal autonomy as well as the negative conception of liberty. Property was the source and guarantor of an individual's freedom, while the state, now backed by mechanical and manipulable majorities, posed a constant *threat* to individual liberty" (1996, 24).

6. In the context of this study, I cannot provide a detailed discussion of property's relationship to gender. Rose engages with gender aspects in her work; see also the historical studies by Norma Basch (1982), Laurel Clark (2010), and Richard Chused (1983).

7. For an extended discussion of the relationship between law and violence, see Austin Sarat and Thomas Kearns's *Law's Violence* (2009).

8. The Declaration of Independence, of course, is not a legally binding foundational document. Nevertheless, it constitutes an important reference point in the cultural discourse on property and property rights.

9. On developments within property law during the early United States, see, for example, Claire Priest's study (2006). For general studies of (early) American law, see Lawrence Friedman's *History of American Law* (2005) as well as Morton Horwitz's *The Transformation of American Law*, vol. 1 (1992a).

10. For a concise overview of the constitutional history of property rights, see Ely (2008). Gordon S. Wood (1993) provides a detailed narrative of the Revolution's social, political, and economic consequences. Focusing on rhetoric and

political concepts, Nedelsky (1990) has meticulously studied the debates during the Constitutional Convention and aptly demonstrated the significance that the founders attributed to the protection of property rights.

11. Over the past two decades, settler colonial studies have turned into a vibrant field which provides a corrective to the central myths and dominant assumptions of the U.S. settler colonial society. See, for example, James Belich's comprehensive study of the "settler revolution" of the nineteenth century (2009), Mark Rifkin's investigation of the creation and extension of U.S. jurisdiction in the antebellum period (2009), Paul Frymer's account of westward expansion (2017), as well as Lindsay Robertson's legal-historical account of the role of the "doctrine of discovery" in the dispossession of Native Americans (2005). On property theory in the settler colonial context, see especially Andrew Fitzmaurice's *Sovereignty, Property, and Empire, 1500–2000* (2014), Nichols's *Theft is Property! Dispossession and Critical Theory* (2020), and Allan Greer's *Property and Dispossession: Natives, Empires and Land in Early Modern North America* (2017). Brenna Bhandar (2018) engages with legal property concepts by examining historical cases of settler colonialism in Canada, Australia, Israel, and Palestine. Aileen Moreton-Robinson (2015) addresses questions of property, race, and sovereignty in the Australian context.

Chapter 1

Agrarian Justice

Land, Labor, and Early Nineteenth-Century Property Discourse

In his *Notes on the State of Virginia*, Thomas Jefferson famously reflected on the virtues of agrarianism: "Those who labor in the earth are the chosen people of God, if ever he had a chosen people, whose breasts he has made his peculiar deposit for substantial and genuine virtue." According to Jefferson, owning one's own soil and laboring on it ennobled the independent farmer. The pursuit of agriculture distinguished the farmer from the wage laborer, whose dependency on an employer "begets subservience and venality, suffocates the germ of virtue, and prepares fit tools for the designs of ambition." A large class of landowning farmers, Jefferson believed, was vital to a successful republican government and the new nation's stability, and much more preferable than an urban working class, which he associated with "degeneracy." He concluded: "While we have land to labor then, let us never wish to see our citizens occupied at a work-bench, or twirling a distaff" ([1785] 1982, 165).

While the rapid economic transformations of the following decades forced the third U.S. president to revise his views on manufacturing, he nevertheless continued to highlight landownership as the guarantor of political stability twenty years later, when he proposed that homestead farming in the West would provide subsistence for an excessive supply of immigrant laborers in the Eastern metropolises—an early version of what later came to be known as the "safety valve theory" (H. N. Smith 1970, 203). Jefferson's agrarian beliefs—which viewed the yeoman farmer as "the proper subject of civic virtue, republican liberty, and self-rule" (HoSang and Lowndes 2019, 24)—would become a central reference point during the industrial revolution in the United States. As the country transformed into a market economy, dominated by wage labor rather than land property, and as dynamic and fungible forms of property—such as moneyed capital and land as the object of financial speculation—gained in importance, relative to more static forms of property, producerism emerged as a moral conviction and partisan identity.

If Jefferson was one hero of agrarian reformers in mid-nineteenth-century America, Thomas Paine was another. Paine's *Agrarian Justice* pamphlet proposed a plan to address economic injustices that rooted, in Paine's view, in land monopolies. Reminiscent of John Locke, Paine held that "the earth, in its natural uncultivated state," belonged to humanity as "common property" (1797, 7). However, while Locke had argued that one could appropriate land by mixing it with one's labor, Paine suggested that land itself always remained common property—only through the value added to it through labor could it genuinely be considered to be private property. Since the improvements made to the land could not be separated from the soil, Paine reasoned, landowners owed a "ground-rent" to the rest of the community—money which would compensate the landless for their loss of a natural right. Paine's ideas on "agrarian justice"—particularly the notion of natural property rights—would later acquire much currency, several decades after they were first published, when access to land became a contested political issue during the industrialization of antebellum America, and movements for land reform sparked a battle over the very foundation of the social order, pressing for a more democratic distribution of the land.

Significantly, in a society structured around land, Paine explicitly promoted "agrarian justice," not "social justice" (Marangos 2008, 317). Paine argues neither against the legitimacy of private property nor for a full redistribution. As Robert Lamb explains, "Paine's egalitarian case for redistribution is intimately bound up with his libertarian defense of private ownership" (2010, 485). By making a distinction between the natural property given jointly to all humans and the property acquired through labor and improvement of the soil, Paine separates common from private property, defending the individual ownership rights to the latter (Paine 1797, 10). Paine ultimately aimed to critique excessive inequality in an unregulated market-based capitalism. He wanted to humanize that system rather than abolish it (Little 1999, 69). He also advocated voting rights for all members of society, without making property ownership a criterion, suggesting that those excluded from political participation would also refuse to give their support to the government, thereby potentially endangering the social order (Paine 1795, 17–18).

Jefferson's and Paine's texts forge a nexus between property ownership and democracy. Their Revolutionary Era writings helped found an aspirational discourse based on the egalitarian promise that defined the United States as a society of class mobility, where property ownership, deeply intertwined with a producer ethic, functioned as a defining characteristic of citizenship (Saxton 2003, 248–49). This aspirational discourse relies on an inclusionary rhetoric, as it foregrounds the equality of all citizens in partaking in economic progress and prosperity. Yet, producerism also entailed significant exclusions, even as it constructed itself as a democratic alternative to slavery, the omnipresent symbol of dependence, and "the specter of feudalism on American soil" (Kazin 1998, 14). It was an alliance of fractions of the elite and working-class whites who considered themselves to be the productive classes, "in opposition to those cast as unproductive and threatening, including bankers and speculators, slaves, and indigenous people" (HoSang and Lowndes 2019, 25).

The following discussion focuses primarily on how U.S. political and cultural discourses negotiated and mediated class conflict and property ownership during the industrial revolution, a time when increasing economic and social inequality began to undermine the credibility of the egalitarian promise. I argue that private property—and particularly property defined as the ownership of land and labor—held a key position in radical socialist critiques of American capitalism in the decades before the Civil War. Unlike contemporary European movements, which rejected private property as a bourgeois institution and advocated communal forms of property, American socialists embraced the right to privately owned property. Property ownership thus served as a key indicator for social justice and as an important mediator of class conflict in the antebellum United States. Social reformers invoked a proprietarian conception of property ownership which was based on natural rights discourse. They thereby relied on the definition of property as being the ownership of a thing—a theory in profound tension with contemporaneous legal definitions of property. Legal property discourse, at the time, conceived of property in increasingly abstract terms and as a private contractual relationship between two parties. Within the capitalist economy, property primarily possessed instrumental value. The public discourse invoked by the social movements, in distinction, emphasized the material dimensions of property, thereby resisting and negotiating these transformations.

This chapter shows that land conceived as property became a crucial mediating device in the social relations of the antebellum era. During the intertwined processes of market and state formation in the early nineteenth century, formerly uncommodified land was transformed into property by appropriating it from its native occupants. Westward expansion thus entailed the creation of land as "a new juridicial and conceptual object—an abstraction—that serve[d] to anchor relations, rights, and, ultimately, power" (Nichols 2020, 31). The socialist and utopian projects I investigate in this chapter crucially rely on a discourse of dispossession, by following Paine's arguments and claiming a "natural right" to the soil for the country's constituents that directly depended upon the actual dispossession of Native Americans and the negation of indigenous land rights. Instrumental for the Anglo-American settlement of the continent, these actors rhetorically helped construct the homesteader as the quintessential American citizen, "in explicit opposition to Indigenous forms of life that presented radically distinct and divergent visions of the relationship between human societies and the lands on which they lived" (35).

The following section will introduce the discursive framework within which property was being debated in the antebellum era. Subsequently, I will analyze the rhetoric of three interrelated land reform movements that originated in New York State in the 1830s: anti-rent, associationism, and National Reform. Anti-rent constituted a large-scale revolt of tenant farmers against their landlords, with whom they had lived in a quasi-feudal relationship, often for multiple generations. As the transforming economy increasingly threatened the income of both farmers and landlords, the tenants resisted what they experienced as an oppressive system and began to demand ownership of the soil. Associationism, or Fourierism, adapted the ideas of the French social reformer Charles Fourier to the American context, advocating the establishment of small rural communities, where the alienating conditions of the capitalist labor system were replaced by a more wholesome producer economy. Popularized in the United States by Fourier's American disciple Albert Brisbane, associationism was most prominently propagated by Horace Greeley, a Whig politician and influential editor of the *New-York Tribune*. Greeley was also one of the most prominent supporters of the National Reform Association, a working-class movement which advocated the free distribution of the public lands to settlers in the West.

The three land reform movements thus supported each other. A number of Associationists, like Greeley, were also National Reformers; the latter propagated their ideas among Anti-Renters and in turn publicized Anti-Rent issues in the National Reform journals, *The Workingman's Advocate* and *Young America!* Their concerted efforts for land reform eventually had concrete legislative results: after decades of congressional debates on the disposal of public lands, Congress passed the Homestead Act in 1862, granting 160 acres of free land to settlers. The last section of this chapter shows how radical demands were mainstreamed into a middle-class endeavor in congressional speeches in the 1840s and 1850s. Closely reading newspaper articles, pamphlets, essays, and other contributions published in the context of land controversies in the antebellum North, I map how the rhetoric of property served to mediate racialized class conflicts, while simultaneously carving out the ways in which ideas about property themselves were shaped and constrained by these conflicts.

PROPERTY AS COMMODITY AND PROPRIETY IN ANTEBELLUM LEGAL AND CULTURAL DISCOURSE

Theories of classical liberalism conceive of property as an individual right that simultaneously serves to define the boundaries between the private and the public realm. Adam Smith, in his *Lectures on Jurisprudence* from the 1760s, much like John Locke before him and the framers of the American Constitution after him, suggested that the major objective of government was to secure individual private property rights, "to prevent the members of a society from incroaching [sic] on one anothers [sic] property, or siezing [sic] what is not their own" (qtd in Rose 1996, 332). This notion of property being the objective of private economic pursuits, free from government coercion and the infringement of others, however, covers only part of the meaning that property has assumed within the American cultural context. Gregory Alexander and Carol Rose both have pointed out that the conception of property as a commodity exists in a dialectical relationship with a second, less familiar but equally important idea of private property as "the material foundation for creating and maintaining the proper social order" or "property as propriety" (Alexander 1997, 1; see also Rose 1994, 58–62). This idea situates the individual as part of a collective and in a public role in which property ownership comes with social rights and obligations. Tellingly, Smith implicitly alludes to this moral dimension by attributing governments with the central moral function of maintaining justice—which, for him, is the same as protecting individual property rights.

The idea of property being both commodity and propriety are intricately interrelated and continue to be articulated even in today's property debates, which foreground the commodity function. The notion of what constitutes the public good, however, varies during different historical periods or is typically contested by particular groups or individuals at a singular moment (Alexander 1997, 2). Historically, conceptions of propriety have especially relied on "the civic value of landed property" (Blomley 2005, 622), which associates landowners with a notably hierarchical governing authority (Rose 1994, 59). This was especially true in European monarchical and aristocratic political systems, but it also applies to the American republicanism that prevailed after the American Revolution. Conceived as a country governed by "the people," the new republic required a greater diffusion of landownership—as most strongly advocated by Jefferson—yet it continued to exclude those who possessed little or no property from civic participation, such as women, children, and the poor (61).

The American political and intellectual elite maintained that only property ownership made people independent and hence capable of exercising political rights.[1] Moreover, they believed that owning property gave people a greater stake in society, making them more committed members of the community because they held a private interest in the state's public policies (Keyssar 2000, 5)—a belief the George W. Bush administration would still echo in the early twenty-first century (see chapter 5). Property requirements thus limited access to the franchise in colonial America and during the early decades of the United States. All thirteen original colonies maintained property qualifications for the ballot. During the Revolutionary Era, many states made substantial changes, in most cases broadening the franchise. Except for Rhode Island, Virginia, and North Carolina, all states had eliminated property qualifications by the mid-1820s, but in many of the former colonies tax-based requirements existed into the 1850s and beyond (Engerman and Sokoloff 2005, 896–98). Though the electorate expanded to eventually include all white men, new lines of exclusion were more narrowly drawn according to identity categories, often explicitly denying women, people of African descent, and Native Americans the vote—property-based franchise laws had usually granted suffrage to members of these groups if they met the qualifications. The notion that only self-governing individuals should be able to vote remained in place, yet the definition of what constituted personal independence was reconfigured: self-ownership replaced property ownership (Steinfeld 1991, 185–86).

Property interests were thus instrumental in defining the nation's political institutions, processes, and conception of citizenship. At the same time, dimensions of propriety had to be constantly renegotiated in the context of the market revolution at the beginning of the nineteenth century, which foregrounded property's commodity dimension and began to move it into the realm of private contractual relations between individuals (Steinfeld 1991, 186). Early American property law, in distinction to the constitutional discourse, was built upon the model of British common law and the colonial statutory legislation instituted prior to Independence. However, these legal foundations became subject to rapid transformations between 1780 and 1820 (Horwitz 1992a, 30). In his preface to the 1803 edition of Blackstone's *Commentaries on the Law of England*, Virginia law professor St. George Tucker spoke of an "almost total change in the system of laws relative to property" (qtd. in Luck 2014, 10) in the United States in that era. Due to multiple factors, British common law had lost much of its applicability in the United States, which subscribed to different moral values than the mother country. As the new nation developed its market economy, profound economic changes necessitated further adaptions, as did unresolved issues relating to westward expansion and indigenous land possession as well as the institution of slavery.

Some of the most basic changes related to the nature of landownership. As Stuart Banner explains, in Britain, all land was considered the property of the sovereign. Everybody else only had tenure, implying that the rights to the land were connected to duties and responsibilities vis-à-vis the Crown. In the United States, by contrast, landownership was considered absolute: though landowners did receive titles through the government, no further duties were related to the grant. Whereas in Britain, land was closely tied to class status, giving its owner a number of intangible property rights—such as noble titles or the right to appoint ministers to a church—such customs did not take hold in the United States, or only very briefly. Simultaneously, traditional central principles of property law were also changing profoundly: primogeniture, the stipulation that the oldest son would inherit an estate, and entails, which regulated that land would remain within one family as long as it continued to produce offspring, were abolished (Banner 2011, 5–10).

Property law adapted to the principles of the new government, which emphasized widespread landownership instead of a landed aristocracy; it also responded to economic demands of greater flexibility and productivity. In Morton Horwitz's account, the two visions of property as commodity and propriety corresponded to competing theories of economic development, mirroring a "fundamental transformation [. . .] from a static agrarian conception entitling an owner to undisturbed enjoyment, to a dynamic, instrumental, and more abstract view of property that emphasized the newly paramount virtues of productive use and development" (1992a, 31).[2] Alexander, however, characterizes the same conflict differently, as one between two competing camps committed to economic development: "Entrepreneurial republicans" believed that "vested rights" of established American entrepreneurs should be protected against competition from newcomers, in order to guarantee the stability of economic development; "democratic entrepreneurs," on the other hand, strove for more egalitarian access and stressed the importance of competition for economic progress (1998, 672).

Historians of property have stressed the increasing abstraction of the concept of property, in the early nineteenth century, from the idea of ownership being a thing toward the notion of property as a bundle of rights (Luck 2014, 12). Though this development does not necessarily correspond to an actual shift from property in tangible things to a set of intangible rights, as Banner rightly points out,[3] legal theory began to interpret property as the rights and interests that parties in property disputes claimed regarding particular objects. While this abstract conception of property as a bundle of rights emerged concurrently with the new market society, the notion of property as an embodied, corporal existence remained influential in the American cultural discourse during and after this time (Luck 2014, 12). And if American property law had all but abandoned the natural rights theory already before the turn of the nineteenth century, the liberal ideology of natural property rights continued to resonate within political and public debates.

Within theories of political economy in the early United States, the natural rights ideology expressed itself through the firm principle that a just distribution of wealth in society rested on a labor theory of property and value (J. L. Huston 1998, 7). As James Huston notes, already during the Revolutionary Era "the public atmosphere in North America was saturated with the phrase *the fruits of labor* and with explicit allusions to the labor theory of property/value" (8). According to this theory, individuals deserved only the fruits of their own labor, and the transference of these fruits from a laborer to a non-laborer was considered unjust. Locke's liberal philosophy provided one of the chief pillars of this labor theory of property. In his *Second Treatise of Government*, he famously stipulated:

> Every Man has a *Property* in his own *Person*. This no Body has any Right to but himself. The *Labour* of his Body, and the *Work* of his Hands, we may say, are properly his. Whatsoever then he removes out of the State that Nature hath provided, and left it in, he hath mixed his *Labour* with, and joined to it something that is his own, and thereby makes it his *Property*. ([1689] 1988, Second Treatise, §27)

For Locke, the sanctity of private property rights derived from an original ownership of one's body; the individual improved the natural resources of the earth by adding his or her own labor and thereby increased their value. The property right emerged in this process of enhancement; only labor, then, according to Locke, created both property and economic value.

The labor theory of property and value provided one of the major justifications for the American Revolution. The colonial elites rebelled not only against "taxation without representation" but also against what they perceived as economic exploitation, namely a dispossession of the fruits of their labor by the British aristocracy. They constructed an egalitarian vision of an American Republic against the model of that aristocracy, where the few earned the profit of the labor of the many. In distinction, the political system of the republic, they believed, required independent citizens, and independence was best achieved through widely diffused landownership. Yet, this conception relied on the notion of an equitable, as opposed to an equal, distribution of property: importantly, the labor theory of property was simultaneously instrumental to the justification of economic inequality in the new American republic. Since individuals possessed different talents and aptitudes, the fruits of their labor also naturally varied and hence the amount of property they were able to accumulate. In other words, property ownership and wealth were based on individual merit, which could differ widely across the population (J. L. Huston 1998, 19–28).

During the industrial revolution, the idea of self-ownership and the ownership of one's own labor gave rise to what historians have called the "free labor" ideology, reconfiguring the civic importance of landownership. Amy Dru Stanley has described the nineteenth century as the age of contract, which "idealized ownership of self and voluntary exchange between individuals who were formally equal and free." Contract as a worldview emerged in the antebellum era as an antislavery position, as "a dominant metaphor for social relations and the very symbol of freedom" (1998, x). But it also gave rise to debates about the ambiguities of wage labor: as previously suggested, to work for wages and thus to submit to the authority of a master was traditionally imagined as a state of dependency, even if the individual laborer voluntarily entered in such a relationship. Moreover, in the eyes of the working class, the notion of contract freedom glorified workers' independence and veiled the asymmetry of power between the contract partners in the context of industrial capitalism. Workers' movements such as the National Reform Association challenged the contract metaphor by insisting that the workers' situation amounted to "wage slavery" or "white slavery." The contrast between wage and slave labor, however, also served to further sharpen and legitimize the ideology of capitalism and to picture the United States as a classless utopia, where industrial laborers were upwardly mobile and could achieve property ownership through hard work, thereby escaping their state of wage labor (E. Foner 1995, xi). As a profoundly malleable term, "free labor" could refer both to a more narrowly defined form of self-employment, of which the small farmer remained the ideal, or more broadly to all non-slave working arrangements. The free labor ideology thus celebrated "the ability of each person to obtain a competence by the act of labor, to rise in wealth and status by merit and talent; it celebrated the dignity and nobility of labor, embraced the market system of competition, and glorified continuous expansion" (J. L. Huston 1998, 69).[4]

These ideas were also central to the project of expanding the American settler society over the entire continent, thereby displacing and dispossessing Native American populations and ultimately installing Anglo-American practices and values by eliminating alternative social systems. Locke already provided the groundwork with his claim that "in the beginning all the World was *America*" ([1689] 1988, Second Treatise, §49), insinuating that the American continent, prior to European settlement, resembled a state of nature, a "vacant place[]" (Second Treatise, §36; see also Tully 1994, 167). The right to property through land, for Locke, depended on its enclosure and agrarian cultivation—both of which the indigenous population allegedly failed to do; instead of working the land and thereby increasing its value, they were leaving it as "wast[e]" (Second Treatise, §42). Therefore, in Locke's argument, indigenous people lacked dominion over the soil; they did not improve the land and therefore did not appropriate it as private property. He did not categorically exclude them from landownership; but the legitimacy of their claims to the land would be based on the condition that they adopt an agrarian lifestyle and thus blend into the settler society (Arneil 1996, 166). Locke's argument, which based private property on agricultural labor instead of occupancy, and which was incorporated into the legal discourse via Blackstone and Emeric de Vattel, served as a major justification for westward expansion and the continual dispossession of the indigenous peoples (Arneil 1996, 169; Frymer 2017, 39).

While access to and the distribution of land became a contested issue in the antebellum United States, the related social and economic conflicts were thus resolved at the expense of the indigenous populations, whose dispossession occurred concomitantly and often not merely through treatises and purchases but through consistent violent confrontation. Conquest did not precede the formation of the United States, but most land was taken over the course of the nineteenth century, "often for inadequate compensation and against the will of the Indian nation whose lands were greatly diminished" (Singer 2011, 767). It took until the 1850s for the United States to fully incorporate the land within its 1783 borders, by establishing new states to cover all the land east of the Mississippi River, which entailed coerced resettlement of about one hundred thousand Native Americans and the deaths of many thousands more (Frymer 2017, 4). Basing their land claims on the doctrines of discovery and racial superiority, the United States justified their conquest as being legitimate. In 1823, the U.S. Supreme Court ruled in *Johnson v. M'Intosh* that land in the possession of Native Americans existed under "Indian title," distinguishing between an "ultimate title" held by the United States and the Indian nation's "title of occupancy" (*Johnson v. M'Intosh*. 21 U.S. 543, 543 [1823]).[5] Landownership was thereby legally transferred from the indigenous communities to the U.S. government (Black 2015, 34).

The notion that Native Americans held no property rights in their lands did not reflect the approach of early American settlers but was a retrospective view that came to dominate the discussion in the nineteenth century. Early explorers and settlers in fact reported that indigenous people did cultivate the land and allocate it to private property systems (Banner 2005, 19).[6] The idea that they were nomadic hunters who occupied but did not own their territory emerged in the context of a transformation in legal thought between 1790 and 1823 (150). Politicians and intellectuals began to voice the opinion that it was wasteful if the indigenous peoples occupied so much land that could be used more productively. Thus, President James Monroe, in his annual message to Congress in 1817, argued that "the earth was given to mankind to support the greatest number of which it is capable, and no tribe or people have a right to withhold from the wants of others more than is necessary for their own support and comfort" ([1817] 1839, 206).

The discourses that I will examine in the following sections relied on the construct of the "Indian" as a vanishing figure, whose only right to the land he occupied was the right to sell. Within the settler colonial logic, property rights in land and in labor played a pivotal role in visions of a just social order. Therefore, it should not be surprising that both land and labor would assume central significance in the property conflicts that arose in the mid-nineteenth century, as traditional egalitarian concepts came under pressure and more people than ever worked as wage laborers. It is tempting to view the emphasis on landownership in the cultural discourse during the industrial revolution as an anachronism, an insistence on agrarian values in the face of a reality determined by the prevalence of manufacturing and wage labor. Yet, the expansion of industry went along with rapid growth in the agricultural sector, as both mutually reinforced each other. In the first seventy years after Independence, the number of farms and plantations quadrupled, only to triple again between 1860 and 1920. Though the relative position of farming vis-à-vis other sectors declined—nine-tenths of the population were engaged in farming in 1790; the number dropped to 72 percent in 1820 and to 27 percent in 1920—farming expanded overall (C. Clark 2012, 14–16).

The conflicted processes and discursive negotiations I have sketched over the last few pages give an idea of the complexity of property matters in the early nineteenth century and provide the analytical framework for my analysis of three interlinked social movements in the 1840s and 1850s. In the following, I will carve out how Anti-Renters, Associationists, and National Reformers advanced their property claims in an era that was, on the one hand, characterized by profound social and economic transformations but which, on the other hand, remained committed to the protection of established property rights. I thus highlight a discourse dominated by competing conceptions of property, on the level of both economic and moral claims.

THE PROPRIETY OF LANDED PROPERTY: THE NEW YORK ANTI-RENT WAR

The American democratic vision glorified both the farmer as an independent proprietor of his own freehold estate and the aim of perpetual territorial expansion to the West. These ideas gained currency in the first decades of the nineteenth century and even sharpened with the market revolution and the intensification of the antebellum sectional conflict. The movements for land reform, backed by tens of thousands of farmers, urban workers, and middle-class reformers, constituted a battle over the very foundation of the social order, "rival[ing] in level of support the other great social movements of the era" (R. Huston 2000, 5).[7] Among these interlinked populist movements, anti-rent was one of the largest, sustained by 25,000 New York tenants who signed petitions and organized themselves in associations, vigilante groups, or within the political party system. As an uprising against the feudal structures of land tenure in the state, the Anti-Rent conflict revolved around a competition between vested legal rights and a moral claim to property.

In New York, unlike in most of the other original states, large estates established in colonial times were preserved during the Revolutionary Era, with a leasehold system that continued to expand until the early nineteenth century (R. Huston 2000, 14). The landlords managed their estates as benevolent hierarchies; leases typically ran for decades, with rent payments due in natural produce and labor, many of which remained unpaid. With changing economic and legal circumstances, this system became unsustainable. In the first decades of the nineteenth century, landholders found themselves in more precarious economic situations and therefore became more dependent on rent payments to keep up their lifestyles. Tenants, similarly, had to cope with an altered economic situation, as production began to shift from grains to livestock and costs rose. Changes in the political order from the 1820s onwards also shifted the balance of power between tenants and landlords and contributed to the latter's erosion of power (R. Huston 2000, 45–58).

The effects of the economic panic and depression of 1837 sparked the Anti-Rent conflict, which first broke out in Albany County in 1839, after the death of Stephen Van Rensselaer III, landlord or "patroon" to more than 3,000 families on the Manor of Rensselaerwyck. Leasehold farmers protested the collection of back rents, through which the patroon's heirs sought to meet the deceased landlord's financial obligations—many of the tenants had believed that the unpaid rents would be forgiven upon Van Rensselaer's death. Pressed to pay their debts under dire economic circumstances, they started to rebel against their state of dependency. The protests were not the first of their kind: leaseholders had challenged the land monopoly and aristocratic domination of New York manors several times in the eighteenth century, but in each instance, government authorities had squashed the insurrections (McCurdy 2001, 1–4). In 1839, however, the newly elected Whig governor William Henry Seward showed himself receptive to the farmers' grievances. While he called upon the militia to suppress violent protests, he also denounced the land tenure system as "oppressive, anti-republican, and degrading" (Seward 1884, 369). Seward thus gave legitimacy to the tenants' demands and identified them "as a public problem that required a public solution" (McCurdy 2001, 4).

Such a public solution, it turned out, was rather hard to come by, not least due to the complex and contradictory structure of the contracts between landlords and tenants, which were at odds with property law in considering the farmers at once being both tenants and owners of their land (McCurdy 2001, 22–31). Seward requested that the legislature find measures "to assimilate the tenures in question to those which experience has proved to be more accordant with the principles of republican government" (1884, 221), yet he did not explain how the matter could be addressed without infringing on the vested property interests of the landlords (McCurdy 2001, 34; Kades 2002, 953). One possible solution discussed in the legislature was to use the power of eminent domain, in order to force landlords to sell their rights to the state; tenants were critical of this plan, however, as they then would have been required to buy their land from the state. In 1844, former president Martin van Buren suggested that the inheritability of the landlords' rights be abolished, a political decision that was tantamount to the abolition of entails. For many of the tenants whose landlords were young or middle-aged, this would have meant years or even decades in which they still owed rents. Tenants themselves put their hopes in challenging the legitimacy of each landlord's titles. Yet, despite imperfections in these titles, the courts rejected all legal claims—had they granted them, no land title in the state would have been secure (Kades 2002, 947).

Rhetorically, the Anti-Renters fought for a social vision which revolved around agrarian ideals. They posited landownership as the basis of freedom and were also inspired by the labor movement's use of the labor theory of value (R. Huston 2000, 107–11). Crucially, they based their claims on alleged natural rights tied to property in land, "the enjoyment of the fruits of their labor, personal dignity, independence from the will of others, economic security, freedom to trade" (113). Thomas Ainge Devyr, an Irishman who had emigrated to the United States in 1840 after having partaken in a Chartrist conspiracy to overthrow the British government, emerged as one of the most vocal—and one of the more radical—voices of the Anti-Rent cause, while also advocating the tenets of National Reform. He served as an editor of the *Albany Freeholder*, the largest Anti-Rent magazine, at its founding in 1845. But he soon broke into open conflict with the more moderate wing of the anti-rent reform movement and therefore started a new publication, the *Anti-Renter*, which allied that cause with that of National Reform (R. Huston 2000, 164). The main point of contention related to the conception of property rights. The Anti-Rent leadership by no means consisted of penniless people; most often, they were freeholders who belonged to the most prosperous segment of their communities (109). As men of property themselves, they tended to focus on the right to their own fruits of labor and economic independence.

But they were not likely to subscribe to demands that limited the amount of land an individual was allowed to own.

More radically inclined, Devyr had already advocated land reform in Ireland before coming to the United States. In 1835, he had published a pamphlet entitled *Our Natural Rights*, which he updated and reissued with an appendix on the American situation and the Anti-Rent trouble in 1842. In that pamphlet, he decried the evils of land monopoly and argued that the concentration of landownership in the hands of landlords and speculators violated natural rights. Referencing Thomas Jefferson, Devyr held that "every man who comes into this world has an equal right in the soil" (1842, 56). He explicitly did not advocate equal distribution of land—given that different people engaged in different pursuits. He also rejected communal forms of ownership and cooperative communities like those advocated by associationism. Indeed, reminiscent of Adam Smith, he thought of the present economic organization as "one vast system of co-operation": people producing in different trades and exchanging goods with each other seemed to him like "a system as much superior to the little hole-and-corner communities that have been proposed" (57). Accordingly, he also distinguished between personal property, with which he did not want to interfere, and what he saw as the evils of concentration in landed property. Devyr thus linked the fate of the American republic to equal access to land. "The sole cause of American freedom is," he wrote, comparing the New World to the Old, "that the energies of her people, and her political influence, is not under the dominion of landlords" (38). People's freedom and independence were only guaranteed by a wide distribution of land, Devyr thought, but he feared that the whole public domain would be converted into the private property of land monopolists within a century, or even faster.

Devyr's pamphlet directly addressed the Anti-Rent grievances: in the stipulations of the rent contracts between landlords and tenants, he recognized "the spirit of British feudalism in its most barbarous days" (51). The leases left the tenants at an economic disadvantage, as they granted the landlord the exclusive ownership of all mines and minerals as well as the right to build mills and dams. This meant that the farmers depended on the infrastructure provided by the patroon. Moreover, through the so-called "quarter sales," the landlord received one-quarter of the revenue each time a farm changed hands, and he thereby also had the opportunity to buy the land himself at a reduced price. "This clause," Devyr argued, "open[ed] a door through which, in time, the title of the farmers can be easily extinguished, and the unlimited ownership of the Patroons established over the whole property" (51). Devyr endorsed both an agrarian vision of independent freeholders that harked back to the Jeffersonian ideal of the yeoman farmer, protected by legal limitations to landownership, and a form of modern liberal capitalism. For him, these ideas were compatible, as both renounced the aristocratic, feudal structures associated with the manor system and conceptualized the farmer as an independent economic agent.

The Anti-Rent agitation also became a subject of the broader public debate. A central voice in this debate, as in all the land controversies discussed in this chapter, was the *New-York Daily Tribune*,[8] with its editor, the Associationist and National Reformer, Horace Greeley. Greeley was one of the most influential actors in the discourse on land distribution in the antebellum period. Born in Amherst, New Hampshire in 1811, Greeley moved to New York City in 1831, where he embarked on a career as a newspaper editor. In 1848–1849, he briefly represented the Whig Party in Congress, and, in 1872, he unsuccessfully ran for president before dying later that year (Snay 2011, 1). The *Tribune*, founded in 1841, constituted Greeley's attempt to reach Manhattan's working class with its advocacy of Whig ideals; eventually, the paper "would become the greatest single journalistic influence in the country" (Borchard 2011, 22), reaching a circulation of 11,000 newspapers per day.

As a close ally of Whig New York governor Seward, Greeley took a sympathetic position toward the farmers. The *Tribune* thus showed itself to be friendlier to the protests than most papers in the city, yet it also condemned eruptions of violence. While Greeley believed that the farmers had a right to the soil they had been laboring for generations, he also respected the property rights of the landlords. In a number of editorial articles published in 1845, Greeley positioned himself not strictly on either side of the debate. He acknowledged the grievances of the tenants as well as the constrictions and obligations the landlords faced. Greeley did not call into question the legal or moral rights of the landlords to their property; but he held that the tenants equally had a "moral right to [their] *improvements*" (*New-York Daily Tribune,* September 2, 1845). He insisted that the issue must be resolved through compromise between the parties concerned, not through legal action—there was little that could be done by the legislature without infringing on individual property rights.

Greeley held that "the soil of our State ought not to have been granted as it was—that all the wild land should have been held by the State until needed for actual settlement, and only disposed of in lots suitable for single farms to those who should desire to subdue and cultivate it" (*New-York Daily Tribune,* September 12, 1845). But infringement on the present property rights of landlords to correct a previous wrong was not an option; if the state were to reappropriate the land, it would have to fully compensate the owners. Instead of focusing on past grievances, Greeley urged that the mistakes of the past be not repeated with the public lands in the West. Instead, future land concentration had to be avoided, to "secure [...] future freeholds for the cultivating many" (*New-York Daily Tribune,* August 18, 1845). Greeley's position on the Anti-Rent issue illustrates his broader views on wealth distribution and the morality of landownership. He favored an economy of landowning producers, though his vision was not one of subsistent agrarianism. For the Whig, economic progress was important, but it was to be achieved by small producers who owned their own farms and fully profited from the fruits of their labor.

The landowners also had strong advocates who defended their property rights. In a long contribution to the *American Review*, Daniel Dewey Barnard, a New York lawyer and confidant of Stephen Van Rensselaer, and one of the gentry's most important spokespeople, emphasized the fact that the tenants had voluntarily agreed to the terms of contract instead of outright buying land with no rent obligations, thereby defending that position. The occupants of the land had taken possession of it without payment of purchase money and instead agreed to pay an annual rent. Barnard strategically chose to speak of the tenants as the "owners of the soil in fee simple" rather than as leaseholders; it was simply the case that "the original proprietor had not absolutely given away his inheritance," but he still held some rights to part of the farmers' annual profit and their labor, as payment for the land they had acquired (Barnard 1845, 579). The farmers were full owners of their soil; but they had acquired a debt as they purchased the land. Conceiving of landlords as grantees, like Van Rensselaer did, and of tenants as freeholders, Barnard denied that there was "something degrading to the landholders, inconsistent with the spirit of our institutions" (583).

Barnard addressed the particular stipulations in the contracts that farmers and other observers considered feudal. The fact that rents were to be paid in produce and labor, Barnard admitted, might sound peculiar to modern ears; but in a farming context, this was a practical way of ensuring a consistent measure of value. Moreover, in practice, cash payments instead of payment in kind were possible, if this appeared more convenient to the involved parties. The reservation of mill-sides Barnard interpreted as an act of benevolence, an attempt by patroons to provide infrastructure for the farmers. And he described the quarter sales as an institution which served to exclude unwanted intruders but encourage permanent settlement and speedy cultivation. He also pointed out that quarter sales were presently only executed in a fraction of land sales (591–93). "Th[e] point is," Barnard generalized, "whether private property, existing in the form of rents, is any longer to be held and deemed to *be* property in the State of New York, and protected and preserved as such under law?" The larger implication of that question, he claimed, was "whether private property, in any form, or of any description, can be respected and preserved, if property in the form of rent is sacrificed" (595). Barnard thereby raised the stakes of the matter and insisted that the anti-rent movement not only constituted an attack on vested property rights, but it more gravely endangered the sacred institutions of the republic. The political institutions of the state, he concluded, had to abandon any attempts at interfering with the private contracts between the parties (596).

However, it was the novelist James Fenimore Cooper, himself the offspring of a landholding family, who provided the most elaborate defense of the manor system. In 1845 and 1846, Cooper published the *Littlepage Manuscripts*, a trilogy designed as a conservative intervention into the Anti-Rent wars. Cooper issued *Satanstoe*, *The Chainbearer*, and *The Redskins* as three separate novels but conceived them as a series. The narrative is set in the New York of the colonial era, the Early Republic shortly after the Revolution, and the 1840s, respectively; it spans multiple generations of the Littlepages, a landowning family, with each book being narrated by the male heir of the Littlepage estates at that particular time. Cooper assumes the persona of an editor of manuscripts that his narrators allegedly have left behind, commenting on the main narrative in footnotes and prefaces. In deliberatively repetitive plots, each text thus features a narrator in his early twenties who travels to the northern part of the state to see about the family's two estates, "Mooseridge" and "Ravensnest," which were originally acquired from the Mohawks. Invariably, each novel climaxes in a violent conflict about property rights between the landholder's party and varying opponents.

Cooper's novels strongly emphasize the proprietarian character of property and downplay the economic power connected to it. Though he wrote at a time when people increasingly thought of land as capital, Cooper's political vision depended on the image of a "rightful owner of the land [. . .] who resisted the tendency to turn it into a commodity" (Thomas 1984, 102). Cooper advocated a decidedly hierarchical model of society, where landlords assume the position of political and moral leaders (Schachterle 2009, 93) and property descends over multiple generations in one family. The Littlepages acquire Ravensnest, their leaseholding estate, specifically not for speculation or quick profit but as an investment to provide for future generations. For Cooper, who was inspired by Locke, Blackstone, and James Kent, property rights marked the existence of civilization and political order.

In *The Chainbearer*, narrator Mordaunt explains that civilization requires political institutions built on "great principles." Mordaunt argues: "When the rights of property are first established, they must be established fairly, on some admitted rule; after which they are to remain inviolable—that is to say, sacred" (Cooper 1845, 101). For Cooper, these sacred laws, as represented in the political framework of the U.S. Constitution, were derived from deeper moral principles, which protect a property-owning minority from demagoguery and the interests of the unpropertied majority. These deeper principles, Cooper suggested in his preface to *The Redskins*, were threatened by the Anti-Rent agitation, which proposed that "the interests and wishes of numbers are to be respected, though done at the sacrifice of the clearest rights of the few" (Cooper 1849, iv). While Thomas Devyr had argued that land monopoly and the hierarchical order of the manor system violated the principles of republicanism, Cooper insisted that "not only is the spirit of the institutions in harmony with these leases, but so is the letter also" (vi). At the same time, he denounced the egalitarian "notion that every husbandman is to be a freeholder" as being "utopian in practice, as it would be to expect that all men were to be on the same level in fortune, condition, education and habits" (xiv).

Cooper's novels stage a discourse on property, when his characters themselves debate on questions of distributive justice. The Littlepages receive support from the Native American Susquesus and the chainbearer Andries Coejemans, two central characters who represent moral integrity. Their opponents are the squatter "Thousandacres" and the renter Jason Newcome, both of whom are portrayed as selfish, uncivilized, and foremost interested in monetary gains. While the Littlepages refer to their right of first possession and their legal titles, the squatter and the renter claim a right to the land because they have improved it, that is, they have invested their work to make it more productive. Thousandacres's claim to the land rests on occupancy; but he cannot present a convincing argument as to why he should have a right to possess "a spot" that another one, General Littlepage, in similar fashion had "crave[d]" a quarter-century earlier (Cooper 1845, 282). Thousandacres tries to apply the ruling laws—which indeed recognized a right of tenants to their "betterment"—to his situation; but since he is not a tenant, but a squatter, his actions are not legally sanctioned, and he is actually stealing from the owner. Persons such as the squatter, our narrator explains, claim "a moral and legal interest in the soil; though in the eye of the law, and of unbiased reason, each new step taken in what is called the improvement of a 'betterment' is but a farther advance in the direction of wrong-doing" (232).

The novels portray characters with an entrepreneurial spirit, such as Thousandacres and Newcome, in consistently negative terms, as they insist on the stability of property relations over alternative conceptions. The indigenous character Susquesus, however, seems to undermine Cooper's legal reasoning. Susquesus, the "Upright Onondago," appears in all three novels, reaching the mythic age of "one hundred and twenty winters" and the status of the texts' moral center by the end of *The Redskins*. Each of the novels contains a dialogue between the respective narrator and Susquesus, whereby the Native American challenges the legitimacy of the Littlepages' claim to the land. In *Satanstoe*, for instance, Susquesus asks Cornelius how it was possible for the family to acquire their land not only by buying it from the Mohawks but also through a grant by the British king. This unleashes a lengthy explanation, which Cornelius directs not at his interlocutor but at the reader:

> This was rather a puzzling question to answer to an Indian. We white people can very well understand that a human government, which professes, on the principles recognised by civilized nations, to have jurisdiction over certain extensive territories that lie in the virgin forest, and which are used only, and that occasionally, by certain savage tribes as hunting-grounds, should deem it right to satisfy those tribes, by purchase, before they parcelled out their lands for the purpose of civilized life [. . .]. The transaction is simple enough to us, and it tells in favour of our habits, for we have the power to grant these lands without 'extinguishing the Indian title,' as it is termed [. . .]. In point of fact, the Indian purchases give no other title, under our laws, than the right to sue out, in council, a claim to acquire by the grant of the crown [. . .]. Still, it was necessary to make some answer to the Onondago's question, lest he might carry away the mistaken notion that we did not justly own our possessions. (Cooper 1852, 2:132)

Cornelius's protracted legalese might indeed lead the reader to "carry away the [. . .] notion" that the Littlepages "did not justly own [their] possessions." Cooper here actually paraphrases a passage from Kent's *Commentaries on American Law* (Kent 1832, 3:380–81). With Kent, he argues that the indigenous population, though the original occupants of the soil, were not legally entitled to their land because they allegedly did not improve it and used it only "occasionally" as "hunting-grounds." And while only the king could issue a valid grant, it was still common practice to purchase land from its inhabitants, in order to "extinguish their title." Thus, indigenous property rights were in fact acknowledged in the act of compensation, yet, at the same time, the existence of such rights was legally rejected. As Vine Deloria has succinctly put it, the logic of the doctrine of discovery denied Native Americans "their title to their land and gave them the right only to sell" ([1969] 1988, 30).

Susquesus's contributions to the discourse are rendered in broken dialect—that is, until he gives his long eloquent speech at the end of *The Redskins*. Here, he returns to the question of rightful landownership, which he had debated almost a hundred years earlier with Cornelius Littlepage, as he states:

> The wicked spirit that drove out the red-man is now about to drive off the pale-face chiefs. It is the same devil, and it is no other. He wanted land then, and he wants land now. There is one difference, and it is this. When the pale-face drove off the red-man there was no treaty between them. [. . .] When the pale-face drives off the pale-face, there is a treaty [. . .]. This is the difference. Indian

will keep his word with Indian; pale-face will not keep his word with pale-face. (Cooper 1849, 422)

Again, this passage implies that the native inhabitants were unlawfully dispossessed. But here, Susquesus insists on the difference between the first dispossession and the one about to happen through the insurgency of the Anti-Renters: "there is a treaty." The whites allegedly never entered a legally binding contract with the indigenous population and therefore did not break their word. Rather than challenging white landownership in principle, Susquesus puts himself on the side of the law, acknowledging the alleged superiority of white "civilization" and progress, thereby denying his own dispossession. Cooper needs Susquesus, in order to advocate a conception of property that is allegedly built on "eternal" and just principles, while at the same time suggesting that laws distinguish a state of nature from civilization.

In *Our Natural Rights*, reaffirming the same discourse on indigenous land rights, Devyr had similarly dismissed the notion that the indigenous populations could be considered the original owners of the soil and that they thus had the legal power to transfer ownership to settlers. "The poor Indian has a right to glean a sustenance from the hunting field," Devyr writes, "but it is extremely childish to suppose that he has a title in the soil, stretching beyond his own lifetime, and extending beyond his own wants. Before I admit that the Indian can convey an absolute and unending ownership of the soil, it must first be shown to me that he is in possession of such ownership himself" (1842, 44). Although they were on opposite sides of the Anti-Rent struggle, Cooper and Devyr perfectly align in their denial of indigenous property rights.

At the end of *The Redskins*, the Littlepages and their allies manage to quell the Anti-Rent rebellion. But the prospect of larger political changes is still looming, with laws pending in the New York State Legislature that would ultimately annihilate the land monopolies. Hugh Littlepage, the editor lets us know, plans to move to Washington and challenge these statutes before the Supreme Court. And should he fail, he will seek exile in Florence as a victim of popular tyranny. This ending portrays the Littlepages' dogmatic insistence on the rule of the law being increasingly stale. Hugh, a gentleman of leisure who lives comfortably on the means provided by the foresight of his ancestors, is not a credible benevolent patriarch. Though the narrative denounces the self-interested squatter and renter, this representative of the gentry is also driven by no higher moral concerns than protecting his property.

Cooper's three-volume contribution to the Anti-Rent conflict certainly betrays ambivalent feelings and the awareness that his moral framework of property no longer remained sustainable in an industrial economy that increasingly foregrounded the fungible qualities of property and hence its commodity dimension. The squatters and renters in Cooper's fiction are reminiscent of what Alexander has called the "democratic entrepreneurs" of the era, those who demanded egalitarian access into the economic sphere for newcomers, while Hugh Littlepage fits the category of the "entrepreneurial republican" who insisted on his vested rights (Alexander 1998, 672). Yet, both parties to the conflict claimed their property rights by means of moral arguments, rhetorically tying their positions to the values of the American republic: the renters insisted on their equal right to the soil, while landlords foregrounded their vested rights in the land.

From the height of the confrontation between landlords and farmers in the mid-1840s, the anti-rent movement continued to drag on into the 1850s. All political attempts to resolve the conflict failed. And while the landlords won all legal challenges to their titles in court, it ultimately proved impossible to sustain the land tenure system. In fact, many of the patroons had already begun to sell off their land prior to the Anti-Rent conflict, and most of them reached settlements with their tenants during the late 1840s and early 1850s. The remaining movement became further entangled with the free soil and antislavery movements, and, instead of concentrating on resolving the Anti-Rent issue, legislators increasingly began to support the distribution of the public lands in the West and the effort to establish a homestead bill—a tactical move to evade the question of vested property rights.

THE EMANCIPATION OF LABOR: ASSOCIATIONISM

Access to property provides an important mediating function in conflicts between social classes in the United States. While the claim that socialism never took hold in the United States may be disputed,[9] if a form of a socialist movement existed in the antebellum period, it certainly distinguished itself from the socialist critiques of capitalism that were unfolding in Europe at the same time. Crucially, most American reformers did not completely reject private property ownership as a feature of bourgeois oppression, nor did they see the relationship between the economic elite and the working class as an irreconcilable antagonism. Instead, they envisioned a meritocracy in which everybody was a producer and enjoyed the fruits of their own labor. While for Marx the solution to economic inequality was the abolition of capitalism and the establishment of a common property system, American socialists instead strove to turn every worker into an owner of productive property. Having an abundance of land at their disposal, Americans did not experience a scarcity of resources, as compared to Europe, which made a capitalist order of small property owners a realistic vision.

As the preceding discussion has shown, the anti-rent movement was not anti-capitalist per se—rather, they demanded land redistribution as a claim to ownership of capital. In distinction, the associationist movement I examine in this section voiced a more fundamental critique of the alienating aspects of capitalist production. Of the three movements investigated here, the Associationists held the most radical ideas about the economic reorganization of society. The *Phalanx*, one of their newspapers, proclaimed "the right of every human being to the Usufruct of the Earth, or the use of its surface, to draw therefrom subsistence." Instead of the "principle of 'division'"—the division of land into individual parcels—Associationists advocated the "principle of Unity," envisioning cooperative communities which held "a joint-stock property in the land" and where labor was not "a burthen to be avoided [. . .], but a blessing, which will be to man the source of the most exalted happiness" (*Phalanx*, August 10, 1844).

Charles Fourier developed associationism as a comprehensive reform in France. Albert Brisbane, his American disciple, promoted it through various publications in the United States, among them being the newspapers *The Phalanx* (1843–1845) and its successor *The Harbinger* (1845–1849). He began by writing a column every week between March 1842 and September 1843 for Horace Greeley's *New-York Daily Tribune*, which explained the principles of associationism to the paper's audience. While Greeley at first distanced himself from Brisbane's paid posts and the editorial content of the paper, he soon came to embrace the reform movement (Tuchinsky 2009, 24–25). Seeking to devise a program to empower workers, the centerpiece of Greeley's reform ideas revolved around the ownership of land. Greeley argued that the origins of many contemporary social problems derived from real estate monopolies. In England, Greeley observed, labor had become twenty times more productive than two centuries prior through the technological innovations introduced during the industrial revolution. The laborers, however, "are worse fed, lodged, more severely worked, and hardly better clad nor taught" than their ancestors were, since "Capital, monopolizing Land and Machinery, takes all the profit of Labor to itself" (Greeley 1850, 22). Though the situation in the United States was not as grave as in Europe and land had been comparatively accessible, Greeley saw concentrations of landownership in his native country as well, which threatened "to sink the landless multitude into a state of more abject dependence" (314).

Greeley proposed a limitation of the amount of land each man might acquire and hold, arguing that land must be made more accessible to the working classes. Yet, he warned that simply distributing land freely or cheaply could not be a remedy—only a strict limitation of land that any one person was allowed to own would help to fight concentration. As a first step, Greeley proposed to apply the principle of land limitation to the public lands in the

West, in order to battle land speculation and concentration. Furthermore, he advocated a reform of inheritance law, which would counteract large concentrations of land through inheritance, thereby forcing heirs of larger estates to sell part of their soil to someone who owned no land, or so far owned less than was legally allowed (Greeley 1850, 20). He pointed out that restrictions of individual property rights were not unprecedented if they served the public good; and land limitations were already in place for banks and corporations as well as for noncitizens (315). He also emphasized the primary importance of the workers' relationship to the soil:

> By Nature's Law, use and improvement can alone vest in any individual a right to call some spot of earth his own, and to exclude all others from the enjoyment and benefit thereof. Nothing can well be a more palpable subversion of the order of Providence than the assumption by Governments of a right to grant a province or county of virgin soil to some favorite, whether with or without consideration, to be held by him and his heirs for their own use and benefit, and to be cultivated and improved by others on terms which make the landlord class rich without labor or useful doing, and keep the tenant class mainly poor and subservient, though they do their best. [. . .] Man has a natural right to such a portion of the earth not already improved by others as he can cultivate and make fruitful. (18–19)

Here, Greeley echoes Locke's argument that man appropriates land by improving it, but he suggests that the government has wronged its citizens by instituting laws that disrespect the natural right to property, by granting more land to some individuals than they could cultivate themselves and allowing them to exploit the labor of an unpropertied class of workers. While Greeley advocated a reform of landownership, he emphasized that he did not seek to redistribute property from the wealthy to the poor. Property was not to be transferred from diligent, hardworking people to sluggards, but to the contrary, the rights of those who actually labored should be restored: "Not to transfer the toiler's earnings to the idler, but to *prevent* such transfer, is the object of Land Reform" (316).

Greeley grounded his program in the philosophical tradition of agrarianism and with the argument for a birthright to the soil that went back to James Harrington's call for land limitation, which intended to preserve the land from being monopolized by a capitalist class (Sklansky 2002, 30). Moreover, land reform was to accompany a comprehensive labor reform: Greeley advocated a limitation of work to a maximum of ten hours per day. But, more importantly, he proposed more thorough social changes to the workers' lives, whose occupations seemed "mechanical merely" and "consecrated to drudgery" (Greeley 1850, 33) in a way that was detrimental to their physical and mental health. Associationism intended to bring about a mental and moral improvement of the laboring classes, through a greater diversity of work tasks as well as an increase in productivity.

Brisbane's and Greeley's associationist movement sought to render labor more attractive and efficient by organizing it along with communitarian principles instead of the rationalizing principles of capitalist economy, which divided labor into small, repetitive tasks. An association was to be a "phalanx" of approximately three hundred families who lived and worked together on a communally owned tract of land. All household chores would be organized communally as well: instead of individual kitchens for every family, all members of the phalanx would eat together. Housework would thus be all but abolished. Brisbane envisioned that, through communal organization, all members of the population, including women and children, would conduct playful, age-appropriate tasks, become part of the productive force, and thereby produce six times the amount of wealth compared to the current capitalist system (Tuchinsky 2009, 26).

Though class was an important category of analysis for them, Brisbane and Greeley stressed that they did not advocate a social(ist) revolution, nor did they call into question vested property rights. Instead, their program depended on the benevolence of the property-owning classes. In an article entitled "To the Laboring Classes," Brisbane stated: "The Reform we contemplate is constructive, not destructive; we do not wish to take from the Rich to give to the Poor [. . .], but we wish to elevate and to give Prosperity and Education to every human Being" (*New-York Daily Tribune*, April 28, 1842). Greeley echoed Brisbane, affirming that the concept of Association "wars upon no Rights of Property [. . .], but it does solicit the Wealthy, the Refined, the Philanthropic, the Religious, to invest some of their pecuniary means in and give something of their countenance and good wishes to all earnest efforts of the Laboring Class to emancipate and elevate themselves" (Greeley 1850, 40).

Greeley and Brisbane's vision of a social harmony of class interests was not a purely idiosyncratic theory. Their framework was indebted to the well-known antebellum political economist Henry C. Carey, who, between the 1830s and the 1850s, "formulated the most comprehensive case that capitalist development naturally led in the direction of class harmony rather than strife" (Sklansky 2002, 80; see also Tuchinsky 2009, 39). For Greeley, Carey was an important authority who challenged the implications of the labor theory of value, as formulated by Adam Smith, Thomas Malthus, and David Ricardo, whose assumptions had come to dominate the work in political economy in the early nineteenth century. While Ricardo foresaw an exacerbated class divide in the future of capitalism, Carey optimistically assumed that new efficient technologies and other innovations would lead to an ever-increasing productivity, from which both owners of capital and laborers would profit. Carey's theories guided Greeley's Associationist vision of a social structure which was ultimately defined by cooperation between economic classes.

Despite such assurances, Greeley's scheme alarmed the more conservative members of his own party. In particular, the rivaling paper *Courier and Enquirer*, with its editor Henry Raymond, a former protégé of Greeley's, attacked the *Tribune*, which led to an extensive debate over socialism, in a public exchange of letters published in both papers in the fall and winter of 1846–1847 (Tuchinsky 2009, 42–43). By the time of this debate, Fourierism was already on the wane, as it became obvious that the practical communal experiments were about to fail.[10] Their exchange consisted of twenty-four—somewhat repetitive—letters, twelve by each editor, with Greeley introducing the features of associationism and Raymond responding to these. Subsequently, Raymond and Greeley also published the collected letters in book form, under the title *Association Discussed* (1847).

Greeley grounded his argument for radical socialist reform in a liberal theory of natural rights: he asserted that all human beings had an equal right to the soil and a birthright to use any part of the earth not cultivated by any other person. In light of this premise, the large land grants given to individuals by state governments "were made thoughtlessly or recklessly" (Greeley and Raymond 1847, 5). Yet, since positive law had suspended natural law, in a civilized society only the owners of title-deeds were the rightful and legal owners of the land. Greeley argued that "this surrender of the original property of the whole to a minor portion" could only be morally justified if it served the public good of the entire community. He claimed that this was no longer the case: land monopoly leads to the effect that "the income of the wealthy owner of land increases while the recompense of the hired or leasehold cultivator is steadily diminishing" (5). Since the land distribution could not be undone, Greeley suggested that the landless receive compensation for the loss of their natural inheritance—he thus implicitly took up the argument advanced by Thomas Paine in *Agrarian Justice*. Unlike Paine, however, Greeley did not envision a plan of financial remuneration but proposed that everybody's "Right to Labor" had to be secured, "that is, to constant Employment with a just and full Recompense" (6). This required a thorough reorganization of the economy, which associationism would offer.

In his response, Raymond seized upon Greeley's property argument, claiming that the latter's position equaled denial of property rights and thus attempted to discredit the very foundations of Greeley's approach. The theory of equal rights to ownership in the soil, Raymond suggested, meant that, with an increase in population, the shares for the individual necessarily must become smaller—the original owners would ultimately have to forfeit part of their property. Yet, owning property equaled the right to retain it and to exclude others from its use. Following the *Tribune*'s theory to its logical conclusion, Raymond insisted, would amount to denying that anybody could rightfully own land at all. Further, this also extended to the ownership of the land's produce: adding labor meant to transform the soil, not create a product out of thin air. Raymond concluded: "The original proposition, therefore, from which the Tribune starts [. . .] is a denial of the Right of Property in Land; and inclusively a denial of the right of Property in any thing whatever" (7).

Raymond also claimed that Greeley misrepresented the relationship between property rights and society. Delineating the principal Lockean argument that the laws of society were introduced in order to protect individual property rights, he suggested that Greeley reversed the causality by "insist[ing] that Society creates property, when in truth it is its creature. Property is the root of the tree in which Society is the trunk; and Society, in turn, as it is the product, becomes guardian of the right of individual property" (8). Raymond contended that Greeley's basic assumptions called into question the very foundation of the political and moral order. To further discredit his position, Raymond associated Greeley's approach with that of controversial social reformer and abolitionist Fanny Wright as well as the work of labor activist Orestes A. Brownson. In a widely discussed article in the *Boston Quarterly Review*, separately published under the title *The Laboring Classes*, Brownson had argued six years earlier for the abolition of hereditary property. He had suggested that private property rights were a matter of positive, not natural law; therefore, upon a person's death, his property should revert back to the state (Brownson 1840, 3). For conservatives like Raymond, Brownson's claim that governments instituted property constituted a threat to vested property rights. And even though Greeley shied away from such radical implications, and despite all his rhetorical references to natural property rights, Raymond correctly detected that his framework in fact relied on the unacknowledged premise that governments should regulate property in the interest of society.

Greeley naturally disagreed with Raymond's characterization, reaffirming his stance on equal rights to land and stressing again that he considered individual appropriation of land as justified, provided "that the *general* good is thereby promoted" (Greeley and Raymond 1847, 9). The main point of contention between the two editors, then, was the question of whether the protection of individual rights or the flourishment of the entire community was the main object of society. Raymond emphatically took the former position, while Greeley's social reform rested on the latter. For Raymond, any attempt to limit individual property rights—for example, Greeley's proposal to restrict the amount of land a person was allowed to own—amounted to an attack on property rights as such. Greeley countered that the right to property originated in labor.

In his second letter, Greeley moved on to the practical details of the program of associationism, outlining the main benefits that the new social order would bestow upon its members: a home, education, a guarantee of subsistence and the right to labor, as well as a fair recompense for that labor, close ties of social relations, and access to knowledge. He further delineated which opportunities for an economy of scale the phalanx would provide, including a more economical use of land, building materials, and household labor, reductions in the cost of education, and improved commercial exchange and legal and medical attendance. In his response, which again in part addressed property rights, Raymond raised questions as to the feasibility and practicability of the scheme: "In whom is the property to be vested? How is labor to be remunerated? What share is capital to have in the concern? By what device are men to be induced to labor?" (12). Greeley explained that the Association would be property of those who invested the capital and that workers would be remunerated proportionally, according to the proceeds of their labor, as would the investors of capital. Workers would be induced to labor because they would be rewarded according to their input (14).

To Raymond, Greeley's proposed scheme sounded less like a social revolution than a return to a landlord-tenant relationship of sorts: capitalists would own the land, and laborers paid them with part of their produce. If the members of the community were unable to contribute any capital at the outset, how were they to become owners of the land they worked? Greeley suggested that the investment would be organized through a stock company: the original suppliers of capital would not own the land but a certain amount of stock in the company. As laborers improved the land, the value of the company would grow, enabling it to give out new stock and apportion it to the members of the Association. With increasing value of the company, laborers would thus hold an increasingly larger part of it (21).

Raymond certainly addressed some of the weak spots of the Associationist model: Greeley started from the assumption of essential social harmony and cooperation; his plan insinuated that there was one superior way of social organization upon which, under the right external conditions, all members of society would agree. Essentially, Greeley and Raymond assumed opposing views of human nature: whereas Raymond believed that individuals acted first of all in their own interest, Greeley believed that a cooperative spirit would prevail among the members of the Association.

VOTE YOURSELF A FARM: THE NATIONAL REFORM ASSOCIATION'S LAND REFORM PROGRAM

As Robert C. Williams notes, "Greeley's own variant of Fourierism was a kind of utopian middle-class capitalism, where laborers could become property owners, and where hard work would lead to individual rewards and civic virtue" (2006, 63). After the decline of the Associationist movement in 1848, Greeley shifted his efforts to the more pragmatic goal of land reform. "Every day's reflection inclines us more and more to the opinion that the plan of holding and settling the Public Lands of our Union proposed by the little band who have taken the name of 'National Reformers' is the best that can be carried, and probably in substance the best that can be devised," Greeley noted in the *Tribune*. The reformers proposed to populate the public lands with an "independent, substantial Yeomanry, enjoying a degree of Equality in Opportunities and Natural Advantages such as the world has not seen," Greeley argued (*New-York Daily Tribune*, January 23, 1846). In comparison to the comprehensive reorganization of the social order envisioned by Associationists, land reform was only a partial reform, but it was also "a characteristically American attempt to construct an egalitarian utopia without violence and class conflict" (Tuchinsky 2009, 138).

The National Reform Association (NRA) was founded by George Henry Evans, John Windt, and Thomas Ainge Devyr in 1844 and actually had its roots in the American workers' movement and the social radicalism that emerged in the United States after the Panic of 1819 (Lause 2005, 10). Unlike previous workers' movements, Evans's organization revolved around the land ownership and the land reform, taking up essential ideas from Jefferson, Paine, and Thomas Skidmore, as well as from European thinkers such as Fourier, Henri de Saint-Simon, Robert Owen, John Gray, and Thomas Spence (16). The National Reformers set up their organization as a lobbying machine, which pressed its cause in Congress and state legislatures, supported agrarian political candidates, and drafted legislation and petitions. In addition, they attempted to educate the public through the press, in town hall meetings, and by sending traveling lecturers to cities all over the North and the West (Bronstein 1999, 16–17).

The NRA's politics and ideas were publicized through its newspaper organ, *The Workingman's Advocate* (1844–1845), a continuation of a paper of the same name Evans had published between 1829 and 1837, which he later renamed *Young America!* (1845–1849). The organization advocated three specific policies: first, they sought to end the seizure of homesteads to settle debts, thereby hoping to protect small family farms and putting a limit to land speculation; second, they advocated a homestead act to allow landless people of small means to settle on public lands; and third, as also proposed by Greeley, they advocated limiting the amount of land any individual could own (Lause 2005, 3).

Though the movement began to disintegrate in the 1850s, "National Reform was clearly responsible for publicizing the homestead issue" (Bronstein 1999, 17), which was subsequently supported by the new Republican Party to induce workers to abandon their allegiance with the

Democratic Party. Reprinting articles from the *Workingman's Advocate*, a large share of American newspapers also came to endorse land reform. The organization spread into twenty states, with fifty National Reform chapters in small towns and larger cities, mostly north of the Mason-Dixon line. Its far reach is illustrated by the impressive amount of pro-homestead petitions sent to Congress: between 1845 and 1855, 533 individual petitions, with a total of 64,000 signatures, reached the federal government (Bronstein 1999, 168–69). The authors of these petitions, as Bronstein has shown through her examination of land reform in Massachusetts, by far, did not merely hail from the factory floors or the radical workers' movement. Rather, "land reform was a project capable of uniting factory workers, small proprietors, and farmers" (173). The NRA slogan "Vote Yourself a Farm" was taken up by Abraham Lincoln's 1860 presidential campaign.

In the *Workingman's Advocate*'s first issue of March 16, 1844, editors George Henry Evans and John Windt delineated the objective of the new reform movement and the conditions of the working class, which, they believed, necessitated such a movement. The equality of all, as announced in the Declaration of Independence, had not become a reality in the United States; to the contrary, inequality between the rich and the poor was on the rise, as laborers did not receive just compensation for their work, and those who produced the most earned the least. To many, the labor situation in the North may have seemed much less dire than in the South, with its system of slavery, yet Evans and Windt argued that the northern economy merely worked with a less obvious system of slavery, which nevertheless was even more oppressive. Although the masters in the South coerced slaves to labor by violence, the slaves were at least being provided with the necessities of life. In the North, however, "the master has a lash more potent than the whip-thong to stimulate the energies of his *white* slaves; *the fear of want*." And in the West, those who wanted to escape northern industrial capitalism by becoming settlers had to struggle with "mercenary capitalists," speculators who bought up the land, solely to make a profit by reselling it (*Workingman's Advocate*, March 16, 1844).

Inspired by a distrust in government institutions characteristic of Jacksonian Democracy, Evans and Windt proposed a vision of human progress which aimed at limiting government as much as possible. With the independence from Great Britain, they suggested, Americans asserted their right to self-government in the new nation, but this was only a preliminary step: "self government will be followed by *less* government; less government, perhaps, by none at all. The time for *less* government has arrived." People should have the liberty to make voluntary contracts with each other and "seek their own markets, without let or hindrance" (*Workingman's Advocate*, March 16, 1844). Clearly, Evans and Windt relied here on the notion of self-ownership as well as classical liberal ideas of contractual freedom. They depicted government, with its hierarchical institutional structures, as an obstacle to egalitarian market relationships, thereby locating the source of economic inequality in the political institutions. Government, in this conception, constituted the problem and not a potential source of protection for workers.

The "right to the soil" soon emerged as the key demand of the national reformers: the goal they most consistently advocated was the freedom of the public lands and the abolishment of all land speculation. They held that land should be given to actual settlers, not to monopolists or people who already owned land. The equality proclaimed by the Declaration of Independence could only be realized if the natural right to the land was recognized. The NRA condensed these points in the slogan "Vote Yourself a Farm." A widely distributed flyer served to popularize its two main political demands, the limitation of individual landownership and the free distribution of public lands to actual settlers. The flyer and the slogan linked the issue of landownership to citizenship, addressing the reader directly in a number of rhetorical questions in its first passage: "Are you an American citizen? Then you are a joint-owner of the public lands. Why not take enough of your property to provide yourself a home? Why not vote yourself a farm?" (*Young America!* October 4, 1845). The NRA here advertises property ownership of land as a right that comes with citizenship. Americans, the passage insinuates, are entitled to a portion of the public lands as their private property—clearly, the organization envisions citizens as homestead farmers. The short text repeats the slogan "Vote yourself a farm" at the end of every paragraph, appealing to the reader as "a party-follower," a man of reason, a Christian, and a man.[11] The last paragraph most emphatically ups the stakes: "Would you free your country, and the sons of toil everywhere, from the heartless, irresponsible mastery of the aristocracy of avarice? Would you disarm this aristocracy of its chief weapon, the fearful power of banishment from God's earth?" Not coincidentally, the text appeals to the sentiments of the American Revolution, as it likens the exploitative structures of industrial capitalism to that of feudalism.

Reminiscent of the utopian project of associationism, National Reform advocated the establishment of agrarian communities on public lands, giving every worker a right to his share of the soil. In the *Workingman's Advocate*, the reformers envisioned townships where every farmer owned 160 acres of land, which were to be populated by "farmers, mechanics, manufacturers, merchants, and what not." They would have little use for bankers, brokers, and lawyers, though doctors and clergymen would actively engage in the community to disseminate their knowledge and thereby educate people, "instead of hiding [their] learning under an impenetrable veil of mystery" (*Workingman's Advocate*, March 30, 1844). Like the Associationists, the agrarian reformers emphasized the egalitarian nature of their envisioned townships but stressed that each family was to inhabit their own home. The agrarians were also critical of the corporate model of investment proposed by the Fourierites, which would allow capitalists to invest in Association stock and thereby reap profits from the labor of the Association (*Workingman's Advocate*, March 30, 1844).

In a series of articles, the *Workingman's Advocate* engaged in a conversation with the Fourierist *Phalanx*. One controversy between them concerned the exact nature of the "right to the soil": "The *Phalanx* does not recognize the right of man to the use of a *portion* of the soil, because the natural right is to the *common* use of it. But when men chose to cultivate the earth instead of hunting and fishing for subsistence, had they not the right, either to cultivate in common, or to divide it in such a way as to secure the equal right to all?" (*Workingman's Advocate*, September 7, 1844). The difference, however subtle it may seem, relates to the question of the property system advanced: should the land be privately or commonly owned? This was important because the model chosen would have implications for the organization of society and the level of cooperation within it. The NRA also understood itself as an ally of similar land reform movements, such as the Anti-Renters, even though Evans carefully distinguished their goals from his own in his paper: the Anti-Renters were fighting for "justice" and for their right to the soil, "a right as unquestionable as the right of our forefathers to attempt to throw off the British yoke," but the goals of National Reform were "more comprehensive," since the NRA "propose[d] to provide, not only for those who are in *possession* of their land, but for ALL" (*Workingman's Advocate*, December 21, 1844). Nevertheless, Evans saw the agitation against the landlords in New York State as a sign of the times that the current system of land speculation and workers' exploitation could not be sustained.

The NRA's program of land reform also entailed a critique of wage labor. In an article entitled "The Slavery of Poverty," Orestes Brownson argued that wage labor was "no improvement" to slave labor. The wage system cemented a division in society between the working class and the capitalist class, which did not allow for upward mobility. Though there were possibilities to rise in American society, wealth did not grow out of wages: "No man born poor has ever, by his wages, as a simple operative, risen to the class of wealthy." Accumulation had to happen through investments, not through one's own manual labor. The conditions for workers, Brownson argued, had grown worse over the past fifty years, making the prospects of becoming independent landowners more dire. He concluded: "The system of wages must be supplanted by some other system, or else one half of the human race must forever be the virtual slaves of the other" (*Workingman's Advocate*, May 4, 1844).

Responding to the binary of slave versus free labor, the labor movement adopted the metaphors of "white slavery" and "wage slavery" to criticize capitalist work relationships. By characterizing labor relationships as a form of slavery, reformers called into question their alleged freedom and highlighted the coercive and unfree aspects of their situation (E. Foner 1995, xviii). Importantly, as David Roediger notes, "a term like white slavery was not an act of solidarity with the slave but rather a call to arms to end the inappropriate oppression of whites" (2007, 68). Invoking a comparison between northern wage laborers and southern slaves, the "New-York Society for the Abolition of All Slavery" published a pamphlet on *The Slavery of Poverty* (1842) through the National Reformer Windt's press. Advertised and excerpted in the *Workingman's Advocate* in 1844, it staged a fictive dialogue between an abolitionist and a slaveholder, in order to criticize the abolitionist position and the concept of "free labor." The fictive slaveholder explains to the abolitionist the alleged failure of the free labor position to recognize that Southern slave labor and Northern wage labor were not qualitatively different kinds of labor but really only gradually different forms of unfreedom. Distinctly emphasizing the economic component of freedom (Bronstein 1999, 92), in this conception, wage labor even appeared like a worse form of slavery because it was not acknowledged as such—the wage laborer was generally considered to be the owner of his own body and labor. In fact, the laborer's situation of poverty coerced him into selling his labor for less than it was worth, that is, merely for subsistence wages. Poverty, the fictitious slaveholder claims, was the root to both southern slavery and northern wage labor. A southern slave was "so poor that he does not legally own his own body—and hence he is all his life compelled to till another man's field, and earn money for another man's pocket." The plight of the northern worker was similar: "His poverty is as much the result of LAW—of LEGISLATIVE CRIME—as that of the negro. The law, it is true, generally allows the poor white to be the owner of his own body, but denies his right to every atom of matter besides" (emphasis is in the original) (Society for the Abolition of All Slavery 1842, 6).

The fictive voice thus appropriated ideas propagated by southern ideologues who justified slavery as a positive good.[12] Yet, in the pamphlet, these ideas were employed not in order to advocate southern slavery but to provocatively propose far-reaching reforms to mitigate the system of poverty. The claim advanced was that abolitionists, in focusing solely on the abolition of southern slavery, would, if successful, cast those slaves into the same condition of relative unfreedom that the northern working class was already experiencing. The remedy advanced against the "slavery of poverty" was to "repeal[] every social regulation whereby the rich are enabled to derive wealth from the toil, or to levy taxes on the existence, of the poor" (Society for the Abolition of All Slavery 1842, 10). Since labor was properly owned by the laborer and every person had a right to the soil, no person should be allowed to own more land than he himself could toil. Finally, the "slave-holder" argued that the liberation of the white laborer would also eventually bring about the freedom of the black slave. Since the reforms advanced would be the end of all "False Rights," the southern exploitation of blacks would also come to an end (15).

Horace Greeley shared the NRA's basic convictions about slavery and free labor. *Young America* published an article by him, copied from the *Cincinnati Morning Herald*, in which he addressed the question "What Is Slavery?" Here, Greeley called slavery "a greater evil" than northern exploitation, "more hideous in kind and degree," but he also argued for a strict separation between the races (*Young America!* June 28, 1845).[13] He also echoed the idea, pervasive among northern opponents of slavery, that "Slave Labor always did, always must, degrade and discourage Free Labor, where the two are brought fairly into contact." The reason that European immigrants opted to go west, rather than south, despite higher land prices, was "very plain" to him: skilled workers would not engage in the same kind of labor done by slaves "because this (they reason) would debase them to the level of negroes" (*New-York Daily Tribune*, July 24, 1848).

As Roediger has argued, "whiteness was a way in which white workers responded to a fear of dependency on wage labor and to the necessities of capitalist work discipline" (2007, 13). Even as they protested their economic "enslavement," the white working class could measure their own fear of unfreedom against the existing slavery system and reaffirm their entitlement to the status of free men, superior to enslaved black laborers (56). In popularizing the terms "white slavery" and "wage slavery," the NRA closely tied working-class identity to self-ownership and economic autonomy, while deploying a deeply racialized class critique. Their reform program envisioned an emancipation of working classes that associated freedom with individual agency, derived from propertied labor, harking back to the ideals of Jeffersonian republicanism. Based on the ideal of free contractual relationships between autonomous individuals, the National Reformers' ideas of property ownership had deeply moral connotations, and they were populist and libertarian in spirit.

HOMES FOR THE HOMELESS: THE PUBLIC LANDS IN CONGRESSIONAL POLITICS

In the pages of the *Tribune*, Greeley relentlessly pressed Congress to curb land speculation and prohibit the sale of public lands, except to settlers—which he believed to be in the legislators' own interest. "Though Congress would seem indifferent to Land Reform, the People are not," Greeley wrote in March 1848 and warned: "The men who agitate for Land Limitation may be undistinguished and apparently few: but they will hold the balance of power in many Districts at the ensuing elections to Congress, and in their view Land Reform has an importance which dwarfs all other questions of the day" (*New-York Daily Tribune*, March 28, 1848). While the National Reform Movement did not chalk up many successes as a political organization, it exerted significant influence on political processes and managed to mainstream its major concerns with regard to the public lands. It ended as an independent movement when the Republican Party both appropriated the topic of land reform and shifted the rhetoric of this discourse. Instead of focusing on a natural right to the soil, advocates of reform now tended to emphasize the more affective terms "home" and "homestead," thereby turning it into a concern of the white middle class.

The homestead movement intersected with larger debates on how to settle the public domain in the West and revolved around competing political and economic interests and actors—government agents, financiers and speculators, as well as homesteading squatters—all of whom, however, coalesced in a systemic denial of indigenous land rights. This is best illustrated by the controversies regarding squatters in indigenous territories. In 1785, Congress forbid unlawful settlement by proclamation, and in 1807, the Intrusion Act legally prohibited U.S. citizens from taking unauthorized possession of lands outside the nation's borders. Yet, this legislation proved to be unenforceable in practice, due to the sheer number of settlers who, over time, grew into a viable social force. What is more, "the distinction between legality and illegality that operates in the land acquisition process of a settler state is particularly fraught and unstable" (Nichols 2020, 38) because the state's claim of a monopoly over an acquired territory only becomes a reality through the act of its assertion. In that sense, U.S. expansion itself depended on an extralegal force, by which western territories successively became incorporated. This is mirrored in the acts of squatters who settled beyond the territorial boundaries of the state and were thus acting extralegally. To frame squatting on land that was still awaiting incorporation into U.S. territory as being illegal posed the danger of calling into question the legitimacy of the settler state itself (37–39).

A preemption law appeared as one possible instrument to legalize squatter's claims, giving them the right of first bid on the property at a reduced price, if they had occupied and "improved" the land for a certain period of time. Various temporary preemption laws had been passed between 1799 and 1838. In 1840, Thomas Hart Benton, one of the earliest advocates for a permanent preemption law, advanced the so-called 'Log Cabin Bill' which would have allowed preemption of public lands at a minimum price of $1.25 per acre, provided that the preemptor built a house and cultivated the land. The law that was finally passed, the Distribution-Preemption Act of 1841, decreed that 10 percent of the revenues from public land sales within the boundaries of Ohio, Indiana, Illinois, Alabama, Missouri, Mississippi, Louisiana, Arkansas, and Michigan would be paid to these states, with the rest of the proceeds to be divided between the twenty-six states of the Union. Heads of families, widows, and single men over the age of twenty-one, who were citizens or who intended on becoming citizens, received preemption rights to tracts of land up to 160 acres, on the condition that they build a dwelling and improve the land (Stephenson 1917, 45–65). Crucially, the legalization of "preemption" occurred at the very moment that the American Indian law defined "Indians" as "occupants," not owners of their land. While their right of occupancy bore some resemblance to squatter rights, "the Indian form of preemption was, however, the inverted mirror reflection of that accorded to settler homesteaders. Whereas homesteaders possessed the preemptive right to *purchase*, Indians held the preemptive right to *sell*" (Nichols 2020, 41).

The western states continued to press for a law that gave land to settlers, and the NRA was a driving force of that development, organizing petitions demanding that public lands be distributed to settlers. The advocates of a homestead bill in Congress appropriated some of the rhetoric of National Reform, while squarely seeking to distance themselves from charges of "agrarianism" or "socialism." Andrew Johnson, representative of Tennessee, the *Congressional Globe* reported on July 25, 1850, "wished to be distinctly understood that he was no agrarian, no leveller, as they were termed in modern times; but he did feel anxious [. . .] to adopt a system that would take the man who was unfortunate in society, and elevate him to the condition of those who had been more favored" (Johnson 1850, 952). Johnson supported the free distribution of public lands to landless settlers, in order to better their conditions and stimulate economic production and future tax revenue. But his arguments were not purely instrumental. He also provided a natural rights argument reminiscent of National Reform: the government, he stated, "had no authority [. . .] to withhold the usufruct of the soil from its citizens" (950). Keeping "the use of the soil from the actual cultivator," he claimed, violated "one of those principles essential to human existence" and might lead to revolution (951).

However, Johnson went quickly beyond such philosophical deliberations to advocate property ownership as the route to loyal citizenship. Property ownership promised to bring about not only political stability and economic growth but also better citizens: a property owner "becomes qualified to discharge the duties of a freeman. He comes to the ballot-box, and votes without the restraint or fear of some landlord. He is in fact the representative of his own homestead, and is a man, in the enlarged and proper sense of the term" (951). Johnson presented a pastoral image of the citizen-farmer in his rural domicile, in which "he and his wife, with their little fair-haired, white-headed ties of affection, sit down at the same table together to enjoy the sweet product of their own hands, with hearts thankful to God for having cast their lot in this country where the land is made free, under the protecting and fostering care of such a Government" (951). Becoming a property owner not only increased the landless person's economic prosperity but properly turned him into a citizen, and a man; women were envisioned to be partners in the endeavor but not as owners themselves. Characterizing the bond between husband and wife as "fair-haired, white-headed," Johnson furthermore carefully underlined that the new citizenry would be white. Indeed, the proponents of homesteading saw it as "a very conscious means of getting more and more white settlers onto lands populated with people perceived not to be white, enabling the government to manufacture demographics while expanding and incorporating these lands more easily and quickly" (Frymer 2017, 133).

George Washington Julian, another fervent advocate of homesteading, argued in similar terms as Johnson. He, too, emphasized that he was "no believer in the doctrines of Agrarianism, or Socialism" (Julian 1872, 51) and that the proposed reform did not attempt to interfere with existing property laws of the states, nor did it touch upon vested rights of private property owners. Yet, like Johnson, he invoked the "natural right of the landless citizen of the country to a home upon its soil" (51–52). The idea of an independent farmer-citizenry held the promise of economic stimulus as well as patriotic loyalty, thus raising the homeless from a status susceptible to crime and starvation "and plac[ing] them in a situation at once the most conducive to virtue, to the prosperity of the country, and to loyalty to its government and laws" (54). Ownership of the soil would instill them with gratitude to the government, appreciation for free institutions, and a sense of responsibility; therefore, the formerly idle and poor would rush to defend their country in the case of war against a foreign power.

Julian also framed his argument for the homestead bill explicitly in anti-slavery terms: he believed that settling the land with small, independent farmers would, in effect, constitute "an anti-slavery measure": "It will weaken the slave power by lending the official sanction of the government to the natural right of man, *as man*, to a home upon the soil, and of course to the fruits of his own labor. It will weaken the system of chattel slavery, by making war upon its kindred system of wage slavery, giving homes and employment to its victims, and equalizing the condition of the people" (57). The homestead bill was thus framed as a northern program of westward expansion, capable of halting the expansion of slavery into the new territories and states, and as a measure benefiting white settlers. Like Johnson, Julian, in his speech, celebrated farm life, pleading for "the inviolability of the homestead," which as the "family hearth-stone should be 'hallowed ground'" (61). Reminiscent of Jefferson, he considered farming to be "peculiarly favorable to virtue" (61) because it meant a life neither in luxury nor idleness.

Both Johnson and Julian projected visions of homesteading as a form of social boost for the poor working classes toward a life of respectability, economic well-being, and patriotic citizenship. Neither of them envisioned these farmers as the future elites but as the backbone of the country. Their projections revolved around the image of the individual family farm, invoking traditional values of family life and celebrating the small farm as a home, rather than merely as alienable property. They called up the natural rights argument popularized by the workers' movement and the National Reformers in the two previous decades, which, however, had undergone a profound rhetorical transformation. What originally had been a critique of industrial capitalism and a denunciation of the structural inequalities of American society, advocating large-scale social reform, was now mainstreamed as an almost philanthropic government project to uplift the poor. Referred to as "landless" or "homeless," the prospective future settlers were portrayed as deficient and prone to crime and starvation. Farming life provided a remedy against these social ills and promised to turn the underprivileged into proper citizens.

In spite of the land reformers' rhetorical appeals to traditional values, conservatives were critical of the homestead plan. Eastern conservative newspapers, in particular, denounced the bill, attacking it as socialist, agrarian, and demagogic. Considering the public domain the lawful property of the older states, donating land to settlers would mean robbing the lawful owners by depriving them of revenue, and would thus invite more poor immigrants from the Old World (Zahler 1941, 151–53). Referencing both Johnson's and Julian's speeches, the Washington *National Intelligencer* raised doubt about the claim that homesteading "would add to [the cultivator's] individual happiness, or promote the common interest of the country." The newspaper accused Julian of surpassing even the Anti-Renters with his agrarian proposals and of echoing "an extensive popular delusion" which "threaten[ed] to subvert the very foundation of our social structure." The *Intelligencer* also questioned the natural rights argument brought forward by the bill's supporters. Property, the publication held, was from the outset a social institution; property was conventional, based on the laws of a country, not on natural rights: "In a regular organized society, every one may have a 'right' to any property which he can acquire in a mode recognised and sanctioned by the law of the country, and he is a wrong-doer if he gets it any other way. It is preposterous to allege that a man must have land as a 'means of living'" ("The Homestead Bill" 1852). What would happen, the newspaper worried, if all the available land was disposed of—would landowners be obliged to share their property with the landless because these had a natural right to the soil? For the *Intelligencer*, natural rights discourse, in that case, posed a distinct threat to vested property rights.

From 1850 onward, both chambers of Congress took the homestead issue seriously, yet they were unable to pass a bill, due to a united southern opposition and the issue of slavery. After 1856, the homestead law became part of the Republican Party program.[14] Only after the secession of the southern states was Congress able to successfully pass a homestead bill, signed into law by President Lincoln in 1862. The law granted a head of a family or person of at least 21 years of age—who was a citizen or who had filed a declaration of his intention to become a citizen, and who had never fought in a war against the United States—the right to up to 160 acres of land for which he had filed a preemption claim or which, at the time of application, was subject to preemption. He had to cultivate it and pay a charge of $10; patents were only issued after five years; and if the settler abandoned his land for more than six months, the land would revert back to the government (Stephenson 1917, 243).

In the end, the Homestead Act was thus passed, not due to a victory of the natural rights argument but as a result of the North unifying against the southern confederacy and its economic system. In opposition to southern plans of expanding slavery further into the West, northern politicians rallied behind the concept of the small producer economy. Though it did not prevent land speculation, railroad monopolies, or capitalist exploitation, while also not fulfilling the populist dream of landownership for all who desired it, the homestead bill did stabilize the cultural ideal of the yeoman farmer and the civic values associated with landownership. It also had significant material consequences: 270 million acres, or 10 percent of the U.S. territory, were ultimately claimed by settlers under the Homestead Act (Anderson 2011, 120).

LAND AND LABOR: PROPERTY DISCOURSE IN THE ANTEBELLUM ERA

The legal concept of property transformed significantly during the first decades after the founding of the American nation. As the United States became an industrial market society, an increasingly specialized and utilitarian legal discourse regulated property rights, now understood as a private contractual relationship. The cultural discourses examined in this chapter, however, illustrate that the public discourse on property, by far, exceeded a merely instrumental function and continued to be associated with a just social order. Within a broader public debate, the idea of property as propriety remained significant and figured prominently in the producerist rhetoric of antebellum social movements. Addressing the social and economic inequalities that the market revolution had generated, farmers, urban workers, and other social reformers in the 1840s and 1850s provided a radical social critique, which put equitable access to property at the heart of the liberal democratic republic and which revolved around the agrarian ideal of the small producer economy as a morally just social order. Crucially, this discourse relied on a rhetoric of dispossession, as its agents claimed a natural right to the soil of which they had been allegedly deprived by the capitalist elites. They conceived of this natural right as one which pertained specifically to white citizens being the truly productive members of the body politic, from which indigenous peoples and slaves remained excluded.

The image of the property-owning subsistence farmer as a model citizen endured remarkably in the face of profound economic transformations; as an alliance between the white property-owning and the unpropertied classes, the democratic ethos that tied political agency to producerism helped mediate social changes and class differences when increasing economic inequality called into question the viability and validity of the egalitarian promise. In distinction to European socialist traditions, which rejected private property as a bourgeois institution, American radical movements in the antebellum era, for the most part, endorsed private ownership of resources, particularly of land. Anti-renters, Associationists, and National Reformers called up the thoughts of Jefferson and Paine, Smith and Ricardo, as well as the foundational American documents, in order to critique unequal wealth distribution as being unjust, aristocratic, and un-American. They engaged in a populist discourse which assumed that a more egalitarian distribution of property would reinstate more democratic political structures. In this sense, they invoked what Margaret Canovan has called the "redemptive" face of democracy (Canovan 1999, 2), which situates itself in opposition to pragmatic institutionalized political structures. This redemptive vision was never fully anti-capitalist, nor did it aim at a coercive redistribution of wealth. Instead, American socialists and social reformers overall respected vested property rights, but they demanded more egalitarian opportunities for people of all classes to become property owners. Only the availability of vast tracts of yet uncultivated land made such a vision feasible, and it required the negation of any legal rights held by the native occupants of that soil.

The reformers' efforts ultimately culminated in the Homestead Act of 1862, which granted white citizens a portion of the public lands in the West for settlement. Though this law provided many families with new economic opportunities, its greater significance perhaps lay in the further perpetuation of the farmer ideal in the cultural imagination and its contribution to what historians have termed the "free labor ideology." As a floating signifier, "free labor" could refer to both the self-employed property owner as an alleged truly independent economic agent and to the wage laborer as an owner of his own labor who entered into a free contractual relationship with an employer. The slippage between both meanings ultimately contributed to preserving racialized class structures and the capitalist order.

As I will discuss in the next chapter, the aspirational property discourse informed the antislavery position in the sectional conflict between the North and the South. Ideas of self-ownership and the right to the fruits of one's labor provided powerful arguments for abolitionists and other adversaries of slavery. Most prominently, they objected to the alleged degradation of white labor when subjected to competition with slave labor. However, the proponents of free labor referred to quintessential American values and the foundational documents, just as advocates of slavery cited the same sources, from which they claimed to derive the protection of their vested property rights. Chapter 2 will analyze this complementary discourse.

NOTES

1. Keyssar attributes the first formulation of this argument to William Blackstone's influential *Commentaries on the Laws of England*, in which he stipulated that the propertyless have "no will of their own" (qtd. in Keyssar 2000, 10). However, the political leaders were simultaneously concerned with the tyranny of the propertyless majority that would leave the property-owning minority unprotected. "Remarkably," Keyssar notes, "the argument that the poor should not vote because they had 'no will of their own' coexisted with an altogether contradictory argument, often expressed by the same people: the poor, or the propertyless, should not vote because they would threaten the interests of property—that is, they would have too much will of their own" (2000, 10–11).

2. Claire Priest suggests that these traditional accounts of changing property law in the Early Republic are somewhat misleading since they overlook that land was already treated as an alienable commodity in colonial times. Land was treated differently in laws pertaining to the colonies than it was with respect to English landed property (2006, 389).

3. Banner delineates that, before the turn of the nineteenth century, property in intangible things, such as political offices, existed. He suggests that "the transition would not be from physical property to nonphysical property, but rather from one group of nonphysical property rights to another" (2011, 13).

4. Historians debate whether the free labor ideology was rooted in fact, that is, in how far American society was upwardly mobile during the nineteenth century, thereby enabling farmers and workers to rise economically. Thus, while James Huston suggests that (agrarian) labor did allow economic advancement before 1890 (1998, 130), Robert Fogel and Robert Margo, in their studies, have pointed out that

long-term trends, showing increases in wages, conceal the workers' actual experiences of periodic short-term declines in real wages, particularly during the depression of 1837–1843 and between 1848 and 1855 (Fogel 1989; Margo 2000; see also Glickstein 2002).

5. Singer points out that this legal status remains valid even today, as lands held by indigenous nations are still coowned by the tribes with the United States: "This assertion of co-ownership is an act of conquest that continues to this day" (767).

6. As Kenneth Bobroff (2001) has shown, the myth that Native Americans did not recognize private property rights and needed to be "educated" in this respect, in order to assimilate into U.S. society, also guided late nineteenth-century federal Indian policy in the so-called era of allotment, when government agencies assigned small parcels of land that formerly belonged to tribes to individual Native American families. Allotment resulted in significant further land loss for the indigenous population. In fact, as Bobroff demonstrates, many tribes adhered to distinct private property systems.

7. Reeve Huston and Charles McCurdy have both provided excellent comprehensive and in-depth studies of the history of the movement and its political contexts, on which I draw extensively in this section (R. Huston 2000; McCurdy 2001). For an early history of the Hudson River Valley region's land tenure system, see Kim (1978).

8. The paper was named *New-York Tribune* in 1841; between 1842 and 1866, it circulated as *New-York Daily Tribune* as well as in a weekly edition, the *New-York Weekly Tribune.*

9. Sociologist Werner Sombart's famous question "Why is there no socialism in the United States?," raised in 1906, has been the subject of extensive yet inconclusive debates among historians, in part, as Eric Foner argues, because of the diverse and often contradictory definitions of socialism (1984, 58). Foner discusses the problematic ramifications of these debates in detail, calling into question some of its premises. The studies by Adam Tuchinsky (2009) and Mark Lause (2005) have thoughtfully engaged with the workers' movements in the United States, making a case for an American socialist tradition.

10. Brook Farm, the best-known communal living experiment, was founded in 1841 and adopted Fourierism in 1844. The community was never financially stable. After a devastating fire in 1846, Brook Farm closed its doors for good in 1847.

11. As Jamie Bronstein notes, the NRA operated with traditional notions of gender relationships, seeing land reform as a way to reinstate women in their rightful place in the home. The factory environment was seen as detrimental to women's virtue and their health. While land reform was considered beneficial for both sexes, the movement did not grant women an active part. The very slogan "Vote Yourself a Farm" rhetorically excluded women, who were not allowed to vote, from participating (1999, 81).

12. Southern slavery ideologue George Fitzhugh's tract *Cannibals All!* for instance, provided the following comparison between northern capitalism and southern slavery: "Capital exercises a more perfect compulsion over free laborers than human masters over slaves: for free laborers must at all times work or starve, and slaves are supported whether they work or not. [. . .] Though each free laborer has

no particular master, his wants and other men's capital, make him a slave without a master, or with too many masters, which is as bad as none" (1857, 49).

13. Greeley's contention that black and white people could not live together in communities was a widely held position at the time, among opponents of slavery, with many favoring the colonization of blacks outside the United States—as did Abraham Lincoln who, as president, made several practical attempts to send away African Americans, for example, in 1862, to Haiti (Vorenberg 1993, 22).

14. In 1860, the Republican Party Platform contained the following stipulation: "We protest against any sale or alienation to others of the Public Lands held by actual settlers, and against any view of the Homestead policy which regards the settlers as paupers or supplicants for public bounty; and we demand the passage by Congress of the complete and satisfactory Homestead measure which has already passed the House" ("1860 Republican Party Platform" 2014).

Chapter 2

"That Is Property Which the Law Declares to Be Property"

Debating Slavery in Antebellum America

On February 7, 1839, Senator Henry Clay of Kentucky delivered an impassioned speech in the U.S. Congress. What infuriated him was the demand, voiced by a group Clay called the "ultra-abolitionists," to immediately end slavery in the District of Columbia. "With them," Clay ranted, "the rights of property are nothing. [. . .]. A single idea has taken possession of their minds, and onward they pursue it, overlooking all barriers, reckless and regardless of all consequences" (1839, 4). The abolition of slavery, Clay suggested, would not merely result in an upheaval of the social structure of the United States and a struggle for power between the white and black races, but it would also threaten the "immense amount of capital which [was] invested in slave property." He explained:

> The total value [. . .] of the slave property in the United States, is twelve hundred millions of dollars. This property is diffused throughout all classes and conditions of society. It is owned by widows and orphans, by the aged and infirm, as well as the sound and vigorous. It is the subject of mortgages, deeds of trust, and family settlements. It has been made the basis of numerous debts contracted upon its faith, and is the sole reliance, in many instances, of creditors within and without the slave States, for the payments of the debts due to them. And now it is rashly proposed, by a single fiat legislation, to annihilate this immense amount of property! To annihilate it without indemnity and without compensation to its owners! (11)

Delivered during a time when both the Senate and the House of Representatives had to deal with a growing number of petitions submitted by abolitionists, demanding the end of slavery in the District, Clay's speech contributed to the ongoing antebellum debate on the issue of slavery within the chambers of Congress. His argument forcefully underlines the fact that, from the perspective of the South, the prospect of abolition entailed the severe threat of dispossession: many Southerners considered slaves, first of all, as valuable personal property. Contrary to a common conception of the South as a feudal or precapitalist society, we can deduct from Clay's speech that slavery was intricately interwoven with capitalist economic processes. Moreover, Clay relies on arguments clad in the language of liberalism: he denounces the abolitionists as being disrespectful of individual property rights, one of the foundational pillars of American society. Donning his position as a democratic garb, he also stresses that slave property is owned by "all classes," even "by widows and orphans, by the aged and the infirm." The abolitionists, he thus makes it seem, attack underprivileged groups of society. His opponents' argument "that negro slaves cannot be the subject of property" Clay dismisses as a "speculative abstraction," as he declares: "That *is* property which the law declares *to be* property" (11). He thus refuses to entertain the notion that property rights precede governmental legislation.

Clay's Senate speech draws our attention to the significance of property and property rights within the antebellum sectional conflict. It illustrates that southern leaders considered slave property to be of systemic relevance, tightly interwoven with the financial structures of the South. Indeed, the claim of a—constitutionally guaranteed—right to slaves as property was one of the major southern arguments for the continuation of the peculiar institution. Clay's speech forcefully illustrates the enslaved persons' de facto legal status as commodities. As Gavin Wright has noted, "Slaves constituted legal property, a form of wealth and a basis for credit and exchange" (2006, 6). Slavery thus needs to be conceptualized as a property system—in distinction to a system of labor or a system of oppression—in order to understand its relevance for the antebellum economy.

I focus on the antebellum slavery debates for several reasons: not only did slaves function in the legal sense as commodities and thus as property, but the debate over slavery also, in many ways, overarched the political discourse during the three decades leading up to the Civil War. And—as I will argue throughout this chapter—this debate was determined by a battle over property rights and the right to define property. When senators and members of the House of Representatives argued about slavery, they negotiated the distribution of political, economic, and social power in the nation, as well as the shape of the latter's institutions and self-conception. Applying Laclau's terminology, we may think of the sectional conflict as an antagonism of two forces—identified as "the North" and "the South"—struggling for hegemony and thereby aiming to define social reality. Property acted as a central signifier in this rhetorical battle. The debates around issues of slavery were crucial for the definition of the legal and cultural concepts of property as such, which simultaneously circumscribed the American self-conception and its social exclusions and inclusions.

The slavery debates are also central for this book, precisely due to their rhetorical nature: over multiple decades, the battle was fought with words, underlining the power and significance of rhetoric as well as its performative character. Rhetoric mattered because the pro- and antislavery arguments significantly shaped the course of events leading to disunion and the Civil War (Ericson 2000, 3). Representatives and senators crafted intricate legal, political, and moral arguments to convince listeners (as well as readers of the written records of the speeches, often publicized in newspapers) of a specific conception of social reality and American political history, thus contributing to the perpetuation of the nation's institutions and material practices. Therefore, this chapter focuses mainly on oratory, on speeches and debates in the chambers of Congress and in the General Assembly of the state of Virginia. Of course, slavery was discussed in many forums: in newspapers and book publications, novels and pamphlets, in courts and in speeches and, most crucially, in abolitionist activism outside of legislatures. The contributions examined here constitute only a small fraction of the entire debate, and, considering the length of the struggle, they are necessarily selective. I chose to focus on political oratory because both sides' material and ideational interests become best visible in the arguments advanced by the political elites. In other words, I concentrate on debates I consider to be paradigmatic for the larger discourse because they best illustrate the intricate relationship between slavery and property.

The present chapter has three main objectives. First, I intend to show that the sectional struggle over slavery exposes property's nature as a fundamentally contested, political concept. Property is far more than merely a person's right to a thing; property rights involve collective decisions about what can or cannot be property, and the claim that something is "naturally" property is always a political statement. Second, I draw attention to the close relationship of the concept of property between violence, coercion, and exclusion. Property excludes others from the enjoyment of a resource, but property rights are also more generally based on power relationships. The negotiation of property rights in the antebellum era entailed the exclusion of people of African descent from the category of legal personhood and the participation in civic life, and racial theories served as justification for their exclusion and dispossession. Third, I want to highlight that the debate on slavery played out as a property discourse within a liberal argumentative framework. Both pro- and antislavery forces drew on the same philosophical foundations and rhetoric; in this light, slavery does not appear to be the antithesis of liberalism—instead, the unfreedom of some was the condition for the freedom of others.

Focusing on the southern institution of slavery in the antebellum period, this chapter complements the primarily northern perspectives on property rights laid out in chapter 1. My analysis of the struggles over the concept of "free labor" has highlighted that northern negotiations of class relationships and property ownership were intricately tied to the slavery debate. The following sections trace the political debate over property and slavery from 1828 to 1850, analyzing its rhetorical shifts and developments. I will first delineate the systemtic relevance of slaves as property in that period before scrutinizing select debates in federal and state legislatures, starting with a dispute in the 20th Congress over the question as to whether or not the federal government should compensate a private citizen's loss of his slave property in the War of 1812. Property rights in slaves were the subject of heated discussions in the Virginia General Assembly in 1832, when the state's legislature probed the possibility of abolition in the wake of the Nat Turner rebellion. The Virginia debate, widely credited with introducing the southern argument that slavery constituted a "positive good," put the major arguments in place which would dominate the slavery debate in the following decades. The chapter's final sections analyze the congressional debates prior to the Compromise of 1850.

THE VALUE OF THE UNION: PROPERTY, SLAVERY, AND THE SECTIONAL CONFLICT

Current historical scholarship on the antebellum period has revised previous understandings of the significance of slavery for the American economic development: the works of James Huston (2003), Sven Beckert (2015), Edward Baptist (2016), Gavin Wright (2006), Calvin Schermerhorn (2015), Michael O'Malley (2012), Bonnie Martin (2010), and many others have reconceptualized the role of slavery within American capitalism and refuted earlier descriptions of the South as a feudal, pre-, or even anti-capitalist society with an inefficient form of labor organization. While some of this previous research suggested that slavery was antagonistic to modern capitalism, contemporary scholars explore "the history of American capitalism [as] a history with slavery" (Beckert and Rockman 2016, 3). Concomitantly, reframing the country's economic history also prompts a revised understanding of the conflicts that led to the Civil War, which was hitherto regarded in terms of a binary opposition of two monolithic systems. Recognizing the intricate relationships between the northern and southern economies, we may think of the sectional conflict as a political construction in a struggle for political and economic hegemony, exacerbated by the industrial revolution and westward expansion (Hahn 2009, 16).

As Stephen Hahn has pointed out, the common narrative of Emancipation being two discreet events in U.S. history that took place during the American Revolution in the North and with the Civil War in the South veils a much more gradual process which took place over the course of several decades. The Emancipation statutes in Pennsylvania, Rhode Island, Connecticut, New York, and New Jersey between 1780 and 1804 did not free any enslaved persons; these laws only decreed the emancipation of enslaved children when they reached a certain age. In this way, slave owners did not suffer the loss of their properties. Legislation in New Hampshire and Massachusetts was less gradual, but even here, slavery in practice did exist even in the first decades of the nineteenth century (Hahn 2009, 8). At the same time, politicians in both Maryland and Virginia, two of the southern slave states, debated about the prospect of abolition and the possibility of a forced exile of African Americans in the 1830s (9). African American free men and women, even in the North, were in many instances without rights; only some states granted them citizenship rights, and fugitives had to live with the fear of being discovered by their former masters, whose pursuit of their property was protected by the Fugitive Slave Acts of 1793 and 1850.

The rhetoric of "free labor" and its association of capitalism with democracy and personal freedom in northern discourse, before and during the Civil War, shaped the work of historians who saw slavery primarily in terms of an inferior labor system (see, e.g., E. E. Williams 2005; Genovese 1965; Stampp 1956). In the light of slavery's persistence and even expansion in the early nineteenth century, Gavin Wright has challenged the idea that the antebellum South systemically relied on slaves as cheap labor. Instead, he points out, "it was a society whose economy and polity revolved around the scarcity and high price of slave labor" (2006, 71). Though enslaved persons themselves generally did not receive wages and lived at subsistence levels, they yielded high prices at slave markets, and increasingly so with the rise of the cotton economy in the middle of the nineteenth century. Thus, one of the reasons that there was no significant opposition against the abolishment of the slave trade in 1807 was that slaveholders actually profited from it: no new import of slaves meant that prices of slaves would remain stable or even increase, with supply lagging behind demand (Gavin Wright 2006, 71–73; see also Ransom 1989, 33).

Considered as a labor system, slavery provided owners with a workforce at their complete disposal, which could be moved freely at their own will. This allowed a quick reallocation of labor, according to the particular needs of a given situation. Slaves were therefore valuable assets for the expansion of farming to new western territories. For southern slaveholders, moving a large-scale farm operation to a new area was less risky and more manageable than for their northern compatriots, since they did not have to attract potential migrants and could rely on a steady, highly mobile supply of labor. Perhaps most crucially, owning slaves enabled them to acquire mortgages with the slaves as security and thus to raise capital in a way which was impossible for non-slaveholders (Gavin Wright 2006, 122).[1] As the United States expanded into new territories in the West, southern slaveholders therefore held distinct advantages in settling the new land—a competitive edge that disquieted many Northerners.

Racial difference took on a crucial significance within this property system, providing the framework for "decid[ing] who could be a slave and who could not" (Morris 1996, 29). Racial categorization assumed persons of African descent to be property, while associating whites with the freedom of personhood. Though the legal and social definitions of who was considered black or white were historically malleable, slavery relied on a system of phenotypic differences that people assumed to be stable. Legal scholar Cheryl Harris has therefore suggested that property in the United States is conceptually tied to a system of racial subordination and that it is intricately racialized. Within the system of slavery, "race and property were [. . .] conflated by establishing a form of property contingent on race": only blacks could be slaves[2] and thus be treated as a kind of property (1993, 1716). At the same time, whiteness itself assumed the status of property, providing "a shield from slavery" (1720) for those who possessed it. According to Michael O'Malley, due to the alleged stability of racial categories, owners saw slaves as objects that stored value, who even served as a stabilizer for the entire financial system of the region (2012, 44). As a result, slaves provided the very foundation of the southern economy, replacing gold as the standard that guaranteed value. The value of slaves significantly exceeded the value of all currency in circulation in the antebellum era, as well as that of gold: "slaves formed a stock of actual capital that supported the issue of paper credit," which in effect turned African Americans into "a commodity of natural value" (81).

As collateral for sophisticated financial products, slaves not only were the motor of the southern economy but also an integral part of the entire country's financial capitalism. Slavery transformed the South into the major producer of cotton for the global market in the early decades of the nineteenth century and drove the expansion of the country into new territories in the West. Cotton production increased from 1.2 million pounds in 1790 to 2.1 *billion* in 1859, thereby dominating the global market (Baptist 2012, 75); and cotton accounted for more than half of all U.S. exports between 1815 and 1860 (Beckert 2015, 119). By the 1830s, the cotton grown by enslaved people in the southern United States and its territories was the most widely traded commodity worldwide and the motor for the Industrial Revolution in the United States, Britain, and the rest of Europe. Industrial expansion was enabled by an immense interregional movement of slaves: between 1820 and 1860, 10 percent of the Upper South's slave population were moved each decade (Tadman 1989, 7); between the ratification of the Constitution and the secession of the Confederacy, more than a million African Americans were uprooted from their original environments (Baptist 2012, 74). In short, slavery was a profitable business for slave traders, plantation owners, national and international financial investors, and a major driver of the market revolution that took place in the antebellum era. This raises anew the question of the underlying causes of the sectional conflict: if American capitalism as a whole profited from the business of slavery, why did the North strive for its abolition, risking the union of the nation and endangering its prosperity?

Leonard Richards and others have pointed to the "slave power thesis" as an explanation for the mobilization of the North against the South, particularly in the 1850s. Northerners increasingly believed that the slave states aggressively pursued the expansion of their system and dominated key positions in the federal government—the presidency, the speakership in the House, the Supreme Court—and thereby also threatened the liberties of northern whites (Richards 2000, 1–27; see also Holt 1983). Recent research investigating the intersections of antebellum congressional politics and the abolitionist movement emphasizes the centrality of abolitionist agitation and tactics not only in convincing the Northern publics of the immorality of slavery and the human rights of the enslaved but also for how the sectional conflict was fought out in Congress. "Among abolitionists' key contributions to the politics of sectional conflict," Corey Brooks notes, "was their effort to elaborate and disseminate the critical rhetorical device of the Slave Power" (2016, 3). Starting in the 1830s, political abolitionists were major drivers of a widespread antislavery sentiment and charged the cross-sectional Whig and Democratic Parties with sustaining the supremacy of slavery interests. Seeking to extricate themselves from the two parties, they managed to build a political platform on the idea of "slave power" that would drive a wedge into the Second Party System, leading to the formation of the Liberty Party in 1840 and importing the sentiment into the Free Soil Party and, eventually, the Republican Party (C.M. Brooks 2016; see also Harrold 2019; Sinha 2016).

While the moral force of the abolitionist movement must not be underestimated, opposition to slavery was also underwritten by economic considerations. As Eric Foner has argued, the antislavery position rested in part on the "affirmation of the superiority of the social system of the North—a dynamic, expanding capitalist society," built on the idea of the dignity of free white labor (1995, 11). Similarly, John Majewski suggests that the Republican Party opposed slavery, due to their commitment to education and democratization (2016, 278). According to James Huston, not only the southern but also the northern position can be explained with reference to property rights: northern resistance to slavery "stemmed from a number of sources, but the crucial one was economic" (2003, xiv). And the economic systems in both parts of the country were built around property rights, with the crucial difference being that the South allowed property rights in human beings, while the North did not. The ways in which wealth and means of living could be accumulated thus followed different rules and were invested in distinct ideologies.

The conflict between the sections intensified at a historical moment when the two property systems threatened to mix. As discussed in chapter 1, by making certain types of jobs unattractive to workers, Northerners feared that if free labor had to compete with slave labor, the latter would hold an unfair advantage and ultimately replace the former. In the territories, the collision of the two types of labor became first visible, but many Northerners worried that slavery would affect labor conditions everywhere. With the transportation revolution, markets became nationally integrated and the effects of slavery were no longer confined to the South. Southern economic practices threatened to invade the North—and the northern unease was aggravated by the fact that, in the decades before the Civil War, slavery had begun to expand into new occupations other than agriculture, including manufacturing and transportation (J. L. Huston 2003, 68–102). The perception of the South as an economic aggressor threatening the foundations of the northern way of life was further bolstered by the northern commitment to the ideal of the yeoman farmer, who earned the fruits of his own labor and was dignified by landownership. In this context, the rhetoric of the superiority of the free labor model also assumed crucial significance.

The material property interests of the sections informed the contentious political debates on the subject of property rights in slaves. Who had the power to define what could or could not be property? The southern position, illustrated by Clay's dictum—"That *is* property which the law declares *to be* property"—usually amounted to a form of legal positivism: whatever lawmakers chose to categorize as property henceforth belonged into the category of property. Defining the subjects of property was thus a politico-legal decision made as part of the social contract. In this legal conception, human beings could be considered a form of private property; enslaved people may be characterized by human personhood, but they were not legal persons—the two forms of personhood were not necessarily congruent. Opponents of slavery rejected this kind of legal positivism and relativism: they insisted on the priority of human personhood with inalienable rights, due to which the institution of slavery was deeply immoral. In the antislavery position, two competing strands emerged: some held that slavery violated true and natural property rights; others suggested that property rights were purely instrumental, conventions introduced by the state according to the country's economic needs. Both views held, however, that "property rights were second to human rights" (J. L. Huston 2003, 104).

Southern slaveholders were acutely aware that property systems were creations of the law. Yet, while they held legal ownership rights in (natural) persons, this system could only be upheld through coercion and subjection and by glossing over the paradoxes inherent in a social order that treated human beings as objects. They also knew that a shift in the political will could threaten their peculiar institution—with all northern states abolishing slavery in the decades after the nation's founding, southern slaveholders feared an encroachment on their legal rights. Thus, in the early stages of the sectional conflict, Southerners were obsessed with receiving a guarantee that the federal government would acknowledge and protect their property rights.

Historians and legal scholars have well established the significance of property and property rights in the American Revolution and the deliberations of the Constitutional Convention in 1787 (see, e.g., Nedelsky 1990; Bell 1987; Beard 1913). The seeds of the sectional conflict were planted during the Convention and in the compromises enacted in the foundational document, which avoided a clear definition of property. As I have already outlined in the introduction, there was no question whatsoever among the delegates to the Convention that the protection of property rights was a paramount goal of the new nation. Yet, according to Huston, "what functioned as a definition of property was entirely circular. Property was an object of personal possession that the law protected; yet possession was secured by the right to property" (2003, 12). Despite their discomfort, all members of the Convention realized that independence from Britain would not have been possible without the wealth provided by slavery and that the country's future economic well-being hinged on the institution's preservation. In the eyes of many, while slavery was an evil, it was a necessary evil inherited from colonial times; and without the consent of large slaveholding states such as South Carolina or Georgia, there would be no Constitution and ultimately no unified American nation (Bell 1987, 29–36).

For Derrick Bell, the Constitutional Convention set a precedent in American history for future policy decisions with similar patterns, in which "white supremacy [served] as a catalyst to negotiate policy differences, often through compromises that sacrifice the rights of blacks" (1988, 768). Slavery not only "provided the wealth that made independence possible, but also [. . .] afforded an ideological basis to resolve conflict between propertied and unpropertied whites" (772). The framework of racial differentiation between blacks and whites, enslaved or free, created an alliance between lower-class and elite whites; the latter were willing to grant more rights of political participation to the unpropertied, as the profitable institution of slavery secured their own positions of economic and political power (772). Such views were advanced, for example, by Thomas Roderick Dew, in his *Review of the Debate in the Virginia Legislature*, who argued that slavery created a "perfect spirit of equality [. . .] among the whites of all the slaveholding states. [. . .] Color alone is here the badge of distinction, the true mark of aristocracy, and all who are white are equal in spite of the variety of occupation" (1832, 112–13).

While some slave states demanded an explicit declaration that the new government recognized slave property in the Constitution, its principal author James Madison, a slaveholder himself, did not want to sanction slavery in a foundational document based on liberal ideas of freedom and inalienable rights. According to his diaries of the debates, Madison "thought it wrong to admit in the Constitution the idea that there could be property in men" ([1836] 1941, 478). In the Federalist No. 54, he publicly intimated, however, that the Constitution recognized slaves "in the mixed character of persons and of property" (Hamilton, Madison, and Jay [1788] 2009, 278), thus indirectly acknowledging the federal government's acceptance of property in slaves. The finished text of the Constitution carefully avoided direct references to slavery altogether and merely distinguished between "free Persons" and "all other Persons." Yet, the Constitution also made important concessions to the slave states that cemented their influence in the new nation: it determined the number of representatives on the basis of the population of each state, counting each slave as three-fifths of a person (U.S. Constitution, art. 1, sec. 2), and the same ratio was used for matters of direct taxation through the federal government.[3] Two further major accommodations of the interests of the slave states relate to the provisions that Congress could not abolish the international slave trade before 1808 (Art. 1, sec. 9) and that individual states were prohibited from emancipating fugitive slaves and therefore had to aid in their return to their masters (Art. 4, sec. 2).

As we will see in the following rhetorical analyses, these stipulations would become a central reference point for both the pro- and the antislavery camps, as both sides deduced the validity of their arguments from the alleged intent of the framers. Both advocates and opponents of slavery sought to ground their arguments in the nation's foundational documents and in the private property rights that they thought to find established there as a cornerstone of a free democratic society. Given the nature of the compromise, the resulting interpretations of the legal text and the historical legacy were diametrically opposed. Representatives of the free states could argue that the Constitution thought of slaves only as persons, while their colleagues from the slave states would insist that the term "other persons" did not grant them legal personhood and that the Constitution de facto recognized property in slaves.[4]

The nation experienced its first great debate over slavery during the sixteenth term of Congress (1819–1820), when Missouri applied for statehood as a slave state; this threatened to tilt the balance of power, established by an equal number of free and slave states in the Union, favoring the South. In a compromise brokered by Henry Clay, Congress ultimately reestablished the equilibrium between slave and free states by admitting Missouri as a slave state and Maine as a free state, yet it outlawed slavery in any future state north of the 36°60′ parallel. As we will see in the following sections, which analyze slavery debates in the decades after the Missouri Compromise, the accord only managed to gloss over the emerging fissures in the slavery question.

PROPERTY OR PERSON? (I): THE CASE OF MARIGNY D'AUTERIVE (1828)

I begin my exploration of antebellum property debates with what might appear as a peculiar discussion of minor importance during the second session of the 20th Congress in 1828: a debate in the House of Representatives on a compensation claim filed by a private citizen who had suffered a property loss after his slave had been impressed by the government during the War of 1812. The claimant, Marigny D'Auterive, a citizen of New Orleans, had petitioned Congress for compensation under the Fifth Amendment, arguing that his slave property had been confiscated for public use. Indeed, the government had taken D'Auterive's slave and other personal property, in an effort to defend New Orleans against the British in January 1815. The specific legal basis for the slaveowner's claim was an 1816 law which provided that government would compensate civilian losses during warfare (Dauber 2003, 297).[5]

The petition was not the only one of this kind, but it stands out because of the intensity with which the representatives pondered it for several weeks, in a debate in which more than thirty of them felt urged to participate. More importantly, the case is typical insofar as it involves the conflict between federal and state rights and engages in the difficult interpretation of the Constitution's unresolved issues. The fact that the amount of money in question was "nothing; [. . .] not to be spoken of," in the words of Congressman Edward Livingston (U.S. Congress 1828, 899), underlines that the claim touched on highly politicized matters: at stake was not merely whether the slave owner deserved compensation but, more significantly, the questions of who defined the nature of property and what was the Constitution's position on slavery, thereby shaping the power relationship between free states and slave states.

Through the prism of this compensation case, we get an insight into how the concept of property and the debate over its definition structured the sectional conflict. In General Andrew Jackson's attempt to defend the city of

New Orleans against British troops in the famous Battle of New Orleans in early 1815, D'Auterive's slave Warwick had been impressed, along with a horse and cart, and had been shot twice by the enemy, in the eye and in the arm. D'Auterive was now trying to claim compensation from the federal government for his property. The contentions were regarding the compensation claim for hospital charges and the treatment of Warwick by a private surgeon, as well as the slave's inability to work during convalescence and his diminished value, due to his injuries, which left him blind in one eye and with a weak arm. The congressional Committee of Claims initially granted D'Auterive compensation for his lost horse and cart but refused to pay an additional sum of 239 dollars for Warwick.[6] The case was brought before the House on January 4, 1828, where Congressman Edward Livingston, a Jacksonian Democrat from Louisiana, proposed to amend the committee's bill, providing additional compensation for the damage to D'Auterive's slave property. The committee had contested the compensation claim, Livingston explained, because they did not consider the federal government liable to pay for injured or lost slaves, since it did not consider them to be property. "Slaves not property?" Livingston exclaimed. "What are they then? If not property, they are free: if they are not our property, we have no right to their service; if they are not property, the whole foundation on which the Constitution of this Union rests, is shaken" (899).

Livingston's remarks illustrate what was at stake for the slave states in this debate—or perhaps he willfully raised the stakes of the case by turning it into a discussion of general principles. For some of the southern representatives, the matter provided them with the opportunity to press their case with the federal government, to formally recognize their property rights in their slaves, thereby creating a precedent to fortify these rights. Granting D'Auterive compensation would acknowledge that the federal government formally recognized slaves as property—a concession that the language of the Constitution avoided. Alternatively, if the House refused to grant compensation, Southerners would conclude that the government did not fully protect their ownership rights and wealth—and would therefore question the value of the Union. A rejection of the claim would pose southern property "within the grasp of the national arm, without just compensation," feared Congressman Clement Dorsey of Maryland, "while the property and the wealth of the non-slaveholding States is shielded against its power by the restrictions imposed by the Constitution in protection of private property" (982). How could the federal government guarantee that it would not abolish slavery everywhere in the Union if it established a precedent case that allowed dispossession without compensation?

In January and February of 1828, the representatives sparred over the federal government's position on the institution of slavery and its legal standing within the Union. The debate did not consider the rights of people of African descent; only a few members of Congress argued that slaves were legal persons, and even those that did would not derive any political rights from that. Most northern Congressmen did not dispute that slaves were property in the South; yet, they wanted to contain slavery as a local institution to the states that had not yet abolished it. We need to keep in mind that, in 1828, slavery was also still a reality in the North: New York had only freed its last slaves in 1827;[7] in other northern states, slavery continued to exist into the late 1840s. Thus, the debate focused primarily on whether slaves were persons or property according to Constitutional law and, in particular, on whether the Constitution's Fifth Amendment protected property rights in slaves.

The Committee of Claims had decided that slaves constituted a different kind of property than other possessions and thus were not protected by the amendment. Elisha Whittlesey of Ohio explained the committee's reasoning: they did not take the position that slaves were not property—instead, the report only held that "slaves are not put on the footing of property, and paid for when lost to the owner, in the public service" (900). After carefully considering several previous compensation claims, all of which had been rejected, the committee did not find any precedent where the government had compensated damages in slave property on any other occasion, whether the slave had been hired out to the government by his master or had been impressed. The government, Whittlesey suggested, had no right to impress slaves, as the country was supposed to be defended by free men, and the option to impress slaves would enable southern slaveholders to send their slaves in their own place. William McCoy, a fellow committee member from Virginia, added that the 1816 federal law regulating compensations for losses in the War of 1812 did not include provisions for the loss of slave property; Congress had debated and ultimately rejected an amendment to that effect (905). Whittlesey and McCoy introduced several arguments against the claimant's right to compensation: apart from providing legal evidence that Congress had rejected analogous cases in the past, they claimed that there were other classes of private property which enjoyed different levels of governmental protection, and they argued that one could see a slave impressed for public service as an analogy to a minor or an apprentice being called up for public service. If the federal government impressed a son or an apprentice, it surely would not pay compensation to the father or the apprentice's master if the person was killed or wounded in battle. Why, then, should a slaveholder be able to claim remuneration from the government for his slave?

Southerners contested all of these arguments. They did not believe the precedents cited by the Committee to be applicable to the claim at hand since, as Livingston claimed, in those earlier cases, owners had offered their slaves for hire to the government, which did not constitute a taking in the sense of the Fifth Amendment (904). Congressman William Drayton, of South Carolina, further disputed that the law of 1816 did not cover slave property: though it failed to mention slaves in its third section, which listed other items of personal property, the fifth section stipulated that compensation would be paid for "every species of property" lost (970). According to the southern position, nothing warranted treating property in slaves differently than other objects of material possession. What constituted property was a matter of legal definition: slaves were property by virtue of the state laws in the South, and the federal government was bound to recognize these laws. "Slaves are property by laws that Congress can neither enforce nor avoid," argued George W. Owen of Alabama, "it can neither add to, nor diminish, the right vested in the master by the respective States within which this people [*sic*] exist" (907). Southerners thus sought to limit the competencies of the federal government—its role was to protect and to recognize the laws that the individual states had enacted, but it could not exert positive legislative power. "Slavery is a municipal institution, as unconnected with any control of the United States, as our corporations, our colleges, or our public charities. We would as soon permit others to invade the sanctuary of our dwellings, as to touch it," added Drayton and continued with an implicit threat: "Much as we value this Union, we would rather see it dissolved than yield to such a violation of our rights" (975).

Whittlesey's analogy between the slave and the apprentice troubled southern representatives, as it put slaves on the level of persons, not property, in the eye of the law. The comparison, they felt, was inadequate. In their view, a slave was comparable to an ox. To Dorsey, the differences between apprentices and slaves were "obvious": the apprentice was a free man and therefore legally subject to government authority, which may call him up to join the militia. The governmental power in this case superseded the contractual agreement between apprentice and master. The Constitution, however, did not give the government an analogous right to regulate a master-slave relationship. Moreover, apprentices, in distinction to slaves, were not considered property for the purpose of taxation. Slaves, Dorsey pointed out, had been subject to a direct war tax in 1813. D'Auterive himself, as the owner of Warwick, would have paid taxes on his slave (985–86). Philip P. Barbour (Virginia) reaffirmed Dorsey's views: "A son and an apprentice are citizens of the State—they are members of the political community; and, in that character, they owe, in their own persons, a share of service to the public. [. . .] The slave, as an item of property, is not a member of the body politic; he owes no service on his own account to the Government" (1010). The government thus could gain access to the slave through the "ordinary process of taxation" or the "extraordinary exertion of power, under a pressing public emergency" (1010), that is, through exercising the power of eminent domain.

Tristram Burges (Rhode Island) took issue with Barbour. "Are not all natural persons, who are within the protection of the law, members of the body politic?" (1108), he asked. Samuel C. Allen (Massachusetts) disagreed with the Southerners as well: slavery, he stated, was merely a local institution in some of the states. "When the slave is impressed into the public service," he explained, "the relation created by the municipal law is suspended between him and his master, and he is brought under the public law which regards him as a person and not as property—subjects him to discipline, and makes him answerable for his acts, and punishable for his delinquencies" (1061). John C. Clark of New York argued "that slaves, for certain purposes, are persons; that their masters have in them only a qualified property" (919). Slavery existed at the time the Constitution was established, and it adopted the same conception of slavery as the slaveholding states at that time, "as property of a peculiar character—property so far as their liberty and services were subject to the uncontrolled will of their master—property so far as they were the subjects of sale; but persons so far as the lives and limbs were protected from violation—so far as the right of trial, in some cases by Justices, and in others by a Jury, was concerned; and so far as they increased the national representation of the States owning them." The fact that the Constitution based political representation not on property ownership but on the number of inhabitants in a state suggested that slaves were legal persons as well. Clark also cited Madison's acknowledgement of slaves' "mixed character of persons and property" and stipulated that "the slave is no less evidently regarded by law as a member of society, not as a part of the irrational creation" (918).

While Southerners fought for the position that slaves be considered property, they also stressed that this did not mean that slaves could not be persons at the same time, and they did not perceive this as a contradiction. John Randolph (Virginia) ostensibly confirmed Clark's view: "What new distinction is this, about persons not being property—as if there were any incompatibility between the two? Sir, there is none: there never has been any. Property is the creation of the law. What the law makes property, that is property; and what it declares to be not property, that is not property. There is no other distinction" (920). Yet, while Clark and Randolph seemed to agree on the "mixed character" of slaves, they really held antagonistic positions. For Clark, the humanity and personhood of the slave constrained his status as property; for Randolph, both were unrelated dimensions—in terms of legal definition, it did not matter whether the object of property was a human being, an ox, a horse, or a cart. The representative from New York wanted to grant legal personhood to slaves; his colleague from Virginia denied them such a status.

Rudolph Bunner of New York elaborated on the particular property character of slaves, by insisting on a distinction between "property which has no rational will, and that which has" (977). The fact that a slave is a rational being gives his master only "a right to his services, the right to his bodily and intellectual labor" (977). Returning to the analogy of the son or the apprentice, Bunner suggested that a claim for compensation was warranted in neither case (978). Fellow New Yorker Henry C. Martindale similarly proposed that the services of slaves were precisely valuable because they were rational beings: "Has not the master the same interest, the same in kind, if not in degree, in the services of his apprentice, or his hired servant?" (1073). Martindale was one of the few representatives who argued for the legal personhood of slaves and called into question their status as property; he stressed that a slave had an unalienable right in his life, which the government had to protect: "Strictly, and legally speaking, [. . .] I deny that slaves are property" (1076).

Ultimately, the controversies sparked by Marigny D'Auterive's compensation claim remained unresolved. The House recommitted a revised bill, including a payment for D'Auterive's slave property, to the Committee of Claims in February 1828, which did not further discuss the issue. The House finally passed the bill two years later, but D'Auterive never received any compensation for his slave. The case of D'Auterive is an interesting episode of the sectional conflict because it occurred at a historical moment when the moral arguments about slavery were not yet firmly in place. Both southern and northern representatives had moral reservations about the institution; at best they saw it as a necessary evil. But the debate centered on political and legal, not moral, aspects. Both sides considered their material interests and the costs and benefits of a federal recognition of property rights in slaves. If representatives invoked the rights of African Americans at all, they did so in a purely instrumentalist manner, and not even the few delegates willing to grant them basic natural rights advocated a position of political and social equality. The debate negotiated legal rights and relationships between white men—slaves were objects of the law, not legal subjects.

"THE VERY LIGAMENT WHICH BINDS SOCIETY TOGETHER": DEBATING SLAVERY IN VIRGINIA (1832)

As the previous section has suggested, the congressional debates in the D'Auterive case focused on the federal government's relationship to the institution of slavery, the protection of property rights, and the negotiation of power between free states and slave states. Moral arguments were only peripheral. In this section, I analyze a related debate in the General Assembly of the state of Virginia in the wake of the Nat Turner rebellion. Prior to all the major debates on slavery in the antebellum Congress—and indeed one of the catalysts of these later confrontations—the battle on slavery in the Virginia legislature put most of the major pro- and antislavery arguments in place. This debate also underlined that slavery was not merely a contested topic between the North and the South: in 1832, Virginians intensely discussed a possible emancipation and colonization of the state's slave population in what was "possibly the greatest contest over the peculiar institution to have occurred in any southern state before the Civil War" (Root 2010, 1). The controversy also had special pertinence because Virginia was the largest slave state in the Union, with more slaves than Louisiana, Mississippi, Alabama, and Tennessee together (U.S. Census Office 1832, 46).

In August 1831, Nat Turner and a group of black insurgents had killed more than sixty people in a revolt in Southampton County and thus shaken the state's white inhabitants to their core. Turner himself was captured and hanged, as were most of his accomplices. Yet, in response to the incident, white Virginians grew increasingly concerned for their safety and felt uncomfortable at the thought of being outnumbered by the enslaved and free black population in their state. They circulated petitions, demanding that the state's General Assembly take measures to protect them. The issue intensified an existing rift between the eastern and western parts of Virginia: the east, where the majority of slaveholders resided, defended their right to their slave property, whereas the inhabitants west of the Blue Ridge Mountains generally favored emancipation.[8] However, none of the participants in the debate harbored much concern for the well-being of the people of African descent; all contributors acted out of concern for white safety, as well as white economic prosperity: the economy of Virginia had been in decline, mostly due to an extended depression in the tobacco industry, and many blamed the institution of slavery for the state's lack of development in the manufacturing sector.

The Turner insurrection was a catalyst for the debate on slavery, with deeper causes in longer-term structural issues related to legislative representation. Virginia's 1776 Constitution based suffrage on property ownership, a requirement which heavily favored large freeholders in the east and disfranchised the growing population of merchants and manufacturers in the west, who did not own the fifty acres that would entitle them to vote. The Constitutional Convention of 1829–1830 extended suffrage to include more property owners and taxpayers, but the compromise plan still favored eastern residents because western reformers were not able to pass a representational apportionment system based on the white population. Easterners insisted on a representational system that combined population and taxation, keeping property central to suffrage (Curtis 1997, 31–32).

In response to citizen petitions and pressure generated by the press coverage in the newspapers of the state, the newly elected Virginia legislature took on the issue of possibly abolishing slavery in December 1831. Thomas Jefferson Randolph revitalized a plan that had already been suggested by his grandfather and namesake: Thomas Jefferson had proposed *post nati* emancipation, that is, freedom for slaves born after a certain date when they reached adulthood. According to Randolph's proposal, all enslaved people born after July 4, 1840, would be emancipated: males were to remain in bondage until the age of twenty-one, females until the age of eighteen—after that, they would become public property and work until enough money was raised to pay for their deportation. Slaveholders were free to remove or sell their young slaves out of state before they reached the critical age, thus circumventing automatic dispossession. For Randolph and other proponents of this plan, such a gradual emancipation scheme could serve as a compromise to honor the property rights of slave owners, thereby limiting disruptions of the southern economic system (Root 2010; Curtis 1997, 45).

In the revolutionary era, many of the southern leaders—and slaveholders—considered slavery to be an evil that contradicted the values of the new nation. "There must doubtless be an unhappy influence on the manners of our people produced by the existence of slavery among us," wrote Thomas Jefferson in his *Notes on the State of Virginia*. "The whole commerce between master and slave is a perpetual exercise of the most boisterous passions, the most unremitting despotism on the one part, and degrading submissions on the other" ([1785] 1982, 162). In the *Notes*, Jefferson denounces slavery for causing despotic tendencies in the masters, and for destroying white people's industriousness. Yet, while he believed it to be a disgrace to "permit[] one half [of] the citizens to trample on the rights of the other" (162) and therefore proposed an emancipation scheme, he also rejected the idea that a free black population be incorporated into the body politic (137–38). Upon emancipation, Jefferson insisted, removal was necessary, in order to avoid that the freed slave "mix[ed] with" and "stain[ed] the blood of his master" (143). Like Jefferson, many Virginians in the antebellum period advanced the necessary evil thesis, which provided "not a defense of slavery, per se" but "a defense of the slaveholders" (Curtis 1997, 7), insisting that it was impossible to abolish slavery because of the state's economic dependency upon slave labor; slavery was the only means by which the large black population could be controlled; and the sanctity of private property rights made impossible any governmental interference with slavery without full compensation for slave owners (7–20).

Unlike in the congressional confrontation between the North and the South, in the case of Marigny D'Auterive, the delegates in the Virginia General Assembly all acknowledged the legal property rights of slaveholders—all participants were aware that, within the legal and political system of the state, slaves functioned as property and their owners held legally sanctioned rights, even if they condemned slavery from a moral standpoint. Delegates absolved themselves from responsibility in the matter, insinuating that it had been Britain who originally introduced slaves into the colony, leaving the state in a position of dependency on the British property and labor system after Independence. "We are not responsible for the existence of slavery among us," thus claimed James Gholson (Brunswick County), the most vocal defender of the proslavery position (Root 2010, 49). And Rice W. Wood (Albemarle) suggested that "the present race of Virginia were no more responsible for its [slavery's] existence here, than the Quakers of Pennsylvania"—the institution "had been forced upon their forefathers" (131). In Wood's account, southern slaveholders appeared as victims, not as responsible agents. But the advocates of emancipation similarly assumed a passive tone: slaves "were cast upon our shores at a period when we had not the authority to exclude them by legislative provision," explained Charles J. Faulkner (Berkeley), who also blamed the current situation on "the inexorable tyranny of the British government" (109).

With the institution being increasingly called into question, however, its defenders began to shift their argument from "necessary evil" to slavery being a "positive good"; that is, they began to defend not merely the slaveholders but the institution of slavery itself as being beneficial for society (see Curtis 1997; Root 2008; A. G. Freehling 1982). Its advocates claimed that slaves in Virginia were, in the words of Gholson, "as happy a laboring class as exists upon the habitable globe"; they were better taken care of than the miserable laboring classes in Europe, and they were not only a "happy" population but "a contented, peaceful, and harmless one" (Root 2010, 49). Alex G. Knox (Mecklenburg) hailed slavery as "indispensably requisite in order to preserve the forms of a Republican Government" and part of the "inherent nature of society" (148). He, too, argued that slaves profited from their status, which he considered to be an improvement to their lives in Africa, prior to enslavement, and better than that of free peasants and workers.

Thomas R. Dew, in his *Review of the Debate in the Virginia Legislature of 1831 and 1832*, summarized the proslavery "positive good" arguments for the first time—his text is generally credited with providing the intellectual basis for the defense of slavery in subsequent decades. Refuting the "necessary evil" conception, he acknowledged that "slavery is against the spirit of Christianity," an "original sin" committed by colonial Virginians. He did not find any proof in Scripture, however, where it stated that continuing it was a moral offense—after all, the Biblical patriarchs had held slaves themselves (Dew 1832, 106). Addressing Jefferson's idea that slavery fostered despotic tendencies in the masters, he asserted that, in reality, the master-slave relationship strengthened "benevolence and humanity" in the former (109), while a "merrier being does not exist on the face of the globe, than the negro slave of the United States" (111). Slavery also allegedly strengthened the republican spirit of the nation, as it fostered a sense of equality and community among whites of different classes, while the dangers of insurrection, Dew claimed, were really miniscule—after all, most slaves were content with their situation, and cases like that of Nat Turner were the exception. Lastly, he also discredited the notion that slave labor was less productive than free labor, suggesting that the current demise in the southern economy was largely caused by disadvantageous federal policies (106–130).

The representatives of the eastern part of Virginia, then, the region where most slaves were concentrated, were, for the most part, highly critical of Randolph's emancipation plans. Taking up the public demand for immediate action, they insinuated that the scheme would aggravate the danger of more violent insurrections. To be sure, the plan would not emancipate any slave for several decades; yet the debate itself might stir up more unrest among the enslaved: if they got the impression that the Turner rebellion had brought them closer to freedom, would they not get the idea that further revolts would result in their emancipation? "If *one insurrection* has been sufficient to secure the liberty of *succeeding* generations, might it not be inferred that *another* would achieve the freedom of the present?" asked Gholson (Root 2010, 53). Moreover, the gradual emancipation scheme would differentiate arbitrarily between slaves who could hope to achieve freedom and those who would remain in bondage forever, depending on their dates of birth. This could also be cause for unrest and revolts.

The main arguments of proslavery forces, however, were economic and legal ones. Even a gradual emancipation, they stated, would be an infringement on their property rights. They repeatedly invoked the legal maxim of "partus sequitur ventrem"—the idea that the offspring followed the condition of the mother, meaning that a child born to a slave mother was also a slave, irrespective of paternity (45). This law hailed from an act passed by the Virginia Assembly in 1662, which, contrary to the English Common Law of villeinage, stipulated that the status of a slave was to be determined by the status of the mother, not the father (Morris 1996, 43–49). One of the arguments for *post nati* emancipation was that only yet unborn slaves would be freed; if at all, this would only touch on prospective, future property rights but not lead to dispossession. Proslavery delegates disagreed. For them, their property rights were not merely attached persons living at the time, but part of the value of their slaves derived from the expectation of a future increase in property. A female slave was more valuable because of the prospect that her offspring would also be property; gradual emancipation would thus drive down the value of female slaves and deprive the owner of his future property. Gholson argued that Randolph's plan would lead to "much pecuniary embarrassment and distress" for his constituency, who looked upon slaves as their major stock of capital. He pleaded:

> Sir, we are in debt; and professing to be an honest people, we are anxious to pay. Our slaves constitute the largest portion of our wealth, and by their value, regulate the price of nearly all the property we possess. Their value on the other hand, is regulated by the demand for it in the western markets; and any measures that should close those markets against us, would essentially impair our wealth and prosperity. (Root 2010, 54)

Proslavery forces were also highly skeptical about the political expediency of emancipation. What would happen with the freed population? It was generally agreed upon that free blacks in large numbers should not remain in the state of Virginia. All representatives in favor of emancipation also advocated for deportation, possibly back to Africa, where the American Colonization Society had already established a colony of free blacks in Liberia. Haiti and other places in the West Indies were also destinations they took into consideration. Some thought about sending blacks to Mexico or to a specifically designated territory in the West. Yet, how would this removal be paid for? Slaveholders feared that they would not only be dispossessed but they would subsequently also have to pay taxes to finance the deportation of their former property.

James Gholson pronounced Randolph's plan to be "monstrous and unconstitutional" (43). The proposed scheme amounted to "the confiscation of property, without crime—the appropriation of private property to public uses, *without just compensation*" (44). For Gholson, it violated the stipulation of the Fifth Amendment to the Constitution as well as the state constitution of Virginia. But he went even further by announcing that it infringed upon "principles of justice" and civilization. The right to property, he held, "is the very ligament which binds society together." Gholson's argument was based on John Locke's liberal idea that men entered the social contract to form a society that protected their property through mutually agreed upon laws: "The great and *chief end* therefore, of Mens [sic] uniting into Commonwealths, and putting themselves under Government, *is the Preservation of their Property*" (Locke [1689] 1988, Second Treatise, §124). According to Locke, then, without the inviolability of property rights, the state would lose its raison d'être, and Gholson likewise insisted that if that ligament was severed, "society itself is no longer worth preservation—nay, a statue of nature itself would be desirable" (Root 2010, 44). In a state of nature, he continued, there would at least be no tyranny of a majority, which infringed on the rights of a (property-owning) minority. Gholson here appropriated the idea, prominent among the founders of the nation, that the property-owning minority must be protected from usurpation by an unpropertied majority. He likened the popular pressure to end slavery in Virginia to James Madison's vision of a tyranny of the majority which posed a threat to the vested property rights of slaveholders.

William Brodnax (Dinwiddie) explicitly elaborated on this idea: "What, sir, are constitutions, and charters, and bills of rights, ever made for?" he asked. "Are they not devised to protect the rights of the few, against the aggressions of the many? They are necessary to secure to *minorities* their privileges and their property—to stay the lawless hand of public violence." Like Gholson, Brodnax characterized Randolph's plan as "monstrous" and "a disruption of all the ties, which bind society together" (67). Slavery, he demanded, which preceded the federal and state constitutions, must be treated as any other kind of property and receive the same protection. Only in the case of absolute necessity, should public safety and prosperity be endangered, did the state have a right to infringe on private property rights, and only if just compensation was provided.

While the proslavery forces saw private property rights, including the property rights in slaves, as the very foundation of society, those representatives in favor of emancipation built their arguments on an entirely different conception, on one which emphasized the right of eminent domain and the police powers of the state. For them, people's safety was superior to the right to property. They argued that if a property posed a threat to the public well-being, or even if its perpetuation did not benefit society overall, dispossession was justified, even without compensation. Slave property, they suggested, was a nuisance to society, and it was not a part of the common law, it was merely introduced as a statutory right. As such, it was subject to regulation through the legislature.

Apart from seeing slavery and the enslaved as a dangerous threat to society, its opponents also believed that it had caused the state's recent economic downturn. They argued that slavery was an inferior form of labor because slaves had no interest in the products of their labor, and the menial tasks they performed did not require much or any education (151). The slavery system also did not encourage white immigration. The state's white population stagnated, whereas the number of blacks rose dramatically, an increase only dampened because Virginia was one of the main exporters of slaves to other states and territories in the West. With a further increase of the black population in the future, white people would be outnumbered by black people. For many, the abolition of slavery would thus provide for the safety and prosperity of future generations of whites.

Charles Faulkner, a representative from Virginia's western part, argued that property was not the highest law, as some of his colleagues maintained, but "a right *contingent*." "Property is the creature of civil society," he suggested. It was granted to the slaveholder "solely by the virtue of the acquiescence and consent of the society in which they live" (106). Therefore, society had the right to abolish this property, if it became a threat to its own best interests. Faulkner's conception of the relationship of private property rights and the state thus notably differed from the Lockean conception advanced by his opponents. If the safety of the state demanded it, a property owner could be dispossessed without compensation. Faulkner drew a distinction between the condemnation of private property for public use—as regulated in the Fifth Amendment—and the removal of property "which is ascertained to be a positive wrong to society" (107) and which thus remained uncompensated. The state, he explained, did not have the means to provide full compensation; pushing emancipation into the future thus acted as a compromise.

William B. Preston (Montgomery) took on Gholson's argument that emancipation infringed on the slave owners' constitutionally guaranteed property rights. He dismissed the idea that the U.S. Constitution's Fifth Amendment protected the right in slaves because it was only applicable to actions of the federal government, not those of a state. Although the Constitution of Virginia, in the 11th clause of its 3rd article, included the same phrase as the Fifth Amendment to the federal constitution, Preston denied Gholson's claim that this stipulation included the protection of slave property. Preston invoked a quote from Thomas Jefferson's original draft of the Declaration of Independence, which charged Great Britain with "violating its most sacred rights of life and liberty in the persons of a distant people," by subjecting them to slavery (qtd in 137). People were not considered property under common law; blacks became slaves only "by statutory enactments" (137–38). The legislature therefore had the power to define what was or was not property, and society's well-being and the necessity of self-preservation demanded the abolition of slavery, even at the cost of infringing on property rights.

Preston also insisted that "the slave has a natural right to regain his liberty" (137), thereby debunking the argument voiced by Gholson and others that Virginia's slaves were happy and content: "happiness[] is incompatible with slavery. The love of liberty is the ruling passion of man; it has been implanted in his bosom by the voice of God, and he cannot be happy if deprived of it" (138). George W. Summers (Kanawha), another representative from western Virginia, added that property in slaves did not derive from the common law, like property in land, but that human beings "become property only by force" (158). Human property had a dual character, since, according to the very laws of Virginia, a slave was also "on some respects" considered a person: "Personal rights are secured to him. The master is bound to feed and clothe him, and to provide for him in old age. Not so with his horse. To kill him is murder" (158).

Toward the end of the debate, James McDowell (Rockbridge) summarized the emancipationist argument. Like Faulkner and Preston, he insisted that private property rights were not absolute but werc, instead, secondary to the right to security: "The rights of private property and of personal security exist under every government, but they are not *equal*. Security is the primary purpose for which men enter into government; property, beyond a sufficiency for natural wants, is only a secondary purpose" (241). Indeed, to put it the other way around would be, yet again, "monstrous": "it would [. . .] make man with all his rights of life and liberty and happiness, subordinate to the workmanship of his own hands—to the very commodity, the very property by which he intended to aid and accommodate his person. [. . .] There is no sacredness in this property which is equal to the sacredness of personal security" (242). McDowell here notably diverged from the Lockean conception, arguing that rights were conventional and granted by the state—the rights of the state were thus primary over the private rights of the individual, and the state could regulate and qualify these private rights.

The debate in the Virginia legislature lasted for two weeks, without generating any substantive resolutions with regard to slavery, but it did intensify the sectionalism between the eastern and western parts of the state (Root 2008, 165–66). The major argument focused on the definition of property rights and the relationship between the private rights of the individual and the powers of the state. While the proponents of slavery adhered to a traditional, Lockean conception of private property rights, their adversaries challenged this position by invoking the power of eminent domain, "an assumed and largely undefined power" in 1832 Virginia (Curtis 1997, 77). Though takings of private property for public purposes, such as the building of roads, had existed since colonial times, in these cases, owners were compensated for their losses. The advocates of emancipation in the Virginia debate suggested that the state could take property without compensation under the power of eminent domain, on account of its police powers. In arguing that property rights were granted to individuals by the state—rather than conceive of them as natural rights antecedent to the social contract—they relied on older, European conceptions, which gave the state prerogative ownership rights rather than placing the sovereignty in the people (Huffman 2013, 58–59). At the same time, the view that granted the state greater legislative power can also be aligned with an emerging instrumentalist conception of property, which promoted economic development and prioritized the latter over the idea of vested rights (Horwitz 1992a, 31–62).

PROPERTY OR PERSON? (II): THE CASE OF ANTONIO PACHECO (1848)

The controversy over slavery in the Virginia General Assembly foreshadowed a larger national political debate that intensified in the 1830s, as abolitionism developed as a mass movement in the North and increasingly turned its attention to the U.S. Congress. Both William Lloyd Garrison's paper *The Liberator*, founded in 1831, and the Declaration of Sentiments issued at the founding of the American Anti-Slavery Society in 1833 urged for federal restrictions on slavery. Abolitionists demanded that Congress uses its power to immediately end slavery in the District of Columbia, to reject the admission of new slave states, and to bar slavery from U.S. territories and federal property. They were also well aware that bringing slavery into the highly publicized congressional debates constituted an effective means to widely disseminate their arguments to a northern audience (C. M. Brooks 2019, 7). In order to force politicians to address the slavery question, antislavery societies sent political petitions to federal and state legislatures by the thousands. Congress responded with a gag rule, through which abolitionist petitions were automatically tabled, but this only had the effect of further abolitionist mobilization. According to Manisha Sinha, more than six hundred thousand petitions with nearly two million signatures were sent to Congress and state legislatures during the antebellum era (2016, 252). Abolitionists framed the gag rule as an assault on their civil liberties, their right to petition, and thus as further evidence that the spirit of slavery encroached on northern peoples' rights as free citizens (C. M. Brooks 2019, 20).[9]

Between 1836 and 1845, legislators in both chambers sought to suppress a discussion on the topic of slavery. With the United States's war against Mexico from 1846 to 1848 and the subsequent expansion of the country's territory, the question of whether the new future territories would be slave or free states, and therefore an open sectional crisis, could no longer be evaded. In the context of the 1848 presidential election, antislavery Democrats and Whigs joined the abolitionist Liberty Party to form the Free Soil Party. Their candidate for the presidency, former president Martin Van Buren, drew 10.1 percent of the popular vote, the largest share of votes for a third-party candidate up to that point in history.

Twenty years after the case of D'Auterive, in late 1848 and early 1849, the House of Representatives discussed a similar compensation case relating to the petition of the legal representatives of one Antonio Pacheco. Representatives again deliberated at length as to whether slaves, in the legal sense, were property, persons, or both. The issue concerned a compensation claim for the loss of a slave during the Florida war against the Seminoles. During the second Seminole War, Antonio Pacheco had lent his slave Lewis to act as a guide and interpreter for the command of Major Dade. When the Seminoles captured and massacred the command, they took Lewis, one of the few survivors. Subsequently, when the tribe surrendered, its chief, Jumper, claimed Lewis as his property since he had captured him in battle. According to contemporary reports, Lewis was an educated man who spoke four languages and knew how to read and write. General Thomas Jesup, one of the commanders during the war, was convinced that Lewis had been conspiring with the Indians. After having lived with the Seminoles for about two years, Lewis returned to Fort Peyton, near St. Augustine, but was sent west by Jesup, who considered Lewis to be a traitor, working against the Americans.[10]

In the aftermath of the war, representatives of the now-deceased Pacheco claimed government compensation for the loss of their property, on the grounds that the government's employment of Lewis constituted a taking for public use under the Fifth Amendment of the Constitution. At the point of the debate discussed here, the claim had already been circulating in Congress for several years. Antonio Pacheco's widow, Quintina Pacheco, had first petitioned to Congress through her attorney on November 9, 1839. The claim was forwarded to the Committee of Claims in 1841. The Committee twice introduced bills to the House, in 1842 and 1844, neither of which was successful. The third attempt passed in the House but was never brought to discussion in the Senate. In the last attempt, Mrs. Pacheco's claim was again brought before the Committee of Military Affairs in 1850, but again nothing came of it and Mrs. Pacheco never received any money (Amos 2006).

In 1848, the five southern and four northern delegates in the Committee of Military Affairs could not come to an agreement and thus filed a majority and a minority report (U.S. Congress 1848). The House of Representatives had to decide whether a claim for compensation of 1,000 dollars was justified, that is, whether Lewis could be considered private property taken for public use. The basic legal questions in the Pacheco case were thus identical to those debated in the D'Auterive case: did the federal government recognize property in slaves or not? Were slaves property, persons, or both, in the eye of the law? The rhetoric of the participants, however, had shifted significantly. The lines between the North and the South had been drawn in a more sustained way, and the words of the representatives became more confrontational.

Armistead Burt of South Carolina submitted the majority report for the Committee on Military Affairs, which argued that Pacheco was deprived of his property when Lewis was sent away with the Seminoles and that he rightfully claimed compensation under the Fifth Amendment. Aware of the issue's controversy within Congress, Burt proceeded with detailed arguments to make a case for the claim. During the Seminole War, he explained, Lewis was lost to the indigenous tribe but later returned to the custody of military officers, though not to his previous owner. Referring to Emeric de Vattel's treatise on international law, he characterized this as a case in which the rule of postliminy applied. According to Vattel, governments in international conflicts had the duty to protect their citizens' property; if private property was lost in the course of war, but later restored under the power of a nation, ownership rights must be restored as well. Since Lewis was not returned to his owner, the government was liable to pay compensation.

Moreover, Lewis, in this case, was withheld from his owner for public benefit: Jesup, the commanding officer, "justified the act solely by considerations of public policy, the evil character of the slave, and the necessity to the quiet and tranquility of the community, that he should be transported with the Indians to the west" (U.S. Congress 1848, 5). The case was thus analogous to many other cases in which the government had compensated the loss of private property—the only argument to refuse compensation would be that slaves could not be property, which, Burt held, was contrary to historical practice. The Constitution only omitted slaves as property in terms of phrasing, but not in spirit. The executive of the federal government also recognized property in slaves, for instance in its peace treaty with Great Britain from 1783, which contained a stipulation that Britain would withdraw from American soil without "carrying away any negroes or other property of the American inhabitants" (8). A similar provision was found in the peace treaty of 1814 between the two countries. Burt furthermore cited a number of treaties with indigenous nations, which similarly referenced slaves as property. Relying on several Supreme Court decisions, Burt showed that the judicative, the third branch of government, had also recognized property rights in slaves.

The four northern committee members, John Dickey, James Wilson, David Fisher, and Dudley Marvin, rejected the arguments of the southern majority. Even if one, for the sake of argument, acknowledged that Lewis was Pacheco's property at the time given, Dickey wrote on behalf of the dissenters, the question was whether he was legitimately taken for public use. By sending the slave west, he argued, the officer had exceeded his authority to act in the name of government—setting a slave free did not constitute public use. Yet, more gravely, the representative claimed that the character of slavery and the federal government's as well as the free states' relationship to the institution spoke against making compensation payments.

Dickey advanced a moral argument by stating that "the inhabitants of Africa are seized in violation of the dictates of humanity and of the natural rights of man" (16). He thus introduced the idea of natural personhood rights, an argument that had not yet been used in the D'Auterive case. Since the capture and enslavement of a person constituted a violation of their natural rights, they did "owe no allegiance whatever to our government" (16). Lewis therefore had a moral right to leave his state of bondage when the opportunity arose; thus, by going with the Indians after Dade's defeat, he became free. When he was returned into the custody of government, he did so as a prisoner of war; in the absence of any law in Florida that would justify his re-enslavement, his former master no longer had any legal claims to him.

Dickey also considered at length the federal government's relationship to the institution of slavery, and, like Burt and the southern majority, he used the Constitutional Convention and the papers of James Madison as a central reference point. Citing extensively from Madison's notes on the Convention, he highlighted the concerns of delegates at the time to not sanction slavery in the foundational document. Speaking of "persons" whenever referring to slaves, Dickey emphasized that, with respect to the Constitution, slaves were never to be regarded as property. Madison himself had been opposed to acknowledging property rights in slaves because he believed that it was "wrong to admit in the Constitution the idea that there could be property in man" (19). Dickey capitalized on this statement, citing a direct quote from Madison, to underline his main point.

Dickey also countered Burt's argument that the executive and judicial branches of government had ever affirmed the property character of slaves. Referring to the case *Groves v. Slaughter* (40 U.S. 449 [1841]), which upheld Missouri's state law that prohibited the importation of slaves, he held that the decision merely relied on the local law of the state, which the federal government accepted and protected but did not positively enact. Dickey also pointed out that the Committee could not rely on any precedent cases where compensation for a slave had been paid by the government, since many similar claims had been rejected. Throughout, the dissent emphasized the local character of slavery and the powerlessness of the federal government to interfere with local laws. All states possessed "equal and perfectly reciprocal" rights (24), and the federal government equally belonged to all of them. In the case of slavery, it meant that the federal government needed to act neutrally. If it were to pay compensation in the Pacheco case, the four representatives felt that this would mean that the Northerners supported slavery, as federal funds would be appropriated in the payment.

The House of Representatives began debating the Pacheco case on December 23, 1848. Relying on the arguments presented in the minority report, both Dickey and Wilson attempted to convince the delegates that the claim was unjustified. The abolitionist and Free Soiler Joshua Giddings, representative of Ohio, delivered the most impassioned speech on behalf of the northern position. Giddings's speech made frequent reference to the liberal values expressed in the Declaration of Independence and the Constitution, emphasizing that these meant to ensure freedom to all living under the jurisdiction of the United States. Like the authors of the minority report, Giddings quoted from the Madison Papers, relating the views of some members of the Constitutional Convention who had been careful not to sanction the institution of slavery. He also pointed out that there were no precedents of paying for slaves and, moreover, that such claims for compensation were a relatively recent phenomenon, unknown before 1816, when many of the founders were still part of the legislature. Southern representatives, he thus argued, were refuting the foundational patriotic values:

> Statesmen, now, in the high councils of the nation, deny that 'all men are created equal;' that 'they are endowed by their Creator with the unalienable right to their lives and their liberties;' or, that 'Governments are instituted among men to secure the enjoyment of those rights.' It is now urged, that this Government was instituted for the purpose of robbing men of those rights; of disrobing a portion of our race of their humanity, and reducing them to the state of brutes, and making them the property of others. (U.S. Congress 1848, 174)

Giddings here not merely drew attention to the contradictions between liberal constitutional values and the institution of slavery, but also used this rhetoric to increase the polarization between the North and the South. He explicitly put slaves on the same level as free persons; in speaking of "our race" he referred to the human race, not the "white race." Considering persons as "the property of others," he emphasized, meant to deny them their inherent humanity in a criminal act: they were "robbed" of their rights, "disrobed." Giddings certainly did not expect to convince the southern delegates of this position—to the passage just quoted, he subsequently addressed his fellow Northerners in a number of rhetorical questions: "Will northern members assist to commit this outrage upon the honor of the nation and constitutional rights of the northern States? Is there a member from the free States who will vote to tax his constituents to pay for the blood, and bones, and muscles, of southern slaves?" (174). Giddings repeatedly stressed that Northerners, in agreeing to compensation claims, "would render *northern freemen* subsidiary to the support of *southern slavery*" (174). In addition to patriotic arguments, he also appealed to the representatives' moral consciences: the legislative branch, he stated, may very well have the power to change the country's foundational laws, but doing so, with respect to slavery, would mean "to deface the work of God" (174). Giddings thus clearly designed his speech to mobilize fellow northern representatives, with an eye to the public discourse outside the halls of Congress,[11] thereby highlighting the immorality of ascribing a commodity value to a person and drawing attention to Lewis's education, which, he claimed, may have surpassed that of some of the members of the legislature:

> He is said to be very intelligent and learned, reading and writing four languages. In this respect he has, probably, few equals in this Hall. [. . .] I regard the moral qualities of a man as the proper criterion by which to graduate my respect. In this light, I know not whether the comparison be unjust to him or to those who estimate his value at precisely a thousand dollars. I would be as willing to enter into an inquiry as to the value of the body of the honorable member reporting this bill, as I am to estimate the value of a man, who, as a linguist, probably has not a dozen equals in this body. (174)

Concluding his remarks, Giddings again quoted from the Madison Papers, reemphasizing the constitutional equality of all men. He suggested that the northern states were willing to grant Southerners the right to their local institution. However, "we will have no participation in its guilt" (177). For the constituents of the free states, he claimed "the constitutional right of being exempt from support[ing]" slavery (177).

Giddings's speech certainly was the most provocative intervention in the debate on the Pacheco case, due to its fiery rhetoric and also in terms of the arguments he provided. He, in fact, advanced the same ideas that abolitionists had propagated since the 1830s, with perhaps the most influential being that of Theodore Weld in his *American Slavery As It Is* (1839), a damning account of southern paternalism, which insisted that African Americans had the same constitutional rights as white Americans. No other members of the House pressed as distinctly the point of the slave's equality to the white citizens of the United States. But the insistence on moral arguments—and the concomitant characterization of slavery being immoral and evil—achieved much more prominence in this debate than it did in the discussion that had taken place on the D'Auterive case twenty years earlier. In 1848, the rhetorical dominance seemed to have shifted to the North, and the arguments against property rights in slaves were now moral ones, deeply embedded in abolitionist discourse, which resulted in a radicalization of each side's rhetoric.

STATES' RIGHTS, CONGRESSIONAL POWER, AND NATURAL LAW: SLAVERY IN THE TERRITORIES

In 1850, the Union came precariously close to dissolution—the North and the South seemed irreconcilably opposed over several unresolved and evermore pressing issues, most of which pertained to slavery. After the United States's victory in the Mexican War (1846–48), which had been provoked by President James Polk with the objective of a large land grab, the United States acquired massive amounts of additional land, comprising most of the territory covered today by California, Nevada, Arizona, and Utah, as well as parts of New Mexico, Colorado, Wyoming, Oklahoma, and Texas. The new additions reignited the debate on slavery in the territories, which had been previously put to rest in the Missouri Compromise. The conflict was further fueled by Texas's claim of part of New Mexico; California's sudden surge in population due to the gold rush, making the territory eligible for statehood practically overnight; strong southern demands for a fugitive slave law that would authorize the federal government to persecute fugitives in northern states and return them,[12] which enraged abolitionists in the North; and the pressure exerted by abolitionists to end the slave trade in the

District of Columbia, which infuriated southern slaveholders (Finkelman 2012b, 1–12).

The key issue debated in Congress pertained to the question as to which governmental entity had the right to legislate over the status of slavery in the territories. In 1846, when the House of Representatives appropriated two million dollars for President Polk to negotiate an end to the Mexican War, freshman delegate David Wilmot of Pennsylvania introduced an additional paragraph to the bill which would have outlawed slavery in all of the acquired land. The so-called Wilmot Proviso ended up later polarizing the debate, until the South seceded and the Civil War began. With Congress being more divided than ever, Senator Henry Clay introduced five compromise resolutions on January 29, 1850. This was followed by seven months of intense debate, before the resolutions, modified by senator Stephen Douglas of Illinois, were finally passed. These laws included the establishment of two new territories (New Mexico and Utah), the entrance of California into the Union as a free state, and the infamous Fugitive Slave Act that required the North to persecute escaped southern slaves.[13] In the bill that was passed, Southerners managed to modify the resolutions to their benefit; they ensured that slavery could be extended to multiple new states in the West, thereby burying the hope of a United States where slavery was on the wane and bound to disappear.

Again, the conflict was a contest about political and economic hegemony, and property rights played a central role in the debate. As Huston notes: "From the beginning of their defense of slavery's ability to expand into the West, southerners used a property rights argument, and that defense continued unabatedly until the moment of secession" (2003, 119). Southerners once again insisted that the purpose of government was the protection of property rights, and since slaves were property, this extended also to property rights in slaves. They also reiterated their claim that the Constitution itself was the result of a compromise in which Northerners had agreed not to attack southern property rights. The western territories commonly belonged to the North and the South. They were the property of all the states, and therefore all property rights needed to be respected. To restrict slavery in the territories, the Southerners asserted, was a discrimination against the slaveholder who would be prevented from taking his property anywhere he pleased. Once more, they thus emphasized states' rights over federal rights, in order to protect the property rights of slaveholders (126–28).

Senator John Calhoun of South Carolina, the preeminent voice of the proslavery South, was the main architect of the southern legal argument for the constitutionality of the western expansion of slavery. In his speeches, he defended slavery as "a positive good" (Calhoun 1854, 2:631), in the tradition of Thomas Dew: African Americans, he argued, had never before in history "attained a condition so civilized and so improved, not only physically, but morally and intellectually"; under the condition of slavery, they had become civilized and increased in numbers, which, to Calhoun, constituted a proof of "the happiness of the race" (2:630). The emancipation of slaves, as desired by the abolitionists, Calhoun warned, would not only upset the institution but would also lead to equality between blacks and whites, thereby reversing the situation and turning whites into slaves (2:633). Contrary to Henry Clay and many other Southerners who had insisted that human beings became property only by positive law, Calhoun argued that there was no distinction between slaves and other property and that slave property needed no special enactment by legislation, no more than any other forms of property. While laws regulated slavery and legislatures had the power to prohibit the institution, the master-slave relationship as such constituted a preexisting relation.

Calhoun held that the states had adopted the Constitution as sovereign entities, in order to profit from more security and to achieve political and social advantages. At the same time, however, the individual states retained their own "domestic institutions and police," institutions upon which other states were not allowed to encroach (3:140). In this scheme, the object of the federal government was to ensure the stability of the states' institutions and to protect them from attack by one or a number of other member states. The equality of rights of the individual states would no longer be given if the southern states were limited in expanding their institutions to new territories "under the pretext that the institution of slavery [. . .] is immoral or sinful, or otherwise obnoxious" and would "in effect, disfranchise the slaveholding States, by withholding from them the advantages, while it subjected them to the burdens of the Government" (3:141).

Calhoun also emphasized that the territories were common property of all the states: Congress, in this setup, was merely the "representative of the States of this Union" and thereby held no right to pass any laws discriminating against individual states. If a law passed by Congress hindered citizens of the states to move to the territories with their property, this would constitute such discrimination and violate the Constitution. Moreover, a prescription by Congress as to the status of a territory would infringe upon the liberties of its inhabitants to self-determine their government and laws, their "unconditional right to form and adopt the government which they may think best calculated to secure their liberty, prosperity, and happiness" (4:348–49). Congress could not establish rules which gave preference to one state over another, "without depriving the State or section over which the preference is given, or from which the advantage is withheld, of their clear and unquestionable right, and subverting the very foundation on which the Union and Government rest" (4:497).

Along with Calhoun, Jefferson Davis, the future president of the Confederacy who, at this time, served as Democratic senator of Mississippi, was one of the most vocal voices of the extreme southern position. Davis insisted on the "national character" of property and a constitutionally guaranteed right to "property in persons held to service" (1848, 2). In a speech delivered on February 13 and 14, 1850, he declared: "The claim is set up for the Federal Government not only to restrict slavery from entering the Territories, but [. . .] in fact, to strip it of every protection it derives from Government. [. . .] As a property recognized by the Constitution, and held in a portion of the States, the Federal Government is bound to admit it into all the Territories, and to give it such protection as other private property receives" (1850, 3–4). Davis here appealed to the shared liberal values of Americans, particularly to the sanctity of property which was the federal government's job to protect. Notably, he did not attempt to ethically justify slavery; in fact, he hardly even mentioned slaves as human beings, preferring to speak of "slave property":

> [S]lave property, like all other, is not the creation of statute, it is regulated by law like other tenures and relations of society, but like other property, must have existed before laws were passed concerning it [. . .]. [. . .] This kind of property was not established here by law, nor did it originate here. It came into the colonies as all other property, subject to the common law which then governed them; and from time to time, laws have been passed to regulate it, but never to establish it. (15)

Davis here naturalizes and universalizes slavery, justifying "slave property" as something that existed prior to legislation. His whole argument rested on the vocabulary of liberalism, framing southern interests in terms of individual rights and Constitutional protection. This entailed the complete objectification of the enslaved population, denying them any degree of legal personhood, or even humanity. Davis thus sought to rhetorically empower the South and protect southern slaveholders' material interests by attempting to construct a hegemonic narrative which relied on a particular interpretation of the nation's history and the Constitution, as well as a specific understanding of property rights.

In sharp contrast, Northerners, who were for the most part in favor of the Wilmot Proviso, claimed congressional authority over the territories. If a territory did not have slavery prior to its acquisition by the United States, they argued, then the federal government could and should not establish it—and, as it happened, Mexico had abolished slavery in 1822. Only once a territory achieved statehood and gave itself a constitution could state legislators assume the power to allow slavery in the new state. Furthermore, Northerners could refer to precedence: in the Northwest Ordinance of 1787, which was taken up by the Constitution, and in the Missouri Compromise of 1820, Congress had already regulated slavery in the territories. They also referred to

Article 4, sec. 3, par. 2 of the Constitution, which granted Congress the power to create the rules and regulations for territories belonging to the United States (J. L. Huston 2003, 121–23).

But the Northerners were not united in their support for Clay's proposal. Less than a month after Davis's speech, on March 11, 1850, William Henry Seward of New York, one of the most prominent antislavery politicians, delivered an equally defiant address because he believed that the compromise would actually lead to an extension of slavery. Seward first attacked the assumption of the need for a political equilibrium between "free" and "slave" states, derived from the premise (attributed to Vattel) that states, as an accumulation of individuals with equal rights, must be equal in terms of their natural rights as well. He then went on to refute the notion that Congress had no power to regulate the subject of slavery in the territories, pointing to the constitutional powers of Congress to admit or reject new states, which also gave the legislative branch the power to impose conditions, among those being rules and regulations concerning the public domain. Seward concluded his speech by insisting that slavery was a temporary institution and emancipation inevitable. At the same time, he reassured his southern colleagues that the North would not interfere with the internal affairs of the slave states: "No free state claims to extend its legislation into a slave state. None claims that Congress shall usurp power to abolish slavery in the slave states. None claims that any violent, unconstitutional, or unlawful measure shall be embraced" (1994, 315).

The Compromise of 1850 helped postpone the dissolution of the Union for another ten years and temporarily settled the question of slavery in the territories, which however resurfaced with the debate on the status of Kansas and Nebraska in 1854. Another three years later, the Supreme Court—under Chief Justice Roger B. Taney and with a southern majority—famously ruled in *Dred Scott v. Sandford* (60 U.S. 393, [1857]) that the federal government did *not* have power to determine the status of the territories as being either free or slave, thereby in effect declaring the Missouri Compromise void.

SLAVERY AND THE DISCOURSE ON PROPERTY

The political debate over slavery in the antebellum era was mainly about the nature of property and the right to define it. What was or could be property was a matter of contestation during the period, and the debate on these issues was intricately interrelated with questions of political and economic power. Conceptions and justifications of property were tied to ideas about the social order and the material distribution of resources. They defined the relationships between the states and the federal government, as well as the position of the individual within that order. One of the major philosophical issues of the time was whether property or property rights were a matter of natural or common law, or whether property was always a function of positive law. Over the course of the decades examined here, the discourse underwent major shifts, especially with regard to the question of slavery. At the outset of the debate, the proponents of slavery were mostly inclined to argue that slaves were property according to positive law: they were property if the law said that they were property. This relativist position emphasized the power of the states to enact property laws, but it also constituted a weak spot for the South: positive laws could more easily be overruled by new legislation, making the abolition of slavery a threatening possibility. The early argument that slavery was a necessary evil, inherited from British colonialism, was later replaced by a stronger assertion of slavery being a positive good. Along with this change in the line of reasoning went a naturalization of property rights in slaves: politicians like Jefferson Davis would draw attention to slavery as being an "eternal" institution which already existed according to common law. They thereby came up with the idea of a natural right to slaves at the very moment that antislavery forces insisted on the natural rights of the individual to their freedom.

The antislavery positions voiced in legislative debates also developed over the course of time, spurred on by the abolitionist movement, which developed the strategic argument of that the "slave power" was threatening to encroach on the rights of free Americans. The northern ideal of property ownership was that of the small yeoman farmer, for whom property had emancipatory potential and was associated with self-ownership and autonomy. The commodification of human beings, denying them their liberty and the fruits of their labor, was increasingly framed as a threat to the economic model of the North and an assault on human rights.

The sectional conflict between the North and the South emerged as a struggle for hegemony between two different political forces. With Laclau, we may think of the two sections not as two stable opposing entities that preexisted the conflict which ultimately led to the Civil War but as an antagonism which was produced by that very conflict. The abolition of slavery was a gradual phenomenon, and the economies of the North and the South were deeply interlinked. As the example of the debate in the Virginia General Assembly has shown, fissures ran through parts of the South, while northern states also widely discriminated against their free black population. Over time, the identification of the South with the institution of slavery fortified—even though only a fraction of Southerners actually possessed slaves—and so did that of the North with the cause of antislavery.

Within this antagonism, the concept of property assumed the role of a floating signifier; since property essentially remained undefined legally, each side attempted to fill it with its own definitions. Significantly, the debates on slavery revolved around the major legal documents of the nation's history, particularly the Constitution but also the Declaration of Independence, as well as other major legislative achievements, such as the Missouri Compromise or the Northwest Ordinance. They also referenced the writings and (supposed) intentions of the Founders, especially James Madison and Thomas Jefferson. The nineteenth-century debates around slavery and property were thus preoccupied with the very identity of the nation.

Over the course of the past two chapters, I have established the framework of the property discourse in the antebellum United States. As we have seen, the concept of property at that time operated in a field of tension defined by economic transformations that were interrelated with social conflicts. Significantly, in these conflicts, property figured prominently in its thing-like qualities as the ownership of objects, be they land or slaves. Moreover, though some actors occasionally invoked the idea that property was a legal creation and hence could be regulated and even redistributed by governments at will, public and political discourses emphatically relied mostly on natural rights arguments to advance property claims. As the following chapter will show the discursive framework of property shifted at the beginning of the twentieth century, as the corporate revolution challenged established ideas about property, and the U.S. transformed from a producer into a consumer economy.

NOTES

1. Bonnie Martin's study of informal credit networks in Virginia, South Carolina, and Louisiana suggests that using human property as collateral was a widespread practice in the South to raise capital, also allowing the purchase of slaves on installment credit. She notes: "Slaves were valuable capital assets, and they were used as collateral for some of the same reasons homes are used today. [. . .] If [people] wanted to buy a slave or slaves and could not pay the cash price, they asked the seller for a purchase-money mortgage. The buyers made a down payment, promised to pay the rest of the price plus interest in installments, and used the same slaves they were buying as collateral for the loan. The seller kept legal title of the slaves until the final payment was made" (2010, 822).

2. In distinction to black slavery, white indentured servitude was considered as a free contractual relationship between individuals—the indentured servant voluntarily sold his labor to another person for a specific period of time. Enslavement, by contrast, was never established by contract, as a slave was denied the status of a legal person and thus the right to enter a contractual relationship. Indentured servitude came to be recognized as unfree labor only in the early nineteenth century (see, e.g., Steinfeld 1991, 5–7).

3. For a detailed discussion of the American history of taxation and the significance of slavery in this context, see Einhorn (2006).

4. Within the abolitionist movement, the question of whether slavery was constitutional was famously subject to much controversy. William Lloyd Garrison, the founder of *The Liberator*, insisted that the Constitution was a proslavery document and thus needed to be discarded completely. Frederick Douglass, who first endorsed Garrison's views, later distanced himself from them; in his famous speech "What to the Slave is the Fourth of July?" (1852) he would argue that slavery was not constitutional. Both Alvan Stewart in *A Constitutional Argument on the Subject of Slavery* (1838) and Lysander Spooner in *The Unconstitutionality of Slavery* (1845) provided legal justifications of the view that the Constitution, in fact, did not endorse slavery.

5. The law was officially entitled "An Act to Authorize the Payment for Property Lost, Captured, or Destroyed by the Enemy, while in the Military Service of the United States, and for Other Purposes."

6. D'Auterive had asked for 24 dollars "for medical attendance for his negro Warwick," 15 dollars "for a month of his time lost," and 200 dollars "for the value of the injury done to him" (U.S. Congress 1826).

7. New York had passed an emancipation law in 1799 according to which all slave children born after July 4, 1799, were legally free, but they had to work through an extended period of indentured servitude; all older slaves were turned into indentured servants. The state thus provided compensation for slaveholders (Gellman 2006, 11).

8. According to the U.S. Census of 1830, Virginia's slave population counted 469,755; this meant that 38.8 percent of the state's population lived in bondage. At the same time, 47,348 free people of color lived in the state, accounting for 6.4 percent of the total free population. The census numbers illustrate the stark difference in the distribution of slaves within the state: whereas the ratio of enslaved people in Eastern Virginia was 50 percent, only 14.1 percent of the population lived in bondage in the western part of the state (U.S. Census Office 1832; see also A.G. Freehling 1982, 287).

9. William Miller (1996) recounts the battle in Congress about the abolitionist petitions in his book-length study; see also W. W. Freehling (1990). On attempts to stifle the debate in the Senate, see Wirls (2007).

10. Alcione Amos (2006) has extensively researched Luis Fatio Pacheco's life; according to her research, it is highly unlikely that he betrayed Dade's command and gave up any information to the Seminoles. Amos uses a different spelling of the African American's first name—I follow the use in the *Congressional Globe* here.

11. Representatives were very conscious of the fact that their speeches in Congress would be publicized; when the debate on the Pacheco case commenced on December 23, 1848, Congressman Stanton of Kentucky pointed out that he was not inclined to speak before the House with most of the reporters being absent; the debates of the day were quickly terminated after his remark (U.S. Congress 1848, 96). Joshua Giddings's speech was also published in pamphlet form.

12. The Constitution had provided only a vague formulation with respect to fugitive slaves. A 1793 fugitive slave law passed by Congress had already provided for federal enforcement, yet most of Northern states had passed personal liberty

laws which were meant to ensure that free blacks could not be legally captured and brought to the South. The U.S. Supreme Court ruled these personal liberty laws to be unconstitutional in *Prigg v. Pennsylvania* (1842), but also held that Northern states were not constitutionally required to help enforce the fugitive slave law. Southerners therefore sought to extend federal powers to capture and return fugitives (Finkelman 2012b, 11).

13. For two recent historical accounts of the Compromise of 1850 see, for example, Bordewich (2012) and Remini (2010). While both Bordewich and Remini emphasize the work of political personalities to save the Union, others, like Paul Finkelman (2012a), see the compromise more critically as an appeasement of proslavery forces, which, however, failed its major goal of diffusing the sectional conflict.

Chapter 3

A Nation of Homeowners

The Transformation of Property in the Emerging Consumer Economy

When the women's magazine *The Delineator* announced a nationwide "Better Homes in America" campaign in its October 1922 issue, it relied on the support of officials in the federal government, among them Vice-President Calvin Coolidge, the Secretaries of Commerce and Agriculture, Herbert Hoover and Henry C. Wallace, as well as the governors of twenty-three states. While Hoover celebrated "The Home as an Investment" in his contribution, Coolidge envisioned the future of a "Nation of Home-Owners." He cherished the "sacred" character of the home in saccharine and highly gendered terms, relating homemaking to "that wisdom born of affection which we call the intuition of woman." Coolidge's article argued that the United States, after dedicating much of its efforts to the development of public infrastructure, should refocus its vision onto the welfare of the individual and the home. Past achievements, including the construction of railroads and highways, had contributed to the nation's progress but were lacking in providing stability and security for the people, as those projects did not respond to the "natural" desire to own something. They were undertaken "for the people, but not of the people"—they did not emerge bottom-up from the democratic realm of the citizenry (Coolidge 1922, 17).

Coolidge's reference to the public infrastructure projects of the nineteenth century—advanced by corporations that had shed their public character and become highly controversial agents of private economic power in the last decades of that century—illuminates one of the vice president's implicit aims in his dedication to homeownership: to counter people's disenchantment with the capitalist order. By advocating the ownership of homes, he sought to reinstall the belief in "American institutions," which included "the right to acquire, hold and transmit property." Coolidge asserted that this right was valuable only if it was to "be enjoyed in a fair degree by all"

(17). And he proposed that homeownership could provide the route to such democratized enjoyment. In attributing homeownership with the ability to stabilize the nation—fortifying it against the lures of socialism and communism—Coolidge ascribed specific public functions to private property, while simultaneously constructing a dialectical relationship between the state and the individual, the nation and the home, the public and the private spheres. In this dialectic, he associated the individual, the home, and the private sphere with the natural order, somehow preceding the forms of the social. Clearly, by labeling public institutions as "detached" and "remote," he insinuated that they were secondary, subordinate to the ontologically prior categories of the individual and the family (17).

In Coolidge's framework, the dichotomies of state/individual, nation/home, and public/private act as homologies, through which the individual, the home, and the private property are constructed as hegemonic concepts. Jeff Weintraub has discussed the multiple and often confusing ways in which the private/public distinction has been brought into the scholarly discussion, emphasizing that it must be understood "not as a single paired opposition, but a complex family of them" (1997, 2). Read with Weintraub, Coolidge's article relies on a distinction between the family and the larger political and economic order, in which the market economy assumes a public role (7). Yet, as will become apparent in the subsequent discussion, a second conceptualization of the private/public distinction situates governments in opposition to private economic activity, "demarcating the sphere of the 'public' authority of the state from the sphere of formally voluntary relations between 'private' individuals" (8). Thus, the economic sector may, at the same time, be contrasted with the domestic and situated in the private realm, in opposition to the political sphere. Both binaries converge in the equation of public and political, private and nonpolitical (36).

As I demonstrate in this chapter, Coolidge's short article is but one contribution to a larger discourse in the early twentieth century that engaged the boundaries between the private and the public and, more specifically, the public functions of private property. On the one hand, this debate was nurtured by the corporate revolution at the beginning of the twentieth century, which fundamentally changed the character of private property, generating an array of political movements that were highly critical of this emerging form of capitalism. On the other hand, in part responding to these developments, government agencies, progressive reformers, academics, and the real estate and financial industries in a concerted effort turned scrutiny onto the home and the virtues of homeownership. In unprecedented ways, the state got involved not merely by promoting private property but also by intensely regulating the terms of ownership.

These debates were highly interlinked with an altered understanding of the legal concept of property that emerged in the second half of the nineteenth century, culminating in the metaphor of property being a "bundle of rights," which became widely accepted in the legal profession in the first decades of the twentieth century. Positivist and utilitarian, this reconceptualization of property as a set of legally enacted rights squarely contrasted with the natural rights-based ideas of private property at the heart of classical liberalism. In the natural rights tradition, property, based on a physicalist notion of ownership, figured as the boundary and limitation of state power, a private right that existed prior to the state and which had to be protected and preserved by the government. The new property of the twentieth century, by contrast, was recognized as a legal creation, granted and enacted by the government. It was also understood as an abstract set of multiple rights, fundamentally social in nature.

Though this highly technical reformulation of the property concept remained confined to discussions among legal scholars and professionals, it nevertheless resulted in broader public debates. This chapter shows first how, as the relationship between state and individual was renegotiated, a very different discourse on the public functions of private property emerged. Governments gained unprecedented normative power through which they regulated the forms of private property. Second, I propose that, in contrast to the highly utilitarian legal concept of property, the public advocacy of individual private property ownership focused on the affective relationship between owners and their property. It aimed at the continued legitimation of private property by strengthening people's emotional ties to their possessions, particularly their homes, thereby constructing the homeowner as a model citizen. And third, I suggest that the normative and affective dimensions of the debate were not only highly gendered but thoroughly racialized as well. Though democratic in rhetoric, the promotion of homeownership was instrumental in constructing a specific form of white middle-class subjectivity which was highly exclusive.

After first delineating the legal redefinition of property in the late nineteenth and early twentieth centuries in the following section, I will analyze two interconnected property debates in the progressive era. One of these debates focused on the role, responsibility, and proper social place of corporations: how did the rise of large manufacturing corporations between 1890 and 1905 alter the concept of private property? In which ways should corporations be regulated? The second debate relates to functions ascribed to the home and homeownership: how did governments and the private sector promote private property ownership? Which public functions were—implicitly and explicitly—ascribed to homeownership? And in which ways were the lines between the private and the public redrawn?

REDEFINING THE LEGAL CONCEPT OF PROPERTY

The idea of property underwent a major redefinition during the second half of the nineteenth and at the beginning of the twentieth century, from the natural rights conception to property to a "bundle of rights." The latter idea highlights three significant insights about the concept of property: "First, it indicates that ownership is a complex legal relationship. Second, the metaphor illuminates the fact that the constitutive elements of that relationship are legal rights. Third, and most important, it underscores the social character of that relationship" (Alexander 1997, 319). These insights, first formulated explicitly by legal scholars in the first decades of the twentieth century, constituted a major adjustment to the legal concept of property from the previous century. These jurists propagated a positivist conception of property that considered it to be an aggregate of different rights, which established (power) relationships between people. This reconceptualization effected the disintegration of the property concept and helped to give rise to the regulatory state.

The judicial process in the early nineteenth century, Morton Horwitz has argued, created a distinction between private and public law, whereby property law was firmly situated in the private realm. According to the Constitution's Fifth Amendment, private property could be taken for public purposes; but in their deliberations on eminent domain cases of the era, the courts clearly differentiated between legitimate and illegitimate actions of the state, seeking to prevent state redistribution of private wealth (Horwitz 1992b, 10). The legal understanding of what constituted a "taking" according to the amendment, however, was fairly narrow: governments were only required to compensate owners for the complete loss of their property, not for damages or injuries to their property rights. If the building of a railroad or a bridge harmed a neighbor's business, courts, in most cases, did not demand that the state agency pay compensation (Banner 2011, 45). Thus, if courts in the early nineteenth century sought to separate the private from the public realm and to protect private property from governmental interference, they nevertheless did not consider all state regulations of property to be an infringement. Instead, they distinguished between "vested" and "non-vested" property rights. Vested rights were those that could not be changed retroactively by the state, whereas non-vested rights were subject to regulation—a distinction which became increasingly difficult to uphold (Horwitz 1992b, 149). Overall, there was a sense that, in a conflict between private rights and public aims, "private interest must be made subservient to the general interest of the community," as James Kent formulated in his *Commentaries* (1832, 2:340).

Beginning in the 1850s and 1860s, however, state courts increasingly began to rely on a more differentiated understanding of property rights. State court decisions had already begun to weaken the no-compensation rule, particularly when the U.S. Supreme Court, in the 1871 case *Pumpelly v. Green Bay Company,* found that the flooding of an owner's land constituted a taking. In the following year, the New Hampshire Supreme Court issued the first national decision that explicitly argued in terms of the bundle of rights theory. This new conception of property served to strengthen the rights of property owners, as courts had to consider the specific rights that were injured by state action (Banner 2011, 57–60).

James Wilson, one of the original Supreme Court justices, already relied on the idea of property being made up of a number of specific rights in the 1790s (Banner 2011, 57). The influential English lawyer and legal theorist John Austin first popularized the concept of a bundle of rights with his influential *Lectures on Jurisprudence* in the 1860s, and various legal treatises during the 1880s and 1890s discussed the modification of the term "property." Thus, in 1882, Arthur Sedgwick systematically reviewed the court decisions in property cases and found that they no longer considered the "thing" itself as property but as the subject of property relations. "In its legal signification," Sedgwick wrote, property "means only the rights of the owner in relation to it." Property needed to be understood as "the right to possess, use, enjoy, dispose of, rent, sell, give away, devise the thing owned" (1882, 255). John Lewis, author of *A Treatise on the Law of Eminent Domain*, echoed these thoughts: "A person's right of property in things [. . .] consists of the right to possess, use and dispose thereof in such manner as is not inconsistent with the law of the land" ([1888] 1900, 56).

While some historians explain the acceptance of the bundle of rights metaphor in the late nineteenth century with the emergence of new, nonphysical forms of property—such as patents, copyright, and trademarks—which necessitated a more abstract concept than the one based on the ownership of land (Horwitz 1992b; Vandevelde 1980), Banner suggests that such abstract forms of property had already previously existed. He locates the reason for the shift in defining property in the political climate of the times (2011, 71). At a time in which socialist and populist movements gained currency and even began to enter governments, conservatives sought to strengthen constitutional protections of property, in order to fend off unwanted regulation. The more abstract conception of property allowed for defining various rights as property rights, thereby expanding the property concept. A third and most convincing explanation, provided by Thomas Grey, sees the reasons for property's transformation in the logic of capitalism and its being "intrinsic to the development of a free-market economy into an industrial phase" (1980, 74). The way in which the concept of property fractures in the late nineteenth century, Grey suggests, mirrors "the voluntary decompositions and recombination of elements of simple ownership, under a regime in which owners are allowed to divide and transfer their interests as they wish" (75).[1] This interpretation concurs with William Roy's observation that the corporate revolution in the late nineteenth century gave rise to what he terms "socialized property" (1997, 10). This new type of property conceptualized ownership as highly "fungible and alienable" and entirely separate from the management and operation of a business. As institutions of finance became crucial to this type of economy, corporate capital distinguished itself fundamentally from other parts of the economy (98).

If the redefinition of property contributed to an expansion of the protection of private interests, it ultimately worked toward a disintegration of the concept itself. The new property derived from a positivist tradition, represented by the English philosophers Jeremy Bentham and John Austin, which was at odds with the idea of natural law and instead saw property entirely as the creation of the law. Bentham, in his *Theory of Legislation*, had insisted that "there is no such thing as natural property" ([1802] 1864, 111). Bentham instead defined property as "the expectation of deriving certain advantages from a thing which we are said to possess, in consequence of the relation in which we stand towards it" (111–12). This expectation, he held, entirely depended on a legal promise, a law that guaranteed the future profit. Famously, he concluded that "property and law are born together, and die together. Before laws were made, there was no property; take away laws, and property ceases" (113).

Responding to the viewpoints of the Bentham-Austin school, conservative jurist Christopher Tiedeman acknowledged that, from a jurisprudential perspective, there was "no room for the assertion of natural rights, except so far as they are recognized and protected by the existing law" (1890, 73). But for Tiedeman, popular notions of rights and justice mattered because they were important sources for the development of actual law. He recognized the ultimately fictitious character of the conception of natural rights as well as the historical and social variability of what social and moral discourse assumed to be natural rights. Unlike Bentham and Austin, however, he refused to make a clear-cut distinction between the law and morality. Having become "a part of the organic law of the land," the rights instituted in the federal and state constitutions needed "to be respected and enforced" (78). Tiedeman's view was one that conservative lawyers fervently advocated in the 1890s. While they recognized the conventional character of the law, they simultaneously insisted that the constitutional conception of property must remain sacred. If they welcomed the new understanding of property as being a bundle of rights, they did so because it promised greater protection of individual rights. Yet, ultimately, the bundle of rights metaphor paved the way for a positivist reconceptualization of property, which would later most forcefully be undertaken by legal progressives and realists in the first decades of the twentieth century.

Legal scholar Wesley Newcomb Hohfeld systematically conceptualized the relational character of property in the early twentieth century. Hohfeld discussed property in two *Yale Law Journal* articles published in 1913 and 1917. His original contribution attempted to formalize property in terms of eight basic legal relationships: as a right, a duty, a privilege, a no-right, a power, a liability, an immunity, and a disability. These rights, he argued, had to be conceptualized as pairs in two ways: On the one hand, each of these terms appeared as the opposite of another, for example, rights opposed privileges and powers opposed immunities. On the other hand, Hohfeld described them as correlatives, meaning that, for instance, the existence of a right necessitated the existence of a corresponding duty. In that sense, a correlative pair expresses a legal relationship in that it considers the perspectives of both parties (Singer 1982, 987). Thus, if A had the right to keep B off her land, then B's duty was to stay off that land. "By stripping away the conventional thing-centered vocabulary of property," Banner points out, "Hohfeld's scheme emphasized the nature of property as relations between people rather than between people and things" (2011, 103). Importantly, Hohfeld's goal was to illuminate the distinction between rights and privileges, which he believed were often conflated (Singer 1982, 987). In Hohfeld's terminology, a privilege equaled a "liberty" to do something in a legal relation but without a corresponding duty of third parties not to interfere. In distinction, a right granted by the state implied that the "correlative" must be "the general duty of every one not to prevent" (Hohfeld 1913, 37).

To understand property as social, as a complex web of legal relationships, meant that property could not be reduced to one essential element, nor could one person's ownership interest be protected absolutely, as each use of a property implicated the rights, duties, and privileges of others (Alexander 1997, 323). Hohfeld's analysis showed that property rights were fundamentally political in nature: granting legal rights comes down to policy decisions, and the question of which interferences by the state are legally permitted or prohibited cannot be answered merely analytically (Singer 1982, 1059; Alexander 1997, 323). A second implication of Hohfeld's conceptualization, and more generally of the shift to the "bundle of rights" metaphor, was the disintegration of a unified concept of property as such: if property does not refer to a single thing but to an abstract set of rights and a web of social relations, it loses the special status upon which natural rights theorists had conferred. Advocates of this new conception thus understood property in predominantly technical, instrumental terms.

The discussion I have traced in this section took place mostly in a specialized discourse among lawyers and legal scholars, not in the public realm. And that legal debate notably diverged from popular understandings of property. However, as I will argue in the following sections, the specialized debate on property also bore deep implications for the turn-of-the-century public debate on how corporations redefined common ideas of private property and economic competition.

PROPERTY DISINTEGRATED: DEBATING CORPORATE CAPITALISM IN THE PROGRESSIVE ERA

Between 1890 and 1905, the large manufacturing corporation became the dominant form of business enterprise in the United States. Concomitantly, the country was shaken by repeated financial panics and depressions, growing out of a heavily financialized economic system, with—foremost in the railroad industry—frequent bankruptcies, mergers, and financial speculation. As disparities of wealth grew between the new corporate capitalist class and the increasingly organized working classes, so did the frequency of labor protests and strikes, while, at the same time, populist and socialist political movements emerged. Among the intellectual elite, lawyers, economists, social scientists, and journalists began to engage in a debate about the new economic reality that corporate capitalism had created.

The new economic order had its roots in developments that reached back into the early nineteenth century. Governments had originally begun to institute corporations to undertake tasks of a public nature that were unsuited for individual business enterprise, for example, because they were too financially risky, unprofitable, or expensive (Roy 1997, 41). Thus, at the outset, corporations were quasi-public in character (Berle and Means 1991, 11), engaging in state-building activities while also developing a private economic sector. Chartered by the government, the corporate form was selective and exclusionary, a form of business organization strictly limited to particular ventures. As an incentive for private investment, corporations often received monopoly rights (Roy 1997, 52). By 1830, about 1,900 corporations had been created in New England; during the following years, incorporations reached an early peak, with New York forming almost 200 new companies in 1836–1837 alone, just before the panic of 1837 hit. Ohio created more than 150 and Pennsylvania 100 corporations in the same time span (J. P. Davis [1905] 1961, viii).

The privileged and exclusionary nature of the corporate form gave rise to an early anti-corporate movement; in Andrew Jackson's America, corporations were often perceived as aristocratic institutions, as antithetical to the egalitarian promise. For many Jacksonians, the involvement of the government in private business enterprise contradicted the idea of popular sovereignty. They favored a radical separation of the private and public spheres and the reduction of state power. As Gregory Mark explains, "In a remarkable innovation in political economy, the Jacksonians sought to foster legislative purity as well as restore equality when they demanded und ultimately won universal access to the corporate form, with restrictions on the power of the legislature to grant special perquisites" (1987, 1453). Blaming the economic crisis of the late 1830s on state involvement and supervision and claiming that private businesses were more efficient, these critics were able to pass constitutionally binding prohibitions on state investments in public works corporations. "Business corporations became entirely distinct from other corporations and fully privatized through general incorporation laws that virtually eliminated the accountability of corporations to ongoing supervision" (Roy 1997, 72).

During the nineteenth century, the legal institution of the corporation transitioned from the status of a public entity into a private institution in U.S. law, establishing the corporate capitalism that became dominant at the turn of the century. As Joshua Barkan has argued, this process brought with it a reworking of political culture and the role of government. From the beginning, corporations were "contradictory objects" that straddled the spheres of public power and private interest. They were instituted to promote the public welfare, with the state holding priority over private interests, yet this commitment to public welfare was increasingly framed in economic terms. The liberalization of the state incorporation laws in the late nineteenth century gave corporations new powers, effectively terminating the close relationship between corporation and state and the claim that the corporation must directly provide for the common good (Barkan 2013, 53–54).

The railroads were of seminal significance for the development of the institution of the corporation. Transitioning from a semi-public agency to a form of private property in the last third of the nineteenth century, corporations retained many privileges for serving a public function, while shedding their public accountability (Roy 1997, 83). Nevertheless, the privatization of the railroads concurred with heavy government involvement, in the form of loans, tax breaks, and legal exemptions, and the donation of a significant amount of public lands (96). The rise of the railroad corporations resulted in the emergence of a corporate capitalist class and the concentration of capital. As the railroad industry collapsed in the 1890s, massive amounts of capital became available for investment in new industrial corporations (223).

Not only were new institutions of finance associated with the corporation crucial for the shape of the corporate form, but the law played an important role in shaping the corporate organization of property as well: "Corporate law contributed to creating the corporate form of property in two ways: by giving the corporation rights and entitlements not available to individuals or individually owned businesses and by solidifying institutional relations among corporations that are specific to the corporate system such as the stock market, investment banks, and interlocking directorships that structured the socialization of capital and of authority" (Roy 1997, 145). Roy identified three crucial aspects that define the legal form of the modern corporation and contribute to its dominance of the economic system: the right of corporations to own stock in other corporations, the reduction of personal ownership liabilities, and the legal powers vested in the board of directors (144).

Perhaps most crucially, however, the metaphor of corporate personhood powerfully impacted how legal and nonlegal actors imagined the social position as well as the internal structures of the new business entities—and they still continue to do so.[2] In an extensive discussion of the personification of the corporation, Gregory Mark has traced how the corporate business came to be understood as a real person, "as an autonomous, self-directed entity in which rights inhered" (1987, 1442). As he argues, the consequences of the metaphor are far-reaching, as it "implies a single and unitary source of control over the collective property of the corporation's members," thereby situating the corporation as an autonomous being and allowing corporations to claim rights, even constitutional ones, thus "giving corporate property unprecedented protection from the state" (1443). With corporations figured as persons, the state was largely removed from the equation, and "corporations were placed in a position of formal equality with other individuals in the market" (Barkan 2013, 60).

Populist and Socialist Critiques of Property

The corporate revolution in the United States significantly shifted economic power relations, creating upheavals in the American economy that led to frequent crises. In response to the new corporate structures and the political culture related to them, diverse and dispersed populist movements emerged in the 1880s and 1890s. In 1892, members of various social movements came together in St. Louis to form the People's Party of America, a coalition that aimed at uniting small farmers, the urban workers of the Knights of Labor and the American Federation of Labor, socialists, as well as middle-class reform movements such as the Temperance movement. Diverse in their positions and interests, these groups found common ground in their perception that the development of the U.S. post–Civil War economy had turned the country into a grossly unequal society, dominated by a corrupt economic elite, while the common people no longer received a fair reward for their labor. In the age of corporate expansion, the principles of laissez-faire economics, they felt, no longer worked to create a society of equal opportunity (Kazin 1998, 30).

The rhetoric of the populist movement built on the ideological heritage of Jeffersonian and Jacksonian times, a tradition that relied on the battle of the "plain people," as the People's Party Platform formulated it, against a corrupt financial elite, which could be redefined for the contemporary moment (Laclau 2005, 203). In the attempt to unify the interests of such diverse groups, the populists had to construct "the people," by establishing a chain of equivalences between these particular interests.[3] Calling up the producer ethic already prevalent in the populist working-class movements of the antebellum era, the party conceptualized the people as the "producers," whose work created all economic value. The party platform presented in St. Louis pictured a nation in a mode of crisis, on "the verge of moral, political, and material ruin" and ruled by fundamental injustice against workers. "The fruits of the toil of millions are boldly stolen to build up colossal fortunes for a few, unprecedented in the history of mankind" ("People's Party Platform" 1892), the text stated in its preamble in hyperbolic tone.

The moralist rhetoric and the rather abstract category of the producer veiled stark economic differences between various kinds of producers, denying the existence of an economic conflict between different classes. Instead, the populists constructed the political vision of "a moral community of self-governing citizens" (Kazin 1998, 35). As both Michael Kazin and Ernesto Laclau note, due to its abstractness, the signifier of the producer could easily be appropriated by the establishment parties (Kazin 1998, 35; Laclau 2005, 205)—which indeed it was, particularly by the Democratic Party, which mainstreamed some of the populist demands by adopting William Jennings Bryan as its candidate in the 1896 presidential election.[4]

Like the National Reform and anti-rent movements in the antebellum period, the populists invoked the nation's foundational documents as their preeminent rhetorical reference point. Jefferson, in particular, as the author of the Declaration of Independence, was enlarged in his significance. As Norman Pollack explains, the populist movement thereby did not challenge property rights but instead made property one of its main pillars. Significantly, it relied on "the conception of property [. . .] prevalent in Jefferson's time—or, more accurately, that associated with individual ownership and the absence of the market control later attained through major aggregations of wealth" (1987, 115). Accordingly, the populist reformers were rather ambivalent about the expansion of government power. On the one hand, they called for the nationalization of important industries, especially the railroad corporations; on the other hand, they simultaneously feared that this might unduly enlarge government influence.

One influential source for populist reformers was political economist Henry George's Single Tax proposal, which he advocated in *Progress and Poverty* (1879) as a remedy for economic inequality. George proposed abolishing existing property taxes and replacing them with a "single tax" on the unimproved value of land. Arguing that land speculation was the major social ill, which the tax would curb, his plan sought to promote economic production and land improvement through tax relief. This would allow entrepreneurs to invest in their businesses' infrastructure and create jobs for workers. Laborers and farmers, in turn, could expect better living conditions and the option of home or farm ownership, as land would no longer be in the hands of real estate speculators (Postel 2007, 229).

Texas lawyer and politician James Harvey "Cyclone" Davis was among the Populists' most powerful orators. Davis, who earned his nickname due to his relentless debating style, toured the country in the 1890s to give public speeches and participate in political debates (Postel 2007, 159). In 1894, Davis compiled his thoughts in *A Political Revelation*, a lengthy book that drew its political vision from his exegesis of the Declaration of Independence, the Constitution, and the Populist Party Platform. The political demands, as outlined by Davis, centered on three areas: land, transportation, and finance. The populists aimed to establish regulations against "all kinds of monopoly and all kinds of aristocracy of wealth," while "encourag[ing] individual industry in the acquisition of property." Drawing upon the familiar labor theory of property, and echoing James Madison, Davis suggested that the government's main objective should be the protection of property and persons and that its tasks included the prevention of land monopolies: "The earth is the source from which all property is derived, and hence when any government grants and makes lawful a monopoly of the land of that government in the hands of a few of its people, it commits a crime against nature's laws, and violates the very objects for which society is organized into government" (J. H. Davis 1894, 93). Speaking of "the land of that government," Davis crucially positions the government not as a protector of property, individually acquired through free-market relationships, but as the agency that owns and distributes land in the first place. Second, Davis argued that the protection of personal and property rights was only possible if the government controlled the means of communication and transportation. To allow corporations to operate and commercially use infrastructure would "convert[] a public necessity into a private benefit" (94). Third, he demanded that the power to issue a national currency remains with the government, prohibiting the transfer of any control over the money supply to banking corporations.

Davis claimed the term "socialism" for the kind of governmental organization he envisioned, yet he assured his readers that the term "need not alarm" them (96). Though he recognized "the right and recognition of private property" as "the dividing line between socialism and Democracy" (96), he ultimately muddled the differences between the systems by implicitly claiming that socialism and the public interest were identical. A government, in this context, could be "more or less a socialism" (95), depending on how large a part of the economy was brought under public ownership. Davis left no doubt, however, that he favored a "democratic" organization: "There is a proper limit at which government should stop" (96). Socialism, then, for Davis, only meant to curb the unfair advantages of some individuals in society, in order to restore equality of opportunity for all citizens—he did not call into question capitalist structures as such. Instead, he favored an entrepreneurial capitalism, "in which the sacred rights of home in reasonable amounts of acres, and the production and enjoyments of comforts are held inviolable" and "all men would be equal in production and distribution of wealth" (100–101). Davis thus ultimately refused to engage with the structures brought about by corporate capitalism, instead projecting a nostalgic vision that revolved around home- and landownership and the individual as an autonomous producer.

While, for Davis, a democratic capitalism seemed compatible with elements of socialism, Eugene Debs, five-time presidential candidate for the Socialist Party, advanced a more radical position. In his early career, Debs had backed the People's Party but joined the Socialists after Bryan's loss to William McKinley in the presidential election of 1896 (Kazin 1998, 67). He took issue with the belief that the Democratic Party represented the poor and the workers—an idea that he found untrue because the Democrats subscribed to the same general ideas about economic organization as did the Republicans. The workers' interests, Debs felt, were represented neither by McKinley, who addressed the "large capitalists," nor by Bryan, who focused on the "small capitalists" (Debs 1908, 89). In distinction to the more moderate populists, Debs believed that a class war was inevitable, and he advocated the abolition of capitalism. To end workers' exploitation was "a question not of 'reform,'" Debs held, "but of revolution. The capitalist system must be overthrown, class-rule abolished and wage-slavery supplanted by cooperative industry" (90). Unlike Davis's attempt to blur the lines between capitalism and socialism, Debs emphasized the antagonism between the systems: "It is simply a question of capitalism or socialism, of despotism or democracy" (92).

Debs's argument built on the idea that the industrial revolution had irreversibly altered the economic structures in the United States, creating an antagonism between the capitalist and the working classes. He proposed that the interests of the people could only be served in a society organized around the collective ownership of the means of production. The dispossession of the capitalist class would, however, not abolish private property but give rise to an egalitarian (re)distribution of it: "We are not going to destroy private property. We are going to establish private property—all the private property necessary to house man, keep him in comfort and satisfy his wants. Eighty per cent of the people of the United States have not property today. A few have got it all. They have dispossessed the people, and when we get into power we will dispossess them" (489).

As an advocate of a socialist revolution, Debs could not rely on the familiar tropes derived from the foundational documents. Instead, he rooted socialism in the workers' movements and communitarian experiments of the 1840s, referencing Fourierism and the leadership of Albert Brisbane and Horace Greeley, whom he hailed as important precursors in the socialist struggle (96–100). He also associated the socialist movement with abolitionism. In 1908, Debs claimed: "We are today where the abolitionists were in 1858," suggesting that, like the coming of the Civil War ended the system of slavery in the South, a similar system change would come to end the northern capitalist version of labor exploitation (488). Instead of looking backward to the allegedly better days of a small producer economy, Debs hailed socialism as "a coming phase of civilization [. . .] in which all will have equal right to work and all will cooperate together in producing wealth and all will enjoy all the fruit of their collective labor" (142–43).

The Conservative Defense of Property Rights

Though their impact ultimately remained limited, populist and socialist assaults on established property relations caused considerable turmoil in the political and cultural establishments. Yet, like the populists, conservatives turned to national foundations and the labor theory of property to defend their view of property rights. In an 1894 commencement address he held in front of law graduates at the University of Michigan, Federal Judge William Howard Taft—who would later become president (1909–1913) and subsequently chief justice of the Supreme Court (1921–1930)—chose to speak on the constitutional right to private property, which, he felt, was being assaulted by a "resounding din of anarchy, socialism, populism and the general demagogy which is so wide spread to-day" (Taft 1894, 232). His talk intended to remind the future practitioners of law of their proper duty to defend the Constitution and to maintain the foundational principles it guaranteed, first among these being the "sacred [. . .] right of private property" (233). Taft located the reason for the contemporary disenchantment with private property in the intense class conflicts between capitalists and laborers, which were manifested in frequent strikes and unions' violent agitations. A growing fraction of the public had begun to argue that the rich were getting richer, at the expense of the poor, citing the immense accumulation of wealth by a few individuals and the corporations they had formed. In Taft's view, this discourse weakened people's trust in the benefits of private property and threatened the social order.

In his defense of the institution, Taft's property narrative harked back to the justifications of private property ownership that were familiar since Locke's contract theory and the American Revolution: it was "a principle of natural justice that one should enjoy what [one's] labor produced" (220). Adapting the labor theory of property and value to times of industrial capitalism, he extended this stipulation to justify the private and corporate accumulation of capital: surplus profits might be accumulated for future investment; and since capitalists and laborers both benefited from the combination of their resources, they arranged agreements as to their respective shares. Moreover, the guaranteed security of private property also encouraged productive individuals to save capital for future generations, thereby providing "the strongest motive for industry" (220): to accumulate more than immediately necessary. For Taft, capital accumulation amounted to economic progress because it increased productivity. The investment of wealth into further production resulted in falling labor costs for each new unit of production and therefore in cheaper products. Laborers profited because consumer items became more affordable, allowing them to buy more products beyond the bare necessities of life. "It would seem, therefore," Taft explained, "to be plainly for the benefit of every one to increase the amount of capital in use in the world," which could "only be done by maintaining the motive for its increase, which we have found to be in the institution of private property" (222).

Given that every member of society profited from economic growth, calling into question the security of private property "is a direct blow at the interests of the working man," Taft argued (222). He insisted that the corporate economic model was "for the general good" (224) and rested on "free labor [and] free right of contract" (223). Not corporate capitalism as such was the problem—but it had come into disrepute as individual corporate managers sought to influence legislative processes, thereby trying to gain "unjust advantages over the community at large" (225). Such undue influence, as well as irresponsible union leaders influenced by "socialistic ideas which prevail among the laboring classes of Europe," was the root cause of people's resentment of corporations (227). In fact, movements against corporations themselves had led to unjust regulations, causing insolvencies and thereby discouraging the further investment of capital.

Taft's remedy for the social upheavals of his time was to renew the sense of appreciation of the institution of private property, with a Jacksonian vision of the social that promulgated a view of the market as self-regulatory and the role of legislation as an essentially neutral one. For the social and economic order to work properly, the state had to avoid granting privileges to specific social groups or classes, be they capitalists or laborers. For Taft, the right of individuals to freely enter contracts reigned supreme—ironically, the very idea to which populists on the political left also subscribed. Taft here represented the dominant judiciary view at the turn of the twentieth century. While later generations have often characterized this legal approach as an endorsement of laissez-faire economics, more recent historians have revised this image. Judges like Taft and members of the Supreme Court, Howard Gillman has argued, proposed a social vision in which the state should refrain from encouraging or supporting factional interests, which they considered to be socially divisive (1993, 10). Attributing to governments a position of neutrality in economic conflicts, they implicitly denied the political nature of property relationships.

A year after Taft's speech, former federal judge and legal scholar John F. Dillon delivered a similar defense of private property in an address to the New York State Bar Association. Like Taft, Dillon denounced socialist attacks on property, considering "class power and class legislation" as the gravest threat to the democratic republic. The state was to serve all members of society equally and protect the individual from the intrusion on his rights. But he simultaneously stressed that property "has in an important sense a public as well as a private side." The property owner, Dillon (1895) held, was "a debtor to the community" because property was a social institution established by the state. More importantly, Dillon distinguished between the "legal" and the "social duties" of property. The state could regulate private property, for instance, in order to protect the public from the harmful consequences of monopolies. Overall, however, he was reluctant to endorse specific measures to redistribute wealth. Instead, he stressed the social duties of those who possessed large fortunes, to associate themselves with philanthropic projects and thereby contribute to the well-being of the community. Dillon thus favored voluntary actions, instead of government involvement, in the distribution of property.

Theorizing the Corporation, Dismantling the "Magic of Property"

Taft and Dillon's response to the rise of the modern corporation and the social unrest of their time was essentially conservative: in the face of challenges by trade unions and socialists, they reverted back to the traditional idea of natural property rights and the labor theory of property. Thorstein Veblen, writing a decade after Taft and Dillon, came to very different conclusions. His 1904 study on political economy, entitled *Theory of Business Enterprise*, constitutes one of the first attempts to analyze the structures of the contemporary economic conditions created by the corporate system. Veblen's book called into question many of the assumptions and conclusions provided by conservative intellectuals and attempted to describe the ways in which the business principles of modern enterprise impacted "the modern cultural situation" (Veblen 1904, 21) as a whole.

Veblen's analysis refuted the premises that Taft and Dillon's position rested upon. He argued that the contemporary era was "the age of the machine process" (1), with mechanization not only being the dominant mode of industry but also a structural logic that infiltrated all areas of economic and cultural activity. Moreover, the economy was now dominated by the primary motive of "pecuniary gain" (20), that is, businessmen who controlled industrial production by making investments for profit. Contrary to earlier stages in economic development, Veblen outlined that the production of goods and the earning of a livelihood were no longer the central concern of business industry; production had become secondary to the realization of profits on investments that businessmen made into the processes of industry: "Industry is carried out for the sake of business, and not conversely" (26). "The adjustments of industry," he wrote, "take place through the mediation of pecuniary transactions, and these transactions take place at the hands of the business men and are carried on by them for business ends, not for industrial ends in the narrower meaning of the phrase" (27). The distinction between "industry," that is, the production of goods, and "business," that is, the financial transactions between managers, thus was defining for the corporate system, and it also explained that—contrary to the assumptions of classical liberal economic theory—the decisions and interests of business managers did not necessarily coincide with the interests and necessities of the community. Goods were no longer produced to meet consumer demands or to generate a public benefit, but, instead, profit became the sole consideration (63).

Veblen characterized the corporate system as a "credit economy," in distinction to a "money economy" (133). The logic of profit and the focus on the earning capacity of an enterprise rested not merely on the capital owned but also on additional funds, whether borrowed capital or capital generated through the issue of stocks and bonds. As the entire concern became capitalized, management and ownership of a firm were separated. This split introduced a new divergence, as "the interest of the managers of a modern corporation need not coincide with the permanent interest of the corporation as a going concern" (157). The property owners thus had an essentially passive role, since managers made the business decisions. Simultaneously, the managers themselves held bureaucratic positions, as they carried out decisions derived from the structuring logic of business. And the "populace," the larger group of workers employed in industry, figured merely as "raw material" in an economy dominated by financial transactions (267).

While Taft and Dillon insisted on the sacredness of private property and the freedom of contract being crucial American social institutions, Veblen provided a differentiated discussion of how the corporate system called into question established ideas of ownership. He acknowledged that modern business derived its focus on pecuniary gain—what Gregory Alexander terms as the commodity function of property—from the ideology of classical liberalism. The labor theory of property, Veblen suggested, provided "metaphysical authentication" (275) to modern business rule as well as the structural legal institutions within which businesses operated. Yet, if freedom of contract existed *de jure*, it did not exist *de facto*, under conditions of mechanization. In an industry dominated by the machine process, the worker might possess freedom of contract in terms of the law, but he actually did not have such freedom at all because the standardization of the mechanical work process had created a system of coercion, in which the material necessities of the workmen were subjected to the pecuniary logic of the business. The legal system, however, did not recognize this coercion, since the question of the livelihood of workers did not limit the freedom of property owners. This discrepancy between law and fact, Veblen pointed out, could be best observed in court decisions, in which judges regularly sided with property owners and not workers, referencing the inviolability of property rights (276–81).

The modern machine age, Veblen argued, was therefore responsible for creating class distinctions between the business class and the working class, whose habits of life fundamentally differed, due to their different occupations and the various disciplines to which they were subjected. While those engaged in business based their thinking on a natural rights foundation of property, the working classes lacked a metaphysical foundation (318). Crucially, their relationship to the ideology of property had notably altered: "The industrial classes appear to be losing the instinct of individual ownership. The acquisition of property is ceasing to appeal to them as a natural, self-evident source of comfort and strength. The natural right of property no longer means so much to them as it once did" (327).

Veblen read the rise of trade unions and socialism as a response of workers to this experience of mechanization and standardization. Trade unions were at odds with the idea of freedom of contract, as they sought collective bargaining power, standardized wage rates, as well as regulations that cut into conventions of natural rights, though they generally did not dispute property rights as such. Socialism did, however. In contrast to previous social movements that aimed at the redistribution of wealth, Veblen noted that socialism voiced demands that could no longer be stated as pecuniary claims: "With the socialistic element the question is not, what shall be done in the way of readjustment of property claims, but what is to be done to abolish them" (342). In Veblen's view, the logic of mechanization was tearing down the natural rights foundation of the economic system, in effect destroying the metaphysical basis of classical liberalism, out of which the modern corporate economy had grown. Contrary to Dillon, he did not believe that the system, or even civilization as a whole, could be saved through conventional measures, such as the establishment of charity organizations. Rather, the influence of the machine age would have to be met on structural grounds.

In *Drift and Mastery* (1914), journalist Walter Lippmann, cofounder of the magazine *The New Republic* and an important voice during the progressive era, came to similar conclusions as Veblen. The modern corporation had fundamentally changed the meanings and functions of private property as such, Lippmann argued, or, rather, private property in the traditional sense was fast disappearing. And it was not socialism that was responsible for this development: "The trusts are organizing private property out of existence, are altering its nature so radically that very little remains but the title and the ancient theory" (Lippmann [1914] 1917, 50). In the modern world created by the corporation, the stockowner had a very different, far more distanced and abstract relationship to his property. The sole connection, Lippmann explained, rested in learning about one's stock's value and waiting for the payment of a dividend. Profitmaking was not even connected to any knowledge about the business, as professional brokers took care of placing the investments. "All the rugged virtues that are supposed to be inherent in the magic of property," Lippmann wrote, "have gone a-glimmering with the revolutionary change that the great industry has produced" (55–56). Within modern capitalist relations, the person and morality of the property owner was of no consequence: "He cannot fulfill any responsibility to the property he owns" (56).

The separation between ownership and management resulted in a diffusion of ownership, but ownership also thereby lost its traditional meaning. Socialism was not responsible for attacking private property, but the corporate system itself. If the government were to decide that private property in the railroads should be abolished, Lippmann mused, this could very easily be done by exchanging stocks for government bonds. The owners, Lippmann predicted, "may feel far happier as creditors of the United States than as representatives of the institution of private property" (60). Therefore, the issue was not a matter of choosing between government and private ownership, as proposed by socialists, but a challenge of how to combine popular control and administrative power. In the corporate economic system, the success of an enterprise was no longer determined by the influence of the property owners but by the decisions of management. The problem of the trusts, therefore, concerned the relationship between centralized authority and democracy. "It is obvious that the trusts have created a demand for a new type of business man," Lippmann wrote, "for a man whose motives resemble those of the applied scientist and whose responsibility is that of a public servant" (63). Lippmann thus redefined the relationship of the private and the public sectors, with respect to the role of corporations. With the concept of private property dramatically being altered by corporate structures, the social order had also shifted fundamentally. As a form of socialized capital, the corporation was more properly situated in the public realm than it was considered a private enterprise.

Both Veblen and Lippmann recognized that the economic situation of the United States had been fundamentally altered with the rise of the modern corporation. But the altered economy not only led public intellectuals of the time to reevaluate the current relationship between private enterprise and public responsibility; it also prompted progressive reformers to scrutinize the validity of the foundational myths and cultural narratives of the United States. In accounts such as Charles Beard's *An Economic Interpretation of the Constitution of the United States* (1913), Herbert Croly's *The Promise of American Life* (1909), and Walter Weyl's *The New Democracy* (1912), a very different view of the foundation generation and the egalitarian promise emerged.

Materialist historian Beard set out to document that the movement for a new centralized government was largely determined by property interests, with many of the Constitutional Convention delegates standing to gain personally or to represent the interests of their class. For Beard, the alleged democratic character of the foundational document was seriously compromised by the fact that only a small, unrepresentative fraction of the population participated in the drafting and ratification process: primarily due to property qualifications which disfranchised many voters, three-fourths of adult men did not vote on the ratification (Beard 1913, 325). The controversy around the Constitution, Beard held, was actually a controversy between groups with different property interests, some of which would profit from a strong national government (investors of capital, owners of public securities, and those with manufacturing and shipping interests), while others would be disadvantaged (owners of real estate, debtors) (19–51). Eventually, the moneyed interests, "the dynamic element in the movement for the new Constitution" (51), would prove to be the more influential group. Beard concluded: "The Constitution was essentially an economic document based upon the concept that the fundamental private rights of property are anterior to government and morally beyond the reach of popular majorities" (324). For Beard, the egalitarian rhetoric surrounding the Constitution was merely a mask for underlying class interest. His work explicitly attempted "to weaken the aura of sanctity surrounding the U.S. Constitution" and to call into question its alleged neutrality (Ely 2008, 122).

Beard was not alone among progressive reformers in his aim to dethrone the founding fathers. "For over a century we have piously exclaimed that our Constitution is the last and noblest expression of democracy," wrote Walter Weyl. "But, in truth, the Constitution is not democratic. It was, in intention, and is, in essence, undemocratic. It was conceived in a violent distrust of the common people, and was dedicated to the principle that 'the minority of the opulent' must be protected from American sans-culottes" (1912, 13). Herbert Croly held similar critical views on the foundational myths, yet he embraced the aspirational sentiment in the American national creed—the idea that the country was constantly working toward a better future. But, he found fault in what he perceived as a general expectation that economic and social benefits would continue to automatically realize themselves. In the past, the country had economically profited by westward expansion, but the conditions had significantly changed since the "Gilded Age." As "the discontented poor are beginning to charge their poverty to an unjust political and economic organization," Croly suggested, "the sincere and candid reformer can no longer consider the national Promise as destined to automatic fulfillment" ([1909] 1963, 20). Croly faulted the American system for its excessive emphasis on individual economic freedom and a socially undesirable concentration of economic and political power. This concentration had to be regulated, by getting to the root of the problem. The individual, Croly held, had to be subordinated "to the demand of a dominant and constructive national purpose," and the state had to make "itself responsible for a morally and socially desirable distribution of wealth" (23).

Croly built his vision by forging a new narrative of American economic and political history that went back to the conflict between Federalists and Anti-Federalists—represented by Alexander Hamilton and Thomas Jefferson, respectively—and the question of how much power should be concentrated in the federal state. He criticized Jefferson's approach as being "meager, narrow, and self-contradictory" and prone to "extreme individualism" (43), while praising Hamilton for his insight that the national good had to be achieved by a strong executive branch. "The triumph of Jefferson and the defeat of Hamilton enabled the natural individualism of the American people free play," Croly deplored (49). In its wake, the role of government was constructed as an essentially negative one. Croly's account was a highly constructed one,[5] aimed at promoting a strong national government. The weakness of the political institutions, he believed, was the reason for the rise of specialized interests, be it corporations, unions, or individual politicians, all of whom sought to exploit the political organization for their own benefits (138). These specialized interests had to be countered by a "democratic social ideal" that provided social cohesion without leveling "desirable individual and class distinctions" (139). Croly's social vision aimed at replacing a predominantly negative conception of liberty—defined as the noninterference of the state with individual economic activity—with a positive definition of liberty, which worked "expressly and intentionally for the welfare of the whole people" (207). While he did not suggest the abolition of private property, he argued that its nature and status within society had to be radically transformed, as the state assumed the responsibility to create a more equal distribution of wealth (209).

The foregoing discussion illustrates the tenaciousness of the ownership model of property and the rhetoric of the producer economy in a radically altered social and economic environment. The discourse on private property at the turn of the twentieth century had to negotiate established values, the most important of which was the notion of property being a private, individual right. The progressive reformers decisively altered the public discourse on private property, successfully calling into question the idea of an absolute private right to property and an individualist conception of wealth. Though they did not manage to fully replace the natural rights idea of property, they revised the relationship between the private and public aspects, granting the state unprecedented powers to regulate private property. Moreover, they reconfigured private responsibility for the public good. The rise of the manufacturing corporation, with its new and specific structuring logic, contributed greatly to the new thinking, as did the populist and socialist challenges to the corporate system. Yet, neither the corporation's redefinition of property ownership nor the socialist attempt to replace private with socially owned property eradicated the American belief in the fundamental importance of private property. Instead, as the following section will show, property made a comeback in a different form: the American dream of homeownership.

THE WORKING MAN'S REWARD: PROMOTING HOMEOWNERSHIP IN THE CONSUMER ECONOMY

"As late nineteenth-century workers relinquished control over the processes of production," argues Elaine Lewinnek in a study on Chicago's suburbanization, "they were promised control over issues of consumption, especially housing, which elites imagined to be a purely residential respite from work" (2014, 4). Taking my cue from Lewinnek's observation, in this section I will investigate a decisive shift in property's position in the American cultural imagination after World War I. At this particular historical moment, the image of the homeowner as the model American citizen emerged, thereby replacing the yeoman farmer. This shift was not merely symbolic but indicated the rupture in the country's political economy, brought about by the economic transformations discussed in the first half of this chapter. Within the modern corporate system, the majority of workers became employees and subordinates rather than agents in the processes of production. At the same time, enterprises with nationwide operations created a new, standardized consumer culture and an unprecedented supply of consumer goods. As corporations and progressive reformers redefined the concept of property, new affective relationships to objects of property concomitantly emerged in the realm of consumption, the most important of which was the owner-occupied home.

By addressing a perceived "housing problem" and a slack in the building industry, the federal government, for the first time, became involved in the promotion of homeownership after World War I. As the following sections will show, it thereby contributed to newly legitimizing the private property system as well as to forming the (white) middle class. In the progressive era, the home, as an object of property, coincided with a discourse on the home as a locus of social and individual improvement. Homeownership became "a means to cultivate a nation of disciplined, honorable, civic-minded men" (Quinn 2019, 88). As Scott MacKenzie has pointed out, "home" is a "hegemonic cultural object [which] serves and helps to maintain modes of governance, class supremacy, and capitalist production" (2013, 15). Homeownership and home improvement were progressive reform projects, looking to bring scientific efficiency into the home and encouraging a specific (thoroughly gendered and racialized) vision of middle-class home life. Yet while the rhetoric of home and property ostensibly promoted a more inclusive ideal, it simultaneously generated social divisions, thereby sharpening the separation between the private and the public spheres.

Homeownership Campaigns prior to World War I

The conception of the home as a sphere separate from public life and as a site of middle-class subjectivity did not originate in the progressive era but has been traced by historians and other scholars to the sanctification of the domestic sphere in the early nineteenth century (Blumin 1989, 184; see also Douglas 1977; Cott 1997). The emergence of a middle-class ideal was intimately related to the fashioning and furnishing of the domestic sphere. "Early in the nineteenth century," Mary Ryan has argued, "the American middle class molded its distinctive identity around domestic values and family practices" (1981, 15). Catharine Beecher was perhaps the most influential voice in that respect. Her work situated women in the home and demarcated a firm line between the private and the public realm. Sarah Josepha Hale, the editor of the popular nineteenth-century women's journal *Godey's Lady's Book*, advanced an "Own Your Own Home" campaign between 1846 and 1898, which included model house plans (Hutchison 1989, 46).

The home has always been associated with moral implications relating not only to gender but also to social class. In 1848, Andrew Jackson Downing, an American landscape designer, horticulturist, and writer, mused on the "Moral Influence of Good Houses." Downing imagined the resettlement of the working classes into open country spaces—aided by the means of modern transportation—to encourage social and moral stability and to avoid European-style tenant systems (Jackson 1985, 117). As MacKenzie argues, "the middle-class private home—as an epistemological construct, an affective complex, and an administrative instrument—was first invented by, but not *for*, the emergent middle classes; it was invented for the poor" (2013, 7). Homeownership promised to increase civic virtue and to pacify the labor force (Quinn 2019, 90–91). The Carnegie Steel Company thus began loaning money to employees, for the purpose of building homes, recognizing that "it is an advantage to a mill-town employer to have property-owning employes [*sic*]. The labor force is more stable and there is less likelihood of a strike, the employes not wishing to jeopardize their position after a house has been acquired, lest they have to move" (Fitch 1910, 193).

In a similar vein, the Boston philanthropist Robert Treat Paine made it his mission to supply workers with affordable homes. In his 1881 publication, *Own Your Own Home*, Paine advertised building and loan associations as the way to homeownership (Hayden 2003, 78). Paine's housing development of 116 single- and two-family homes in a suburban development in the Boston area, constructed in 1891, aimed at providing members of the working class with a middle-class lifestyle, an alternative to dense and unsanitary tenement housing. Through his cooperative bank, the Workingman's Building Association, he offered the new financial instrument of the amortized mortgage (Warner 1962, 103-16).

Around the same time, Chicago commercial developer Samuel Eberly Gross constructed twenty-one large-scale subdivisions and ten thousand homes in the Chicago area, most of which were explicitly targeted at the working-class population (E. Clark 1998, 135). Gross advertised his houses widely, investing considerable energy in the design of his sales materials, which would be distributed outside factory gates. He also advertised in newspapers with graphics and stories, like "The House that Lucy Built," in which a thrifty young woman manages to not only achieve homeownership but also to build a business (Hayden 2003, 80–81; E. Clark 1998, 141–42). In one often reproduced image from his *Tenth Annual Illustrated Catalogue of Famous City Subdivisions and Suburban Towns* (1891), Gross promoted homeownership as "the working man's reward" (Gross 1891, 62): in the ad, a worker with a shovel and a hoe sits on a concrete platform and beholds a dark sky; to his right, the angel of justice projects the image of a large sun, at whose center the working man sees the reward for his toil—a single-family, pastoral home "at $10.00 a month." At its top, the ad promises: "Where all was darkness, now is light." Underwritten by religious connotations and imagery, the aspirational dream of one's own home appears here as a respite from strenuous manual work; the home provides the worker with a reason to continue his toil rather than to leave it for other endeavors (figure 3.1). As Lewinnek has pointed out, the actual suburban subdivision advertised here—Ashland Avenue and 47th Street—was less than pastoral, located in the immediate neighborhood of Chicago's extremely polluted stockyards (2014, 67). Gross's booklet, however, did not attempt to dupe its prospective customers but instead pointed to the advantage of owning a home close to the workplace. "Why live long distances from your work when you can buy a home within two-minute walk of your work with the money you now spend for rent and car fare?" Gross asked in another ad, explaining, "350 men now working in the Packing Houses have bought homes from me in my New City Subdivisions. Why shouldn't you?" (1891, 60).

Gross apparently not only recognized the potential of workers as a class of consumers but also managed to perform a public role as a benefactor who provided the poor with opportunities to uplift themselves. Furthermore, he supported the cause of the eight-hour movement for shorter workdays and better pay, as he believed that more leisure time would increase people's desire for commodities—above all, a home of their own (E. Clark 1998, 149). His view echoed arguments provided by labor leaders themselves. Thus, Ira Steward, a major advocate for the eight-hour workday, suggested: "Unless the working classes are *paid* sufficient wages, they will not be able to *buy* certain articles which manufacturers and merchants are so eager to sell. Capitalists remember us as *Producers*, to be paid as little as possible; but not as *Consumers, to be paid enough* to enable us to *buy* their commodities" (1868, 15). Some twenty years later, T. W. Powderly declared that "the adornment of the home became an object with the man who could see his home by daylight, and the demand for articles of home consumption and adornment increased very rapidly" (1890, 465).

Between 1895 and 1919, the *Ladies' Home Journal*—one of the most widely read American magazines at the time—emulated Sarah Hale's series of housing patterns in *Godey's Lady's Book*, by including similar promotional homeownership campaigns on its pages. From its December 1895 issue onward, the *Ladies's Home Journal* printed architectural designs for small- and moderate-income two-story houses, bungalows, and, occasionally, farms and summer homes. Building costs were included in the designs, often already highlighted in the titles of the contributions: "A $3500 Suburban House" (December 1895); "A Stucco House for $3600" (April 1910). Sometimes, cost estimates were broken down for a particular location. Images of facades and, in some cases, interiors were accompanied by floor plans and a descriptive text by the architect. With the publication of these designs, the *Ladies's*

Figure 3.1 "The Working Man's Reward": Advertisement from Samuel Eberly Gross's *Tenth Annual Illustrated Catalogue of Famous City Subdivisions and Suburban Towns* (1891). *Source*: Samuel Eberly Gross. In *Tenth Annual Illustrated Catalogue of Famous City Subdivisions and Suburban Towns*, 62. Chicago, 1891.

Home Journal underwrote a cultural ideal of the family home and proposed specific ways in which domestic life could be most efficiently arranged. The designs suggested a standardized arrangement of rooms, while also emphasizing individuality. The plans were not aimed at mass production but could be adapted to individual needs, nor were the houses presented as part of a community; each image projected the home in a pastoral setting rather than in a lot next to other houses.

A staunch advocate of progressive reform, the *Ladies's Home Journal* reveled in visions of cooperative household arrangements during World War I. The most prominent of these was the community kitchen that could replace individual home-cooked meals. Inspired by national kitchens in England during the war, as well as a food service operating in several New York City districts, contributors such as the architect Charles Harris Whitaker believed in a future for the kitchenless home.[6] According to Whitaker, to outsource cooking from the individual home held several advantages. For one thing, it provided a solution for the scarcity of servants: "When servants are not to be had, and the burden of caring for these necessities falls wholly upon the mistress of the house, there is a general tendency to ask what are the actual necessities in a house." Cooperative forms of domestic work would provide women with "more time for other activities—for their children, for wider social contact, for a little play"—though apparently not for paid work outside the home, an opportunity Whitaker failed to mention. More efficient forms of preparation and overall higher quality food would make up for the replacement of the cultural ideal of the home-cooked meal. "Life will not be poorer and less homelike and intimate through the banishment of menial work from the house," predicted Whitaker, "but the home will be made richer and a better instrument for enlarging the field of life" (1919, 66).

Many contributions projected a better life for citizens, once the government was granted a stronger involvement in private living arrangements. Yet, though some articles displayed communitarian impulses, partly reminiscent of the associationists discussed in chapter 1, the *Ladies's Home Journal* did not subscribe to a social vision beyond private property. Instead, the magazine promoted foremost a vision of domestic efficiency, which incorporated the dominant image of the individual family home and conservative gender roles. The published housing designs made clear that its efforts were mainly directed at a lower middle- and working-class clientele, making homeownership a possibility for people with smaller incomes.

A number of revisionist suburban historians have recently emphasized that the expansion of cities in the late nineteenth and early twentieth centuries was much more diverse in terms of class, race, and ethnicity than scholars commonly have assumed (see, e.g., Lewinnek 2014; Nicolaides 1999; Harris and Lewis 1998). The dichotomy between inner-city poverty and the affluent middle and upper classes in the suburbs, familiar from post–World War II images of suburbia, does not do justice to the historical developments of the first decades of the century. As the examples discussed in this section make clear, the cultural imaginary around thc home and homeownership that developed in the nineteenth and early twentieth centuries was largely aspirational in character. Magazines like *Godey's Lady's Book* and the *Ladies' Home Journal*, as well as advertisements by builders and developers, did not necessarily address the affluent or well-to-do middle classes but sought to expand the dream of homeownership to the working classes. Yet, the limited financial means available to them and the largely informal lending practices made homeownership a precarious state for most workers.

Homes as Commodities

During the nineteenth century, prospective homeowners had to either make cash payments or rely on complex financial strategies, in order to buy a home. One widely used strategy to build a house for 3,000 dollars, for instance, was to first save 1,500 dollars in a savings bank, using 500 dollars to pay for the property and the rest as a down payment for construction costs. Then, the builder would take on a mortgage with a savings bank or a private investor of 1,200 dollars at 5 or 6 percent interest. Nearing completion, a second mortgage at 6–8 percent would be raised from a real estate professional (Calder 1999, 65). In the absence of a bank mortgage system for private borrowers at the time, the building and loan associations thus emerged as important mortgage lenders. The first B&L was founded in Philadelphia in 1831; in 1893, 5,838 B&Ls were in operation, making them the third largest lender, after private individuals and savings banks. By 1900, the building societies had accumulated over half a billion dollars in assets and boasted at least 1.4 million members, collectively (Quinn 2019, 94). The B&Ls worked as cooperative societies: in order to be eligible for credit, prospective homebuyers would invest in the shares of the association and then borrow against them at low interest rates (Calder 1999, 66–67).

National banks first became authorized to provide mortgages for private individuals in 1916 (P. J. Davies 1958, 95). During the 1920s, home mortgage lending grew faster than in any other period during the twentieth century, despite the fact that comparatively few financial instruments for home financing existed. Though forms of installment credit became available in the 1920s, non-amortized "balloon mortgages" were most common, whereby the principal was due in full at the end of a mortgage period of usually three to five years. Balloon mortgages covered no more than 60 percent of the property value, which meant that buyers had to take on second mortgages, through nontraditional lenders, at higher interest rates. In comparison with installment plans, a prospective homeowner was thus able to borrow more money. Speculators hoped to sell their property with a profit when the borrowing period ended; the majority rolled over their mortgages every three to five years (Hyman 2011a, 47). These kinds of mortgages had long been used in the commercial and farming sector; in 1916, the U.S. Congress established the Federal Farm Loan System, which offered farmers long-term amortized mortgages, but, at the time, it did not set up an equivalent system for nonfarm borrowers (Fishback, Rose, and Snowden 2013, 12).

The introduction of installment credit changed real estate finance in the first decades of the twentieth century (Weiss 1987, 31). Between 1920 and 1930, owner-occupied housing rose from 10.9 to 14 million homes, usually financed through building and loan associations, which offered loans over a twelve-year period (O'Toole 2012, 51–53). Though mortgage lending through mutual savings banks, commercial banks, and life-insurance companies existed, the fastest growing mortgage lenders were the building and loan associations, operating in every state by 1920. They offered "share-accumulation" mortgages, which enabled the borrower to repay his loan without a large payment at the end. In comparison to amortized mortgages, the principle was not reduced over time through monthly payments; instead, the noninterest part of the monthly payment was invested in shares of the B&L association, paid into a sinking fund which earned dividends until the funds equaled the principal. The borrower thus would use the sinking fund to pay for the loan in full. These share-accumulation mortgages had some advantages, compared to loan contracts: as shareholders, the members of the associations were full owners and therefore received higher returns than they did on saving accounts at commercial banks. Also, these contracts created larger incentives to pay back the loan, since failing to do so would mean the loss of not only the home but also the accumulated funds. This generated an additional security for the B&L and enabled the association to offer longer maturities as well as larger loans that could amount to up to two-thirds of the property value (Fishback, Rose, and Snowden 2013, 14). However, during the Great Depression, the strengths of the B&L system grew into a weakness, when borrowers' investments in their sinking funds no longer generated profits but produced losses. As financial assets lost in value, paying off one's mortgage required larger payments into the sinking fund, thereby making it more difficult to fully amortize one's debts (18).

The 1920s not only saw an expansion of mortgage financing but also an early form of securitization: mortgage guarantee companies began to offer private mortgage insurance as well as a form of mortgage-backed securities. These two forms of securitization "played a significant role in the urban building boom of the 1920s and the general financial distress of the 1930s" (Snowden 1995, 283). Mortgage guarantee companies began to provide insurance policies against the default on mortgages for investors who had either created these mortgages themselves or who had bought them from independent mortgage companies. Some of these guarantee companies would also make loans on properties themselves and then sell these loans with default insurance policies. By 1930, "some fifty mortgage guarantee companies had written nearly $ 3 billion of default insurance in New York alone" (284). The inherent weaknesses in the mortgage securitization business greatly contributed to the system's downfall in the 1930s.

The expansion of homeownership at the beginning of the twentieth century was thus, in significant ways, the result of a restructured credit system after World War I. Furthermore, the availability of credit and the question of who would receive credit and under which conditions helped to shape capitalist production, distribution, and consumption through categories of race and gender. As Louis Hyman has noted, "the modern credit system of the twentieth century was built by white men for white men, leaving other Americans to borrow in older, more expensive and dangerous, ways" (2011a, 7). While other racial groups were not completely excluded from official credit systems, they often received credit only at less favorable conditions, or they had to rely on informal lending. In fact, a significant number of African Americans, who went north or west during the Great Migration, moved to the suburbs, as Andrew Wiese delineated in his study on Evanston, Illinois (1999, 429). Many of them became homeowners, despite the fact that they had faced housing discrimination.[7]

While residential areas had been fairly well integrated in cities like Atlanta or Chicago in the late nineteenth century (see, e.g., Lands 2009; Connolly 2014; Gwendolyn Wright 1983; Garb 2005), legally sanctioned forms of segregation nonetheless arrived with the suburbanization and professionalization of the real estate business. In 1908, realtors had formed a national professional organization; as the United States entered World War I, the National Association of Real Estate Boards (NAREB) already represented 150 local boards with more than 7,500 members (Hornstein 2005, 14). These newly organized realtors emerged as major agents in the transformation of urban and suburban spaces after the war, promoting homeownership and championing city planning and extensive regulations such as zoning ordinances (19). The realtors believed it to be their "civic duty," Jeffrey Hornstein suggests, "to intelligently create great cities" and "to bring the benefits of homeownership to every American, especially the workingman" (35). This commitment, however, was biased toward white customers and to the protection of property values.

With large numbers of African Americans and new immigrants coming into American cities, both realtors and progressive reformers reacted by advancing racial zoning as what they believed to be an effective means of social control: "The homogeneous suburb, populated by middle-class homeowners, offered the hope of good government and local control" (Wolf 2008b, 31). Racial tensions and violence in American cities between 1917 and 1921 further contributed to the emergence of these new institutional practices that sought to contain conflicts (Jones-Correa 2001, 554).

NAREB's amendment of its "code of ethics," adopted in 1924, therefore contained a stipulation that realtors "should never be instrumental in introducing into a neighborhood a character of property or occupancy, members of any race or nationality, or any individuals whose presence will clearly be detrimental to property values in that neighborhood" (qtd. in Jones-Correa 2001, 564). The development of large-scale suburban subdivisions thus went along with practices of zoning, redlining, as well as, in some instances, racially restrictive covenants.

"Own Your Own Home!" Federal Homeownership Initiatives

After World War I, the residential home became an object of investment, not only for prospective homeowners but also for an emerging professional financial industry. These financial aspects cannot be separated from the promotion of homeownership in the political and cultural discourses of the time. In 1919, NAREB conducted an "Own Your Own Home" campaign, to educate white middle- and working-class families on the benefits of buying a home on mortgage credit. This propagandistic effort was orchestrated first by the Department of Labor and then moved to the newly founded Housing Division within the Department of Commerce (Hutchison 1989, 62). Realtors throughout the country would conduct "Own Your Own Home" campaigns during the 1920s. Though soon discontinued as a government project, the campaign foreshadowed subsequent government involvement under Secretary of Commerce and later president Herbert Hoover in the 1920s, as well as New Deal legislation. Whereas homeownership had previously been organized locally, the federal government was now responding to housing shortages and urban blight, as well as the perceived threat of socialism. The "Own Your Own Home" campaign was only one of several efforts with government involvement that targeted the private home; the federal government also endorsed the "Better Homes in America" movement (a nonprofit organization of which Hoover acted as president over several years in the 1920s), the Architects' Small Service Bureau (a professional organization), and the Home Modernizing Bureau (Hutchison 1997, 184).

Mortgage credit became a crucial mechanism of social inclusion and exclusion, serving to expand urban and suburban home ownership to the white working class, while all but excluding other social groups, such as African Americans and recent immigrants. As various scholars have noted, the campaign advertisements operated with normative, standardized ideas about the family and home, gender and race (Dunn-Haley 1995; Hutchison 1997; Lands 2008; Luken and Vaughan 2005; Altman 1990). The effort to expand homeownership hinged, to a large extent, on making homeownership not only available to but also desirable for a larger fraction of the (white) population.

According to the 1920 census, only 45.6 percent of American families owned their homes (Halbert 1932, 51); in fact, the number was even declining and several percentage points lower than in 1890. In 1917, NAREB's executive secretary, Tom Ingersoll, observed: "Capital has for some years been more and more inclined to seek other channels of investment than housing. The characteristically American impulse toward the making of a permanent home for the family in a place of its very own, while still strong and general, appears to be losing rather than gaining among people of small means" (qtd. in P. J. Davies 1958, 129).

Then, homeownership had not yet been established as a prerequisite of middle-class identity, and many families found it more convenient to rent a place in the suburbs, while investing their money elsewhere (Dunn-Haley 1995, 102). While middle-class suburbanites often did not see homeownership as an end in itself, a home of one's own remained unavailable for many members of the working class, due to the weak institutionalized mortgage system. In the early twentieth century, many workers simply found their wages to be too low, relative to the cost of acquiring a home (Garb 2005, 204).

The "Own Your Own Home" campaign sought to destigmatize debt and sell the idea to Americans that mortgage financing was a form of thriftiness. B&Ls supported the campaign, as becomes evident in a four-page publication issued by the Building and Loan Association of San Francisco in May 1919. The cover image shows, as the caption aptly summarizes, how "The Building and Loan Association Mistress Opens the Gates of Opportunity and Tenders the 'Key' to Home-Ownership" to what appears to be a white middle-class family. The sketch does not show the family members' faces, as they are meant to stand in for a generic "Mr. and Mrs. Homehunter," an American couple on the brink of becoming homeowners. However, their formal dress insinuates their middle-class status; a little girl with a dog on a leash complements the picture. As they stride through the "Gates of Opportunity," their gaze falls on a street of detached single-family homes in a suburban environment. The mistress on the left—who bears some resemblance to the Statue of Liberty—provides them with a large key, which represents a Building and Loan savings account. The "good habit" of making monthly savings to this account, the accompanying text highlights, will pave the way to homeownership (figure 3.2).

The image depicts homeownership as being exclusive, with the building and loan mistress as the gatekeeper. The couple's social status as white middle class suggests who will be left out of this suburban "gated community," implying that you need to be a particular kind of subject to become a homeowner—or, perhaps, that homeownership will transform you into such a subject. Interestingly, the text refrains from referencing debt altogether, putting

INCORPORATED IN 1885—34 YEARS AGO.

CITIZEN'S REPORT

BE YOUR OWN BANKER | BE YOUR OWN LANDLORD

SAN FRANCISCO, MAY 12TH, 1919.

The Building and Loan Association Mistress Opens the Gates of Opportunity and Tenders the "Key" to Home-ownership

Our illustration above, tells its own story, almost. Mr. and Mrs. Homehunter, tired of rent-paying, approach the gateway of opportunity. The Mistress of the Building and Loan Association, hospitably opens the gates for them, and cheerfully bids them enter. She tenders them the key to home-ownership, meaning a building and loan savings account.

But let us drop the allegory here and express the idea in another way. If you, reader, are really anxious to escape the burden of rent-paying and sincerely desire to own a home all your own, the usual problem may confront yau. You may want the home alright, but have you the necessary cash to start it? This is not the age of Knight Errantry, when one may hope to be enservilized by the witchery of a tin-pot knight. Rent shackles may not be released by your own efforts. Do not look for dream entities to pour from the sunset lands of Nowhere, the liquid gold of life's fortuitous opulence.

Then why not start about the idea in a rational way. Take a few shares and begin a building and loan association monthly saving account? The habit once formed, like all good habits, you will find easy to persevere in. When you have saved enough to buy a lot, then you will know that you are the happy possessor of the key that unlocks the door to home-ownership.

DURING THE WAR IT WAS PATRIOTIC NOT TO BUILD; NOW YOU CAN BEST SHOW YOUR PATRIOTISM BY BUILDING.

Figure 3.2 Building and Loan Association of San Francisco, *Citizen's Report*, May 12, 1919. *Source*: Box 461, USHC Real Estate Division, Record Group 3, National Archives at College Park, Maryland.

an emphasis on savings instead. Paying deference to a reigning morality that eschews spending money that one does not own, the text urges the reader to invest in a savings account, without mentioning that saving is only half of the bargain and will merely provide for the down payment on a house. The rest of the buying price would be financed, typically, with two mortgages. The ad thus caters to an audience that associates debt with guilt and insolvency with immorality.

Other ads were more forthright in advancing the benefits of debt. The "Own Your Own Home" Committee of Philadelphia published advertisements elucidating the advantages of these amortized mortgages. One of these ads, titled "The House that Bought Itself: The story of a young couple, a small salary, and a strong desire to own a home," is typical of the campaign's use of both visual and narrative elements. To the right of the headline, a white couple gazes in awe at a single-family detached home; on the curb, three little children play under a tree. The accompanying narrative relates, in the husband's voice, the couple's journey to homeownership. Having entered their married life twelve years ago, financially unprepared and having given up their prospects of ever owning a home on their modest salaries, the couple is being saved by their friend Jack Wise's financial smartness. Jack manages to disperse the narrator's doubts about getting into debt and his fears of foreclosure, detailing the financial ramifications of buying a $2,000 house with a $300 down payment and two mortgages. Convinced of Jack's reasoning, the couple embarks on the adventure of homeownership, managing to pay off their debt after only eleven years, through monthly installments, and, in effect, not having spent any more than they had previously paid for rent. Through its imagery and narrative, the ad proposes that getting into debt is a form of thrift because, unlike a renter, you invest in a sustainable good. A rented dwelling, in this vision, can never rightfully be a home. The fact that the ad features a $2,000-house suggests that its target audience was lower income families—according to a 1929 report of the Bureau of Labor Statistics, the average single-family home cost $3,972 in 1921 (qtd. in Halbert 1932, 53). Operating with a down payment of less than 25 percent and at comparatively low interest rates, the narrative downplays the financial barriers to homeownership and the very real risk of foreclosure, which the text's alleged financial expert dismisses as "nonsense" (figure 3.3).

Other ads published by the Philadelphia "Own Your Own Home" Committee operated in similar ways, projecting images of idealized white middle-class life and the benefits of buying on installment credit. They also starkly perpetuated traditional gender roles. In one example, the ad's headline appears to quote a happy wife, who exclaims: "How glad I am that I agreed with John when he proposed that we 'Own our Home'!" In the accompanying image, a woman behind a curtain takes a peak at her husband and two children, comfortably playing in what appears to be the family's living room. The text, in the woman's voice, addresses the stress and uncertainty of living as renters, being frequently required to move and dependent on a landlord for repairs. Their own home, in contrast, provides security and neatness: "Our home is always in order and much pleasanter and more livable than any rented house could be. Our lawn is well kept, our garden is blooming—in short, we live in a real home atmosphere." Another ad directly addresses the male citizen, appealing to traditional ideas of masculinity as well as patriotism. The headline boldly states: "The Man Who Owns His Home—is a better—Worker—Husband—Father—Citizen and a real American." The accompanying text, too, is characterized by imperatives that appeal to the

Figure 3.3 "The House That Bought Itself": Advertisement by the "Own Your Own Home" Committee of Philadelphia. *Source*: Box 5, USHC General Records, Own Your Own Home Campaign, Record Group 3, National Archives at College Park, Maryland.

reader's pride and sense of responsibility. Homeownership, the ad claims, will mark a man as successful and place him "among the bigger men of your community" (figure 3.4).

The ads of the "Own Your Own Home" campaign make use of narratives and images that consistently picture homeowners as members of the white middle class. Crucially, the ads work with first-person narratives,

Figure 3.4 "The Man Who Owns His Home": Advertisement by the "Own Your Own Home" Committee of Philadelphia. *Source*: Box 5, USHC General Records, Own Your Own Home Campaign, Record Group 3, National Archives at College Park, Maryland.

thus establishing textual subjectivities that provide the audience with figures of identification. Within these narratives, debt plays a crucial role: the ads encourage, even demand, that citizens get into debt, in order to become homeowners. They depict homeownership on the installment plan as a prudent form of investment, a promise of a future happy family life, a moral and patriotic duty. Moreover, these ads contain implicit assumptions about the morality of debt: getting into debt includes the imperative to meet one's financial obligations, to pay one's monthly installments. By buying into the American dream of homeownership, citizens thus become "debtor subjects" (Lazzarato 2012, 11): they are subjected to the social control inherent in the creditor/debtor relationship. Debt has a disciplining function because it causes debtors to behave in certain socially sanctioned and predictable ways.

As secretary of commerce, Herbert Hoover promoted the "associative state" (Hutchison 1989, 2), in which private business interests and philanthropists cooperated with the government for the public good. Hoover himself entered a strategic partnership with Marie Meloney, the editor of the women's magazine *The Delineator*, with whom he developed the "Better Homes in America" campaign, to promote homeownership and, more generally, home improvement (Altman 1990, 287). Janet Hutchison has argued that the campaign was both progressive and conservative, as it sought to apply scientific approaches to the home, yet, at the same time, it worked to reaffirm the woman's domestic position (1989, 3). As Karen Altman suggests, "Better Homes" also "legitimized consumerism by associating it with both the old American values of property and ownership and with the new, modern values of standardization and expertise" (1990, 290).

Activities of the "Better Homes" campaign included a yearly "Better Homes Week," conducted by local committees which erected or furnished model homes in their communities. The "Better Homes Week" began in 1923, with a modest number of seventy-eight model homes throughout the nation. In 1931, over the nine-year period since the initiative's founding, the number of local committees had increased from 500 to 7,200, and they were distributed among all states but one and included the territories of Alaska, Hawaii, Puerto Rico, and the Virgin Islands (Ford 1931, 223). As the participation numbers increased exponentially, many cities diversified their model homes by providing various house types for citizens of different incomes and ethnicities. Addressing various social groups separately—such as the working class, immigrants, and black women—the campaign was premised on categories of difference it itself had helped to construct and reinforce. For instance, a model home erected for black Americans on St. Helena's Island, South Carolina, described as "a small Negro cottage" in the *Delineator*, received a prize for its "perfect demonstration to Negroes" (qtd. in Altman 1990, 296).

The "Better Homes" campaign included the erection of the 1923 "national home," called "Home Sweet Home," on the national mall in Washington, D.C. "Home Sweet Home" brought great publicity to the campaign in its early stages, underlining the immense national importance placed on the housing issue. Located in proximity to the White House, the national home achieved symbolic significance. Designed by architect Donn Barber, it showcased the

Colonial Revival style, and both this style and the name "Home Sweet Home" gave the project a nostalgic ring, alluding to the early American period and John Howard Payne's 1823 song "Home! Sweet Home!" (Hutchison 1989, 126–56). The proponents of the campaign thus took care to locate the idea of home in past history and relate it to the nation's founding. The "Better Homes" campaign shaped a national ideal of home and thereby also helped to produce a cultural imaginary primarily directed at the white middle class. The actual built home, furnished with contributions by private businesses, well exceeded the budgets of the majority of American families and was hence unattainable to large parts of the population (142). In that sense, "Home Sweet Home" also remained a projective surface.

The "Better Homes" campaign also created a yearly award for the best model house. In 1924, Caroline Bartlett Crane, a Unitarian minister and social reformer, received the award for her "Everyman's House" in Kalamazoo, Michigan. She published a detailed account of the project in her book *Everyman's House*, explaining her design choices for "a house built around a mother and her baby" (1925, 1). "Everyman's House" was built according to principles of efficiency and with a focus on women's domestic work. It did away with unnecessary customary features such as hallways and separate dining rooms, instead focusing on making the most of limited space for a family with four children. Crane's book affirmed separate spheres demarcated by gender lines: "Everyman's House" was built for a wage-earning father and a mother who did all the domestic work on her own and who raised the children. Though she pointed to ways in which the house could be adapted to the living situation of working women without children, Crane remained focused on the ideal of a nuclear family. From the outset, she aspired to a free-standing house for the individual owner and advocated professionally designed individual floor plans. And while she promoted the duplication of her principles, she eschewed the idea of "mass production" of identical, interchangeable houses (209). In a commercial age in which prefabricated houses could be ordered from mail-order catalogues by Sears, Roebuck and Company, projects such as Crane's resisted standardization and conformity (Archer 2010, 49).

Insisting on the universality of "Everyman's House" and the domestic arrangements it propagated, Crane and the wider "Better Homes" movement ostensibly posited natural gender relationships, where women assumed the role of homemakers and consumers and men acted as wage earners and homeowners. The scientific approach to home economics elevated the significance of homemaking, making it a subject of science while also underwriting conservative gender values. At the same time, the campaign inscribed the home with national importance, turning homeowning and homemaking into patriotic duties. To be sure, in promoting normative ideas about the home being a cultural institution of national importance, the federal government and its closely allied private organizations did not engage in an explicit discourse about the concept of private property. Yet, by emphasizing that only the privately owned house could ever truly be considered a home, they endorsed and encouraged property ownership and endowed it with an affective dimension. As hegemonic signifiers, the ideas of home and property thus mutually reinforced one another.

THE TRANSFORMATION OF PROPERTY DISCOURSE AT THE TURN OF THE TWENTIETH CENTURY

The corporate revolution during the late nineteenth century and the disintegration of the legal concept of property into a nonphysicalist bundle of rights significantly altered the relationship between the public and private spheres. The rights-based theory of property gave way to a more utilitarian discourse, which prioritized public welfare over individual rights, subordinating private to national interest. Private property no longer marked the boundary of the state but was indeed recognized as a creature of the law.

The institution of the corporation played a significant role in these transformations. On the one hand, its enormous power in the late nineteenth century was based on the enterprises' status as legal persons, which protected their interests as a form of private, individual economic activity, without holding them accountable for the public consequences of their actions. In this sense, corporations were built on the traditional rights-based idea of property. On the other hand, by divorcing pecuniary interest from managerial control over one's property, they contributed to the disintegration of the concept and helped destroy the "magic of property," as Lippmann put it. The corporate system therefore profoundly shattered the traditional ideal of property ownership as a form of individual agency, moral responsibility, and civic participation in democratic processes.

It is thus unsurprising that the turn of the century saw the most violent confrontations between capitalism and labor in the history of the United States. Populists and socialists, as well as more moderate progressive reformers, protested the concentration of wealth and pressed for revolution or reform. Ultimately, the progressive call for more regulatory involvement of the state outlasted the agitation for the abolition of private property in the means of production. The reformers succeeded, in part, because (white) workers were allowed to participate in the emerging consumer economy. They traded control in the workplace for the amenities of domestic life, enjoying property ownership, not through the means of production but through their participation in a new culture of consumption. As the "working man's reward," homeownership expanded significantly after World War I, aided by the professionalization of the real estate business, the introduction of modern credit instruments such as the amortized mortgage, and the active involvement of the federal government. Together, these institutions allowed more people to become property owners and fostered an affective relationship to the home as an object of property. Thus, despite the significantly altered idea of property in the legal realm, the physicalist conception of property survived in the public imagination.

The new consumer culture, however, was also premised on racial divisions and exclusions. The new property regime intensified social stratifications along the lines of race and ethnicity and created segregated urban and suburban landscapes, where especially African Americans were all but excluded from property ownership. Practices of zoning and redlining, which were allegedly introduced to preserve the stability of neighborhoods and home prices, found their way into federal government policy and skewed the distribution of wealth along racial lines. Though overtly discriminatory practices were eventually abandoned, structural forms of discrimination remained. As homes became financial assets to their owners, their whiteness also turned into a kind of property.

NOTES

1. The thing-based conception of ownership in classical liberalism also served important ideological functions and developed in opposition to feudal property. In distinction to the feudal system of complex social relationships, interdependencies, and hierarchies, "property conceived as the control of a piece of the material world by a single individual meant freedom and equality of status" (Grey 1980, 74).

2. The legal fiction of corporate personhood is currently being discussed intensively within interdisciplinary legal studies. See, for example, the symposium on "Imagining Corporate Personhood" in the *Political and Legal Anthropology Review* (2014).

3. In *On Populist Reason*, Ernesto Laclau develops his theory of populism whose mechanism he sees as paradigmatic for political articulation as such. In this context, he addresses the People's Party as a historical example which illustrates the workings of his theory (Laclau 2005, 201–08).

4. In his famous "Cross of Gold" speech, which he delivered at the Democratic National Convention in Chicago on July 9, 1896, and which won him the presidential nomination, Bryan invoked the precise rhetoric of the populist movement, calling upon the principles of Jefferson and Jackson and relying on a producer ethic that sought to unite a variety of groups, from western farmers to urban workers, whose actual economic interests, however, varied substantially or even conflicted.

5. Christopher Lasch (1965) has pointed out that Croly's praise for Hamilton unduly confused the latter's eighteenth-century mercantilism with a specific kind of

twentieth-century social planning and that Croly disregarded Hamilton's nationalism as being linked to particular social and economic forms he promoted.

6. In its advocacy of more efficient homes without kitchens as well as other cooperative arrangements, the *Ladies' Home Journal* echoed reform ideas that can be traced, most prominently, to Charlotte Perkins Gilman's proposals, for example, in her book *The Home: Its Work and Influence* (1903) and in her utopian novel *What Diantha Did* (1909–10). In the latter work, Gilman's heroine pursues plans that involve nothing less than a thorough reconstruction of her entire society. By situating the home as the origin of social change, Gilman also challenges the boundaries between the private and public sectors (Knewitz 2005, 17).

7. In his case study, Wiese shows that, contrary to common assumptions, homeownership and suburbanization were not all-white phenomena. In Evanston, Illinois, African American homeownership was facilitated by the availability of cheap land and was supported by white citizens. African Americans thus had access to receiving credit from mainstream financial institutions and individuals, which also meant, however, that they were dependent on the white financial industry's good will (1999, 451).

Chapter 4

Challenging the "Possessive Investment in Whiteness"

Black Power and Property Discourse in the 1960s

In Lorraine Hansberry's critically acclaimed 1959 play, *A Raisin in the Sun*, the Youngers, an African American working-class family living on Chicago's Southside, come by a modest amount of money thanks to deceased Walter Younger, Sr.'s life insurance policy. Walter's widow, Lena, decides to invest part of the money into a down payment for a house, thus enabling her daughter, her son's family, and herself to leave the cramped, rundown apartment they inhabit together. With house prices inflated in areas advertised to black homebuyers, Lena Younger opts to settle in Clybourne Park, an all-white residential district. It does not take long for the "Clybourne Park Improvement Association," an organization of white gatekeepers, to find out about their prospective black neighbors and raise money to buy the Youngers out. Karl Lindner, the chairman of the "New Neighbors Welcoming Committee," appears at the Youngers' apartment to convince the family to resell the house. The Clybourne Park community, Lindner explains to the Youngers, are "hard-working, honest people who don't really have much but those little homes" (Hansberry [1959] 1994, 117). Accordingly, one should respect their wish, selfish as it may seem, to surround themselves with neighbors of their own liking—which happen to be white people.

This scene, which takes place in the play's third act, is dripping with irony, as Lindner expounds on the reasons why the Youngers should give up their new home, while at the same time trying to deflect any charges of racism. He attempts to put a distance between the people of Clybourne Park and the Youngers by denying that they could share "a common interest in the life of the community" because of their different "background[s]." Yet, his own language betrays him: Having just praised the Youngers as "a nice family of folks, hard working and honest" (117), he subsequently uses the same adjectives for his white neighbors. Like the Youngers, they are working class; their home is the realization of their aspirations for social advancement. Their aims, in other words, perfectly mirror those of the Youngers. However, the white homeowners act on their feelings of entitlement to determine who will be their neighbors; they claim a "right to the neighborhood" that people of color lack. The only thing that truly separates them, then, is, in fact, the very "race prejudice" that Linder disavows. Racism is the driving force, as these people "get awful worked up when they feel that their whole way of life and everything they've ever worked for is threatened" (119). Yet, those who are really threatened are people like the Youngers, who venture out into white neighborhoods—news reports of black people being bombed are ubiquitous in *A Raisin*.

Hansberry's drama, inspired by the author's experience as the child of a black middle-class family that fought housing discrimination in the courts,[1] seeks to unveil the structural forms of racism that people of color had to endure in 1950s America, a time in which white Americans enjoyed unprecedented prosperity. Hansberry's critique does not merely focus on housing discrimination but links it to themes of economic freedom and self-determination. She contrasts Lena's American dream of homeownership with Walter Jr.'s vision of becoming a business owner, by investing part of the life insurance money into a liquor store. Walter sees himself as a rugged individualist, hoping to become a full member of society by acquiring capital. While the Youngers have similar aspirations as white working-class families with respect to housing, Walter, like "them white boys" downtown, believes that "money is life" (74). Walter craves economic success and agency through property ownership. By the end of the play, however, he has to learn that "race and economics cannot be separated, that capitalism was and is founded upon the subjugation of particular raced bodies" (Matthews 2008, 559). As his putative friend Willy fleeces him of the remaining insurance money with which his mother has entrusted him, he understands that "it's all divided up. Life is. Sure enough. Between the takers and the 'tooken'" (Hansberry [1959] 1994, 141).

J. Charles Washington attributes Hansberry with "prescience," by arguing that she engages the question of economic freedom for African Americans, which "Black leaders and intellectuals only began to discuss a decade later" (1988, 120). Black activists in the 1960s confronted what George Lipsitz has called the "possessive investment in whiteness," trying to expose the racial hegemony and shift the distribution of wealth in American society. In this chapter, I investigate a series of attempts by black activists to attack the hegemonic order and the systemic exclusions of blacks from property ownership between 1963 and 1970. I analyze the rhetorical strategies of African American activists who questioned established property rights and of white actors who sought to protect their privileges.

Picking up on the structures of racial discrimination that have already become visible in the construction of and debates on homeownership in the early twentieth century, as discussed in chapter 3, the current chapter proceeds in three steps: the first section draws on Critical Whiteness Studies to elucidate the nexus of race and property in the twentieth century, thereby establishing the framework of racially discriminatory practices in the context of real estate ownership and black economic freedom. Subsequently, I will turn my attention to the efforts of integrationist activists in the early 1960s who battled discrimination in the area of housing. In the wake of landmark legislative achievements, most prominently the Civil Rights Act of 1964 and the Voting Rights Act of 1965, open housing laws in the North and the West of the United States provoked what came to be termed a "white backlash" (Glickman 2020). Though many members of the white middle class supported the idea of granting African Americans equal opportunities in employment and political participation, they were uneasy with respect to education and housing integration. Analyzing the debate over Proposition 14 in California, a ballot initiative challenging the state government's 1963 fair housing law, I show how the language of constitutional rights provided white property owners with an ostensibly race-neutral rhetoric to assert white privilege. Liberal open housing advocates, meanwhile, advanced an ideal of colorblindness, which impeded their ability to confront structural racism.

Addressing this blind spot of the liberal civil rights movement, black power activists, such as Stokely Carmichael and the Black Panther Party, aimed to make whiteness visible and to militantly confront established structures, thereby exposing and challenging systemic exclusions. In the third part of this chapter, I discuss black power's radical challenge and the ways in which its radicalism was normalized and integrated into the discursive mainstream. Though much of the previous scholarship has often characterized black power as a movement of the political left, my analysis shows that it was ideologically diverse. Many of the black elite understood black power as a form of black capitalism and probed the ways in which black economic power could be achieved, by adapting and transforming the structures of capitalism in a way which would benefit the black community.

The political upheavals of the 1960s are very much interrelated with a (re) negotiation of the concept of property. The liberal consensus of the time, in many ways, resulted from the New Deal institutions built on an instrumentalist conception of property in the tradition of the "bundle of rights" model, which granted governments great regulatory power. Against this model, conservatives reintroduced traditional notions of ownership, advancing an originalist interpretation of constitutional rights. In contrast, activists from the political left subscribed to socialist critiques of private property to challenge structural exclusions. Both the right and the left aimed at altering the status quo and its hegemonic property narratives.

WHITENESS, PROPERTY, AND THE POLITICS OF REAL ESTATE

Since the 1990s, George Lipsitz, Cheryl Harris, Charles W. Mills, David Roediger, and many others working in the field of Critical Whiteness Studies have scrutinized the mechanisms through which white supremacy manages to perpetuate itself within liberal social and economic structures. This scholarship is indebted to the movements of the 1960s, when activists such as Stokely Carmichael and the Black Panthers sought to engage with systemic racism in the United States and on a global scale. In the analyses of Critical Whiteness scholars, whiteness is a systemic tool of domination and exclusion that works by making itself invisible or unmarked. In the West, Richard Dyer remarks, whiteness is habitually "felt to be the human condition"; it "both defines normality and fully inhabits it" and "secures a position of power" (1997, 9). Whiteness asserts itself through the absence of racial markers which are only projected upon others. "White supremacy," Lipsitz argues, "is usually less a matter of direct, referential, and snarling contempt and more a system for protecting the privileges of whites by denying communities of color opportunities for asset accumulation and upward mobility" (1998, viii). As my discussion in chapter 2 has already carved out, property rights in the United States are rooted in racial domination, as black people themselves became objects of property; race, here, was the defining factor for the establishment of a particular form of property. With the hybrid status as both persons and property attributed to people of color, the distinction between races became critical in defining the line between slaves and non-slaves. Since blackness raised the presumption of slavery, "whiteness became a shield from slavery, a highly volatile and unstable form of property" (C. I. Harris 1993, 1720). White privilege thereby became embedded into definitions of property itself, "a prerequisite to the exercise of enforceable property rights" (1724).

More importantly, the racialized structures of property did not end with slavery but are continuously perpetuated by social and political institutions. Drawing on Harris's seminal work, Lipsitz speaks of a "possessive investment," in order to signal that whiteness indeed "has a cash value," allowing white individuals to profit financially from advantages created through structural racism. Thereby, "white Americans are encouraged to invest in whiteness, to remain true to an identity that provides them with resources, power, and opportunity" (Lipsitz 1998, vii). The nexus of whiteness and property that Harris, Lipsitz, and others have highlighted may help us analyze the discourse on fair housing in 1960s America, not as a phenomenon of "backlash" of white conservatives against more progressive liberal social forces but as a renegotiation of racialized structures. As African American activists Stokely Carmichael and Charles V. Hamilton already explained in their 1967 analysis of systemic racism *Black Power: The Politics of Liberation in America*, "the so-called white backlash against black people is something else: the embedded traditions of institutional racism being brought in the open and calling forth overt manifestations of individual racism" (56).

As Adrienne Brown and Valerie Smith assert, "the thread historically tying together race, property, and citizenship has been one of racial discrimination and exclusion" (2015, 5). Before the Civil War, free and enslaved blacks living in the South rarely possessed any real estate. Some states, like Georgia in 1818, passed laws prohibiting African Americans from owning property. Florida also imposed severe restrictions on African American property ownership. Nevertheless, there were quite a number of African American landholders in the antebellum era, for instance in New Orleans, where black people owned real estate at an estimated value of 15 million dollars in 1860 (Copeland 2013, 647–48). During the Civil War, northern troops confiscated lands of southern slaveholders on the basis of three confiscation acts passed between 1861 and 1863, with plans to distribute the land to freed men. In 1865, General William T. Sherman issued Special Field Order No. 15, which reserved land in Florida, Georgia, and South Carolina for African American settlement, yet a year later President Andrew Johnson intervened and returned the land to its former owners, dispossessing the black settlers. Further laws ostensibly enabling southern blacks to acquire land, such as the Southern Homestead Act of 1866, remained ineffective (see, e.g., Oubre 1978). Though African Americans were aspiring to integrate themselves into mainstream society, limited access to credit and overt discrimination made it impossible, in most cases, to acquire full political and economic citizenship. They had only the limited options to work as sharecroppers or in service: "Social exclusion paralleled economic disenfranchisement and was facilitated by the absence of mechanisms for African Americans to gain access to real estate" (Fernández-Kelly 2015, 73). These processes of exclusion were not merely tolerated by governments but were also underwritten by policies that supported whites in the accumulation of property, such as the Homestead Act of 1862 (77).

As discussed in detail in chapter 3, the cultural investment in homeownership in the early twentieth century was intimately related to the construction of a white middle class and relied on policies and practices which favored homogenous neighborhoods, all but excluding African Americans from property ownership. In the twentieth century, private and public discrimination of African Americans reinforced each other, materializing in practices of zoning, racial covenants, and redlining. The zoning of cities into different areas for different land use was a relatively new idea at the beginning of the twentieth century; many cities began to employ zoning restrictions, in the attempt to grow and develop on the basis of rational plans. The first city to pass a racial zoning ordinance was Baltimore in 1910, followed by many other cities, particularly in the South and the Midwest. Such ordinances, which presented themselves as race-neutral by allegedly adhering to the standards of 'separate but equal,' were justified by the argument that zoning would help preserve property values, while preventing racial tensions and violence (R. Brooks and Rose 2013, 39). The NAACP challenged racial zoning in the courts. In *Buchanan v. Warley* (1917), the Supreme Court held a zoning ordinance in Louisville, Kentucky, which closely resembled the one in Baltimore, to be unconstitutional. The Court here "emphasized most heavily the point that racial zoning impeded a person's ability to own and dispose of substantial tangible property" (42).

With racial zoning being outlawed, racially restrictive covenants remained the last resort to legally enforce residential segregation. Restrictive covenants were not predominantly used on racial grounds but regulated on a detailed level of how space in a neighborhood should be used, for example, by specifying lot sizes, building types, or the kinds of land uses deemed appropriate (R. Brooks and Rose 2013, 48). Race was just one aspect to be included among others. Since restrictive covenants were held to be private agreements—unlike the public zoning laws passed by city governments—the courts initially agreed that, for example, in the Supreme Court decision *Corrigan v. Buckley* (1926), they were not covered by equal protection limitations and hence were not unconstitutional (53). In 1948, however, the Court reversed its previous ruling in *Shelley v. Kramer*, by holding that the state could not enforce racially restrictive covenants, as these violated the Fourteenth Amendment (141).

The real estate industry was not only at the forefront of segregating cities through restrictive covenants, but it also played a practical role in expanding black ghettos. As African American migration to cities like Chicago increased the demand for housing within black neighborhoods, rents and home prices in these areas inflated and were significantly higher than in white neighborhoods. Some realtors took advantage of this by "opening up" new neighborhoods for black settlement through "blockbusting": the term refers to a practice among realtors to actively interfere in the racial composition of a neighborhood by renting or selling a few homes to African Americans in a so far "white" neighborhood. Subsequently, they would raise fears of falling property values among whites and encourage them to move to other, all-white neighborhoods, while simultaneously augmenting the black demand through advertising. By thus "flipping" a neighborhood, the realtors profited from the property transactions, with many of them also buying up houses themselves. Those neighborhoods constituted an option for black middle-class families to escape the ghetto and become homeowners (Massey and Denton 1993, 37–38). Yet, since they lacked access to the formal credit instruments available to white families, they were often at the mercy of real estate agents who acted as both seller of the house and lender: "The agent would collect a cash advance and several months of mortgage payments before the buyer defaulted; then the family was evicted and the house was resold to another family under similar terms. In this way, agents could 'sell' a home several times in the course of a year, generating extra profits" (39).

Racial discrimination was a common practice in the area of mortgage credit and insurance, through what has become known as "redlining." In the New Deal era, President Franklin D. Roosevelt created the Home Owners' Loan Corporation (HOLC), which refinanced homes in danger of foreclosure, granted loans at low interest rates, and introduced the long-term, self-amortizing mortgage into the U.S. housing market. The HOLC also developed systematic methods of real estate appraisal, whereby residential areas were rated according to "the occupation, income, and ethnicity of the inhabitants and the age, type of construction, price range, sales demand, and general state of repair of the housing stock" (Jackson 1980, 422). With this data, they devised four categories of quality: first, second, third, and fourth grade areas (referred to with corresponding code letters A, B, C, and D). The HOLC's procedures were based on racist assumptions about urban neighborhoods. Thus, the organization assumed that all neighborhoods would eventually deteriorate, due to the age and obsolescence of the physical structures, and, with the decline in value, would be handed down to families of lower income and different ethnicities. In this scheme, "black neighborhoods were invariably rated as Fourth grade," that is, not credit-worthy (423). This appraisal system became crucially influential regarding the financial decisions of other institutions, with private banks relying on the residential maps created by the HOLC and providing loans based on their system.

The methods of the HOLC were subsequently also adopted by the Federal Housing Administration (FHA), which, between 1934 and 1968, insured long-term mortgage loans by private lenders for home construction and purchase. Though it did not lend money itself, the FHA had a revolutionary impact on the home finance industry: Since the U.S. Treasury guaranteed the loans, large down payments became unnecessary, and, with the reduced risk, interest rates dropped by two to three percentage points. The repayment periods for loans were extended to twenty-five or thirty years, and the loans were fully amortized. These changes significantly increased the number of families that were able to become homeowners, yet the FHA programs also heavily impacted residential structures by favoring single-family suburban construction and thereby contributing to the decay of inner-city neighborhoods. Like the HOLC, the FHA relied on criteria for the evaluation of credit risks, which privileged all-white subdivisions in the suburbs, while refusing to guarantee loans in all-black neighborhoods. It also promoted the residential segregation and use of restrictive covenants, often refusing to insure loans in areas of mixed occupancy as well (Jackson 1980, 430–37). Thus, "both FHA guidelines and actual FHA assistance favored new construction over existing dwellings, open land over developed areas, businessmen over blue-collar workers, whites over blacks, and native-born Americans over immigrants" (447).

African Americans were not only subject to discrimination in housing and mortgage finance, but they also had very little access to consumer credit, which, in the post–World War II period, for the white middle class "had become an entitlement [. . .] tightly interwoven with suburban material culture and everyday middle-class shopping habits" (Hyman 2011b, 201). Moreover, the segregation of neighborhoods and the ghettoization of blacks in inner cities actively contributed to credit discrimination. African American citizens were not cut off from the consumer culture that white America enjoyed, but they were subjected to personal credit relations with retailers operating in their neighborhoods. Storeowners in the inner cities were willing to give them credit, yet the consumer products available there came at a much higher cost than the sellers charged for the same items in suburban neighborhoods. But without credit references at these stores, African Americans had no other choice than to buy televisions and other consumer items at less favorable terms. And not only were the products more expensive, but urban merchants would also charge higher interest rates for products on installment credit. Hyman explains that, when the ghetto riots broke out in the 1960s, people's anger was mainly directed toward the stores that sold on credit, due to the resentments of these inner-city inhabitants toward the merchants' credit practices (2011b, 210).

As this brief overview illustrates, African Americans' relationship to property rights has historically been characterized by racial discrimination. However, the political and social climates slowly began to change after World War II. The civil rights movement started to gain momentum in the 1950s, when the landmark Supreme Court decision *Brown v. Board of Education* (1954) and the Montgomery Bus Boycott (1955–1956) achieved the first victories against segregation. People outside the South especially began to embrace antidiscrimination measures. Yet, with respect to housing and property rights, the North and the West remained as segregated as the South, in some areas even more so.

In the 1950s, under the pressure of civil rights organizations such as the NAACP and its National Committee against Discrimination in Housing

(NCDH), several states and cities passed open housing laws, attempting to end discrimination, also in relation to private and single-family homes. New York had been at the forefront, passing the nation's first antidiscrimination law with respect to public housing in 1938; further laws on the state level and in the city of New York extended the protections, though these laws still often lacked enforcement power and excluded small apartment buildings and private housing. From New York, open housing activism spread to the Midwest and the West, with eight states and twenty-one cities having introduced similar laws by 1954 (Meyer 2000, 159). The federal government, both Congress and the Eisenhower administration, meanwhile remained silent on the issue in the 1950s. Yet, with racial tensions and violence increasing, fair housing slowly became an issue on the national agenda. The Civil Rights Act of 1957 instituted the Civil Rights Commission, which, in its first report, published in 1959, drew attention to housing discrimination nationwide and pointed to the failure of the federal government to address these issues (164–65). In 1962, President Kennedy issued an executive order banning discrimination in federally assisted private housing, the first time the federal government committed itself to support open housing (151–52, 171). As Meyer notes, while fair housing campaigns could celebrate successes across the nation, "the debate on civil rights versus property rights remained heated" (162).

A "RIGHT TO DISCRIMINATE"? CLAIMING CONSTITUTIONAL PROPERTY RIGHTS

In 1968, according to a survey on racial attitudes, 56 percent of white respondents believed that whites had "a right to keep Negroes out of their neighborhoods if they want to" (qtd. in Collins 2006, 21). As discussed in the previous section, a large part of this resistance to African American neighbors was "derived from a self-reinforcing set of economic incentives and racial beliefs that were also propagated by realtors, builders, developers, and bankers" (Collins 2006, 27). In addition to several decades of state-sanctioned discriminatory practices in the area of housing, public and political debates on antidiscrimination laws, introduced on city and state levels during the late 1950s and early 1960s, gave currency to the view that there existed a constitutional "right to discriminate" in the private realm.

With established legal forms of racial discrimination on the brink of being outlawed, homeowners' associations grew stronger in many cities. The Greater Detroit Homeowners Council, for instance, represented 200 groups with a potential membership of 250,000 people (Meyer 2000, 176). Though themselves ethnically diverse, these groups "shared a common bond of whiteness and Americanness," which they asserted against others like "'the colored' and Asians (and occasionally Jews)" (Sugrue 2005, 212). Detroit property rights activists proposed a "Homeowners' Rights Ordinance" on the September 1964 Detroit primary ballot. The rights claimed in the ordinance included a right to choose one's friends and associates and freedom from government interference in homeowners' property. A circuit court had initially deemed the proposition unconstitutional, yet the State Supreme Court reversed the ruling and allowed the ordinance to be presented on the ballot. The voters narrowly approved the initiative, which was however again ruled unconstitutional by the Wayne County Circuit Court in 1965 (227).

For the white population in the North and the West, property rights rhetoric became crucial in the attempt to maintain the status quo at a time when the denial of access to property on purely racial grounds was losing acceptance and respectability. As David Freund has argued, before World War II, whereas northern and western whites pointed to a natural racial hierarchy to justify racial exclusion, after the war they invoked "what they viewed as nonracial variables: protecting the housing market, their rights as property owners and, linked to both, their rights as citizens" (2007, 8). Conservative whites seeking to preserve their status frequently employed arguments that emphasized property as an allegedly race-neutral, constitutionally guaranteed right. At the same time, liberals denounced this strategy as being a form of racism and bigotry, arguing for everyone's right to upward mobility. They thus similarly relied on the language of individualism, which failed to account for structural racism.

My following analysis of the debate around Proposition 14 in California, a ballot initiative aimed at repealing the state's "Rumford Fair Housing Act" in 1964, shows two things: first, it highlights how both conservative and liberal arguments were ultimately shaped by the interests of whiteness; second, and most importantly, I carve out the potency of the rhetoric of constitutional property rights to advance specific political positions in public discourse. The conservative defenders of Proposition 14, I argue, were successful because they managed to appropriate the liberal language of individual (property) rights, thereby forging unity among diverse groups. Though their political victory was struck down by the courts and therefore short-lived, the campaign helped to popularize specific argumentative strategies about property rights. Relying on essentially libertarian property arguments, they planted the seeds for a property discourse that would gain prominence in later decades.

In 1960, the state of California was at the nation's forefront in the battle against racial discrimination. Propelled by a political program devoted to racial reform, the Democrat Edmund G. "Pat" Brown had been elected governor in 1958; Democrats also carried both houses of the legislature, the first time since 1878 (Schiesl 2013, 1). Brown and the party's liberal leaders, among them Augustus F. Hawkins and William Byron Rumford, the only

African American members of the State Assembly, immediately began to press for legislative measures prohibiting discrimination in the workplace. The California Fair Employment Practices Act was passed in April 1959, establishing the Fair Employment Practices Commission (FEPC). A second, extensive civil rights bill against discrimination in public accommodations and business dealings was sponsored by Assemblyman Jesse Unruh and passed in May of the same year. Finally, the Hawkins Fair Housing Act prohibited discrimination in all publicly assisted housing (Schiesl 2013, 2). After his reelection for a second term in 1962, Brown insisted on further extending the Hawkins Act to also cover the private housing market, outlawing discrimination in private real estate transactions. Though such transactions were, in principle, already covered by the Unruh Act, antidiscrimination lacked enforcement, as those who suffered damages had to go through the courts—not a realistic means for many of those subjected to discrimination. The bill envisioned by the Brown Administration, eventually passed as the Rumford Fair Housing Act in June of 1963, gave the FECP authority to enforce the law.

In 1960, the urban centers of California were characterized by intense segregation. Los Angeles was the most segregated city in the nation: its black population had almost doubled over the previous decade, with 94 percent of African Americans living in the south-central part (Schiesl 2013, 1). It had not always been that way, however. In the early decades of the twentieth century, homeownership and occupancy was far less restricted by race. In 1910, California had had a black homeownership rate of 38 percent, a rate higher than in New England (17 percent) or the South (22 percent) (HoSang 2010, 55). Many whites, in fact, were willing to sell or rent houses and apartments to people of color at that time. This changed with the widespread proliferation of restrictive covenants and similar agreements, often aggressively pushed by developers and realtors. Like in the rest of the country, the redlining practices by the HOLC and FHA brought additional force to these developments, as did the move toward large-scale suburban developments in the 1950s. Even after the Supreme Court outlawed restrictive covenants, racial segregation still increased in areas such as the San Fernando Valley, north of Los Angeles. In fifteen of the sixteen cities in the Valley, the black population was under one percent in 1960; almost every African American moving to the area moved to the city of Pacoima. Meanwhile, in San Diego, 82 percent of African American residents lived in only 10 of the city's 123 census tracts (HoSang 2010, 58–59).

Realtors had a key role in these developments: as both Daniel HoSang and Robert Self have argued, segregation was not incidental but rather central to realtors' business strategies, as they viewed treating white and black real estate markets separately as the most profitable approach (HoSang 2010,

59; Self 2003, 265). Since the value of homes was partially determined by the racial makeup of the neighborhoods they were situated in, this affected homebuyers and homeowners as well, as "the value and sanctity of their property and neighborhoods [became] dependent on racial distinction and exclusion" (HoSang 2010, 59). In effect, this meant that "racism [was] rationalized as economic calculation" (Self 2003, 160). The California Real Estate Association (CREA) was very active in the promotion and maintenance of segregation. Local real estate boards in California were particularly exclusive: no single black realtor was among the 2,000 members of the L.A. Realty Board in 1960, and only 3 out of 600 realtors in San Francisco did not employ discriminatory strategies in their businesses. In response to the *Shelley* decision, the L.A. Realty Board had campaigned for more than a decade to amend the U.S. Constitution to enforce property restrictions, drawing up a proposed amendment and advocating its adoption before the NAREB (HoSang 2010, 57).

Protest against the Rumford Act originated among the realtors. Mark Brilliant notes that the opponents of the act "were initially little more than a smattering of angry and anxious realtors, apartment owners, and tract developers" (2010, 195). The Act itself really covered only about 25 percent of the state's 3.8 million single-family homes, that is, only those that were financed by loans guaranteed or insured by the federal or state government; multifamily buildings with less than five apartments were also exempt (192). Nevertheless, CREA went ahead, along with the California Apartment House Owners Association and the Home Builders Association, to create an umbrella organization, the Americans to Outlaw Forced Housing. This organization began to collect signatures for a state constitutional amendment initiative—later to be known as "Proposition 14"—to be put on the ballot in 1964. For CREA and NAREB, the initiative held high symbolic significance. With open housing laws proliferating all over the country, they believed that it would be possible to reverse the trend should they manage to overturn legislation in one of the nation's most populous states, which often saw itself as the avant-garde. The initiative sought to amend the State Constitution rather than directly repeal the Rumford Act. If successful, the amendment would prohibit state and local legislatures from passing any similar ordinances, unless the amendment was repealed by another amendment (193).

Early in February 1964, the organization submitted 767,015 signatures, almost 300,000 more than necessary. With additional signatures collected for possible supplemental filings, more than one million voters signed the petition in total (Leitch 1964, 5). Californians ultimately affirmed Proposition 14 in November of 1964 by a 2-to-1 margin; in the same election, they voted against the right-wing presidential candidate Barry Goldwater and instead for Democrat Lyndon B. Johnson, a split which seemed schizophrenic to many observers. A possible reading of this outcome is that, while the majority of Californians did indeed support civil rights legislation and antidiscrimination laws, property rights still trumped antidiscrimination (Brilliant 2010, 206). The outcome was also in large part due to the realtors' rhetorical campaign strategy, that is, to the way they framed the issue as a question of property rights. The opponents of the amendment initiative, who had organized themselves as Californians Against Proposition 14 (CAP 14), did not manage to craft an equally compelling campaign strategy.

Christopher Schmidt provides a legal and cultural context for the rhetorical battle on fair housing in his investigation of the claim to a constitutional "right to discriminate" among segregationists in the 1960s. Schmidt stresses that "the civil rights movement nurtured constitutional rights claims not only among proponents of the black freedom struggle but also among those opposed to the cause" (2013, 420). Supporters of segregation, just like the civil rights activists, saw themselves as fighting for the cause of freedom, yet it was a very different conception of freedom that motivated them. They claimed that there existed a legal right to discriminate in the private realm, in which the government could not interfere—opening up contestation over how to draw the line between individual choices that should be protected as private decisions and those that were publicly accountable (420). Legal claims to a right to discriminate, advanced in court cases, became prominent at a historical moment "when legally enforced discrimination was replaced by legally enforced nondiscrimination" (423). The courts invariably defeated these claims, but the libertarian arguments for such a right gained significant traction in public discourse. In the area of housing, the challenge was more successful than in other areas of legislation, with opponents being able to strike down the open housing law in California. Though the California Supreme Court rejected the amendment to the California Constitution in 1966, which Proposition 14 had introduced—as did the Federal Supreme Court one year later—its underlying idea exerted significant influence.

CREA's campaign essentially advanced a libertarian argument: it asserted a constitutional right of individuals to own and dispose of their property at their own discretion, without the infringement of governments. Importantly, the organization appropriated the language of civil rights for their purposes. The text of the initiative itself was phrased in language that had, according to a September 1964 *Time* magazine article, a "let-freedom-ring sound to it" ("Proposition 14" 1964, 23). The central sentence of Proposition 14 read: "Neither the State nor any subdivision or agency thereof shall deny, limit or abridge, directly or indirectly, the right of any person who is willing or desires to sell, lease or rent any part or all of his real property, to decline to sell, lease or rent such property to such person or persons as he, in his absolute discretion, chooses" (qtd. in "Proposition 14" 1964, 23). Expressed as a matter of individual rights and freedom of choice, the consequences of the amendment did not immediately become clear. *Time* reported on a poll among African Americans who were asked by pollsters whether they supported the amendment. While initially 59.3 percent approved of it, this number was starkly reversed after respondents had been explained the practical effects Proposition 14 would most likely have. Then, 89 percent were against it.

The *California Real Estate Magazine* served as CREA's most effective propaganda tool. CREA had a membership of 38,000 that year; and 75 percent of licensed realtors read the magazine, making it one of the most influential information sources in the business (Mann 2012, 61). CREA thus had an excellent means for disseminating its arguments against the Rumford Act among its members, ensuring a unified message. A large number of articles published in the monthly magazine between October 1963 and the election of November 1964 addressed the issue, consistently referring to the law as the "Forced Housing Act."

In a "Statement of Policy" adopted at CREA's fifty-ninth annual convention, the realtors affirmed "the basic human right of private property ownership" and asserted "that the most precious rights each American has are Civil rights and Civil liberty which guarantee exemption from arbitrary government interference with person, opinion or property" ("Statement of Policy" 1963, 8). CREA president L. H. Wilson insisted that the organization supported the value of equality and nondiscrimination and instead accused the legislators of introducing a discriminatory law:

> The law in California, since the forced housing and other similar legislation was passed, does not treat all of our citizens equally. It takes away part of the property owner's right to decide for himself to whom he shall sell, rent or lease his property. At the same time it grants special privilege to those who want to buy, rent or lease that property. For the almost 200 years since the American constitution was adopted, property rights have been a cornerstone of American freedom; we contend that every American should continue to have, as he has always had, the right to refuse to rent, lease or sell to anyone, and for any reason. ("Housing Initiative Titled" 1963, 5)

Wilson here points out that the Rumford Act prioritizes potential buyers of property over those who already own an apartment or house. Though one might frame this as competing interests—or competing rights—of acquisition and disposal of property, Wilson speaks of the "right" of the property owner but refers to a "special privilege" when talking about the prospective buyer. A demand characterized as a "right" enjoys "presumptive power," which thereby fortifies it against a conflicting claim (Underkuffler 2003, 69); a right is therefore more powerful than a "privilege." The subtle shift from right to privilege, in this passage, allows Wilson to affirm existing property interests over prospective ones. The property rights that constitute "a cornerstone of American freedom," to Wilson, are therefore based on a rather narrow conception of property that favors previously established interests. Framed in this way, the Rumford Act appeared to take something away from those who already owned property, giving it to non-owners. Furthermore, Wilson's rhetoric occludes all issues of racial differences or discrimination: he holds that "every American" should have the right to dispose of their property as they see fit, but that, of course, conveniently omits the fact that in order to sell or lease a home, one must have been able to buy one in the first place.

Another article in the *California Real Estate Magazine* reports about a speech given by NAREB president Daniel F. Sheehan and addresses racial discrimination more overtly. According to Sheehan, the national organization committed itself to combating discriminatory practices such as "blockbusting" and supported the idea of equality of opportunity for everybody. Yet, like the California organization, he strongly rejected plans to achieve antidiscrimination through legislation. Sheehan pitted two approaches against each other: legislation and education. The route through legislation, he argued, deprives the owner of a right and "penalize[s] the real estate broker who seeks to effect the sale or a rental in accordance with the owner's instructions." As "a pillar of free society," the right to property "ha[s] to be defended." It would be much preferable, in his view, to "place[] [one's] faith on education that would replace ignorance and overcome prejudice." In order to achieve integration, Sheehan held, one first needs to address homeowners' lack of acceptance of people of different ethnicities. He called on "every person of good will" to take on the social responsibility of this education, including realtors themselves ("NAREB President Hits Forced Housing Laws" 1963, 5).

Read against the background of the multifaceted discriminatory practices instituted and promoted by realtors, Sheehan's remarks appear rather cynical. He frames racism as a problem of individual attitudes, avoiding to face its structural nature and the realtors' own complicity with racist schemes. Instead, he depicts real estate agents as merely acting at the service of homeowners, insinuating that they would gladly sell homes to minorities if only their clients wished it that way. Sheehan's successor as NAREB President, Ed Mendenhall, confirmed the national association's approach in an address at the CREA Directors' Meeting in March of 1964. He stated:

> The point which unfortunately is so often overlooked in the whole situation is that social acceptance, which is so bound up with human emotions, cannot be legislated. As much as we may deplore snobbery, class consciousness, racial

> bias, or whatever you want to call it, we still must admit its existence and that it can be cured only by education which brings tolerance, understanding, and acceptance. The achievement of social consent will automatically solve any housing problem which may exist. (Mendenhall 1964, 6)

Like Sheehan, Mendenhall asserted NAREB's commitment to equal civil rights and pointed out that NAREB had adopted a policy statement the previous year which mandated realtors to pass on all written offers to their clients, independently of the prospective purchaser's or tenant's personal background. He thus frames realtors as neutral intermediaries.

Mendenhall also decries an alleged "over-protection" of citizens. Criticizing governmental overreach, he points out that one-sixth of workers are already employed and paid by governments, and that the federal government protects and advances consumers through a multitude of agencies. He concludes: "Americans are the most protected people on earth. [. . .] If we, the American people, get much more protection, we'll be smothered to death. We are about to be protected into utter dependency, and when that time comes, we will no longer deserve to have the eagle as our national emblem. The spineless, dependent oyster would be much more appropriate" (6). Mendenhall's rhetoric here seeks to establish a direct connection between the issue of fair housing and American values. To be independent of government aid and protection figures as a form of patriotism, as he evokes the symbol of the bald eagle as the embodiment of freedom and self-reliance, in contrast to a much less heroic figure, the "spineless, dependent oyster." Clearly, Mendenhall makes an ironic statement here, which however captures the libertarian outlook CREA and NAREB sought to establish in the housing controversy.

CREA president Wilson employed national symbolism in an even more hyperbolic fashion, in an editorial published in the July 1964 issue of the *California Real Estate Magazine*, titled "Gettysburg—1964!" appropriating the text of Abraham Lincoln's famous 1863 Civil War speech. One of the most famous speeches in American history, Lincoln's "Gettysburg Address," defined the Civil War as a fight for human equality and the principles of the Declaration of Independence. Wilson begins by quoting Lincoln's first paragraph verbatim, before differentiating between two conflicting civil rights: equality and liberty. He defines the struggle for civil rights as a "great war [. . .], testing whether equal rights for all can be achieved without losing freedom of choice, freedom of association and the sacrifice of private property rights." Again, he pits a right yet to be achieved—equality—against rights already established. The planned California constitutional amendment, he argues, will provide "freedom, equality and equal opportunity for ALL." Depicting the preservation of freedom as a patriotic effort, he proposes that they need to work toward "terminating government of the people by the bureaucrats," thus tying in with Mendenhall's denunciation of government protection (Wilson 1964, 1). The rhetoric of Wilson's editorial seeks to turn CREA's cause into a matter of national importance, portraying the effort as a noble cause and thereby also raising the stakes of the controversy. Appropriating Lincoln's speech for its libertarian framework, Wilson reframes the issue of civil rights.

Throughout the campaign for Proposition 14, articles in the *California Real Estate Magazine* insisted that the amendment would reestablish property owners' constitutional rights, which had been unlawfully taken from them by the government's fair housing legislation. The realtors praised the right to own property as being "the most fundamental right Americans enjoy" ("Editorial" 1963, 1). Thus, another editorial argued: "What possible authority could anyone have to knock on a property owner's door and demand that he be selected as the one with whom to deal, simply because he desires that particular property? To say that he has such a right, and back him with law, amounts to confiscation by the state" (1). CREA's campaign managed to defend white privilege without building their argument on overt racial claims. Instead, they focused on individual freedom, rights, and choices, while denouncing fair housing legislation as an illegitimate, immoral, unpatriotic government intrusion into private affairs. They thereby crafted a consistent message that appealed to voters.

Opponents of Proposition 14, most prominent among them Governor Pat Brown, initially were optimistic that voters would reject the proposed amendment. They formed a political coalition which not only included well-known leaders of liberal, labor, civil rights, and religious organizations, but which also drew moderate Republicans, as well as some realtors who disagreed with the direction of their professional organization (Brilliant 2010, 196–97). The diversity of these groups, however, led to much less consistent arguments, in comparison to those advanced by CREA and its allies. Moreover, many of their points failed to gain traction with the electorate. Edward Howden, the executive officer of the FEPC, directly addressed CREA's main argument that there existed a constitutional right to freely dispose of one's property, by arguing that the right to acquire property superseded this right. "The right to secure [. . .] property," he said in a speech, "is a vital human right [. . .] [that] cannot be a right for white folks only—unless we wish to be classed as liars and hypocrites who pay no more than lip service to the principles of free enterprise and equality of opportunity for all" (qtd. in Brilliant 2010, 199). Howden sought to lift the egalitarian veil from CREA's civil rights argumentation, accusing them of leading a disingenuous campaign. He pointed to a statement published by CREA the previous week as evidence "that when the gentlemen speak of the property rights 'of every person' they mean every *white* person, no more and no less. For they know full well that nonwhite

Americans in our State are generally unable to acquire or occupy housing as are other citizens" (qtd. in Brilliant 2010, 199). Howden emphasized that minority citizens, as they acquired a more prosperous status, should also receive the possibility to lead a similar life as their white middle-class counterparts. Turning racial distinctions into a matter of class, he tried to drive a wedge into people's racial anxiety (Brilliant 2010, 198). He thought this to be an effective way to stress similarities, rather than differences, between established white property owners and aspiring homeowners with "ethnic" backgrounds. By doing so, he also sought to appeal to peoples' sense of justice and their liberal American values.

Nevertheless, CAP 14 had a hard time shaking the perception that they vouched for a form of government redistribution of property. An editorial in *The Healdsburg Tribune* on May 14, 1964, for instance, quoted Assistant Attorney General Howard Jewell, who told an audience at the University of San Francisco that the Rumford Act was a means "of forcing property owners to act like Christians despite themselves." He then affirmed the feasibility of such an endeavor, by drawing a parallel to slavery, saying: "Freeing the slaves wiped out millions of dollars of property rights, too" (qtd. in "What Are Property Rights? . . ." 1964, 4). These statements provided fodder for Proposition 14 supporters, as they conceded the coercive nature of the law and that it ultimately would redistribute—or void—established property rights. The editorial rejected Jewell's slavery comparison by stating that "no man has a moral right to own human beings. Every man has a fundamental right to own real property. The Russians don't think so, but we in America do" ("What Are Property Rights? . . ." 1964, 4). With the last sentence, the text renewed the accusation that the government attempted to introduce a form of state socialism, turning the matter into a morally charged issue of patriotism.

The Anti-Proposition 14 campaign employed a highly moralist tone and cast the advocates of the amendment as bigots, racists, and right-wing extremists. Flyers would associate them with Jim Crowism (Brilliant 2010, 201–02; HoSang 2010, 75). Yet, the campaign focused on white voters and relegated civil rights groups, such as the NAACP, the United Civil Rights Committee and the Mexican American Political Association, to the margins, providing them only with limited funding (HoSang 2010, 78). According to HoSang, this was an intentional decision, prompted by the view that CAP 14 should not set out to defend the Rumford Act but rather focus on abstract values of fairness and antidiscrimination. They feared it would alienate white voters if they stressed that the racism of mainstream society made such a law as the Rumford Act necessary in the first place (80–82). Thus, while they depicted the supporters of the amendment as backward oriented and their campaign as a backlash against the liberal creed of the times, the underlying racial assumptions of both sides shared a common core, as both their efforts were directed at the needs and interests of white voters. The decision to denounce opposition to the Rumford Act, as an expression of individual racism and bigotry, not only weakened the campaign in significant ways, but it also eliminated the possibility of discursively engaging with the systematic racial exclusion in the housing market during the previous decades.

In the end, the legal impact of Proposition 14 proved to be limited: in May 1966, the California Supreme Court held the amendment to be unconstitutional in *Reitman v. Mulkey*, a ruling which the U.S. Supreme Court affirmed the following year. Justice White, in his majority decision, followed the argument of the state court that, with the constitutional amendment, the state "ha[d] become significantly involved in private discriminations [. . .] to an unconstitutional degree" (*Reitman v. Mulkey*. 387 U.S. 369, 378 [1967]). The amendment's major impact, the Court recognized, was in the "the way it helped valorize a set of racial propositions about the 'rights' particular homeowners possessed" (HoSang 2010, 88)—underwriting ideas which Ronald Reagan, in his successful gubernatorial campaign against Pat Brown in 1966, would later mobilize. If the direct legal consequences were contained, the cultural ones appeared more significant.

I have focused in depth on the rhetoric of Proposition 14 supporters because it seems particularly pertinent for understanding the potency of property rights arguments within public discourse and because their approach anticipated the strategies of property rights activists in later decades. Conservatives easily appropriated the language of liberal individualism—which had always based the rights and privileges of some members of society on the exclusion of others. Charles Mills has called this the "racial contract" between whites, "an agreement among white contractors to subordinate and exploit non-white noncontractors for white benefit" (Mills 2008, 1381). The ballot initiative in California thus exemplifies not simply a white backlash against the attempt of the United States to move closer toward the liberal ideal of an antiracist society. Rather, a close examination shows that liberalism itself was complicit in further perpetuating a "possessive investment in whiteness."

The discussion on fair housing in the early 1960s provides us with a context in which the radical critique of the black power movement that emerged in the second half of that decade can be situated. The radicalization of black activism was not least motivated by the shortcomings of the liberal civil rights movement, which the controversy about Proposition 14 so forcefully exemplified. Radical actors such as Stokely Carmichael and the Black Panther Party set out to expose and challenge the racial contract and thereby alter American property relationships. As I will argue in the following, however, black power appeared as a multifaceted concept which could also be appropriated for more conservative ends.

BLACK POWER, BLACK CAPITALISM? CHALLENGING THE RACIAL CONTRACT

On Election Day, November 7, 1968, Republican presidential candidate Richard Nixon courted African American voters with a double-page ad in *Jet* magazine. Portraying an alleged college student by the name of Homer Pitts, it pondered the career chances for a black male graduate in the late 1960s. Instead of a low-paying, working-class job, common for most African Americans at the time, the ad suggested a different option: Homer might become a business owner. Nixon, the ad states, wants to increase the chances for people like Homer Pitts of owning their own businesses because he "believes in black capitalism." The term "black capitalism" remains undefined here—is there a distinct form of capitalism that differs from "white capitalism"? And what would be its specific features? Yet, the next sentence equates "black capitalism" with another, similarly undefined but nevertheless notorious term of the era: "black power." "Black capitalism is black power in the best sense of the word. It's the road that leads to black economic influence and black pride. It's the key to the black man's fight for equality [. . .]." As owners of their own businesses, the ad proposes, African Americans will manage to determine their own destinies and receive access to equal opportunities (Nixon-Agnew Campaign Committee 1968, 9).

This ad is remarkable for a number of reasons: for one thing, one may be surprised to read Nixon's name next to terms like "black power" and "black pride," since, during his 1968 election campaign, Nixon had famously relied on his "southern strategy" to pick up the votes of conservative white southerners, the so-called "silent majority." To cater to this audience, he showed himself to be invested in the idea of "law and order," thereby responding to white anxieties about urban unrest and political protests over the course of the previous years. But for Nixon to speak of "black power" and "black pride" meant to acknowledge and appropriate terms associated with the black radicalism and black nationalism of the mid-1960s that sought to challenge the hegemonic order of the United States. "Black power" and "black pride," in the radicals' dictionary, meant to affirm a black collective identity and to confront white supremacy. The terms referred to African Americans' attempts to liberate themselves from white political, economic, and cultural oppression, in order to shift the power balance between blacks and whites and redistribute the wealth in American society.

How, then, did the concepts of black power and black pride, which derived from activism that often sought to *challenge* the American capitalist system and its commitment to private property ownership, come to be equated with a specifically "black" form of capitalism? In what follows, I explore the travels and transformations of "black power" from its first popularization in the summer of 1966 by Stokely Carmichael, to the political discourse of the 1968 election and the debates about black economic advancement among African American officials and academics, into the early 1970s. I contend that the discourse on black power and its spin-off, black capitalism, presented a challenge to what Lipsitz has termed America's "possessive investment in whiteness." With different strategies and through various channels, African American activists and reformers sought to address the inherently racist nature of the property system in the United States.

With the passing of the civil rights legislation on the state and federal levels, especially the Civil Rights Act of 1964 and the Voting Rights Act of 1965, the United States consolidated its transition from legally sanctioned segregation to an official politics of antidiscrimination. Though the laws were not strictly enforced in many cases, the official doctrine was that of colorblindness, aiming at the integration of blacks into middle-class America. Concomitantly, however, African Americans were also aware that race relations were defined by culture as well as by the law and that "the absence of legal barriers against equal opportunity was not the same thing as the presence of equal opportunity itself" (Condit and Lucaites 1993, 189).

In the 1960s, black Americans still faced severe economic disadvantages: 15 million or 69 percent of African Americans lived in metropolitan areas, many of them in highly concentrated racial ghettos. American cities experienced the most intense segregation in history, which constituted a major source of economic inequality (Massey and Denton 1993, 2). Incomes between blacks and whites differed widely: Black median family income was only 58 percent of white median family income in 1966; and unemployment rates for blacks were twice as high in every income category. At the same time, jobs available for blacks were highly concentrated in low-skill and low-income categories, with little status and little job security. Blacks also held only very few financial assets: they made up 11 percent of the population but owned less than 2 percent of assets (Brimmer 1970, 119). While white Americans experienced a time of great prosperity, little of that was available to African Americans.

Responding to this continued inequality, the activism of the mid- to late 1960s turned to a language of black separatism and nationalism. The advocates of racial integration—most prominently Martin Luther King, with his American dream of equal opportunity—started to lose ground, as new leaders calling for "black power" began to confront the systemic nature of white supremacy, and therefore shifted their tactics from nonviolence to self-defense. Rhetorically, charismatic figures like Stokely Carmichael, national chairman of the Student Nonviolent Coordinating Committee (SNCC), and Huey P. Newton, one of the founders of the Black Panther Party (BPP), were indebted to Malcolm X, who emphasized difference over sameness, describing black and white as two separate, antagonistic cultures.

Though Malcolm X, before his assassination in February 1965, inspired these radical critics of capitalism, he also represented a capitalist tradition of black nationalism, harking back to Booker T. Washington and Marcus Garvey. Stressing that African Americans should build their own businesses and provide for their own housing, Malcolm X described black advancement in terms of a black capitalist economy, whereby black producers, salespeople, and consumers support each other. Blacks, he held, must aspire to economic prosperity to be granted the same human dignity as other ethnicities (Malcolm X [1965] 1992, 300). These ideas resonate in the concept of black capitalism, which was intensely debated among the black elite in the late 1960s and early 1970s. Social theorist Harold Cruse argued in 1967 that, contrary to its Marxist rhetoric, "the Black Power ideology is not at all revolutionary in terms of its economic and political ambitions; it is, in fact, a social reformist ideology." For Cruse, black power was "nothing but the economic and political philosophy of Booker T. Washington given a 1960's militant shot in the arm and brought up to date" (qtd. in Marable 1984, 109). Cruse also drew attention to the continuities of African-American thought from the left to the right in that era, as well as to black power's roots in Black economic nationalism.

Activists like Carmichael and the BPP invoked "black power" to confront the ways in which whiteness functioned as property, thus challenging the liberal consensus and unacknowledged systemic racism. Yet, as my analysis will show, the meaning of "black power" was contested right from the beginning, and it was claimed by very different political camps: as a floating signifier, the term was easily appropriated for various arguments. Tracing black power's trajectory from a radical challenge into a mainstreamed liberal position, I argue that the term's very malleability aided the normalization of the radical movement. Despite black power's alleged opposition to liberalism, I show that the debate on black economic advancement must be considered in dialogue with more liberal, as well as conservative, voices at the time. Even the radical BPP, as Devin Fergus has recently proposed, though relying on a separatist rhetoric, often cooperated with liberals in practice but, in their community work, relied on money from (white) liberal donors and corporations. Fergus has convincingly argued that the black power movement and liberalism transformed each other, while also contributing to the rise of the New Right in the 1960s (2009, 7–12). Far from merely challenging property interests in whiteness, "black power" could also be harnessed for the ends of liberal individualism.

In what follows, I will first closely analyze Stokely Carmichael's rhetoric. As a charismatic figure, prolific speaker, and strong media presence,

Carmichael was the early public face of the nascent black power movement. Exposing structural racism in American society, Carmichael attempted to make whiteness visible and prompt whites to engage in self-reflection. He proposed that there was no "Negro problem" but a "White Problem in America," as a 1965 special issue of *Ebony* phrased it. The BPP radicalized Carmichael's already confrontational style. Though often associated with the advocacy of violence, much of the Black Panthers' work and their actual aims targeted the economic betterment of the black underclass—a dimension of their activism that, in the critical reception, has too often receded into the background. Parallel to the rise of the BPP, figures of the African American establishment like Floyd McKissick, Nathan Wright, and Roy Innis advocated forms of black capitalism. Though their tone differed, Black Panthers and more conservative figures ultimately shared the same goal: more economic and political power for African Americans. The point of contention was whether this could and should happen within the American capitalist system, whether this system needed to be transformed as a whole, or whether it was possible and desirable for African Americans to create a separate, more community-oriented economy.

"An Insidious Subterfuge for the Maintenance of White Supremacy": The Rhetoric of Black Power

In June 1966, only weeks after being elected national chairman of SNCC, Stokely Carmichael introduced the slogan of "Black Power!" during the Meredith March against Fear in Greenwood, Mississippi. The term had been used before by U.S. Representative Adam Clayton Powell Jr., as well as by novelist Richard Wright (Marable 1984, 104), but its proclamation during a highly mediatized rally catapulted Carmichael immediately into the national media spotlight. As Joshua Bloom and Waldo E. Martin note, "Black Power was not so much an answer as a new way of framing the quest for black liberation" (2013, 37–38). This new frame included turning away from the nonviolent tactics of the established civil rights movement and from a politics gearing toward integration of blacks into white middle-class society. Black power, as advocated by Carmichael, represented a critique of liberalism and refused to accommodate the fears of the white establishment. Carmichael's interventions, however, also sought to engage white liberal supporters of the freedom struggle, for instance, by contributing to liberal print outlets such as the *New York Review of Books* and the *Massachusetts Review*.

Carmichael analyzed what he conceived to be the intrinsically exploitative structures of capitalism and white supremacy in American society and on a global scale. Indebted to the thought and rhetoric of Malcolm X as well as

French-Caribbean philosopher Frantz Fanon, he described the position of African Americans in the United States as a colonial situation akin to the colonial regimes in Africa (Carmichael and Hamilton 1967, 6). Politically, he claimed, blacks were oppressed not only through overt suppression that denied them the right to vote but also through the colonial power's installment of black leaders who were accountable to the white power structure. While seemingly letting the black community participate in political processes, the agency of black leaders was circumscribed by a system that rejected them if they failed to conform. At the same time, these black leaders acted as spokespeople for African Americans whose interests they only allegedly represented. Economically, the majority of blacks were forced to live in ghettos and in poverty, while white slumlords and employers exploited their labor. Only a small minority had the chance to rise through education and establish a black middle class, upholding the idea that anyone can make it through hard work. Socially, blackness consistently signaled inferiority in all areas of life (2–32).

For Carmichael, structural racism served capitalism. He explicitly pointed toward the intrinsic link between power and property ownership: "The people who own the property are the people who make the laws," which made the rebellions in the ghettos a "question of property versus propertyless people" (Carmichael [1971] 2007, 72). Accordingly, a major part of Carmichael's rhetoric was a structural analysis of the economic conditions of blacks in American society and an attempt to dismantle the American myth of upward mobility. He emphasized that the United States was a country committed to property rights, not human rights. The idea of "integration" fit very well with this notion: integration, he suggested, meant that the recognition of a black person's humanity depended upon his or her success within the capitalist system. Those failing to integrate and remaining in the ghetto would not be recognized as fully human. Integration was thus part of the myth of American liberalism and capitalism, and those black and white liberals who propagated it actually contributed to the continuity of white supremacy.

Carmichael's demand for economic and political power for blacks accordingly did not aim at merely bringing more blacks into influential positions but at "the creation of power bases from which black people can work to change statewide or nationwide patterns of oppression" (21). Black power would be "that of a community, and emanate from there," with the ultimate goal of changing "the economic foundations of this country" (22). He envisioned a different social order: "Our vision is not merely of a society in which all black men have enough to buy the good things of life. When we urge that black money go into black pockets, we mean the communal pocket. [. . .] The society we seek to build among black people, then, is not a capitalist one. It is a society in which the spirit of community and humanistic love prevail" (29). Carmichael here rejects capitalist forms of private property, insinuating that black dispossession was intrinsic to capitalism. Instead, he advocates a form of black socialism, where capital would be communally owned.

As previously mentioned, Carmichael's rhetoric aimed at making whiteness visible, not least to the white supporters of the civil rights movement, as in the speech he gave at Berkeley on October 29, 1966, in front of approximately ten thousand, mostly white people. The first of many similar talks Carmichael would later give, it was widely noted and commented upon in newspaper editorials (Gallagher 2001, 146). Carmichael's speech dismantles the rhetoric and discursive structures that support the power structures and political discourse in the United States, particularly the rhetoric employed by black and white liberals. He thus attacks the concept of integration, advocated by established civil rights leaders, as being "an insidious subterfuge for the maintenance of white supremacy" (Carmichael [1971] 2007, 47). Integration, he argues, insinuates that whites give black people their freedom, when, in fact, what they must do is "stop denying black people their freedom" (47). Civil rights legislation, he points out, was never directed at blacks but, in truth, meant to discipline the white population: "I am black, I know that. I also know that while I am black I am a human being. Therefore I have the right to go into any public place. White people didn't know that. Every time I tried to go into a public place they stopped me. So some boys had to write a bill to tell that white man, 'He's a human being; don't stop him'" (47). Carmichael here adopts a simple, syllogistic argumentative structure, by which he asserts the right to move freely. As a basic human right, it necessitates an inscription into positive law, only due to the fact that it was previously ignored—civil rights legislation is thus only necessary due to white ignorance. Carmichael ironically reverses the conventional rhetorical frame which suggests that the majority grants new rights to the African American minority. Instead, civil rights legislation appears as an attempt to educate whites with respect to the knowledge that a black person already has, the knowledge of his own humanity. He thus also draws out the implicit connection between whiteness and humanity and to blackness with a less-than-human status. The framework of integration implicitly makes the recognition of blacks' humanity conditional on their becoming a member of the middle-class society, and on shedding their "blackness."

Carmichael further dismantled the myth that wealth correlates with hard work. Juxtaposing the terms "poor" vs. "rich," he defines a poor person as someone who "does not have money" as opposed to someone who does not work, since most wealthy people do not acquire their wealth through hard work either (49). On the contrary, if hard work were truly the indicator for the distribution of wealth, blacks "would own this country lock, stock, and barrel." He continues: "We have picked the cotton for nothing; we are the maids in the kitchens of liberal white people; we are the janitors, the porters, the elevator men; we sweep up your college floors. We are the hardest workers and the lowest paid" (54). Implicitly, Carmichael here attacks the notion that property constitutes the fruits of one's labor, or, more precisely, that each person, regardless of his/her color, is allowed to reap what should be their profits. For him, the myth of hard work is closely associated with the distribution of power; the social structures of the country individualize property ownership as well as poverty, attributing a poor person to personal failure (57).

In the Berkeley speech and similar texts, Carmichael sought to unveil the rhetoric of white supremacy and expose the racial and economic underpinnings of long-established American myths. His major rhetorical strategy, as exemplified by the slogan "black power" itself, was to ironically reverse the rhetorical framework that structured the mainstream social and political discourses at the time. By constructing a group identity and labeling it "black," he simultaneously identified a white group identity, highlighting the existing social hierarchy as a form of "white power." While this strategy may have worked (to some extent) with academic audiences, such as the left-leaning students in Berkeley, his ironic approach did not work as well in the mainstream media, which portrayed Carmichael as militant and confrontational. As recent studies have stressed, during the 1950s and early 1960s the TV networks had grown to be allies of the civil rights movement, which, in return, provided an opportunity for television to establish itself as a legitimate news medium (Acham 2004, 27; Torres 2003). With the emergence of the black power movement, however, the relationship between TV and the black community changed significantly.

On June 19, 1966, only a couple of days after his proclamation of "Black Power!" in Mississippi, Carmichael appeared on the CBS Sunday Newscast *Face the Nation*, where the three journalists John Hart, James S. Doyle, and Martin Agronsky cross-examined him on the concept and on his position of nonviolence. Less than a year after the Watts riots in Los Angeles, *Face the Nation* framed Carmichael as a violent agitator and implicitly contrasted him unfavorably with other leaders of the civil rights establishment, foremost the Reverend Dr. Martin Luther King Jr., whose persona and strategies of nonviolence and integration they had come to endorse.[2] Instead of engaging with the structural injustices Carmichael pointed out, the journalists worked within the dialectical but hierarchical pairs of nonviolence/violence and integration/separation. Since Carmichael refused to embrace nonviolence and the social goal of integration, he was portrayed and perceived as extreme. Nonetheless, interviews such as this one provided Carmichael with high visibility in the mainstream media; he also appeared on NBC's *Meet the Press* and was interviewed by CBS correspondent Mike Wallace for an hour-long documentary entitled *Black Power, White Backlash* in 1966. Looking closely at the latter interview in particular, it becomes apparent that Carmichael had little influence on how he was framed and that the audience got little chance to learn his actual positions. He seemed to proclaim that African Americans should receive special benefits, due to their blackness and their history of oppression, without having to work for them. He was also framed as, once again, endorsing violent insurgencies like the ones in Watts.

In 1966, the civil rights movement was at a crossroads: while the NAACP and the Urban League remained steadfast in their integrationist course and their focus on using legal means, the SNCC and the Congress of Racial Equality (CORE) had altered their previous positions toward a more radical and militant approach. Martin Luther King and the Southern Christian Leadership Conference (SCLC), critical of the rhetoric and tactics of the black power movement[3] but also aware of its threat to the traditional civil rights movement, targeted Chicago and organized a controversial march in the suburban neighborhood of Cicero, Illinois, to protest racially restrictive housing policies. Protesters were greeted by flying rocks and placards reading "White Power!" (*Black Power, White Backlash* 1966).

The activism of the SNCC and its defiance of white supremacy provided a model for Bobby Seale and Huey P. Newton, the two African-American college students who founded the BPP in Oakland, California, in October 1966 (Ogbar 2004, 70). In the late 1960s, the group became the most provocative challenge to white liberal America and "the most influential revolutionary nationalist organisation in the US" (Marable 1984, 123). The BPP began as a small local organization but expanded in 1968, when it opened offices in twenty other cities; by 1970, sixty-eight offices existed all over the country (Bloom and Martin 2013, 2). Carmichael acted as the BPP's Prime Minister in 1968 but soon broke with the party over ideological differences. Originally called the "Black Panther Party for Self-Defense," the organization first gained notoriety for their habit of carrying guns in public and for their surveillance of police patrols in black neighborhoods. The Panthers understood themselves as a vanguard party that would lead the masses into a socialist revolution. Their program combined theory and action: philosophically, they were inspired by Malcolm X and Frantz Fanon, as well as Mao Zedong and Che Guevara; practically, many of their efforts were directed not only toward recruiting members for their cause but also toward providing immediate aid for the poor black community through a variety of "survival programs." By the summer of 1969, an estimated 10,000 children received free breakfasts every day, which "vividly exposed the inadequacy of the federal government's concurrent War on Poverty" (13).

The BPP drew attention mostly through its visual performance of protest, which established a distinct iconography. In her study on photography, Leigh Raiford has pointed out that "many observers and participants viewed the Panthers' style, rhetoric, and image [that] circulated through photography as the outward manifestation and best representation of the party's political platform" (2011, 134). The relationship between the Panthers' aesthetics of protest and the substance of its politics is quite contested, with former activists like Kathleen Cleaver, the BPP's communication secretary, or Angela Davis insisting that the focus on the images was reductive and distracting from the political program (Phu 2008, 167). Yet, the party's "prominence as the visible icon of black power" suggests that the BPP used photography as "a medium for its politics": "The visual field constitutes not a distracting betrayal of radical politics, but rather a crucial site where the form of protest is fiercely, even violently, negotiated" (168).

The public notoriety of the BPP, which also drew the attention of the FBI (see, e.g., Churchill and Vander Wall 2002), was the result of a "dialogic relationship" between the party and the national mass media (Rhodes 1999, 97). Though they could not control their presentation in the mainstream media, the Panthers were not victims but active participants who helped shape their own image, "and they expended considerable energy to become masters of rhetoric and iconography" (100). Their distinctive style of black berets and leather jackets was completed by guns, the movement's crucial symbol. As a warning to law enforcement officers and an important element of their recruiting strategy, the gun, to Huey Newton, was also an "educational" tool, "[to] set an example. We made black people aware that they have the right to carry guns" (qtd. in Sol Stern 1967). Exercising their constitutional right to bear arms, a group of thirty party members congregated at the California State Capitol in Sacramento on May 2, 1967. Calculating that their appearance would provoke massive media attention, they protested the Mulford Act, a bill that would repeal the right to carry firearms in public. It was not their intention to stop the bill but "to project their image in the press and on the screen until the Whites were haunted by it" (Jean Genet qtd. in Raiford 2011, 165). While Carmichael challenged the rhetoric and narratives that make acts of white power legitimate, the Black Panthers similarly confronted hegemonic structures on the visual terrain.

Inspired by the Nation of Islam (Finzsch 1999, 228), Newton and Seale devised the party's program as a ten-point platform in October 1966, which combined concrete practical demands with the BPP's theoretical positions. The requests related primarily to the black community's right of self-determination and economic flourishing, through the provision of employment, housing, education, and the end to exploitation. Further points related to fair treatment by law enforcement and the justice system. In its theoretical justifications of the demands, the platform relied on anti-capitalist positions, declaring, for instance, that the federal government should be "responsible and obligated to give every man employment or a guaranteed income" and suggesting that "the means of production [. . .] be taken from the businessmen and placed in the community so that the people of the community can organize and employ all of its people and give a high standard of living" (P. S. Foner 1995, 2). They also advocated that land be turned over to cooperatives, in order to provide decent housing for the community. Point 3 included the demand for reparations of slavery, calling on the government to live up to the promise of "forty acres and two mules" (2). In the last point, they formulated as their "major political objective, a United Nations-supervised plebiscite to be held throughout the black colony in which only black colonial subjects will be allowed to participate for the purpose of determining the will of black people as to their national destiny" (3–4). Here, the Panthers framed the black community as an internal colony of the United States and advocated a black nationalist position. Interestingly, however, they concluded the platform by extensively quoting from the Declaration of Independence, by which they underlined their right to revolution and affirmed the values propagated in a central document of the nation's political history and self-conceptualization. In previous points, they had already referenced the U.S. Constitution twice by citing the Second and Fourteenth Amendments, the right to bear arms and the right to fair trials in court. Paradoxically, then, the party platform relied on a revolutionary rhetoric which was already incorporated in the nation's self-conception.

To Newton and Seale, the ten-point platform had the status of a "survival program" (Newton 1972, 45) designed to improve the lives of the poor black segment of society in the short term. The long-term goal, however, was a socialist revolution and the abolition of capitalism. Unlike the established civil rights organizations, which focused on the black middle class, the Panthers sought to recruit new members among the most marginalized members of the black community: "Employing Marxist terminology, the Panthers considered the lumpenproletariat the most open to revolutionary struggle, and an effective mobilization of the lumpen was essential to the Black Power struggle" (Ogbar 2004, 94). Ironically, though, most Panthers themselves did not fit the category of "lumpen"; many of them were first-generation college students with working-class backgrounds.

In a 1969 article for *Ebony*, Newton outlined the ideology of the BPP for the magazine's black mainstream audience. The text was framed by a number of images, many of which were taken at Black Panther rallies. A prefacing editorial message justified the publication of Newton's words by stressing the magazine's commitment to presenting a variety of opinions. Despite the controversies stirred by the party, the editor noted, "relatively little is known about the objectives and ideological underpinnings of the Black Panther organization" (Newton 1969, 107). The article's subtitle and image captions—provided by the editors—stressed Newton's current imprisonment and the militancy of the party. The accompanying pictures draw attention to the Panther iconography, such as the Black Panther symbol, the raised fist, the black berets, and publicly displayed firearms. Images also include a portrait of Eldridge Cleaver, minister of information for the Black Panthers, who, as the caption stated, allegedly lived in Cuba to avoid a prison sentence.

The imagery opens up a very different discourse from the text, which centers neither on the Panthers' program of armed self-defense nor on their activism, but instead provides an ideological critique of the system of capitalism. Newton here outlines the BPP's commitment to socialism. He makes a distinction between capitalism and socialism and compares it to the difference between slavery and freedom. The capitalist system, he argues, works only for the owners of the means of production and not "for the benefit of the people." In the United States, "a small group of men has another and larger group of men enslaved simply for profit"—therefore, the system of capitalism constitutes "a slave situation," an updated version of the antebellum agrarian economy under modern circumstances (Newton 1969, 108). Oppression is thus intrinsic to capitalism according to Newton, whereas socialism promises the participation of all members of society in the processes of decision-making and therefore freedom and self-determination.

Newton also addresses the concept of "black capitalism," which had been recently brought into the larger public discourse by President Richard Nixon. He accuses Nixon of trying to widen the differences within the black population, calling black capitalism "a hoax perpetrated on many sincere but misguided black people who still believe they can find their freedom and security in the capitalist system." He compares the notion that a small black elite would form a bourgeoisie within the black community to antebellum times, when a small number of free blacks were slaveholders but did nothing to alleviate the oppression of their slaves. Capitalism, Newton holds, is "the white man's game," "a giant stride away from liberation" (110).

"Black Capitalism Is Black Power in the Best Sense of the Word": The Rhetoric of Black Capitalism

Though the term "black power" was introduced by black activists from the political left, it "quickly became the cornerstone of conservative forces" (Marable 1984, 108). Nathan Wright, a conservative black nationalist closely affiliated with the Republican Party, organized the first Black Power Conference in Newark, New Jersey, in July 1967. Targeting middle-class black professionals, the conference's concern was not to alleviate the conditions in the nation's black ghettos, but the organizers understood "black power" as the quest for a "'fair share' of American capitalism" (108). A second conference in Philadelphia one year later was sponsored by the Clairol company, a "white" corporation whose president endorsed the black power movement as a form of black capitalism (108). Jeffrey Ogbar argues that more moderate blacks appropriated the slogan, in order to "sanitize" it, so as to ensure support by liberal whites (2004, 152); this understanding, however, does not do justice to the fact that, from its beginnings, the black power movement drew on a long tradition of black nationalism and economic empowerment that was also vested in a capitalist tradition. Black conservatives, as well as critics of the "myth" of "Negro Business" on the left (Frazier 1971, 83; see also Ofari 1970), identified black power as the most recent incarnation of a long tradition of fostering black economic development, going back to Marcus Garvey, Booker T. Washington, and even to Martin Delaney during the Reconstruction period. As Joshua Farrington notes, "though *Black Power* remains the defining term in characterizing black political activism in the mid- to late 1960s, it was an elastic concept that covered a plethora of ideologies, ranging from the revolutionary nationalism of the Black Panthers to the conservative nationalism of black capitalists" (2012, 63).

Nathan Wright, a former Episcopalian priest who founded a consulting firm in the late 1960s and later went on to become the founding chair of the Department of African and Afro-American Studies at the State University of New York at Albany, certainly fits Ogbar's description of a black moderate who worked for economic development by enlisting the support of whites. In his book *Let's Work Together*, he called especially on white businessmen to bring power and prosperity to all segments of society and "to eliminate the degrading welfare system as we know it today." According to Wright, "all men should have some kind of responsibility—even if it is clearly 'make-work'—before they receive any money. Earning for self spells dignity. Every man should be allowed this path to dignity" (1968, 94–95). He also advocated investments by blacks into business and housing: "People who own something are not prone to destroy it" (102). Like the militant black power advocates, Wright equaled economic power to "self-determination" and advocated an effort for black people to gain "full control of economic resources in the black community" (147, 251). Yet, he envisioned that this goal would be achieved neither through the intervention of governments nor by a revolution; he relied on more traditional, conservative strategies of uplift through private initiatives. He advocated property ownership through work, which would provide blacks with dignity. Though he recognized a systemic deprivation of blacks from economic opportunities in the past, he suggested that African Americans could "overcome the handicap of business exploitation" through a concerted effort of blacks and whites (251).

Among the civil rights leaders, black power was most vocally advocated by Floyd McKissick, national director of CORE (Ogbar 2004, 62). Leading the organization between 1966 and 1968, McKissick, a personal friend of Malcolm X's who also served as a lawyer for the Nation of Islam, took CORE into a more militant direction. McKissick advocated a redistribution of wealth in American society, so that African Americans could participate in society's affluence (McKissick 1969, 34). He held that "economic power is the first prerequisite for political power" and that blacks needed to, first of all, gain economic independence (42). McKissick left CORE in 1968 to promote black capitalism through his own firm, McKissick Enterprises, which assisted existing businesses and invested in the formation of new companies. Planning to become "a major American Corporation" with the social goal of letting African Americans profit from capitalism (494), the firm drew on the financial support of white institutions and corporations. There was no alternative to capitalism, McKissick argued. Moreover, "if Black Men and Women are to share in the productive wealth of the nation, they have no alternative at this time other than full participation as entrepreneurs" (495). The companies McKissick envisioned, however, did not merely aim at individual profit but at black community development. The projects his corporation attempted to undertake included not only restaurants and shopping centers but also a publishing company, as well as art, music, and drama programs (502).

A brochure advertising McKissick Enterprises celebrated its founder as "the first man in recent times to clearly articulate the meaning of 'Black Power' [and] the only one to draft a realistic program and design a structure for achieving Black Power and self-determination" (McKissick 1970, 496–97). Like the black power advocates on the left, McKissick believed the main problem of African Americans to be economic, but, similarly to Wright, he also attacked welfare: "Black people are fighting for respect and dignity, not a handout" (493). McKissick's largest endeavor was Soul City, the project of a model city where blacks controlled all businesses and institutions, which, in 1972, became the largest publicly funded project ever developed by an African American (Farrington 2012, 64–65).

"Black capitalism" gained some currency in the larger American public during the presidential campaign of 1968, when Republican candidate Richard Nixon started to endorse the black power movement. As Robert Weems emphasizes, though, the term "black capitalism" was most closely associated with Nixon's campaign. There was a longstanding interest of the federal government to promote entrepreneurship among African Americans, reaching back to the presidency of Herbert Hoover. Both the Kennedy and Johnson administrations were concerned with the issue of black economic development, especially after the beginning of urban riots and unrest (Weems 2009, 85; see also Kotlowski 1998, 416). And the Democratic presidential candidate Humphrey and the Republican Nixon claimed in 1968 that, if elected, they would promote African-American businesses, strengthen the Small Business Administration, and create an urban development bank (Weems 2009, 105).

In his campaign, Nixon had to walk a fine line, in order to appeal to blacks without alienating white voters. He pursued his "southern strategy," which emphasized "law and order," while at the same time secretly seeking the support of black power advocates Roy Innis and Floyd McKissick from CORE (Weems 2009, 118).[4] Nixon defined the term "black power" in a March 28, 1968 campaign speech in Milwaukee, Wisconsin, as "the power that people should have over their own destinies, the power to affect their own communities, the power that comes from participation in the political and economic processes of society" (qtd. in Marable 1984, 108). In a subsequent, frequently cited CBS radio address, he elaborated:

> Much of the black militant talk these days is actually in terms far closer to the doctrines of free enterprise than to those of the welfarist '30s—terms of "pride," "ownership," "private enterprise," "capital," "self-assurance," "self-respect." [. . .] What most of the militants are asking is not separation, but to be included in—not as supplicants, but as owners, as entrepreneurs—to have a share of the wealth and a piece of the action. And this is precisely what the Federal central target of the new approach ought to be. It ought to be oriented toward more black ownership, for from this can flow the rest—black pride, black jobs, black opportunity, and yes, black power [. . .]. (Nixon 1968, 13)[5]

Speaking to a general audience, Nixon attempted to domesticate the radicalism of the black power movement, which, in the public mind, was associated with militancy and Marxist critique. Only implicitly touching on the socialist thought of the movement, he dismissed connections to the "welfarist '30s," instead trying to establish a positive connection to mainstream American values such as "ownership," "capital," and "self-respect." The activists, Nixon insinuated, did not mean to break with the system but instead wanted to participate in political and social life, the same way whites did. And he associated this participation, first of all, with ownership: as for white people, the economic ideal was that of the entrepreneur, not the "supplicant." (Black) power, he argued, should derive from "black ownership." Nixon thus associated property ownership with agency and social and economic power.

Drawing on the language of black power, the Nixon campaign suggested that he would provide solutions to the economic obstacles African Americans faced, enabling black citizens to lift themselves out of poverty. He appealed to a longing for agency and self-determination as an alternative to government-sponsored entitlement programs. He thus managed to expertly exploit the inherent instability of the signifier of black power and to domesticate its radical implications: "Nixon's rhetoric of black capitalism was at once problematic and intriguing; one the one hand, he offered an unsophisticated and at times insulting view of black poverty; on the other hand, he used the same language employed by black critics of Democratic liberalism, most conspicuously, black Republicans *and* black militants" (Rigueur 2015, 137).

In the attempt to fulfill his campaign promises, Nixon created the Office of Minority Business Enterprise (OMBE) on March 5, 1969, by Executive Order 11458. His personal involvement, however, remained mostly limited to verbal support, as he left the management to Commerce Secretary Maurice H. Stans. Nixon was also aware of the program's difficulties and limited potential. "Any small business," he stated in a handwritten comment to Stans, "has a 75 percent chance of failing," and "minority small business has a 90 percent chance of failing—good luck" (qtd. in Kotlowski 1998, 420). Nevertheless, Nixon believed that the program was the best way to gain the long-term political support of African American middle-class voters (Kotlowski 1998, 421). Even though the OMBE was slow to get off the ground, due to the diligent work and consistent pressure exercised by African American businessmen and conservatives, it became a viable program during the early 1970s, reaching a budget of more than 91.3 million dollars annually by 1974; it had given more than 400 million dollars in loans and guarantees to black businesses by 1973, while also helping existing businesses to procure federal contracts (Farrington 2012, 70).

"Which Way Black America?": Debating Black Capitalism

Nixon's black capitalism initiative spawned a broad public debate among African-American leaders and black economists over the route to black economic development. A special issue of *Ebony*, published in August 1970, asked on its title page: "Separation? Integration? Liberation? Which Way Black America?" The issue featured articles devoted to controversial discussions of this question, with many contributions positioning themselves firmly in one of two camps: while some argued that the only feasible way to boost the African American was through integration into white society, others believed that at least temporary separation was necessary, in order to truly establish African-American power structures and economic strength. The position of African Americans within the capitalist economy of the United States was at the center of contention. By 1970, many were skeptical of the potential of black capitalism, and many rejected the term, due to the exploitative connotations that "capitalism" held for many African Americans (Haddad and Pugh 1969, 4).

Robert S. Browne, an economist teaching at Farleigh Dickinson University and the founder of the Black Economic Research Center in Harlem, addressed the possibilities and limitations of economic advancement in *The Review of Black Political Economy*, offering "a cautious, realistic assessment of the parameters of present and future African American economic empowerment" (Weems and Randolph 2001, 70). According to Browne, such a realistic assessment included the insight that any efforts could only bring about "achievements [. . .] of limited scope and will certainly not bring into being the Black Nation" (1970b, 23). African Americans, Browne outlined in the *Review*'s inaugural issue, lacked access to the basic sources of power in the United States, of which he identified six: private wealth, ownership of major corporations, the military-industrial complex, federal and state government, the federal legislative apparatus, and "the crime syndicate" (21). With these levers of society firmly being in white hands, Browne only saw limited chances for African Americans to grasp a significant handle of control over society, beyond "a sort of negative power [. . .] over how the white establishment uses its power" (21). Here, he was referring to the possibilities of political participation in the electoral process, as well as forms of organized protest. A movement for economic advancement, Browne emphasized, would have to come up with a strategy as to which goals to prioritize in trying to wrestle some of the power and influence from the white establishment. He identified as the main problem "the task of acquiring a base of wealth for the black community," an all but futile endeavor in a society where all property had already been previously divided and where "it is nearly impossible to acquire wealth unless one already has wealth" (Browne 1970a, 60, 61).

Browne also addressed the considerable hostility of many black intellectuals toward the concept of "black capitalism" and capitalist forms of organization. While he, too, advocated greater control and self-determination for black communities, he warned not to put too much emphasis on institutional differences: cooperatively owned companies may be just as exploitative as those that were privately owned, especially as long as they remained part of "white, capitalistic American society" (Browne 1970b, 24). At the same time, he also critically evaluated the notion of black entrepreneurship, as advocated by black conservatives and the Nixon administration, an idea he thought was important "principally for psychological reasons" (Browne 1970a, 63). To create black companies with significant economic and political influence and communal benefit would require a substantive basis of wealth, which the black community lacked. A possible way to solve this problem would be by means of reparations for slavery, as advocated, for instance, by James Forman. Browne supported this notion in principle but pointed out that this approach, at least at present, was impossible to enforce (64).

In stark distinction to Browne's cautious tone, James Forman, a former SNCC executive secretary and activist in the BPP, took a militant stance and demanded that blacks should "commit [them]selves to a society where the total means of production are taken away from the rich people and placed into the hands of the state for the welfare of the people" (1970, 38). Forman was particularly vehement in his opposition to the notion of "black capitalism." He called the African Americans who supported black capitalism "Black Power Pimps," "people who are clinging to the rhetoric of the Negro," and suggested that "we must separate ourselves from those Negroes who go around the country promoting all types of schemes for Black Capitalism" (36). The interest of the United States, Forman held, was "to make us capitalists," thereby neutralizing the threat by integrating blacks "into the mainstream of American life" (38). He called upon people to resist this integration and instead commit to the fight against racism, capitalism, and imperialism. In his "Black Manifesto," Forman demanded reparations for slavery—a sum of 500 million dollars, or an estimated 15 dollars for every black U.S. citizen—from Christian churches and Jewish synagogues; he targeted the religious institutions because of their implication in capitalist exploitation and complicity in the system of slavery. This money was to be spent in support of a southern land bank and cooperative farms, the establishment of black media industries, research, practical training, and the organization of welfare and labor organizations (40–41).

But the idea that black capitalism was a hoax was also shared by more conservative figures, albeit for different reasons. In fact, Federal Reserve Board governor Andrew Brimmer, an economist, used the very term in his evaluation: "I believe the encouragement of Negroes to look to black capitalism (essentially the ownership of small businesses in the ghetto) as a strategy for economic progress is to perpetuate a cruel hoax" (1970, 121). The state of African Americans within the economy—characterized by high unemployment rates, relatively large debts, and few financial assets—was simply not a proper precondition for successful businesses, Brimmer thought. In addition, such businesses would face national competition from companies seeking to expand into the African-American market, while also running against the trend toward larger, nationally operating businesses (121). While Brimmer saw possibilities for blacks to participate in the economy as owners of businesses and by starting ventures together with whites, he did not think that this would be an approach for the economic advancement of the black community, specifically—indeed, it would just be part of regular capitalism. Instead, he advocated more and better education to achieve integration of blacks into the labor market. Brimmer concluded: "Black people must get *inside* the corporate structure to learn how basic decisions are made and how genuine economic power is exercised. Only then can they be in a position to share this power and to assure that it is used for them—and not against them" (121).

In a critical response to his articles, Charles Tate charged Brimmer with "obscuring the causal relationship between exploitative white capitalism and the economic structure of the ghetto" (1971, 174), putting the blame instead on black businesses and failing to consider the various concepts advocating collective or community ownership. Tate dismissed Brimmer's suggestion that blacks should seek to advance through salaried employment in white firms as "an unrealistic, integrationist concept," which did not take into account the racist structures of white capitalism, that is, "the masses of Black people who are excluded from competition for white-collar jobs" (177).

BLACK POWER ACTIVISM AND THE CONCEPT OF PROPERTY

In what seemed like a striking reversal of ideology, a *Washington Post* article on the BPP, entitled "The Transformation of the Panthers," announced on February 13, 1972, that the party was now to manufacture golf bags in Oakland, California, one of several "enterprises that sound little like the Panthers of old." The business venture, the article continued, intended to purchase "300 to 400 sets of clothing to be given away each month to ghetto residents by the 'People's Free Clothing Program'" (qtd. in Weems 2009, 154–55). Struggling to finance their community programs, the pragmatic wing of the party, led by Huey P. Newton, thus tried to connect with black entrepreneurs.

In *Ebony* in August 1969, Newton had analyzed capitalism as being an exploitative system that needed to be abolished for a socialist one. Less than two years later, he revisited the issue of black capitalism in the pages of *Black Panther*, the party's news organ:

> many people have offered the community Black capitalism as a solution to our problems. We recognize that people in the Black community have no general dislike for the concept of Black capitalism, but this is not because they are in love with capitalism. Not at all. The idea of Black capitalism has come to mean to many people Black control of another one of the institutions in the community. We see within this characteristic the seeds of the negation of Black capitalism and all capitalism in general. What we must do then is increase the positive qualities until they dominate the negative and therefore transform the situation. (Newton 1972, 103)

Almost ironically, at a time when many black public intellectuals had discarded the term "black capitalism" and raised serious questions about the feasibility of a separate black economy and black entrepreneurship, the Panthers discovered the small black businessman. For Newton, the embracement of black capitalism denoted a shift in strategy, recognizing that the black community associated the concept not with exploitation but with prosperity and control. Acknowledging that, in the past, the party had relied on money from "wealthy White philanthropists, humanitarians, and heirs to the corporate monopolies" (105), in order to finance its community programs, while condemning black capitalists, Newton now proposed that the strategies of capitalism should be harnessed to transform capitalism itself. Instead of revolution, he advocated a kind of reform. In Newton's new analysis, black capitalists were not oppressors, but they themselves were "victimized by the corporate capitalist monopolies" (107). The enemy, then, was no longer the small black entrepreneur but corporate capitalism.

The Panthers' unlikely and reluctant embracement of black capitalism signaled that the options for a radical critique of the American capitalist system had become more limited in the early 1970s and that the hegemonic order proved resilient. The concept of black power had started out as a critique of the inherently racist nature of the U.S. commitment to private property ownership. Stokely Carmichael had deconstructed the American myths of upward mobility and possessive individualism as instruments of white supremacy. He and his fellow activists fought for black group power and communal self-determination, in order to change the very pillars on which American society rested. Yet, their strategy of provocation and confrontation ultimately did not succeed, as the public and political discourses managed, in part, to normalize the critique and to outlaw the movement's protagonists.

Though there was an increase in black-owned businesses in the era, partially thanks to the federal government's programs, black capitalism, Nixon-style, most powerfully thrived on the small screen in the end. One of the most successful TV shows of the mid-1970s was the sitcom *The Jeffersons* (1975–1985). Its central character, George Jefferson, in the words of Henry Louis Gates, "epitomized Richard Nixon's version of black capitalism, bootstrap variety, and all of its terrifying consequences" (1989). George Jefferson had worked his way up from humble beginnings by establishing several dry-cleaning businesses, thus allowing him and his wife Louise to move to an upper-middle-class apartment on Manhattan's Upper East Side. As Gates points out, George is not a cultivated character or black professional, like Cliff Huxtable of the *Cosby Show* in the 1980s, but a black self-made man, "pure street, draped in a Brooks Brothers suit." George Jefferson can therefore be read as both a domestication of the militant black males represented in the black power movement and as an affirmation of the culture of possessive individualism.

The *New York Times*, in a 1967 editorial, had argued that "American society is likely to accommodate Negro aspirations only as they express themselves in individual terms. It cannot be otherwise in a society that honors personal effort as its highest value and looks toward integration as its goal" ("What Do the Negroes Want?" 1967). These words seemed to be proven true at the beginning of the 1970s. As the result of a general economic boom as well as the antidiscrimination legislation passed in the mid-1960s, the United States saw a rise of a "new black middle class" (Landry 1987, 3) in the late 1960s and early 1970s, allowing more African Americans to participate in the country's economic prosperity. At the same time, however, Nixon called for a "war on drugs," which intentionally targeted blacks. Also, the 1970s saw the proliferation of a "culture of poverty" narrative, which suggested that lower class people were poor because they had a defective culture (Massey and Denton 1993, 5). This narrative diverted the attention from the structural issues of discrimination that the black power movement had originally sought to make visible.

If material gains for African Americans were thus only possible within the hegemonic order of liberal capitalism, the individualized concept of private property in the American cultural imagination did not merely remain intact but, in fact, intensified during the 1960s and beyond. The conservative narrative of private property as an absolute, individual right, as it was proposed in the battle on fair housing and other antidiscriminatory legal measures, would become a mainstay of public rhetoric in future decades and indeed find its way into the more specialized legal discourse. Starting in the late 1970s, conservative think tanks and public interests group began to appropriate the language of liberalism in similar ways, and successfully so, to advance a libertarian agenda and to wage war against the welfare state introduced in the New Deal era. Chapter 5 will thus investigate the "property rights movement" that flourished in the United States at the beginning of the new millennium.

NOTES

1. Lorraine's father, Carl A. Hansberry, was the plaintiff in the Supreme Court case *Hansberry v. Lee* (1940), which successfully challenged a racially restrictive covenant in a Chicago neighborhood. The Supreme Court ruling was based on a legal technicality and hence did not void racial covenants per se, but it still constitutes an important step in the fight against housing discrimination.

2. As Ogbar notes, "King's philosophy anticipated violence and exploited it" (2004, 42). His commitment to nonviolence was really a rejection of direct action self-defense; in fact, King himself was often involved in violent situations. Malcolm X, by contrast, was perceived as violent, yet, until his death, he actually avoided

violent confrontations. At the same time, of course, "white Americans generally embraced direct action self-defense for themselves" (42). Ogbar also points out that the (print) media's relationship to the integrationist part of the civil rights movement became more favorable, after more threatening radical organizations, such as the Malcolm X's Nation of Islam, gained popularity (56). For a reevaluation of the role of violence in African American activism of the 1960s, see also Simon Wendt's study (2007).

3. In his last book *Where Do We Go From Here?*, King discusses his reservations about the slogan at length ([1967] 2010, 23–69).

4. According to Weems, Nixon secretly met with Innis and McKissick in his New York apartment in May 1968, striking some kind of deal to gain their support. Both appeared on *Meet the Press* on July 14, 1968, where Innis indirectly endorsed Nixon (Weems 2009, 116, 119).

5. *Time* magazine printed much of Nixon's speech in the May 3, 1968 issue, under the title of "Nixon on Racial Accommodation."

Chapter 5

Creating an "Ownership Society"?

The Rise of the Property Rights Movement

In early 2002, the second year of his administration, President George W. Bush began to promote the idea of the United States becoming an "ownership society": "Every American deserves to be an owner in the American Dream," Bush claimed. "That dream includes a sound pension plan and adequate private savings, and it is ultimately completed by Social Security reform" (Bush 2005b, 310). In his speeches, on more than 170 occasions, Bush continued to advocate an American society structured around private property, featuring the concept prominently in his 2004 reelection campaign and until the end of his presidency. The rhetoric of the ownership society interwove concrete policy proposals with ideas of property ownership being a moral, cultural, and quintessentially American value. Bush envisioned a society that made ownership accessible to all its members, thereby bestowing upon them "independence" and "dignity" (Bush 2006b, 929). He depicted property ownership as an intrinsically ethical value: citizens would be enabled to control their own destinies by pursuing economic opportunities and by making their own choices, and they would thus also participate in the democratic decision-making processes of the country. Future-oriented and optimistic, this social vision manifested itself as a utopian blueprint of a better community.

Bush's "ownership society" can be considered the rhetorical apex of a conservative push for more market-driven American social institutions that have evolved since the late 1970s in the United States. Part of an increasingly powerful libertarian movement, which had gained momentum since the Reagan era, it envisioned reform projects that sought to "empower" citizens by shifting responsibility and risk from the government to the individual. In this context, libertarians particularly targeted Social Security, a popular American institution and signature achievement of the New Deal era. In a political climate that increasingly disfavored "big government," they saw the chance to replace a system of solidarity with one of individual responsibility, advocating partial privatization, in a concerted effort to redraw the boundaries between the public and the private spheres, the state and the individual.

In this chapter, I explore the public discourse on property rights as it proliferated in the years prior to the financial crisis of 2007–2008. My aim in this chapter is not to claim a paradigm shift in the cultural understanding of property and property rights in recent years but, rather, to point to a trend that has been evolving over the last several decades. As the previous chapters of this study underline, Bush's concept of the ownership society was neither a particularly creative invention nor an isolated phenomenon. Notions of ownership—and particularly homeownership—as a primary American virtue have long been central to the U.S. cultural imaginary as well as part of presidential rhetoric. Bush's concept, however, needs to be located specifically in the context of the recent "property rights movement," which seeks to "benefit from the creation and naturalization of a mass investment culture" (Soederberg 2010, 24).

Though privatization originated as an effort orchestrated by libertarian legal and economic scholars, think tanks, and public interest law firms, advocates of property rights have meanwhile incited a public discourse on private property that seeks to strengthen individual rights, against an alleged intrusion of the government into private affairs. They address what they see as the "unwarranted" and "severe" expansion of state agencies since the New Deal era, which has led to property owners perceiving "themselves [as] increasingly entangled in a web of regulatory restrictions that have limited what they can do with their property" (Eagle 2005, 1). Proponents of property rights posit the primacy of individual as well as private economic relationships, often by insisting on an originalist reading of the Constitution. This chapter analyzes how these property rights advocates managed to form a populist movement that centers on specific social demands and advances private property as a hegemonic concept.

The discourse on property establishes an antagonism that sees the individual under attack by an alliance of "big government" and "big business." In the view of property rights advocates, ostensibly democratic institutions fall short of offering free democratic participation, while intruding into the private sphere by excessively regulating the affairs of the "little guy." In turn, they see economic enterprise of private individuals as promising more democratic, nonhierarchical interactions. Thus built on an adversarial relationship between the state and the individual, property rights discourse seeks to determine the line between the private and the public, naturalizing property rights as being apolitical and antistatic.

My argument proceeds in two steps: the first part focuses on public debates about the governmental power of eminent domain. The right of the state to take private property for public use, instituted through the Fifth Amendment to the Constitution, represents one of the focal points of current property rights activism. The Supreme Court decision in the case *Kelo v. City of New London* (2005), which held that governments were allowed to take property in order to give it to private investors for economic development, brought the issue of eminent domain into the media and onto the public agenda in unprecedented ways in the mid-2000s. I will delineate the narratives on property and the relationship between the state and the individual this discourse has generated. The second part zooms in on George W. Bush's presidential rhetoric of private property being a moral virtue and the policy proposals the administration advanced in this context. Bush's speeches present a particular—at its core even utopian—vision of political participation, which bears far-reaching implications for the shape of major social institutions and government itself.

A MAN'S HOME IS HIS CASTLE: THE MYTH OF PROPERTY AND THE POWER OF EMINENT DOMAIN

"What is more sacred, what more strongly guarded by every holy feeling, than a man's own home?" William Blackstone, citing Cicero, asks in Latin, in his *Commentaries on the Law of England*, one of the origins of the modern proverb, "A man's home is his castle."[1] The idea that the home is endowed with a special sanctity is a prominent one in popular discourse in the United States—as my investigation in chapter 3 has shown—and is also reflected in specific legal protections for the home. Based on the Fourth Amendment to the Constitution, the Supreme Court granted the home a special status against the intrusion of the state into the private sphere of citizens by forbidding warrantless searches; and the majority of U.S. states have instituted the so-called "Stand Your Ground" laws as protection against trespassing.[2] Following Margaret Radin's theory of personhood, which suggests a close connection between property ownership and personal identity (Radin 1993, 35), the legal discourse has accepted the "home as a wellspring for psychological flourishing" (S. M. Stern 2009, 1095), which is also reflected in American property, bankruptcy, and tax laws. Legal provisions include numerous financial protections and privileges for homeowners, such as homestead exceptions, which offer creditor protection by shielding some or all of the equity in a personal residence, in case of personal bankruptcy. Tax exemptions include, for instance, the federal home mortgage interest deduction as well as property tax deductions and, in many places, the capping of property taxes (S. M. Stern 2009, 1100).[3]

As Stephanie Stern has pointed out, the introduction of many of these latter protections occurred concomitantly with the rise of the New Deal state and the expansive promotion of the American dream of homeownership (2009, 1105). Contemporary advocates of property rights believe that the government has expanded too far into the realm of the private sphere of the home and therefore seek protection by the government against expropriation by state agencies. In the rhetoric of property rights activists, governments appear to abuse their powers, thereby infringing on people's constitutional rights. In this context, eminent domain cases provide a particular focal point, raising the question of when the government may legitimately take private property and what the balance of interest between the public and private spheres should be. The 2005 *Kelo v. City of New London* case allowed conservative activists to stir public outrage about government intrusion into private rights and craft a property narrative around eminent domain which resonates with the tenets of the ownership society.

Kelo v. City of New London: Eminent Domain in Legal Perspective

In 1998, the city of New London, Connecticut, an economically distressed town, decided to redevelop its waterfront area for a new plant owned by the pharmaceutical company Pfizer, with the aim of creating jobs and increasing tax revenues. Utilizing state funding, the New London Development Corporation, a private nonprofit organization, cleared a large area of contaminated land for Pfizer. Additionally, the city condemned the adjacent area on the waterfront of the Thames River, the historic Fort Trumbull neighborhood, in order to make room for a conference hotel, residential housing, a shopping mall, research and development facilities, a state park, and the U.S. Coast Guard Museum. The city sought to buy 115 properties in the 90-acre area, inhabited mainly by older lower-middle-class residents, to give them to a private real estate developer. Susette Kelo, who had only bought and restored her house in 1997, refused to sell, as did several of her neighbors—among them Wilhelmina Dery, a woman who had been living in her house since her birth in 1918. Kelo, Dery, and seven other neighbors did not want to leave Fort Trumbull or relocate their businesses. The city therefore opted to use its power of eminent domain to acquire the remaining lots.

While the homeowners did not oppose the economic development of the area, they believed that the project mainly served the private business interests of Pfizer, with economic development being incidental but not the motivating factor behind the eminent domain decision. They felt that their neighborhood had been sacrificed to corporate interests. Having received eviction notices from the city, they sued for their right to keep their homes and businesses.

In 2005, the U.S. Supreme Court heard the case *Kelo v. City of New London*, in order to decide on the question of whether private economic development satisfied the Constitution's requirement that the government have public use for property that it takes by eminent domain. With a 5–4 majority, the Court ruled in favor of the city of New London, confirming lower court decisions that the city's plan to demolish the neighborhood for development through private investors was valid for the purpose of public use. It thereby dismissed the claim of the plaintiffs, who had argued that the city administration had taken their property to give it to another private party for private benefit.

The ruling caused tremendous public outrage in the following days and weeks, with most national media outlets firmly siding with the homeowners and scolding the justices' decision in favor of "big government" and "big business."[4] In an op-ed published in the *Washington Post* on June 24, 2005, the day after the Supreme Court publicized its decision, conservative columnist George F. Will scathingly remarked: "The question answered yesterday was: Can government profit by seizing the property of people of modest means and giving it to wealthy people who can pay more taxes than can be extracted from the original owners? The court answered yes." The dissenting opinions by Justices Sandra Day O'Connor and Clarence Thomas further fueled such perceptions, claiming that, with its decision, the Court had abandoned the tradition of limiting government power and failed to protect individual property rights. "The specter of condemnation hangs over all property," O'Connor wrote. "Nothing is to prevent the State from replacing any Motel 6 with a Ritz-Carlton, any home with a shopping mall, or any farm with a factory" (*Kelo v. City of New London.* 545 U.S. 469, 503 [2005]).

Before *Kelo*, eminent domain was a topic removed from popular discourse; most Americans regarded it as a legal technicality, bearing little relevance to their own lives (Schultz 2010b, 1). But *Kelo*, to many citizens, implied that their own homes were now potentially up for grabs by government authorities. The *Kelo* case triggered strong public disapproval (Nadler, Diamond, and Patton 2008, 298) as well as a broad debate on private property, characterized by allegations of government power abuse and infringement of citizens' constitutional rights. Such perceptions were seemingly proven right, as the city's development plan ended up turning out disastrous: in 2009, Pfizer closed its heavily state-subsidized facility in New London, which resulted in the loss of the 1,400 jobs the firm had attracted. The area of the Fort Trumbull neighborhood was cleared but still had not been successfully developed fifteen years later, leaving an urban wasteland in the place of historic houses.

The legal debate on eminent domain centers on the Fifth Amendment's so-called Takings Clause: "nor shall private property be taken for public use without just compensation." During the last decades, and in the *Kelo* case, the most controversial has been the meaning of "public use."[5] Should we take "public use" to mean "used by the public?" Or can we equate it with "public benefit?" It is legally uncontroversial that eminent domain can be used to build basic infrastructure (such as roads and power grids) or public buildings (such as schools and libraries). Yet, courts have often interpreted eminent domain in such a way that property was taken from one private owner and given to another, for instance, a real estate developer, for economic development (Schultz 2010b, 82–83). Adhering to the broader understanding of "public use" as "public benefit," the Supreme Court has held it constitutional to exercise eminent domain even if it means to take private property and give it to another private entity.

Justice John Paul Stevens, writing for the majority in *Kelo*, stressed that the Court had long rejected the narrow public use test, which "proved to be impractical given the diverse and always evolving needs of society" (*Kelo v. City of New London.* 545 U.S. 469, 479 [2005]). Given these diverse needs, he argued, the Court had "wisely eschewed rigid formulas and intrusive scrutiny in favor of affording legislatures broad latitude in determining whether public needs justify the use of the takings power" (483). Stevens based his opinion, in particular, on two precedent cases, *Berman v. Parker* (348 U.S. 26 [1954]) and *Hawaii Housing Authority v. Midkiff* (467 U.S. 229 [1984]). In *Berman*, the Court had justified the redevelopment plan of southwestern Washington, D.C., an area deemed "blighted": most houses in this African American neighborhood were found to be beyond repair and torn down, and the land was partly sold to private investors for redevelopment. A department store owner challenged the condemnation, arguing that his store was not blighted and that it had only been condemned because it happened to be located in the targeted area. The Court rejected his argument, instead accepting the judgment by the legislative branch that the development had to occur as a whole. In *Midkiff*, the Court had to decide whether a Hawaii statute, designed to redistribute property ownership from landowners to tenants to break up a concentration of landownership, was in accordance with the Constitution's Fifth Amendment. Here, the jurisprudence held that the statute corrected a dysfunctional residential land market, thus accepting that the takings served public use.

In both *Berman* and *Midkiff*, the Supreme Court had found that a redistribution of property from one private owner to another may validly serve the public purpose and that public ownership could not be seen as the sole basis of community redevelopment projects. Given these two precedents, the Court therefore determined the use of eminent domain in *Kelo* to be valid as well. The majority opinion also rejected the plaintiffs' argument that eminent domain takings needed restrictions, in order to avoid property transfers for allegedly more productive use and the creation of tax revenues. It also did not require "reasonable certainty" that the public benefits would actually come to fruition, deeming such a requirement as diverging from the precedent (*Kelo v. City of New London.* 545 U.S. 469, 488 [2005]). Stevens suggested that it was neither the Court's role to second-guess a city's urban planning nor to measure whether the actual or supposed public benefit did justify the taking. It merely had to decide on the violation of the Fifth Amendment's Takings Clause. By judging the case against the previous jurisprudence, it became clear that this was not the case. According to Stevens, it would be up to the legislative branch to pass stricter legislation and define public use more narrowly (489).

Justice Sandra Day O'Connor, in her dissenting opinion, voiced stark critique of this majority decision, which, to her, failed to protect individual property rights in making "public" and "private use" indistinguishable, thereby effectively extinguishing the public use clause from the Fifth Amendment. She criticized the Court's deference to legislative power, suggesting that jurisprudence needed to keep political power in check as an external force. O'Connor argued that the *Kelo* decision departed from *Berman* and *Midkiff* in eliminating the requirement of public purpose, which she saw as given in those precedents. In the former cases, eminent domain helped to mitigate public harm and thus created public benefit: in *Berman*, the development removed a blighted area in unsanitary condition; in *Midkiff*, it removed a significant concentration of wealth. The Fort Trumbull neighborhood in New London, however, did not present public harm; its removal was solely for economic reasons. Allowing a taking in such a case, which would nearly always entail some incidental benefit to the public, would make almost all economic development takings legal, effectively leaving the power of eminent domain unconstrained. She concluded:

> Any property may now be taken for the benefit of another private party, but the fallout from this decision will not be random. The beneficiaries are likely to be those citizens with disproportionate influence and power in the political process, including large corporations and development firms. As for the victims, the government now has license to transfer property from those with fewer resources to those with more. (505)

Calling the ruling a "far-reaching, and dangerous, result" (523), Justice Clarence Thomas went even further in his critique of the majority decision. Like O'Connor, he believed that the decision especially failed to protect members of poorer communities, putting them at a disadvantage vis-à-vis powerful political and corporate interests. But unlike O'Connor, Thomas suggested that in *Kelo* the Court proceeded on what had been erroneous precedents in the first place. Starting with his interpretation of the original meaning of the public use clause, he suggested that the framers of the

Constitution had had a narrow understanding of "public use" in mind and that the modern interpretation as "public benefit" was not justified by the text. In other cases, Thomas noted, the Court had made a point of specifically protecting the "sanctity of the home," for instance in *Payton v. New York* (445 U.S. 573 [1980]), with regard to the question of when the search of a home was reasonable. He wrote: "Something has gone seriously awry with this Court's interpretation of the Constitution. Though citizens are safe from the government in their homes, the homes themselves are not" (*Kelo v. City of New London.* 545 U.S. 469, 518 [2005]). The Court, in Thomas's opinion, should revisit the original meaning of the public use clause. In his understanding, property constituted "a natural, fundamental right" (510), and the Court should therefore follow the Framers' original intent as closely as possible.

Debbie Becher has pointed to rhetorical differences between the majority and dissenting opinions, noting that O'Connor and Thomas use the terms "property" and "home" much more frequently than Stevens. The dissenting justices invoke "home" nine and eight times, respectively, while referring to "property" on forty-four occasions each. Stevens, on the other hand, uses "property" seventeen times and "home" only once, instead employing the more neutral term "house" (Becher 2010, 78). The dissenting justices' rhetoric thus links the "home" to an ideological concept in American society and also takes up some of the plaintiffs' argumentative strategies. Moreover, both invoke the alleged 'original' intent of the Constitution, weighing the decision against the meaning of the public use clause at the time of the founding of the nation. They take a position that tends to see property rights as historically stable and coherent, and not as time- and location-specific.

To many observers in the legal profession, the Court's decision was not surprising, given that it had traditionally paid deference to the legislative branch in similar cases (Becher 2010, 77; Wolf 2008a, 15). But the public outrage over the decision and the split between the Supreme Court justices signal frictions between different conceptions of private property rights in American society. In one understanding, property is conceived of as the ownership of a "thing." Property rights, in this conception, are natural or immutable. The second understanding conceives of property as a "bundle of rights," or a number of historically variable, discreet rights that regulate relationships among people. The latter describes the dominant conception in the legal profession and contemporary legal practice, as it has evolved since the progressive era.

Clarence Thomas, arguing for a literal interpretation of the Constitution, advocates a "thing-like" position in his dissenting opinion, as do the proponents of the property rights movement. Such a view claims property to be an individual right with a special sanctity that needs to be protected from the intrusion of the state. In the rivaling view, usually championed by those in favor of urban renewal and economic development, property rights are not only created by the state, but they operate on the same level as other legal stipulations and are therefore subject to the political process. The Court's deference to legislative power and its resulting failure to protect the interests of homeowners are informed by this latter view. Responding to this apparent lack of protection, conservatives posit property as being a fundamental component of individual freedom. Thus, law professor Steven Eagle has claimed that "the right to own property is essential to individual liberty and is a birthright of every American. [. . .] [A]s people who cherish liberty have always understood, property is a natural right of free persons. And, when individuals enjoying such rights freely bargain to coordinate the use or sale of their property rights, they assert their human dignity and enhance their mutual welfare" (2005, 4).

Regarding property ownership as an inherent component of human nature and interpersonal relationships, some proponents of property rights imbue these rights with moral significance (see, e.g., Sandefur 2006, 9; Coyle 1993, 7). Others stress the superior efficiency of free-market exchanges: "The protection of private property and the safeguarding of economic liberties," writes legal scholar Richard Epstein, "are the essential hallmarks of a strong classical liberal system, because the third-party effects of these protections are always positive" (2011, 54). Economic development takings, viewed from these perspectives, are morally wrong because they deprive homeowners of their constitutional rights grounded in the nature of human relationships; they also distort market relationships, as governments interfere with what ordinarily would be economic choices between private parties, that is, between homeowners choosing or refusing to sell and private investors seeking to acquire land. Likewise, the media discourse on eminent domain, in the context of *Kelo* and similar court cases, sided with Thomas's originalist interpretation of the powers and limitations of government, which reaffirmed popular narratives about property rights.

The "Court of Public Opinion": Eminent Domain Media Narratives

Eminent domain takings for economic development first became a national media topic when *60 Minutes,* the prestigious and widely publicized CBS news broadcast, took up the issue in September 2003. Reporting on alleged eminent domain abuses, host Mike Wallace explained to the audience that popular beliefs about eminent domain were misleading: under the Constitution's Fifth Amendment, government could not only take private property to build schools, roads, or power grids. Increasingly, homes and privately owned businesses were being taken and transferred to other private owners, in an attempt to not only generate more tax revenue for cities but also create additional jobs. The main part of the broadcast focused on citizens "fighting back" against this reallocation of property. The report also included interviews with Dana Berliner and Scott Bullock, attorneys at the nonprofit public interest firm Institute for Justice, which fights takings for economic development in court, on behalf of affected citizens. Wallace's team, in fact, had been approached by the institute with a study conducted by Berliner, entitled *Public Power, Private Gain: A Five-Year, State-By-State Report Examining the Abuse of Eminent Domain*, published the same year. The study listed more than 10,000 alleged abuses of government power between 1998 and 2003, mainly based on research of local media reports and picturing eminent domain takings as "a nationwide epidemic," as Berliner called it in her interview with Wallace.

Following the lead of Berliner and the Institute for Justice, *60 Minutes* sympathized with the owners whose property was taken for what seemed to be questionable economic projects. Jim and JoAnn Saleet, for instance, an elderly white middle-class couple, faced the condemnation of their home of 38 years in Lakewood, Ohio, in a neighborhood that had been declared "blighted," in order to make room for upscale condominiums built by a private developer, to raise the city's tax revenues. "This is morally wrong, what they are doing here," Jim Saleet told Wallace. Using tropes of rugged individualism, he emphasized that he and his wife had worked hard to be able to buy their house and pay off their mortgage with the prospect of spending the rest of their lives there and then passing it on to their children. To have their house and neighborhood labeled "blighted"—a necessary legal qualification for eminent domain procedures—felt "humiliating" and "degrading" to them.

The broadcast juxtaposes the Saleets' story with an interview with the Lakewood mayor Madeline Cain, who argued that the town's future depended on raising the tax base in the aging community. "Blight," in this context, Cain suggested, must not be understood as an allegation that homes so labeled are not well maintained; it merely denoted, in legal terms, an area that could be employed for "higher or better use." Confronted by Wallace, Cain had a hard time explaining why exactly the neighborhood had to go, especially since, according to the city's definition of "blight"—lack of central air, an attached two-car garage, and at least two bathrooms—most of Lakewood's houses would have had to be labeled blighted, including the mayor's own. Even the mayor considered the area a "cute little neighborhood," Wallace stated in the report, "but without those new condos, it won't produce enough property taxes to satisfy the mayor and the city council."[6]

60 Minutes sides with individual property owners whose constitutional rights are seemingly at the mercy of greedy local governments and more powerful economic interests. The report contrasts Saleet's straightforward sense of justice and morality with the apparently shady legal technicalities invoked by the mayor. Generalizing from individual cases, the show pictures eminent domain as a threat to homeowners all over the United States. As Saleet states: "If my home isn't safe, nobody's home is safe in the whole country, not only Ohio, but this is rampant all over the country, it's like a plague." Wallace does not dwell on the reasoning of Lakewood's city council or explore the process of local decision-making. He does not consider the fact that property taxes constitute a municipality's most significant income base, without which public services cannot be provided. Omitting any discussion of graver structural problems, Wallace instead insinuates that the city's administrators are personally driven by the greed for tax revenues and therefore willing to sacrifice long-term, solid residents and senior citizens for a more affluent clientele. Property, in these cases, seems to be reallocated from poor to rich. This *60 Minutes* report exemplifies narrative patterns that are characteristic of the public discourse on private property and eminent domain, including references to a moral right to property beyond legal regulations and to the American dream of homeownership, as well as suspicions about the motives of government authorities.

A year after the *60 Minutes* report, George Will took up the issue of eminent domain for the first time in his influential column, published in the *Washington Post* and syndicated by hundreds of other newspapers across the United States. Though not acknowledging his source in the article, Will's take was also informed by the Institute for Justice, which had reached out to him after filing its petition on behalf of Susette Kelo with the Supreme Court (Benedict 2009, 301). Will, much like Wallace, sides with the homeowners, accusing the government officials of New London of "despotism" (Will 2004). He frames the city of New London's aims as being primarily the reaping of more tax benefits. Accordingly, the redeveloped area would be stocked with "expensive condominiums, a luxury hotel and private offices." Will emphasizes this point twice throughout the short text, by insisting on the city's alleged intent to generate taxes. He omits, however, that another, possibly more important, rationale for the development had been the creation of new jobs and that the envisioned site would also include a shopping mall as well as a state park and a museum. The narrow focus on taxes helps to cement the negative view of a seemingly cold-hearted government forfeiting their constituents' interests for quick cash. Will further portrayed the city's action as illicit, by linking its effort to the aforementioned precedent case of *Berman v. Parker*. *Berman* had been ostensibly about the removal of urban blight in an African American neighborhood but had, as a consequence, what some called "Negro removal." Will here alludes to the fact that, in the past, eminent domain was frequently used as a discriminatory practice. Without explicitly saying so, he insinuates that *Kelo* constitutes a case of class discrimination against white middle- and working-class homeowners.

The media discourse on eminent domain after the *Kelo* decision, for the most part, proliferated similar narratives, with most editorials being unsympathetic to the Supreme Court's decision and the city's choice to exercise eminent domain. The *Wall Street Journal* published a commentary by law professor Richard Epstein, one of the most prominent legal scholars associated with the property rights movement. Calling the *Kelo* decision "truly horrible," Epstein denounced, in broad strokes, both New London's development plan and the Supreme Court majority opinion (2005, A14). The *Washington Post's* editorial was characterized by a different tone, thereby balancing the overtly critical assessment by George Will published the same day. The *Post* called the ruling "correct," yet held simultaneously that its result was "quite unjust" (Main 2007). Acknowledging the difficulties in setting standards for the public use clause, the editorial suggested that the ruling interpreted the Fifth Amendment accurately in its deference to legislative power. The theme of justice runs through many of the opinion pieces, especially those not disputing the constitutionality of the Supreme Court ruling (see, e.g., Jacoby 2005). The *New York Times*, being more restrained than most other newspapers, though not entirely uncritical, put a slightly different emphasis on eminent domain than most publications, using the occasion of the court decision to report on the longer-term consequences of a local case in Port Chester, New York. Focusing on the lives of people affected by the economic development plan exercised there, journalist Elsa Brenner (2005) provided a more differentiated picture of the outcomes of one specific project. Though reporting on the hardship and economic losses that some of the owners endured, as a result of the redevelopment, her article also included stories of property owners who managed to come to an agreement with the city and who were content with the compensation they received for their property.

Even in the years after the Supreme Court decision, *Kelo* resonated in the media, triggering several book publications, among them Jeff Benedict's reconstruction of the case, *Little Pink House: A Story of Defiance and Courage* (2009).[7] Benedict's narrative leaves little doubt that the New London urban renewal plan was a prestige project invented by ambitious local and state authorities, who worried little about what the redevelopment meant for the inhabitants of the Fort Trumbull neighborhood. In Benedict's meticulously researched account, Connecticut governor John G. Rowland emerges as the original instigator of the project, a Republican in a blue state facing reelection in 1997 and trying to gain votes in Democrat-governed cities. Rowland's attempts at garnering political support included the attempt to turn the New London neighborhood into "a case study in how to revive a community" (Benedict 2009, 101).

Rowland orchestrated a coalition that included officials from Pfizer, members of the city council as well as the dormant New London Development Corporation (NLDC), a nonprofit organization which reconstituted itself under the leadership of the president of Connecticut College, Claire Gaudiani. Though Pfizer, at the time, considered building new facilities in other locations, and the Fort Trumbull site seemed less than ideal for the company's purposes—it was too small and heavily contaminated—Gaudiani and the NLDC managed to broker a deal with the state government, which pledged $100 million in public investments. In addition, the company was promised additional development around its site, according to its requirements, which necessitated the complete demolition of the existing neighborhood. Instead of seeking to compromise with property owners, the coalition, as described by Benedict, single-mindedly pursued their own goals, up to the point of destruction, not merely of the neighborhood but ultimately also of the development plans, leaving "a barren wasteland of weeds, littler, and rubble" (Benedict 2009, 377) in place of a formerly "intact piece of urban neighborhood" (125).

Benedict crafts his narrative as "a uniquely American saga about power and defiance," in which Susette Kelo's "little pink house" comes to stand in for a national epidemic (ix). After the Supreme Court's negative decision, the house had been moved and preserved as a historical landmark, open for visitors, turning it into a national symbol commemorating the owner's David-against-Goliath fight and sanctifying the right to homeownership. Casting Kelo in a heroic role, Benedict, like many of the reporters, sides with the homeowners from the beginning. In an "author's note" prefacing the text, he frames the case as a matter of American values, citing also O'Connor's famous dissent. He begins by explaining the government's power of eminent domain, stressing that "Americans accept this practice" of taking private property for public purposes "as long as deprived property owners receive due process and just compensation. Under the Fifth Amendment" he claims, "that's been the American way since the Framers drafted our Constitution" (ix). With *Kelo*, however, "the Supreme Court changed the rules," allowing transfers to private developers and equating "public *benefits* with public *uses*" (ix). Building up momentum for the story to follow, Benedict gravely overstates the legal significance of the case. Picturing eminent domain as an unchanging practice and the *Kelo* decision as a game changer is more than an oversimplification. As discussed above, the decision did not so much break with a tradition of rulings than confirm precedent cases. Thus, the author sets the stage for a narrative about moral values and justice and elected government officials who have to be distrusted. Turning the New London case into a paradigmatic case representative of a larger social problem, *Little Pink House* supports a conception of politics as a hierarchical endeavor in which officials rule at the expense of powerless citizens.

Beginning with Susette Kelo's purchase of her house in 1997 and ending in 2008 when it has become apparent that the development did not pan out, Benedict narrates the events chronologically, yet with one crucial deviation: the text contains a prologue that—reminiscent of the narrative strategy of many movies—flashes forward to September 2005, when Kelo is asked to testify before the U.S. Senate Judiciary Committee, three months after the Supreme Court had published its controversial decision. This prologue underlines Benedict's desire to emphasize the allegedly larger moral significance of the case. It allows him to introduce Kelo as the inspirational leader of a national movement. The fact that the Senate debates the case and invites Kelo to testify lends gravity to the issue, and her spiritual leadership is emphasized by the concerns that the senators voice about the state of private property rights in the United States. Ending the prologue with a quote from Kelo's testimony, Benedict sets the moral tone of the following narrative: "The battle against eminent-domain abuse may have started as a way for me to save my little pink cottage. But it has rightfully grown into something much larger—the fight to restore the American Dream and the sacredness and security of each one of our homes" (2).

Benedict returns to the scene in the Senate at the end of the book, thus recontextualizing it in the events that led to the testimony and pointing toward Kelo's transformation from ordinary working-class homeowner into "the leader of a national movement" (346). Seated next to the mayor of Hartford, who would testify to defend the power of eminent domain, Kelo feels that "she owed it to millions of other working Americans to do her best to convince the senators that politicians like the one seated next to her didn't care about the little guys" (346). Kelo delivers her testimony wearing a pink sweater—the same one she had worn when attending the oral arguments in the Supreme Court, matching exactly the color of her house and decorated with sneaker footprints "signifying 'They walked all over me'" (1). Owner and home here seemingly become one, the alleged abuse of eminent domain appears as a violation of Kelo's very body.

Throughout the text, Benedict stresses the significance of the house for Kelo's identity and as the locus of her self-realization. Prior to the purchase of her house in the Fort Trumbull neighborhood, Kelo had led an "unfulfilled home life," (3) married to her second husband who "showed more affection for the bottle than her" (4). Hailing from a poor, severely underprivileged background, she had first become pregnant at age 16 and had five children by age 25. Leaving her second husband, the pink house with a view on the water offers her a fresh start. Having never owned anything in her life before, the house provides her with new independence, security, and the possibility to develop her own personality: "Her house represented her only possession. More than that, it was a refuge, the place she went to in hope of becoming the woman she had always put off being while raising five sons" (89).

By thus stressing the affective investment of homeowners into their property, Benedict portrays the *Kelo* case as a matter of social justice and the main protagonist as a woman who, despite (or because of) her lack of education and sophistication, is "guided by an instinctive sense of right and wrong," with an unwavering belief that "taking people's homes was simply the wrong thing to do" (298). Susette becomes a leader because of her authenticity, because "she *was* the people, a plain-talking woman with a story that was too infuriating to be made up" (347). The battle against eminent domain, the text insinuates, turns into a form of civil disobedience—a defiance of unjust legislation and a defense of higher moral laws. Susette comes to see herself as a modern-day Rosa Parks, suddenly cast into a leadership role:

> Rosa Parks hadn't set out to become the mother of the modern civil rights movement when she refused a Montgomery bus driver's order to vacate her seat for a white passenger. Her civil disobedience sparked the Montgomery bus boycott, which elevated Martin Luther King Jr. to national prominence and ushered in a movement that forever changed America. Every so often, an ordinary person has the chance to do an extraordinary thing that alters history. That chance had come to Susette Kelo. (370)

The allusion to the civil rights movement in this passage is striking, as it appropriates the struggle against segregation and for equal rights for African Americans for the battle against eminent domain, seeking to legitimize the defense of individual property rights. Kelo and her lower middle-class neighbors are likened to the victims of racial discrimination. In another instance, Susette had expressed her anger at the developers by saying to a friend: "Rich white people don't like us" (102), implicitly identifying herself as nonwhite, by stressing the race of her opponents. The feeling of powerlessness thus becomes associated with blackness.

The text juxtaposes Susette's integrity with the shady, self-interested motives of the people behind the redevelopment project. In particular, Benedict contrasts her with the head of the NLDC, Claire Gaudiani. A professor of French literature and the president of Connecticut College Gaudiani appears as Kelo's complete antithesis. Having come to New London only a few years earlier, she soon emerged as a rising star in social circles, "the closest thing New London had to a diva" (19). She would wear provocative dresses to public events, "showcasing just enough to tantalize" (18). If Susette becomes a moral leader through sincerity and candor, Claire "possessed an uncanny power of persuasion" (21), which she instrumentalizes for her "quest to satisfy personal drives and ambitions" (35).

Claire Gaudiani, along with Governor Rowland, is clearly cast as the villain in Benedict's drama, and both will be dismantled at the end. Rowland, charged with corruption (though not related to the New London project), has to resign from office and is subsequently sentenced to a year in federal prison; Gaudiani ultimately has to resign as well, both as president of Connecticut College and of the NLDC. Kelo, in contrast, can claim moral victory in the end. As all her neighbors finally settle with the city and give up their homes in the neighborhood, she decides to leave as well, yet continues to refuse giving up her home to the city. Instead, she leaves under the condition that her house will be relocated to a different place in the city and preserved as a "historic landmark and a fitting tribute to the historic battle they had waged" (371).

The Institute for Justice and the Campaign for Property Rights

Most media reports on eminent domain portray citizens who were allegedly morally wronged by their city governments' power abuses, a thrust also prominent in many other popular publications after the *Kelo* decision, which repeat similar tropes of individuals—often members of the white working class—fighting a battle against larger corporate and government interests. These books are joined by a body of literature produced by conservative legal scholars and activists arguing for a better protection of constitutional property rights.[8] The Institute for Justice, a libertarian public interest law firm, has played an instrumental role in putting property rights on the public agenda, along with other similar organizations, most importantly the Pacific Legal Foundation, the oldest conservative public interest law firm. Juxtaposing Dana Berliner's *Public Power, Private Gain* (2003) with the *60 Minutes* story, the George Will articles, and Benedict's narrative, Berliner's report reads like a template from which the main tropes and arguments are repeated. While ostensibly conducted as a scientific study, Berliner employs highly emotional language to discredit "local bureaucrats who are hungry for dollars" (4) as being "deeply immoral" (7). Specifically invoking American ideals of individualism, Berliner projects a normative moral vision of the relationship between the individual and the state, in which individual rights are, by definition, prioritized.

Part of a conservative legal movement that had been developing since the early 1970s in the United States, the Institute for Justice was founded by William H. Mellor and Clint Bolick in 1991. The Institute seeks to advance legal change through litigation in the areas of economic freedom, school choice, property rights, and First Amendment cases (Teles 2008, 65). In his speech at the firm's founding, Mellor described its approach as "a long-term, philosophically and tactically consistent litigation program based on natural rights and the Constitution" (Bolick and Mellor 1991). After having identified these subjects as key issues to advance the cause of libertarians in the United States, Mellor's and Bolick's firm has indeed remained committed to these issues since its inception (Teles 2008, 237). More importantly, the strategy of the Institute for Justice goes beyond mere litigation, including also the training of lawyers in managing the public relations aspect of cases, the funding and publishing of strategic research, reaching out to local grass-root activists, and working in conjunction with legal scholars and think tanks. A portrait of Mellor in the *Wall Street Journal* characterized the organization's approach as "guerilla legal warfare on behalf of individual freedom" (Levy 2012).

The Institute for Justice not only rallies behind the cause of property rights but has been supporting other alleged infringements on citizens' constitutional rights as well. Working on First Amendment rights, the firm won the case *SpeechNow v. Federal Election Commission* in 2010 in the D.C. Court of Appeals, which made unlimited contributions to political action committees during election campaigns possible. The Institute models its strategies on those of liberal public interest groups affecting broad public opinion, such as the NAACP, and adapts this approach for libertarian purposes. This strategy is also reminiscent of that of the California Real Estate Association in the 1960s, discussed in chapter 4, which strategically invoked property rights against a liberal fair housing law, thereby uniting diverse voices.

The Institute's effectiveness is demonstrated by the fact that, in the *Kelo* case, it managed not only to round up the support of conservatives and libertarians but also of traditionally liberal organizations such as the NAACP, the AARP and the SCLC, which together filed an amicus brief on behalf of the plaintiffs. They followed the Institute's lead by stressing that eminent domain requires "individuals or families to give up their most valuable and important possessions—their homes—and even to leave lifelong communities" (U.S. Supreme Court 2004, 4). The brief expressed concern that if the Court were to rule in favor of eminent domain for economic development, then the result would disproportionately hurt racial and ethnic minorities, the elderly, and other economically underprivileged groups. It pointed to the history of urban renewal, which, in the past, had frequently served as an excuse to eliminate minority neighborhoods by use of the power of eminent domain. In these instances, the label of "blight" was invoked as a seemingly neutral term that however contained racial and ethnic prejudice (7). Even in the absence of overt racial bias, these groups, the brief noted, were often targeted by redevelopment projects because they were "less likely, or often unable, to contest the action" (11). Moreover, low-income neighborhoods were particularly attractive for developers because they would be required to pay less compensation than in more affluent neighborhoods, while offering the prospect of a highly increased value in the real estate after the development.

By arguing in favor of Kelo, the liberal organizations that traditionally stand in for minority citizens aligned their cause with that of the (lower) middle class, while also helping the Institute for Justice to realize one of its strategic aims: to change the public image of conservatives. Representing clients usually associated with liberal groups, such as African Americans and members of the working class, the Institute sought "to transform the identification of civil rights with liberalism, and to remove the stigma of racism from conservatives," while devitalizing "the usual assumptions of the media and courts that conservative lawyers were just fronts for big business" (Teles 2008, 239). Bolick's book *Unfinished Business: A Civil Rights Strategy for America's Third Century*, published by the Pacific Research Institute one year prior to the Institute's founding, operates precisely in this vein, seeking to turn civil rights into a conservative cause. Arguing that the movement had been coopted by white middle-class interests but failed to empower members of a black underclass, Bolick pursued a mission of achieving civil rights through "individual empowerment" and based on the natural rights theory, for which a "vigorous and effective litigation strategy is essential" (Bolick 1990, 6). This strategy followed a long-range agenda, with a strategic identification of useful cases with sympathetic plaintiffs who made it easy "to argue the case in the court of public opinion" (142) and thus to exercise agenda control.

The Institute for Justice and the property rights movement do not stop at using litigation to change legislation; an important part of the movement's attempt to garner support derives from its symbolic co-optation of the strategies of the civil rights movement. Reminiscent of Martin Luther King's framework of nonviolent resistance, property rights advocates depict their goals as a fight for moral justice, seeking to create an analogy between African Americans' demands for political rights and racial equality and the fight for a stronger acknowledgement of private property rights. Both movements insist on constitutional rights, which they contrast with state and local laws that appear as morally unjust. It is thus no coincidence that Jeff Benedict's book stylizes its heroine as a modern-day Rosa Parks, likening Kelo to an African American figure of moral authority.

The defense of property rights, as David Schultz has pointed out, is crucially significant in conservatives' "effort to limit state power and promote the free market" (2010a, 12). Aiming at reinstituting property's privileged position under the Constitution—dismantled since the New Deal era by courts' deference to legislatures in property matters—eminent domain cases have become a central field of the Institute for Justice's work. In conjunction with other conservative firms, think tanks and legal scholars, it has most successfully "used the law as a mobilizing tactic, to set the political agenda, and to transform public opinion" (Teles 2008, 241). "In bringing *Kelo* to the US

Supreme Court," William Wilkerson notes, the Institute "was able to recast and reinvigorate historic criticism about 'urban renewal' and 'community redevelopment' in constitutional terms that had their genesis in the neoliberal ideology that emerged in American politics with the election of Ronald Reagan" (2010, 60). Despite losing the Supreme Court case, it managed to win in the "court of public opinion," ultimately garnering the attention of federal and state lawmakers for the issue, who then in many cases worked to restrict eminent domain powers.

Invoking Property as a Natural Right

The property rights movement argues that we should interpret property rights more faithfully to the original intent of the framers of the Constitution, with property acting as a boundary of the state and a limit to state action. Property rights, in this conception, are individual rights that need protection from government intrusion rather than rights instituted by governments. If we view property as a natural or constitutional right, the ownership of property becomes a good in itself that cannot be negotiated and which appears to be neutral and apolitical. This view is problematic, Nedelsky suggests, because it "means that property does tacitly define the limits of legitimate state power" and "which system of distribution of power and goods is natural and what must be justified as a deviation" (1990, 259). If the right to property assumes the role of a natural right, this will affect which policy options are socially and ethically defensible, thereby shaping the regulatory framework. Positing property rights as outside the law, crafted by legislatures, their proponents naturalize a particular social vision, the idea that individuals be best left alone to act in their own self-interest and that the state should not intrude into private economic activities. Such an approach assumes that all market participants are equal; as a consequence, it "cannot account meaningfully for differences among individuals, because doing so would entail acknowledging the influence of social forces like race, sex, and class" (Asen 2010, 126). Furthermore, while the market approach treats all property owners alike, be they homeowners or large corporations, it leaves the interests of nonowners of property completely unacknowledged.

Eric Freyfogle has argued that, while the property rights movement responds to existing problems in property law, it ultimately undercuts democratic governance. In Freyfogle's view, the main problem can be located in the fact that property conflicts are phrased as constitutional takings in the first place. To "argue about takings and the constitutional limits of government power" precludes us from asking "basic policy questions," such as whether development in a region should be limited or who should get to develop and share economic profits (Freyfogle 2007, 67). Such questions are not being asked because "the Court has had essentially no role in updating and applying the basic laws of private property," as property rights and regulations are mostly shaped by state legislatures (68). By no means unchanging, property rights had, for centuries, been subject to common law and were thus shaped through judicial rulings. Lawmaking power began to shift in favor of elected legislatures in the nineteenth century, making land use subject to government regulations and the police powers of the state. Though common law and regulations address the same issue, ownership and the use of land, people tend to perceive these two sets of laws as fundamentally different. Rather than seeing new regulations as a shift in property rights themselves, critics often frame them in terms of intrusions into property owners' constitutional rights, employing "an increasingly abstract vision of landownership[,] an ideal that wasn't really grounded in any body of law" (73).

By interpreting the public use stipulation in the Fifth Amendment, the Supreme Court in effect treats property as an unchanging constitutional right, but it cannot say much about this right, as property rights are made and remade by legislative authorities rather than by the courts. Property rights, understood as a "bundle of rights," are much more differentiated and subject to local and state authorities. The Supreme Court, however, can only decide on whether a particular taking violates the stipulation in the Constitution. If the Court interfered in more detail with which takings are justified, it would impose stronger regulations on local authorities and give them less leeway to make decisions. As Justice Stevens suggested in his *Kelo* opinion, this would cause other problems.

While property as an immutable right has lost its status in actual legal practice, it has increasingly turned into a "cultural ideal" and a "mythic emblem of individual autonomy" (Freyfogle 2007, 74). The inherent failure of the Supreme Court to protect homeowners has empowered property rights organizations to strategically employ the idea of the sanctity of the home. In the aftermath of the *Kelo* decision, the Institute for Justice started a "Hands Off My Home" campaign, organized through their spin-off organization, the "Castle Coalition," which described itself as a "nationwide grassroots property rights activism project" on its website (Institute for Justice 2002). The property rights movement was able to mobilize public support for their cause of a stronger constitutional protection of property rights because the "bundle of rights" approach cannot account for the fact that some property rights may in fact be more important than others and indeed may warrant stronger protection, if only because many people possess so much emotional investment in their homes.

By positing property rights as natural and neutral, property rights activists seek to limit the powers of the state and to reshape the regulatory framework in a libertarian fashion. The property rights movement conflates individual rights and property rights, as well as the concepts of home and property. Employing the rhetoric of the home, its proponents argue for stricter eminent domain laws. As John Fee points out, however, such restriction may "provide[] only incidental protection for homeowners. The public use doctrine focuses on what the government proposes to do with the land after the taking, not its status to the owner before the taking. It makes no distinction between homes and other kinds of property" (2006, 785). Moreover, the rhetorical identification of "home" and "property" may ultimately serve not homeowners but larger corporate interests who hold the majority of privately owned lands in the United States and who have significantly different investments in their properties than homeowners. Thus, Peñalver argues that "providing heightened protection against eminent domain for all private land is an unnecessarily over-inclusive way of protecting people's castles; it permits a politically powerful, well-funded, and well-connected set of property owners to piggyback on the rhetorical power of a conception of property that has nothing to do with their own relationship to the land" (2006, 2976).

A "Track Record on Takings Regulation," published by scholars at Georgetown Law School in 2008, examined the consequences of stricter eminent domain laws in cases where the property rights agenda has been adopted. Analyzing compensation measures in Oregon and Florida, the study found that "while the property rights agenda is generally advertised as being for and on behalf of the 'little guy,' the primary beneficiaries of the property rights agenda have been relatively well to do special interests" (Echeverria and Hansen-Young 2008, 2). Though the legislative changes enacted in various states may have widely differing effects, these results hint at the possibility that even publicly approved measures can potentially aggravate, instead of solve, property conflicts.

PROPERTY AS PRIMARY VIRTUE: THE RHETORIC OF THE OWNERSHIP SOCIETY

Takings of private property under the law of eminent domain most often happen on a local or state level; the federal government, however, takes property only infrequently.[9] Nevertheless, on the first anniversary of the *Kelo* decision, President George W. Bush signed an executive order entitled "Protecting the Property Rights of the American People," which in its first section stated:

> It is the policy of the United States to protect the rights of Americans to their private property, including limiting the taking of private property by the Federal Government to situations in which the taking is for public use, with just compensation, and for the purpose of benefiting the general public and not merely

> for the purpose of advancing the economic interest of private parties to be given ownership or use of the property taken. (Bush 2006a)

Ostensibly, the administration here committed itself to the protection of private property rights against infringements from federal agencies. Yet, in actuality, the text hardly moves beyond already existing protections of private rights—it reaffirms the public use clause of eminent domain regulations and only rules out takings "merely for the purpose of advancing the economic interest of private parties." In this way, it leaves leeway for takings cases in which agencies are able to claim at least a partial public benefit of economic development, for example, the generation of new jobs or tax revenues. Rather than curtailing business interests, the Bush administration's contribution to the protection of property rights appears merely rhetorical. At the same time, however, the aims of the libertarian property rights movement previously discussed tie in precisely with the administration's policies that sought to strengthen individual rights and responsibilities. In championing the United States as an ownership society, Bush relied on the same antagonistic vision of the relationship between the individual and the state, yet he focused more intensely on the individual benefits of property ownership and redefined ownership as a means to participate in political processes and decision-making.

Intending to reform the Social Security and healthcare systems as its signature projects, the Bush administration's concept of the ownership society focalized the conservative push for a more market-driven restructuring of American social institutions. Though they were ultimately unsuccessful in passing their proposed legislation, one must view the project of the ownership society as "more than a short-term, neoconservative exercise in rhetoric" (Soederberg 2007, 93). Or, more precisely, even though the concept operated primarily on the rhetorical level, we have to properly appreciate the shaping power of rhetoric and the long-term consequences it generates—which, during the Trump administration, have resurfaced in congressional Republicans' attempts to dismantle entitlement programs. Policies mediate "rhetorical and material forces" in a society (Asen 2009, 7), while "the process of *policy-making* foregrounds the role of rhetoric as a constitutive force" (9). Rhetoric assumes an important role for the making of meaning and in the definition and framing of social phenomena and social problems. Political actors wishing to alter existing institutions—such as the very popular Social Security system—need to present coherent and attractive alternative visions before they go about constructing the necessity of reforming these established policies (Béland 2007, 93).

The ownership society did not constitute just one proposal of a solution to a preexisting social problem; rather, the Bush administration strategically employed the concept, in an attempt to frame social reality in a particular way, thereby creating the issues that supposedly needed fixing. The remedies suggested were to minimize the state's power and to maximize individual economic liberties. To (re)define the roles of the market and the state and the relationship between the government and the individual thus emerged as a crucial function of Bush's public speeches, in an attempt to formulate a hegemonic vision of a society that necessitated a restructuring along the lines of ownership. And the resulting discourse on property not only circumscribed the debates on policies introduced by the Bush administration but also reinforced similar tendencies to distrust the motives of the regulatory state and the belief in absolute rights of the individual in other contemporary and future discussions on related issues.

A Blueprint for a Capitalist Utopia

Bush's social vision of the ownership society posits a primacy of the rights and responsibilities of the individual citizen, which, in his speeches, can be translated into the recurring theme of the citizen being a stakeholder: "If you own something in America, you own a stake in America's future" (Bush 2005b, 311). Bush likens the citizen to a stock investor: property privately owned here figuratively appears as the shares of the corporation of America, promising the owner a profit for his or her investment through dividend payments and increased future stock prices. The owner-citizen "buy[s] into the future of America" (Bush 2007d, 1782) and participates in the process of wealth creation and the fate of the nation. Like a stockowner, the citizen is invested in the future political development of the country—in particular in the policies that regulate property. According to Bush, ownership is "an important part of making sure people have a [*sic*] interest in the future of our country. If you own something, you want to make sure Government makes the right decision so you can continue to own it" (Bush 2007c, 1225). The citizen as stakeholder, then, is more than a metaphor: Bush understands stake holding here, quite literally, as protecting one's material interests and thereby redefines stake holding as a form of shareholding. He thus advances a form of democracy based on the model of the corporation as a passive mode of control, not an active form of participation. Depicting the state and the citizen in oppositional roles, the property relation (re)emerges as a defining characteristic of the democratic state.

By thus positing property ownership as the prerequisite to political participation, Bush's rhetoric harks back to a time in U.S. history when voting rights were tied to owning property (see chapter 1). Bush's model of democracy seems to distinguish between owners and nonowners or at least potentially delegitimizes the political interests of those not owning any property. Yet, the president emphasizes that, in fact, he does not envision an exclusive society of the few, promising to expand ownership to include all citizens: "We want 100 percent of our people to be a part of the ownership society" (Bush 2003, 159). Bush offers inclusiveness as a distinctly American feature, as he asserts: "I'm talking about ownership for all people, not just a certain type of person. We want ownership to be a part of every neighborhood. And it's happening in America. It's really what makes us such a wonderful country, isn't it, when people from all walks of life can say, 'I own something'" (Bush 2007c, 1225). Citing rising homeownership rates to new all-time highs as evidence, Bush pictures the United States as being in the process of realizing its potential as a community of owners, in which racial and economic differences—the distinction between "certain type[s] of person[s]" with access to property and those without—are becoming ultimately leveled.

For the individual, the ownership society not only holds the promise of financial security—"a nest egg you can call your own and Government can never take away"—but, more generally, seeks to provide "a path to greater opportunity, more freedom, and more control over your own life" (Bush 2007b, 1857). Owners do not depend on the government, neither materially nor for directions of how to lead their lives; they "take responsibility for the decisions they make" (Bush 2006b, 929). Bush frames the absence of government intervention as a gain in individual agency and autonomy. He introduces "responsibility" as a key term that is meant to suggest individual empowerment but at the same time also imbues it with an ethical dimension: responsibility not only to act self-interestedly but also to respect other people and take care of one's community. Ownership, for Bush, entails obligations, most importantly to act compassionately: For him, Robert Asen notes, "responsibility served as the copula connecting compassion and ownership, thereby revealing the spiritual dimension of ownership" (2010, 117–18).

The Cato Institute, a libertarian think tank in Washington, D.C., sought to deliver a philosophical foundation for the ownership society and positioned itself as one of the concept's staunchest supporters. Tom G. Palmer, a political scientist at George Mason University, and David Boaz, Executive Vice President at the Cato Institute, each published an article in 2004 to delineate the "ownership society [as] a society of responsibility, liberty and prosperity" (Palmer 2004), thus reinforcing the themes and key signifiers of Bush's speeches. Framed as a philosophical deliberation, their discussion proceeds without addressing concrete social or political problems and instead focuses on the moral and ethical dimensions of ownership. The three abstract principles Palmer invokes already in his headline—"responsibility, liberty, prosperity"—guide their argument for an allegedly superior form of social organization on economic, political, and personal levels. Private property ownership, they suggest, enables the most efficient use of resources, promises a diffusion of power in society as well as individual agency, and creates an environment for human flourishing. They thus frame, in popular terms, arguments advanced by liberal and libertarian philosophers and economists who favor a private property system.[10]

The belief in the efficiency of markets constitutes the main pillar of the libertarian vision: markets allow for a prosperous society, Palmer holds, because they generate wealth for individuals and are able to coordinate activity without the intervention of a centralized authority. Palmer relies here on the idea that spontaneous, self-interested behavior generates the socially most beneficial outcome. Significantly, Palmer subsequently transposes the notion of market efficiency from the economic to the political sphere, arguing that the market model provides a paradigm for cooperation without conflict, without the "squabbling [. . .] characteristic of political control" (Palmer 2004). Guided by the principle of efficiency, then, political negotiations over resources become dispensable, as people will take care of their needs via private transactions and choices. This approach presumes the existence of only one efficient and just way of distributing resources, making political discourse superfluous.

By relying on individual choice and decision-making, Palmer argues, the market model also "induces people to act responsibly": in a society structured around private ownership of resources, it is in the individual's best interest to take care of one's property—there is no "tragedy of the commons" (Hardin 1968), no squandering or exploitation of shared resources for private gain. In this vein, David Boaz (2004) even proposes that an ownership society would help improve the environment. He gives the example of a timber company, which, acting in its own self-interest, would not cut down all trees on its land at once and would plant new trees to replace the ones they felled. "They may be moved by a concern for the environment," Boaz writes, "but the future income from the property is also a powerful incentive." From this specific example, he generalizes that citizens will have an incentive to worry about pollution and environmental destruction in a private property system only, since they aim to protect "the future value of property." Evidently, this generalization is problematic, as Boaz's example does not account for externalities: different examples, for example, of a chemical plant polluting natural water bodies with sewage, would imply the opposite, namely that destruction increases if the company lacks economic incentives in the absence of government regulation.[11] Here, Boaz strategically tackles an area in which markets are often considered to be harmful, in order to emphasize, in his view, the fundamentally ethical nature of private property ownership.

Both Boaz and Palmer advance their libertarian vision of a private property system by contrasting it with the (far-fetched) alternative of state socialism, thereby invariably focusing on the shortcomings of the latter. In a system in which "government owns all property," Boaz writes, "individuals have little protection from the whims of politicians." Phrased in such an antagonistic way, capitalism appears to be the superior form of social organization because "it diffuses power." In Boaz and Palmer's conception, then, the ownership society appears, almost paradoxically, as the ultimate realization of a classless society in which all members have equal access to political power and resources. Both authors develop the ownership society as a capitalist utopia, which also promises to put into practice the tenets once formulated by the proponents of socialism. By operating with the fundamental contrast between socialism and capitalism, however, they circumvent the much more pertinent question of how the ownership society compares to the actually existing capitalist system in the contemporary United States. They also evade a discussion of any function of governments—in these articles, governments are only mentioned as entities whose powers need to be clipped. Strictly realized, the ownership society would replace all state functions with market mechanisms. In this philosophy, "market modalities constitute an ethically superior realm of society because they enable more authentic expressions of human activity" (Asen 2010, 110).

Boaz and Palmer, like Bush, depict the ownership society as an attractive vision that promises individual autonomy, agency, and ultimate self-realization. The aim of the ownership society is to create the owner as a specific type of subject: owners not only strive to improve their property but also their selves, namely by cultivating "healthy habits of behavior," as Geoff Mulgan, top aide to former British Prime Minister Tony Blair suggested (qtd. in Boaz 2004). Life in the ownership society thus entails the disciplining of the self and demands specific forms of behavior. Specifically, the ownership society asks the individual to take on responsibilities for risks formerly borne by public institutions, as becomes apparent in the reform proposals advanced by the Bush administration.

A Nation of Homeowners?

Between 2002 and 2004, the Bush administration defined specific policy areas to realize the ownership society. Reform proposals included the expansion of homeownership, the privatization of Social Security, health care, and public schools, as well as plans to tighten bankruptcy laws, the replacement of income and wealth taxes with consumption taxes, and the elimination of welfare "entitlements" (Wray 2005b, 7). Bush's focus on homeownership, particularly in the first years of his presidency, held large symbolic significance. With Americans traditionally associating property ownership with the home, an already increasing homeownership rate, and a booming housing sector, Bush could introduce his far-reaching transformations of public institutions by promoting the ownership society in an area already considered a unanimous good and a mainstay of federal policy and presidential rhetoric.

Moreover, by particularly addressing minority citizens, Bush emphasized inclusiveness. His 2003 American Dream Downpayment Initiative (ADDI) supported prospective low-income homeowners unable to contribute a down payment for a mortgage; it provided 200 million dollars annually for down payment assistance, offering grants of up to 10,000 dollars or 6 percent of the purchase price of the home (whichever was greater), as a grant for low-income, first-time homebuyers. ADDI was signed into law in December 2003 and mainly targeted minority families, who were traditionally underrepresented among homeowners.[12] During a time in which the private financial industry was already expanding its credit products to sell loans and mortgages to previously excluded groups with low incomes and no assets, Bush declared as his goal to enable 5.5 million minority families to own their own homes over the next ten years. As Ofelia Cuevas critically notes, Bush's acknowledgement of the gap between Anglo-American and minority homeownership rates "was a significant discursive shift for a president who had shown little concern for black or brown people" (2012, 614). She argues that the actual motivation behind his support for minority ownership was to cater to the industry that sold the financial products involved; African Americans and Hispanics were thus "allowed to enter the housing market not as active agents [. . .] but as consumers of debt-as-commodity" (615).

Tying in with the century-long history of federal homeownership initiatives, ADDI was not merely the least controversial of Bush's efforts to increase private ownership but in fact gathered broad bipartisan support (Mian, Sufi, and Trebbi 2008). More specifically, the act bore stark resemblance to a similar effort by Bush's predecessor, Bill Clinton, who had already sought to increase homeownership with his "National Homeownership Strategy" in 1995.[13] Clinton had taken office when the homeownership rate hovered around 64 percent, having dropped from its all-time high of 65.8 percent in 1980; he aimed to expand homeownership to 67.5 percent by the year 2000 (the rate actually climbed to 67.7 percent in the third quarter of 2000). Clinton did not institute new federal programs to help more families become homeowners but relied on "an alliance of the public and the private sector" (Clinton 1995, 808). In concrete terms, this meant further deregulation of the financial industry, which the Carter and Reagan administrations had already set into motion. Under Clinton, subprime mortgage loans and "predatory lending"[14]—exploitative, high-cost loans—gathered momentum: in 1995, the overall volume of the subprime mortgage loan market was 90 billion dollars; the amount then doubled over the next three years, while the number of subprime lenders also increased significantly (Canova 2008, 43). When George W. Bush was elected president, the mechanisms which would cause the 2007–2008 financial crisis were thus already in place; the housing bubble was already building and would reach its climax in 2004—the very moment of Bush's second presidential campaign and his proposition to expand homeownership.[15]

While supporting policies that advanced the financialization of the housing market, Clinton rhetorically advocated homeownership as something families "were entitled to [. . .] as part of the American dream" (Clinton 1995, 808). He pictured homeownership as being "about the way we live as a people and what kind of a society we're going to have" (806); it enabled people to "have a stake in a better life" (807); it "strengthens our economy [. . .] and builds better citizens" (808). Thus, Clinton advocated many of the values that would become characteristic of Bush's rhetoric as well: homeownership as a unanimous good, the idea of an intrinsic link to American citizenship, as well as the perspective of a better future society. Yet, Clinton remained focused on homeownership and avoided the term "property," whereas Bush usually lists homeownership as only the first of several goals in a more expansive vision. He thus conflates the ownership of houses with that of other financial assets, thereby trying to transport the positive connotations of the home as a place of privacy and security to these other forms of private ownership.

In essence, the promotion of homeownership as Bush's first ownership-related policy proposal strategically served to portray his administration's broader efforts to strengthen privatization in a positive light—further bolstered by the actual steady increase of homeownership throughout the nation at the time, as well as concomitant rising property values. He relied on a prominent conservative ideal in which "land ownership mythologically becomes ownership, and the ideology then mythologically extends to whatever we normally denominate property" (Radin 1993, 12). As Béland has noted, ADDI was actually rather modest in its scope; its objective was to help approximately 40,000 families per year with their down payments and to provide insurance through the FDA for first-time homebuyers who did not contribute a down payment, thus relating only to a fraction of the entire housing market.[16] The limited reach of the policy "contrasts strongly with the president's optimistic and ambitious rhetoric" (Béland 2007, 98). The positive projection, however, was complemented by a less explicit dystopian vision: in the area of Social Security, Bush drew the image of a much riskier future, one characterized by the imminent demise of the retirement system.

Realizing the Ownership Society through Social Security Reform

Bush could point directly to the alleged success of his policies in the housing sector while proposing to reform Social Security, thereby rallying to gather support for a conservative reform project of a popular institution that the public at large did not perceive to be in urgent need of reform (Asen 2009, 199). In 2001, he had already appointed the bipartisan Commission to Strengthen Social Security that recommended partial privatization. After his reelection, Bush promoted a plan that would allow workers to divert 4 percent of their wages into a private retirement account. In its current form, Bush argued, Social Security was "headed toward bankruptcy" (Bush 2005a, 115). According to his administration's calculation, Social Security in its current state would start to pay out more than it took in by 2018 and exhaust its funds by 2042.[17] While Bush promised that he would not change the system for workers over the age of 55, he proposed "a better deal for younger workers," "personal accounts" to "build a nest egg for your own future," and the option "to pass along the money that accumulates [. . .] to your children and—or grandchildren." And he stressed that "best of all, the money in the account is yours, and the Government can never take it away" (Bush 2005a, 116). Bush thus proposed individual profit and security at the expense of collective solidarity.

With its program to reform Social Security, the Bush administration "turn[ed] away from well-established, successful policy strategies of broadening ownership and intensifie[d] the shifting of risk to individuals" (J. L. Brown, Kuttner, and Shapiro 2005, 2). The proposal triggered a large debate on privatization, which, however, ultimately did not result in any legislation being successfully passed by Congress. Many of Bush's critics were doubtful about these promises, fearing that the reform would lead to an even earlier depletion of Social Security funds, as contributions by younger workers would be partly taken out of the solidarity system. They also criticized the notion that individuals would make better investment decisions and generate greater returns than the public fund invested in U.S. treasury bonds. To them, it was more likely that private investments would become more risky and more severely subjected to financial market cycles (Levinson 2005, 33–34). Such privatization, Randall Wray argued, "would produce high management fees for Wall Street and low returns for tomorrow's seniors" (2005a, 3; see also Krugman 2005, 6). Not surprisingly, the plan was backed by its largest benefactors, the financial and insurance industries (Soederberg 2007, 104).

Social Security stands for one of the most significant achievements of the Franklin D. Roosevelt administration and thus exemplifies the New Deal state; it is highly symbolic as an institution that redistributes wealth and risk in society. Paul Krugman criticized "Social Security privatization [as] a solution in search of a problem," a deliberate attempt by the political right to dismantle an institution they had "always disliked" (2005, 8). This view was inadvertently confirmed from inside the administration itself: Peter Wehner, Bush's Director of Strategic Initiatives, in a 2005 confidential internal memo—subsequently published by the *Wall Street Journal*—considered the privatization of Social Security, if successful, "as one of the most significant conservative governing achievements ever." For Wehner, the overarching goal was "to promote both an ownership society and advance the idea of limited government." In this context, "Social Security reform [was] not simply an economic challenge, but a moral goal and a moral good"—and a "battle" that conservatives, "for the first time in six decades," stood a chance at winning. As Asen has pointed out, the Wehner memo underlines that conservatives did not merely believe that the Social Security system had become economically unsustainable in its current form, but that its very principles were at odds with their espoused libertarian values (2009, 201–02).

Intent on pushing Social Security reform after his reelection, Bush prominently addressed the ownership society in his second Inaugural Address on January 20, 2005, emphasizing it as part of his core domestic political vision, in a speech characterized by highly idealistic language. In a 2004 address, he had already argued that the United States was recovering from the September 11 attacks "because we're a strong people, we're resilient, because there's an ownership society, a culture of ownership in America" (Bush 2006c, 311). Speaking while U.S. military were fighting in Afghanistan and Iraq, Bush dedicated his speech to "America's ideal of freedom," using the term "freedom" to bracket foreign and domestic politics. Bush relied on freedom as a floating signifier to invoke the ideals of the American Revolution, extending them to the arena of world politics. Seeing it as America's "mission" to expand "freedom in all the world" (Bush 2007a, 66), Bush employed the term in the sense of a negative liberty, the absence of tyranny and oppression. The term also blends the freedom of the individual with that of a political community; it denotes "the imperative of self-government, because no one is fit to be a master and no one deserves to be a slave" (66). Invoking slavery, Bush also implicitly alludes to the positive connotations the term freedom gained in the struggle of African Americans in the context of abolitionism and during the civil rights movement. Throughout the address, Bush figuratively associates tyrannical government with a master-slave relationship. Due to the abstractness of his terms, "liberty" and "freedom" remain unspecific; by invoking notions of "self-government" and slavery, however, liberty, in this case, can be most strongly interpreted as economic freedom, as the right to one's own body and labor.

As he turns from foreign policy to domestic issues, this very notion of freedom being understood primarily as economic legitimizes Bush to link these two spheres, as he proclaims:

> In America's ideal of freedom, citizens find the dignity and security of economic independence, instead of laboring on the edge of subsistence. This is the broader

> definition of liberty that motivated the Homestead Act, the Social Security Act, and the G.I. Bill of Rights. And now we will extend this vision by reforming great institutions to serve the needs of our time. To give every American a stake in the promise and future of our country, we will bring the highest standards to our schools and build an ownership society. We will widen the ownership of homes and businesses, retirement savings, and health insurance, preparing our people for the challenges of life in a free society. By making every citizen an agent of his or her own destiny, we will give our fellow Americans greater freedom from want and fear, and make our society more prosperous and just and equal. (68)

Freedom, in Bush's rhetoric, possesses a utopian quality: the ideal is both a legacy of the Founding Fathers and a promise of the future, of an ultimately just society, where all citizens are truly equal. When speaking about "dignity" and "security," he endows "independence" with a moral significance and an affective dimension. Giving people in other parts of the world dignity through economic freedom is supposed to foster national security, just as economic independence is a source of security and dignity for American citizens. Moreover, economic independence is contrasted with "laboring at the edge of subsistence," thus implying that individuals can only flourish through economic self-determination. Invoking the Homestead Act, the Social Security Act and the G.I. Bill of Rights as great achievements to the commitment of liberty—three historical instances of landmark legislation that helped to distribute wealth more democratically among Americans in the past—Bush announces his intent to remake these "great institutions to serve the needs of our time." He thus puts his own proposals in line with these former acts, while at the same time advancing legislation that changes their fundamental character, thereby justifying his intervention as being progressive and future-oriented. In Bush's rhetoric, the commitment to ownership appears at the symbolic core of American values, which is also underlined by his allusion to Roosevelt's "Four Freedoms" speech at the end of the paragraph cited above. Here, Bush approximates himself to Roosevelt as being both inventor of Social Security and wartime president, thus reestablishing the link between world politics and domestic policy.

For Bush, freedom, understood as economic liberty, bears a large moral significance: "The public interest depends on private character, on integrity and tolerance toward others and the rule of conscience in our own lives. Self-government relies, in the end, on the governing of the self." The autonomy of the self depends on disciplining the self; successful membership in the ownership society requires an adherence to conservative moral values, that is, "character" which is "built in families, supported by communities with standards" (Bush 2007a, 68). The reform of social institutions through their privatization and financialization is here thus also promoted as "a way to develop the self" (R. Martin 2002, 9). The autonomous self learns to accept and manage ever higher risks at a moment in which the institutional structures, meant to soften these risks, are being dismantled, foremost among them Social Security.

These values can be illustrated by pointing to the influential thought of economists Friedrich von Hayek and Milton Friedman, who characterized Social Security as an instrument of an ever-expanding welfare state that encroached on individual liberties as early as the 1960s. They criticized Social Security's compulsory nature as well as the state monopoly on providing Social Security insurance. They also suggested that Social Security did not work like insurance but more properly had to be understood as a coercive income redistribution scheme (Hayek 1960, 285–305; M. Friedman 1962, 182–89). The system of retirement benefits, Friedman explains in *Capitalism and Freedom*, was to the advantage of those who entered the system at a later age, at the expense of someone who entered young; in such a case, wealth was redistributed from the young to the old, independently of the participants' previous economic positions. Friedman also questioned that such a system would be self-financing in the long run, making subsidies from the general taxpayers necessary (M. Friedman 1962, 184). For Friedman and Hayek, such redistribution is immoral. Even more starkly, Robert Nozick suggests more generally that any kind of "taxation of earnings from labor is on par with forced labor," because it requires a person to work more hours than he or she will effectively be paid for (Nozick 1974, 169). According to Nozick, taxation is equivalent to "seiz[ing] some of a man's leisure [. . .] for the purpose of serving the needy" and therefore deeply illegitimate (170). For Hayek, Friedman, and Nozick, Social Security is ultimately irreconcilable with their understanding of individual autonomy and represents a state-mandated system of redistribution that creates a culture of dependency and undermines self-reliance (Avsar 2008, 126–27). These arguments emphasize that the debate around Social Security centers on a conflict between two fundamentally different visions of society: "Social Security," Mark Levinson points out, "is based on the *socialization of concern*, the vision of society as a community, which even if not based on truly egalitarian principles, at least modulates the heartlessness of 'rugged individualism'" (2005, 34).

Bush's Social Security reform project ultimately failed to come to fruition. Congress did not pass any Social Security legislation before the Congressional elections of 2006, in which Democrats gained majorities in both the Senate and the House. The window of opportunity for conservatives to reshape the solidarity system had—at least temporarily—closed. Yet, despite this setback, the campaign for reforming Social Security had far-reaching consequences, as it raised doubt about the program in the public mind. As a result of these political debates, "insurance no longer reigns supreme as a guiding principle of retirement policy" (Asen 2009, 231). The fact that the fundamental values of Social Security have been called into question impacts future discussions, potentially paving the way for new schemes of privatization and financialization.

THE CONSEQUENCES OF OWNERSHIP DISCOURSE

For most Americans, the home is a sacred place that warrants special protection. The legal conception of property as a bundle of rights, subject to political negotiation, poses a threat to this emotional dimension of homeownership because it does not account for cultural sensibilities or the fact that some property rights may be more important than others. Framing property as a constitutional right pays tribute to the cultural ideal but may, in practice, do little to actually protect homeowners. Instead, it has served to advance the political agenda of a conservative property rights movement during the last decades. Popularizing the idea of property as being a natural right, the property rights movement has succeeded in creating a public discourse on the limits and the legitimacy of government. Invoking the moral dimension of property ownership, the proponents of the movement have worked to naturalize a specific, libertarian ideal of social and economic relationships. Assuming that markets are egalitarian and deny structural inequalities, this vision prioritizes private market relationships and depicts the individual and the state as adversaries. Ultimately, the property rights movement seems to serve a different clientele than it ostensibly addresses, protecting larger property interests from government interference and foreclosing debates on policy options that threaten these interests. To the extent that the movement depoliticizes questions of economic distribution and property allocation, it exacerbates the very inequalities at the heart of economic development conflicts.

Forging a positive vision of the United States as an "ownership society," the Bush administration built on the same ideas about property ownership and the sanctity of the home as the conservative activists in the eminent domain cases, employing the notion of property as the absolute, private right to instigate a fundamental reconstruction of the welfare state. The Bush administration and its conservative allies promoted the ownership society, in order to create a hegemonic social discourse that made the reshaping of the social institutions look desirable and expedient to the public at large. The concept signified a further limitation of public investments which in effect redistributed wealth, thereby resulting in a shift from a communal solidarity to individual risk. The ownership society put trust in the forces of the market as an allegedly more "natural" way of organizing society and adapting to the needs of the times. Its proponents aimed to convince the public that a society that puts the self-interested and responsible individual at its center was more attractive and more future-oriented than the one brought into being during the New Deal era. The ownership society constituted a political vision that attempted to establish the property-owning individual as an identity category, thereby building a political coalition around the notion of property ownership. If citizens were understood as owners with material interests, this would generate a psychological shift—people holding assets would automatically become interested in protecting their wealth, all the more so if they shouldered considerable financial risk. In such a society, "class consciousness would be a relic" and workers-turned-owners would shift their party affiliation to those political forces committed to protecting their property rights (Klein 2008).

The libertarian utopian vision of the ownership society evoked the image of a democratic society in which every individual participated on equal terms in capitalist wealth creation. However, "the ownership-society reforms would have been likely to do the opposite, increasing inequality and concentrating wealth among the owner classes" (Wray 2005b, 30). The image of the United States as an ownership society with widespread wealth largely rested on the idea of the home being a significant asset owned by families across the spectrum of all income and wealth percentiles. Yet, as Wray had already correctly cautioned in 2005—before the crash of the housing market—counting homes as wealth is compromised by the fact that many supposed owners of their homes hold mortgages, with their debts rising quickly—especially so for people in the lower-income percentiles. With respect to other financial assets, such as stocks, the wealth distribution is heavily skewed toward higher-income groups (Wray 2005b, 22–25). Far from creating a hopeful, future-oriented society without structural hierarchies, a community that puts faith primarily in free-market relationships is bound to aggravate inequalities and in fact introduce a new hierarchy between owners and nonowners of property, the latter being excluded as legitimate members of the political sphere.

Ironically, and paradoxically, the vision of the ownership society, with its promise of individual agency and control and nonhierarchical social relationships, appeared particularly attractive in the face of people's increasing experiences with expanding risks and the lack of agency during the past quarter century: less job and wage security; fewer unemployment benefits, more precarious health insurance, and rising out-of-pocket health-related costs; housing insecurity and education-related debt—all, to a large extent, consequences, in fact, of deliberate political choices to deregulate the markets and cut public funding, the very measures which would have further been exacerbated in Bush's ownership society (J. L. Brown, Kuttner, and Shapiro 2005, 3–7).

Though it promised the inclusion of all citizens, the ownership society ultimately distinguished between owners and nonowners, the latter being excluded as allegedly choosing to opt out or failing to take on the responsibilities of ownership. Since the lower and middle-income classes are more exposed to financial risks, asset building for them is less feasible, whereas the new options generated through financialization enable people with higher incomes to increase their investments and secure their own future risks. The ownership discourse thus curiously inverts risks and responsibilities; it holds people responsible for events outside their immediate control—such as job loss and health problems—while framing deliberate political choices as being merely reactive to the demands of a changing world and the realization of a "natural" ideal. The ownership society thus seeks to transform the realm of politics as such, making debates about a social redistribution of resources among citizens appear immoral and illegitimate. To borrow from Adam Smith's *The Wealth of Nations*, the ownership society defends "the rich against the poor, or [. . .] those who have some property against those who have none at all" (A. Smith [1776] 1976, 715).

NOTES

1. "And the law of England has so particular and tender a regard to the immunity of a man's house, that it styles it his castle, and will never suffer it to be violated with impunity: agreeing herein with the sentiments of ancient Rome, as expressed in the words of Tully: 'quid enim sanctius, quid omni religione munitius, quam domus uniuscujusque civium?'" (Blackstone 1915, 4:223–24).

2. In *Kyllo v. United States* (533 U.S. 27 [2001]) the U.S. Supreme Court ruled that law enforcement was not allowed to search a person's home without a warrant, not even with technology that did not physically enter the house, like, in the Kyllo case, a thermal imaging device. "Stand Your Ground" laws allow citizens to protect their property, themselves, or other persons against perceived threats.

3. The overhaul of the tax code in December 2017 reduced these privileges but did not revoke them. I discuss this more extensively in the Coda.

4. The print media picked up the issue nationwide in the days and weeks after the Supreme Court decision. While national newspapers were generally more restrained, most reactions were overtly critical of the Court. The day after the decision, *USA Today* ran a front page article entitled "Seizing Land for Private Use OK'd" (Biskupic 2005), and an editorial in the same edition was headed "Ruling Leaves Door Open to Abuse." *The Wall Street Journal's* headline read: "Local Governments Cleared to Take Private Property If Projects Promise Growth" (Bravin 2005). The Florida local paper *St. Petersburg Times* headlined with "Your Home Could Be up for Grabs"

(Trigeaux 2005), which was followed up by a story entitled "A Person's Home Is the Government's Parcel" (Dyckman 2005) a few days later. One column in the *Hartford Courant* asked "When does Economic Benefit Trump Local Control?" (Jacklin 2005), while another article in the same paper advised: "Plan Expertly Before Grabbing" (Haar 2005). For a more extensive delineation of the media coverage of the *Kelo* decision, see Wolf (2008a, 16–22).

5. Before *Kelo*, one of the most widely publicized eminent domain cases had been the Michigan Supreme Court decision in *Poletown Neighborhood Council v. City of Detroit* (1981), which allowed the condemnation of a neighborhood predominantly inhabited by immigrants for the expansion of General Motors. In *County of Wayne v. Hathcock* (2004), the state court revised its previous decision.

6. The Institute for Justice filed suit on behalf of the Saleets and their neighbors in May 2003 in the Cuyahoga County Court of Common Pleas. In November of 2003, the citizens of Lakewood rejected the economic development plan, and in 2004 they rescinded the blight designation that would have allowed the city to take the properties ("Saleet v. City of Lakewood" 2004).

7. Eminent domain discourse has also entered the genre of film: Benedict's *Little Pink House* has been turned into a movie of the same title, directed by Courtney Balaker with Catherine Keener starring as Susette Kelo. The movie premiered in the United States in February 2017. Eminent domain has further been the subject of two documentaries, as well as another movie in recent years. *Battle for Brooklyn* (2011) documents the fight of citizens against a real estate development project in the Prospect Heights neighborhood of Brooklyn, while the independent film *Greetings from Asbury Park* (2009) follows a 91-year-old woman's defiance of the condemnation of her home in New Jersey. And in *Split Ends* (2009), a movie starring Vincent Pastore and Corinna May, a hairdresser takes on an unscrupulous real estate developer.

8. The popular press featured books with titles such as *Bulldozed: "Kelo," Eminent Domain and the American Lust for Land* (Main 2007), *Stolen Fields* (Boggio 2008), or *Abuse of Power* (Greenhut 2004). In academic discourse, the work of Richard Epstein (2008; 2011) has been particularly influential. Another prominent voice is that of Ilya Somin (2015).

9. An earlier version of this section has appeared in *Finance and Society* (Knewitz 2018).

10. Jeremy Waldron (1988) provides a detailed discussion of philosophical arguments advanced in defense of private property. Libertarian perspectives on property and the role of the state were established, most prominently, by Friedrich von Hayek in *The Constitution of Liberty* (1960); Milton Friedman in *Capitalism and Freedom* (1962) and Robert Nozick in *Anarchy, State, and Utopia* (1974).

11. It is precisely in cases such as this that the "tragedy of the commons," described in Garrett Hardin's famous 1968 article, occurs: without regulations enforced by a government, companies will have no incentive to protect resources that belong to all, like air and water, because their private gain will outweigh their losses which will be imposed on society as a whole. These resources, as Hardin points out, "cannot readily be fenced," and therefore exploitation needs to be averted through different means, "by coercive laws or taxing devices that make it cheaper for the polluter to

treat his pollutants than to discharge them untreated" (1968, 1245). Such regulations, however, require government institutions; rational market actors who maximize their profits will not voluntarily agree to shoulder the losses.

12. In December 2003, the African American homeownership rate was at 49.4 percent (Hispanics: 47.7 percent; non-Hispanic whites: 75.5 percent), which in fact was also its peak—the rate then started to decline again and went down to 42.4 percent in the third quarter of 2015, putting it at roughly the same level as in 1995. The Hispanic homeownership rate peaked at 50.1 percent in 2007 and has now dropped to 46.1 percent. In comparison, the rate for non-Hispanic whites peaked in 2005 at 76.2 percent and has meanwhile declined to 71.9 percent, one percentage point higher than the 1995 rate (U.S. Census Bureau 2020).

13. As Béland has pointed out, Bush's rhetoric also draws on Margaret Thatcher's "popular capitalism," which similarly envisioned an ownership society in Great Britain in the 1980s and which invoked a similar discourse on ownership with its moral and economic inflections (2007, 94).

14. The exact definition of which loans should be considered "predatory" is contested; for an extensive discussion of the term, see, for example, Engel and McCoy (2001, 1259–70).

15. A more detailed discussion of the relationship between Bush's rhetoric and the structural conditions of the housing crisis is beyond the scope of this chapter. Clearly, it would be a mistake to attribute the crisis singularly to Bush's promotion of the ownership society. Congress passed policies which helped the expansion of the subprime mortgage market during the time of the Bush administration, often with bipartisan support, while initiatives to regulate or prohibit predatory lending could not gain enough legislative support (Mian, Sufi, and Trebbi 2008).

16. According to a June 2006 report by the U.S. Government Accountability Office, jurisdictions had spent 98.5 million dollars to aid approx. 13,000 families by December 31, 2005, during the first two years of the ADDI programs; about half of the beneficiaries were minorities (4).

17. These calculations were highly contested. Randall Wray called the idea of Social Security's imminent bankruptcy a "preposterous claim," advanced by conservative think tanks (2005a, 2). Mark Levinson, chief economist at UNITE HERE!, argued that, while Social Security would indeed pay out more than it took in from 2018 onward, these expenses would be funded to a large extent through the fund's investment in U.S. Treasury securities—enabling the system to continue through 2053 without changes. After that, there would be a 20 percent gap in funds needed to pay all scheduled benefits. The missing funds would, however, amount to "only one-half of the tax cut Bush provided the richest 2 percent families" (Levinson 2005, 32).

Conclusion

Contested Property Claims

I opened this study with a reading of photographs of foreclosed homes taken in the immediate aftermath of the housing crisis of 2007–2008. These images speak of both a nostalgia for an American dream perceived as dead and an anger against a predatory financial industry and a government that failed to protect its citizens from financial ruin. Staging the substantial financial and cultural investment in homes as the quintessential form of middle-class wealth, these pictures illustrate the American commitment to property ownership. More than a decade after the Great Recession and in spite of a reinvigorated national economy, the consequences of the crisis still vibrate within U.S. public and political discourses. Its traces are also visible, according to a study by the Pew Research Center, in "a sharp, prolonged decline in the wealth of American families" and an exacerbated wealth gap between white households and Hispanic and black ones (Kochhar and Cilluffo 2017). The Obama administration's response to the crisis—which prioritized saving the banks over helping insolvent homeowners (Judis 2016, 54–55)—sparked populist movements on the right (like the Tea Party) and the left (like Occupy Wall Street), and eventually the presidential candidacies of Donald Trump, Bernie Sanders, and Elizabeth Warren.

These recent developments raise questions about the present and future meaning of property in the American cultural imagination and the country's social and political institutions. However, as I want to suggest in conclusion to my investigation over the past five chapters, the housing crisis as well as the controversial Trump presidency should be read less as a caesura than as a catalyst for processes that have been long in the making. Viewed through the lens of property discourse, current public debates tie in with established antagonisms about the role and functions of governments, the relationship between the individual and the state, and the relations between different racial groups. The profound transformations that capitalism faces in our digital age, however, may challenge our understanding of property and property rights in even more radical ways.

THE POLITICS OF PRIVATE PROPERTY IN THE UNITED STATES

This study has established the long-term trajectory of the rhetoric and politics of private property in the United States and thereby placed contemporary debates on property rights from a historical perspective. I set out to investigate the ways in which discourses about property legitimatize, naturalize, and challenge the social and economic order and how property structures the relationships among individuals and social groups. Scrutinizing instances when the country's social institutions and established property relationships were subject to intense controversy, my discussion has zoomed in on paradigmatic moments in U.S. history: the industrial revolution and the slavery question in the antebellum era, the rise of corporations and the new consumer culture at the turn of the twentieth century, the social movements of the 1960s, and the emergence of a conservative property rights movement in the late twentieth century. Within these historical debates, property issues were subject to continuous conflict about resources as well as to negotiations of political, economic, and social power. Therefore, the property narrative I have crafted in the preceding chapters notably diverts from those put forward in previous studies of U.S. property culture which have—with either a positive or a negative slant—regarded the commitment to private property ownership as being an important part of a national consensus, if not the country's civil religion. In distinction, I propose to view property as a fundamentally political concept, and the contentions over the distribution of material resources as being intertwined with antagonisms within the discursive field. My investigations of property discourses make visible the structural and systemic dimensions of U.S. property culture, which otherwise too often remain veiled.

By providing this perspective on property, my work also helps to map out the intersections of law and culture. Subject to both politico-legal and cultural negotiations, the concept of property cannot be considered merely in the specialized discourse of the law; instead, it exemplifies the interactions between different cultural fields and property as an idea, institution, and cultural practice. *The Politics of Private Property* has underlined that legal property concepts and conflicts have cultural and political dimensions, while popular debates and practices are shaped and structured by property's legal institutions. As C. B. Macpherson proposed, property claims need a justifying framework, in order to be recognized as legitimate in a society. Thus, the idea of property is closely tied to the cultural narratives America tells about itself, which sanction specific property arrangements by naturalizing them, thereby establishing what is perceived as the right social order.

Property debates are conflicts about the continuity and change, the protection of established rights, and the acknowledgement of aspirational claims. Over the past two centuries, the economic and social structures of the United States have undergone profound structural changes, developing from an agrarian to an industrial society, which gave way to corporate capitalism and, more recently, to what has been termed "late capitalism" (Mandel 1978) or "postcapitalism" (Mason 2015). Considering the enormity of these cultural transformations, the endurance of specific rhetorical strategies within the cultural discourse is remarkable. The concept of property continues to assume central significance as a stabilizing force within the American cultural imagination. Property takes on the role of a hegemonic signifier in the negotiation of social and material structures. In conjunction with a number of other terms, most prominently "freedom," "equality," "privacy," and "home," property acts as an abstract, empty term that takes on multiple and conflicting meanings in different discursive figurations. Furthermore, the conservative power of property discourse in the United States is illustrated by the ongoing rhetorical legacy of the framers of the Constitution and the country's foundational documents, which throughout history appear as a central reference point. The American Revolution and the founding of the nation act as an origin myth for the country's cultural self-understanding, and the role of property is perpetually stressed within these documents and the intellectual thought of the time. References to the Declaration of Independence or the U.S. Constitution frame property contests as a matter of national importance; at the same time, this act of framing also stabilizes the concept of property, perpetuating its thing-like qualities.

Yet, despite the rhetorical dominance of property's conservative dimensions, we need to appreciate that the concept of property also dynamically adapts to economic, political, and legal shifts, reacting to and itself enabling transformations within the economic system. In politico-legal practice, property law evolved significantly over the course of American history, as did the way legal practitioners and theorists conceptualized property. Here, the history of property can be characterized as one of increasing abstraction, to the point of a disintegration of the concept of property as such: in a legal sense, property has discarded its thing-like shape and is now considered to be a set of rights, which define legal relationships between people. I therefore see the debates on property crystallize into what can be characterized as two rivaling but unequal legitimizing strategies: the "ownership model" and the "bundle of rights model" of property (Singer 2000, 1–13). The former relies on a static, material conception of property and conceptualizes ownership as an individual moral or even natural right; the latter views property in instrumental terms, emphasizing its nature as being a set of variable rights and obligations instituted by society. These strategies dominate different yet overlapping areas of discourse. The ownership model relates most closely to the idea of property in the American cultural imagination; the bundle of rights model currently defines how property works as a legal institution.

Rooted in the theories of John Locke, William Blackstone, and other liberal thinkers, the ownership model has been foundational for the way Americans think about the relationship between the private and public spheres, the state and the individual. Liberalism claims that individual rights and subjectivity precede social and political institutions. Locating the private realm outside the boundaries of the state, liberal theory posits the protection of individual private property rights as the ultimate end of government. At the same time, property ownership appears to be a prerequisite to attain full citizenship and individual agency. Though explicit property requirements for political participation were abolished in the first half of the nineteenth century, the ownership of property has remained significant for constructions of a U.S. social identity.

Conceived as a negative liberty, the ownership model promises a basic egalitarianism, attributing each individual with a natural right to his or her own body and fruits of labor. It presumes an economy that is structured nonhierarchically, where every individual has the same bargaining power, and the role of the government is at best a neutral one. I have termed this to be the aspirational dimension of property discourse, which surpasses the mere possession of material wealth and imbues property ownership with a moral dimension. Thus, within a culture of "possessive individualism" (Macpherson 1962), property, for the most part of U.S. history, has been framed in a positive fashion, through its association with freedom, individual agency, personhood, and citizenship. Significantly, harking back to the early period of the American nation, when the economy was structured around the ownership of land, this vision is considerably invested in material forms of property. Though wealth and property rights are certainly not limited to real estate and tangible objects, and indeed most property today exists in intangible forms, the cultural imagination still seems to prioritize physical forms of property, such as land or a house.

The rivaling legitimizing framework, the bundle of rights model of property, does away with this physicalist conception and replaces it with a more abstract understanding of property. Building on utilitarian theory in the tradition of Jeremy Bentham, proponents of this model consider property to be a function of the law and therefore focus on its commodity functions. In this sense, the distribution of property in society comes down to policy decisions about the most efficient use of resources, which guides the distribution of rights and privileges among the members of society. Property here means a set of social relationships, which entails both rights and obligations, and is subject to historical change. Rather than merely preserving a fixed order, by protecting established individual rights, the bundle of rights model appears to be more dynamic.

Historically, this model evolved as a theoretical scheme in the context of the corporate revolution in the late nineteenth century, as the law had to engage with changing economic structures which it concomitantly was helping to shape. Property as a bundle of rights more closely corresponded to an economic reality in which various actors simultaneously held different interests in an object of property. Its basic premise, the insight that property is a social creation, however, also provided legal scholars of the progressive era, most prominently Wesley Hohfeld, with the opportunity to devise a legal approach that legitimized government regulations of the excesses of laissez-faire capitalism.

Joseph Singer has argued that the ownership model is "misleading and morally deficient" (2000, 6) because it posits a particular social arrangement as being natural and encourages a framework based on self-interest rather than mutual obligation. In distinction, the bundle of rights model highlights the political nature of property, the fact that all property regimes are the result of choices. In this understanding, government does not "intrude" in the rights of individuals but negotiates choices between competing property claims (Singer 2014, 5). However, this approach is derived from a specific historical and political context, which is no more neutral than that from which the ownership model emerged. It relies on a particular set of values about social justice and claims precedence of public interest over individual property rights. Yet, whereas the ownership model is explicit about the positive values it advances and speaks to people's affective, cultural investment in property, the bundle of rights model tends to operate on a more technical level. It thus fails to offer an alternative legitimizing framework to truly rival the ownership model in the American cultural imagination.

While property in the ownership conception appears to be founded on strongly egalitarian claims, this understanding simultaneously privileges the protection of previously established property rights, thereby fueling potential conflicts between those members of a society aspiring to become property owners and those who have their rights already established. As an individual right, property therefore tends to function in deeply conservative ways: if a person is granted a natural right to what he or she owns, any schemes of redistribution will be subject to challenges, and the established property rights of some will hinder the acquisition of property by others. Historically, this problem, to some extent, was mitigated through the availability of large tracts of land, enabling citizens to become land- and homeowners without impacting established property rights—that is, on property rights recognized by the U.S. government, while the native American population's claims to the land were disregarded.

Accordingly, the American history of property is also a history of systemic exclusions. Indeed, as this study has also demonstrated, the discourse on property is closely tied to the construction of the white middle class, at the expense of indigenous populations, African Americans, and other racial and ethnic minorities. While the dispossession of Native Americans resolved the United States' hunger for land, withholding the fruits of their labor from African Americans drove the expansion of the American economy in the early nineteenth century. Racial minorities were excluded from full membership in the polity and therefore also from the rights to property granted to white citizens. And discriminatory practices did not end with slavery: Black codes and Jim Crow laws ensured that African Americans remained in subservient positions, excluding most from acquiring land and the self-determined use of their labor, while the government promoted and subsidized the expansion of landownership for the white middle and working classes, for instance through the Homestead Act of 1862. In the twentieth century, continued and newly established government-sanctioned practices of segregation continued to exclude African Americans from equal access to property ownership. Most significantly, as white America developed into a nation of homeowners, with the help of favorable government-guaranteed loans and tax subsidies, most African Americans were actively excluded from the credit system. The widespread diffusion of property ownership among the white working- and middle-class population was thus intrinsically connected to racial privilege, creating a social hierarchy based on economic inequality, thus turning whiteness itself into a form of property. Therefore, while major developments in the democratization of property ownership occurred after economic crises and protests against economic inequality—as during the industrial revolution in the 1840s and the corporate revolution at the turn of the twentieth century—the resulting policy decisions regularly provided whites with a larger share of social wealth than African Americans.

PRIVATE PROPERTY IN TIMES OF POPULISM

Though the social safety measures of the New Deal developed out of the bundle of rights approach to property and have become important social and political institutions, programs of social welfare have consistently proven vulnerable to conservative attacks. As the preceding chapter has shown, over the last four decades, a conservative movement has strategically and successfully instrumentalized the idea of property as a natural and quintessentially American right, in the attempt to redraw the boundaries between government and individual responsibilities. Promoting free-market solutions as being allegedly more just and efficient forms of economic organization, the property rights movement has aimed explicitly at dismantling the welfare state, including such highly popular programs as Social Security. Importantly, conservatives have attempted to draw on the positive values traditionally associated with property ownership, such as individual freedom and agency, as well as on a widely prevailing distrust of the efficiency of governments to sell citizens a social vision that values individual responsibility over government "handouts." They strategically employ an originalist understanding of the Constitution, which claims that the document should be interpreted according to the framers' original intents and which ties in directly with the ownership model of property. Conservatives posit that the Constitution stands above politics, thus attempting to disavow the charge that they employ historical positions to advance a specific political agenda. Yet, as Jamal Greene notes, originalism must be understood as a way of casting political positions "in putatively neutral terms and therefore branding the agenda as a whole consistent with constitutional fidelity" (2009, 86).

Since the Reagan era, conservatives have been successful in shifting the political center toward more market-oriented policies, substantially cutting back on government-sponsored welfare programs and market regulations. Paradoxically, however, much of the ire of right-wing protest movements after the financial crisis was not directed at free-market advocates. Though market deregulations had enabled the excesses of the financial industry, which led to the financial crisis in the first place, the Tea Party movement emerged in 2009 in opposition to the Obama administration's handling of the crisis. Tea Partiers rallied around the very libertarian themes of small government and individual freedom that conservative organizations had long been promoting. Through their electoral successes, since the midterm elections of 2010, Tea Party candidates pushed the Republican Party into more conservative positions and mainstreamed a kind of constitutional originalism that was also characteristic of the property rights movement (Foley 2012, xi). The movement built on the belief that solutions to contemporary problems can be found in the text of the Constitution and the framers' intents, with its meaning being fixed and readily available to all who take the time to educate themselves, and that, above all, the overarching purpose of the Constitution is to ensure a limited government (Schmidt 2011, 194).

As a number of studies have demonstrated, the Tea Party cannot be considered a unified movement, and relationships between grassroots organizations, powerful donors, conservative media, and right-wing political organizations are certainly complex[1] and often contradictory. Significantly, many Tea

Party sympathizers actually held favorable views of Social Security and Medicare—which they consider to be social protections earned through their tax contributions—while rejecting welfare programs and the Affordable Care Act as government services for the "undeserving." As John B. Judis notes, Tea Party members' "arguments about 'makers' and 'takers' recalled the 'producerism' of the Jacksonians and the People's Party, which was rooted in a distinction between productive and unproductive elements of society. Bankers, land speculators, and gamblers were typically numbered among the unproductive—as were, for the populists, recent immigrants who took jobs from native-born Americans" (2016, 57). We may also associate the Tea Party movement with the "fruits of labor" ideology that proliferated in the United States after the American Revolution and in the property discourses of the nineteenth century. As Theda Skocpol and Vanessa Williamson point out, the "Tea Party distinction between freeloaders and hardworking taxpayers has ethnic, nativist, and generational undertones" and that, within this binary, "deservingness is a cultural category, closely tied to certain racially and ethnically tinged assumptions about American society in the early twenty-first century" (2012, 74).

Viewed in this context, Donald Trump's candidacy and eventual ascendance into the office of the president seems less like an aberration than a continuity. Trump centrally built on the narratives of producerism in his 2016 campaign (Oswald 2019, 109). In his populist campaign rhetoric, Trump played on popular Tea Party beliefs, such as the racially charged division of citizens being either "makers" or "takers," skepticism about experts and political elites, and the critique of alleged government corruption. In his ads, Trump attacked "the establishment" and stylized himself as an advocate of "the people," arguing that because he was self-funding his (primary) campaign, he didn't "owe anybody anything. I only owe it to the American people to do a great job" (Trump 2016). Picturing the United States as a nation in crisis, Trump tapped into the anger of large parts of the working and middle classes, directed at the country's economic and political elites. Playing up his credentials as a successful entrepreneur and savvy businessman, he also significantly built on his media image as host of the reality TV show *The Apprentice*, flaunting material symbols as evidence of his financial success during his election campaign. His private jet served as an important prop at many of his campaign rallies, as did his properties, such as Trump Tower in New York and Mar-a-Lago in Florida.

While Trump's conspicuous display of personal property may stand in the tradition of Gilded Age captains of industry and robber barons, such as the Vanderbilts, the Rockefellers, or J. P. Morgan (D'Antonio 2016, 6), he would more accurately be placed in the context of the contemporary culture of branding. As Naomi Klein (2017) argues, Trump was less successful as an actual entrepreneur—his career being littered with bankruptcies—than in turning the Trump name into a brand, for which his televised performance of the successful businessman in *The Apprentice* was instrumental (28–34). The material signifiers of his wealth during the campaign reinforced "his brand as the ultimate capitalist success story—power and wealth incarnate" (33). The Trump phenomenon illustrates that, in the context of postmodern celebrity culture, property ownership assumes meaning primarily within an economy of signs: Trump's performance as property owner takes precedence over his actual material net worth.

In 2020, the Trump campaign took to calling up the specter of socialism, in order to discredit his Democratic opponent Joe Biden. In his nomination acceptance speech at the Republican National Convention, Trump framed the contest as a decision about "if we save the American dream or whether we allow a socialist agenda to demolish our cherished destiny"; he also called Biden "a Trojan horse for socialism" (Thrush 2020). On the campaign trail, he repeatedly warned his electorate that voting for Biden would ultimately empower his running-mate Kamala Harris and leave the country with a "female socialist president," once she succeeds Biden (Richardson 2020). Though neither Biden nor Harris advanced any political positions that could be remotely constructed as being socialist, Trump's message had traction with some of his electorate, most crucially with South Floridian Latino voters. As Heather Cox Richardson points out, there is a long tradition in American political discourse, reaching back to the post-Civil War years, to "cr[y] 'socialism' whenever ordinary Americans try to use the government to level the economic playing field by calling for business regulation—which will cost tax dollars by requiring bureaucrats—or for schools and roads, or by asking for a basic social safety net." While in the nineteenth century, white property holders insisted that black voting would result in the redistribution of wealth from hardworking whites to poor black people, thus constituting a form of socialism, the same charge is now voiced against any attempt to equalize access to resources.

The Trump administration, in spite of numerous scandals and its general air of dysfunction, has been successful in advancing many of the positions of the political right. Not coincidentally, Trump's strategist Stephen K. Bannon—meanwhile ousted—in February 2017 announced as one of the administration's primary goals the "deconstruction of the administrative state" (Rucker and Costa 2017)—an aim that seems to explain many of the decisions and appointments of Trump's first year in office. Ruling by executive orders, Trump reversed environmental regulations instituted by Obama and other previous administrations, a field in which property rights advocates have been particularly active in recent years.[2] The president also appointed the wealthiest cabinet in history, populating it with political outsiders whose merits were often derived from their accomplishments in business and finance—and who, in the past, have opposed the very agencies they were now chosen to lead. Thus, former Texas governor Rick Perry, champion of the oil and gas industry, was chosen to preside over the energy department (2017–2019), an institution he formerly believed should be eliminated (Davenport and Sanger 2017). Betsy DeVos, an advocate for the privatization of education, assumed the position of Secretary of Education, and, as head of the Environmental Protection Agency, Trump picked former Attorney General Scott Pruitt of Oklahoma, who formerly had worked closely with energy lobbyists to push back against the Obama administration's environmental regulations. Pruitt later resigned in July 2018.

Despite frictions with the Republican establishment, the administration and the Republican majority in Congress passed an overhaul of the tax code in 2017, which can also be interpreted as an attack on the "administrative state." The tax bill slashed taxes for corporations, while giving only modest tax cuts to individuals. According to an estimate by the Congressional Budget Office (2018), the cuts are expected to add 1.8 trillion dollars to the federal deficit. Defenders of the tax plan insisted that it would act as a stimulus for the economy, thereby compensating for the cuts by bringing in additional revenue. However, as then-Speaker of the House Paul Ryan stated on the TV program *Good Morning, America* (ABC) in December 2017, paying for the deficit would also almost certainly involve "getting spending under control," that is, cutting back on entitlement programs. Ryan suggested that future initiatives would focus on getting people "from welfare to work," thereby implying that cuts would be made on government programs for the needy ("Paul Ryan Reacts to Tax Reform Victory for GOP" 2017). However, the actual size of these programs was dwarfed by much more costly ones such as Social Security and Medicare.[3] Though Ryan denied that these entitlements would have to be reformed, the tax bill was believed to "open[] the door for the [Republican] party to need to cut these programs" (Bump 2017).

Viewed in the larger context of this study, the Trump administration seemed to align closely with the framework of originalism and the property rights movement, which is not least illustrated by Trump's picks for the Supreme Court, Justices Neil Gorsuch, Brad Kavanaugh, and Amy Coney Barrett, as well as more than two hundred lower-level federal appointees.[4] However, the Trump tax reform also broke, in interesting ways, with the established property rights narrative: while the property rights movement—at least in its strategic rhetoric—emphasized the constitutional rights of the individual, the tax bill explicitly favors corporations, reducing the corporate tax rate from 35 to 21 percent and thus encouraging individuals to incorporate themselves, in order to avoid higher individual tax rates. Real estate executives are projected to reap more profits under the new law, while owners of high-end homes and those living in high-tax states are expected to take losses, as the home mortgage interest deduction was capped at 750,000 dollars, and the deduction of state and local taxes from the federal tax bill at 10,000 dollars (Drucker and Rappeport 2017). As Andrew Ross Sorkin (2017) has pointed out, the idea that the tax reform benefits wealthy Americans is misleading; it, in fact, benefits the "ultra rich" who reap income through corporations, while most "merely rich" citizens will face higher taxes due to capped deductions.[5] The Trump administration thus notably diverged from the last Republican administration's "ownership society": the citizen as a homeowner is being replaced by the simulacrum of the celebrity entrepreneur. With his strategy of self-branding and self-incorporation, Trump symbolically erased the distinction between the corporation and the individual, thereby realigning "big business" with the individual and "the people" against "big government."

On the other end of the ideological spectrum, opposition against the neoliberal consensus, in the context of the financial crisis, first formed with the short-lived Occupy Wall Street movement, which claimed "the right of *we the people* to create a world that works for the 99%" (Van Gelder 2011). Relying on a stark binary distinction between the "elite" of the wealthiest one percent and the "people," or the bottom 99 percent, Occupy showed populist family resemblances with the Tea Party. Bernie Sanders's 2016 and 2020 primary campaigns, as well as Elizabeth Warren's 2020 bid for the presidency, also relied on this binary. Announcing his candidacy for the Democratic nomination on May 26, 2015, Sanders, similar to Trump and Occupy, spoke of the United States' "rigged economy" and of building a movement to fight the "same old establishment politics and stale inside-the-beltway ideas." He also promised jobs for "our struggling middle class" and a minimum wage of fifteen dollars. However, contrary to the demands of Tea Partiers and to Trump's agenda, the majority of his proposals concerned the expansion of the social safety net and government programs: universal health care; an expansion of Social Security benefits; tax increases for the rich; and free tuition in public universities and colleges. Sanders, in effect, proposed policy changes which conservatives denounce as being "socialist," but which he and his followers saw as "progressive," echoing the reforms of the progressive era and referencing the institutions of Scandinavian social democratic welfare states. Though Sanders received neither the 2016 nor the 2020 presidential nomination, his proposals have become firmly entrenched in the agenda of the Democratic Party's progressive wing and have contributed to moving the party as a whole to the left.

Conservative and liberal-progressive critics of the current status quo thus rely on opposing cultural narratives about the roles of government and the welfare state. Americans have been starkly polarized on core political values since the Obama presidency, and the gaps have even widened under the

Trump administration. Significantly, partisanship has become "*the* dividing line in the American public's political attitudes, far surpassing differences by age, race and ethnicity, gender, educational attainment, religious affiliation or other factors" (Pew Research Center 2019, 5). Republicans and Democrats diverge in their views about the role and functions of government and the perception of individual responsibilities and structural impediments. Seventy-eight percent of Democrats and Democratic-leaning independents wish that government would do more to solve problems, whereas 71 percent of Republicans and Republican leaners are of the opinion that government interferes too much in areas that should be left to individuals and businesses (24). At the same time, 61 percent of Republicans argue that government regulation of businesses does more harm than good, while three-fourths of Democrats believe that regulation is in the general public interest (24). And while 59 percent of Democrats believe that government should increase aid for people in need, only 17 percent of Republicans say the same (39).

The divide on these exemplary questions corresponds to the divisions between conservatives and progressives outlined above. For many (white) working- and middle-class Americans who sympathize with Trump and right-wing Republicans, the United States is a culture in crisis; they bemoan the loss of traditional values and are pessimistic about their own and their children's economic futures, and they see the government as being harmful rather than helpful (see, e.g., Vance 2016, 188–95). In distinction, progressives seek to harness the powers of government, in order to redistribute wealth more justly, to rebuild and strengthen the institutions of the New Deal, or to even transform the property system more thoroughly.

THE FUTURE OF PROPERTY DISCOURSE

My investigation has carved out the intricate ways in which the concept of property has put constraints on public and political discourses and the material structures of society throughout American history. In particular, it has become apparent that the idea of property as an individual, constitutionally guaranteed right has impeded radical critiques of the private property system. Neither the associationists nor the national reformers of the antebellum era, nor the socialist organizations of workers at the turn of the century, nor the radical branches of the black power movement in the 1960s were able to shatter the American commitment to private property. Although these movements aimed to make visible the systemic exclusions within capitalism and to advance alternative forms of social organization and wealth distribution, the dominant discourse regularly managed to normalize radical demands and reframe them in individual terms—unless it outlawed the proponents of these positions. Associationism, which aimed at creating communitarian living and workspaces, ultimately left its traces in the expanded access to private property ownership for the white working and middle classes after the Civil War. The socialist critiques of corporate capitalism triggered the response of progressive era reforms, which helped create a nation of homeowners and consumers. And the radical black power activism in the second half of the 1960s resulted in an expansion of the black middle class in the subsequent decade, although many of the members of the Black Panther Party were killed by police or jailed; less militant members of the movement, as well as the Nixon administration, meanwhile reframed "black power" as "black capitalism."

These historical experiences cast considerable doubt on the chances for success of contemporary attacks on the property system by the political left. In recent years, a number of critics have prophesied that the cultural investment in property and property rights is now coming to an end. According to Jeremy Rifkin and Paul Mason, among others, the mechanisms of capitalism, including the commitment to private property, were seriously called into question in the information age, when the principles of market exchange no longer worked and the ownership of property lost its importance. The model of the future, they hold, is that of the "sharing economy" (Mason 2015, xv), in which ownership is replaced by access. The idea that "acquiring and accumulating property are integral parts of our earthly sojourn and that who we are is, at least to some degree, a reflection of what we own," Rifkin suggests, will soon be an anachronism (2000, 4). Instead of investing in things, our wealth will be vested "in human imagination and creativity" (5).

Both Rifkin and Mason see in these large cultural transformations "an escape route" (Mason 2015, xv) from a society driven by market mechanisms and private ownership. In an age in which "information technology has reduced the need for work" (xv), new forms of collaborative production and exchange are emerging, which no longer follow the dictates of the market and established hierarchical systems; capitalism in its current form, Mason argues, will no longer be able to adapt. Instead, "info-capitalism has created a new agent of change in history: the educated and connected human being" (xvii). The new technologies, he claims, make "large parts of the utopian socialist project" of the mid-nineteenth century finally possible, "from cooperatives, to communes, to outbreaks of liberated behaviour that redefine human freedom" (xxi).

Neither Mason nor Rifkin believes that the futures they project will arrive automatically; instead, they envision a new route for social activism and a stronger role for the regulatory state that seizes upon the window of opportunity created by the crisis of capitalism. In doing so, they may, however, overstate the transformative potential of info-capitalism. Though technology enables people to connect and work collaboratively, the internet is profoundly shaped by media conglomerates with considerable power over the infrastructure necessary for these interactions. Instead of liberating its users, technology channels interaction in specific ways that are profitable to these companies—as is the case with social media platforms such as Facebook, Twitter, or Instagram. Rather than merely providing connections among users, these media also often participate in the creation of social divisions.

Moreover, it needs to be noted that these visions are written from a particular political vantage point which aligns with the liberal-progressive class position of highly educated knowledge workers. With their explicit rejection of property as a positive value, Mason and Rifkin position themselves in direct opposition to the conservative political right, which, as we have seen, strongly insists on fixed political meanings and a restrained role of the state. The educated "new agent[s] of change" are presumably members of the creative class, not the working- and middle-class Trump voters who currently work in menial jobs. It is possible and even likely that their work will be affected by the digital revolution as well, if only by their jobs becoming obsolete. But is the vision laid out by Mason a positive utopia to which they may want to subscribe? How will the lives of the less educated be transformed in a positive fashion in postcapitalism?

If Mason is right, capitalism has reached the limits of its capacity to adapt to new technological structures, and the culture of ownership rights will soon be an anachronism. Then, possibly, the discursive investment in private property as a positive value of individual freedom and agency will have to be replaced as well. As this study has demonstrated, however, such a transformation would entail an almost complete rejection of the discursive patterns that have guided political debates in the United States in its more than two-hundred-year past and the cultural values in which the country has been invested. In order to transform this ideational framework, I believe, contemporary progressives will have to develop a cultural vision about property rights that goes beyond the mere rejection of the capitalist private property system.

In the past, liberal theorists of property have occasionally attempted to reframe the concept of property within the ownership model in more inclusive terms—one may think of Charles Reich or Margaret Radin—yet, such approaches bear the danger of reinforcing the myth of property and are particularly vulnerable to conservative appropriation. Therefore, a progressive legitimizing strategy must rather build on the bundle of rights model of property and strengthen alternative values that place property in the context of mutual obligation and human relationships.[6] Such a strategy would not only have to take seriously the idea that property rights are social rights, but, more crucially, it would have to foster a cultural dialogue on the political nature of property.

NOTES

1. For some observers, the Tea Party amounts to an "astro-turf" movement that relies on an elite, top-down organization to promote pro-market business interests (see, e.g., Dimaggio 2011, 9). Others describe it as a genuine grassroots movement (Libby 2014). Both these views, however, seem too simplistic to account for the success of the Tea Party; studies like Skocpol and Williamson's (2012) shed light on how bottom-up and top-down elements mutually reinforce each other in this context.

2. The libertarian law firm Pacific Legal Foundation (PLF) has been one influential actor in this regard. For instance, the PLF organized opposition to the Clean Water Rule, introduced by President Obama in May 2015. Obama's executive order regulated the pollution of the waters of the United States, by, among other things, establishing stipulations that limited the use of chemical fertilizers. Invoking constitutionally guaranteed property rights, the PLF accused the federal government of intervening into state and local responsibilities in a "sweeping power grab." According to the PLF (2015), "property owners around the country" were "being micro-managed by federal bureaucrats." On January 22, 2018, the Supreme Court decided in favor of the PLF's challenge to the Clean Water Rule in the case *National Association of Manufacturers v. Department of Defense*. The Trump administration suspended the law and crafted a new version, which unsurprisingly turned out to be more industry-friendly (Davenport 2018; Department of Defense and Environmental Protection Agency 2020).

3. According to the Center on Budget and Policy Priorities, in the fiscal year 2016, Social Security made up 24 percent of the federal budget, and health care programs (Medicare, Medicaid, CHIP, and ACA marketplace subsidies) came in at 26 percent, whereas all safety net programs, combined, accounted for only 9 percent (Center on Budget and Policy Priorities 2017).

4. The Federalist Society, a nationwide organization of lawyers, has been most influential in getting conservative, originalist judges on the bench, and played a crucial role in all three nominations, as well as in those of other federal justices (Toobin 2017; Savage 2017). Justice Amy Coney Barrett's rushed nomination and confirmation on the eve of the 2020 presidential elections made her the 220th federal judge confirmed under President Trump and the leadership of Mitch McConnell in the Senate (Kim 2020).

5. Ironically, high-tax blue states like New York have introduced laws that allow residents to pay part of their taxes as charitable contributions to the state, thereby circumventing the federal cap on state and local deductions (Sahadi 2018). Such schemes not only privilege the upper classes, but they also change the meaning of taxes, by declaring them a voluntary contribution.

6. In their "Statement of Progressive Property," legal scholars Gregory Alexander, Eduardo Peñalver, Joseph Singer, and Laura Underkuffler delineate the contours of such a progressive conception of property. They propose that such an understanding would enable property law to "establish the framework for a kind of social life appropriate to a free and democratic society" (2009, 744).

Bibliography

"1860 Republican Party Platform." 2014. In *A Documentary History of the American Civil War Era: Volume 2, Political Arguments*, edited by Thomas C. Mackey, 71–74. Knoxville: University of Tennessee Press.

60 Minutes. 2003. Reported by Mike Wallace, September 26. CBS.

"A $3500 Suburban House." 1895. *Ladies' Home Journal*, December: 37.

Abraham, David. 1996. "Liberty without Equality: The Property-Rights Connection in a 'Negative Citizenship' Regime." *Law & Social Inquiry* 21 (1): 1–65.

Acham, Christine. 2004. *Revolution Televised: Prime Time and the Struggle for Black Power*. Minneapolis: University of Minnesota Press.

Ackerman, Bruce A. 1977. *Private Property and the Constitution*. New Haven: Yale University Press.

Adams, John. (1787) 1851. *The Works of John Adams, Second President, of the United States*. 10 vols. Vol. 6, edited by Charles Francis Adams. Boston: Little, Brown and Company.

Alexander, Gregory S. 1997. *Commodity & Propriety: Competing Visions of Property in American Legal Thought, 1776–1970*. Chicago: University of Chicago Press.

———. 1998. "Property as Propriety." *Nebraska Law Review* 77: 667–702.

Alexander, Gregory S., Eduardo M. Peñalver, Joseph William Singer, and Laura S. Underkuffler. 2009. "A Statement of Progressive Property." *Cornell Law Review* 94 (4): 743–44.

Altman, Karen. 1990. "Consuming Ideology: The Better Homes in America Campaign." *Critical Studies in Mass Communication* 7: 286–307.

Amos, Alcione M. 2006. *The Life of Luis Fatio Pacheco: Last Survivor of Dade's Battle*. Dade City: Seminole Wars Foundation.

Anderson, Hannah L. 2011. "That Settles It: The Debate and Consequences of the Homestead Act of 1862." *The History Teacher* 45 (1): 117–37.

Appleby, Joyce Oldham. 2010. *The Relentless Revolution: A History of Capitalism*. New York: Norton.

Archer, John. 2010. "The Place We Love to Hate: The Critics Confront Suburbia, 1920–1960." In *Constructions of Home: Interdisciplinary Studies in Architecture, Law, and Literature*, edited by Klaus Stierstorfer, 45–82. New York: AMS Press.

Arneil, Barbara. 1992. "John Locke, Natural Law and Colonialism." *History of Political Thought* 13 (4): 587–603.

———. 1996. *John Locke and America: The Defence of English Colonialism.* Oxford: Clarendon Press.

Arrighi, Giovanni. 2010. *The Long Twentieth Century: Money, Power, and the Origins of our Times*. London: Verso.

Asen, Robert. 2009. *Invoking the Invisible Hand: Social Security and the Privatization Debates*. East Lansing: Michigan State University Press.

———. 2010. "The Ownership Society, or Bourgeois Publicity Revisited." In *Public Modalities: Rhetoric, Culture, Media, and the Shape of Public Life*, edited by Daniel C. Brouwer and Robert Asen, 109–30. Tuscaloosa: University of Alabama Press.

Avsar, Rojhat B. 2008. "A Critique of 'Neoliberal Autonomy': The Rhetoric of Ownership Society." *Forum for Social Economics* 37 (2): 125–34.

Banner, Stuart. 2005. *How the Indians Lost Their Land: Law and Power on the Frontier*. Cambridge: Belknap Press.

———. 2011. *American Property*. Cambridge: Harvard University Press.

Baptist, Edward E. 2012. "Toxic Debt, Liar Loans, Collateralized and Securitized Human Beings, and the Panic of 1837." In *Capitalism Takes Command: The Social Transformation of Nineteenth-Century America*, edited by Michael Zakim and Gary John Kornblith, 69–92. Chicago: University of Chicago Press.

———. 2016. *The Half Has Never Been Told: Slavery and the Making of American Capitalism*. New York: Basic Books.

Barkan, Joshua. 2013. *Corporate Sovereignty: Law and Government under Capitalism.* Minneapolis: University of Minnesota Press.

Barnard, Daniel Dewey. 1845. "The 'Anti-Rent' Movement and Outbreak in New York." *American Review* 2 (6): 587–98.

Basch, Norma. 1982. *In the Eyes of the Law: Women, Marriage, and Property in Nineteenth-Century New York*. Ithaca: Cornell University Press.

Beard, Charles A. 1913. *An Economic Interpretation of the Constitution of the United States*. New York: Macmillan.

Becher, Debbie. 2010. "The Rights Behind Eminent Domain Fights: A Little Property and a Lot of Home." In *Property Rights and Neoliberalism*, edited by Wayne V. McIntosh and Laura J. Hatcher, 75–93. Burlington: Ashgate.

Beckert, Sven. 2015. *Empire of Cotton: A New History of Global Capitalism*. New York: Penguin.

Beckert, Sven, and Seth Rockman. 2016. *Slavery's Capitalism: A New History of American Economic Development*. Philadelphia: University of Pennsylvania Press.

Béland, Daniel. 2007. "Neo-Liberalism and Social Policy: The Politics of Ownership." *Policy Studies* 28 (2): 91–107.

Belich, James. 2009. *Replenishing the Earth: The Settler Revolution and the Rise of the Angloworld.* Oxford: Oxford University Press.

Bell, Derrick. 1987. *And We Are Not Saved: The Elusive Quest for Racial Justice*. New York: Basic Books.

———. 1988. "White Superiority in America: Its Legal Legacy, Its Economic Costs." *Villanova Law Review* 33 (5): 767–79.

Benda-Beckmann, Franz von, Keebet von Benda-Beckmann, and Melanie Wiber. 2006. "The Properties of Property." In *Changing Properties of Property*, edited by Franz von Benda-Beckmann, Keebet von Benda-Beckmann and Melanie Wiber, 1–39. New York: Berghahn Books.

Benedict, Jeff. 2009. *Little Pink House: A True Story of Defiance and Courage*. New York: Grand Central.

Bentham, Jeremy. (1802) 1864. *Theory of Legislation*, edited by R. Hildreth. London: Trübner and Co.

Berle, Adolf A., and Gardiner C. Means. 1991. *The Modern Corporation and Private Property*. New Brunswick: Transaction Publishers.

Berlin, Isaiah. 1969. *Four Essays on Liberty*. London: Oxford University Press.

Berliner, Dana. 2003. *Public Power, Private Gain: A Five-Year, State-by-State Report Examining the Abuse of Eminent Domain*. Institute for Justice. http://ij.org/report/public-power-private-gain/.

Berman v. Parker. 348 U.S. 26 (1954).

Bhandar, Brenna. 2018. *Colonial Lives of Property: Law, Land, and Racial Regimes of Ownership*. Durham: Duke University Press.

Biskupic, Joan. 2005. "Seizing Land for Private Use OK'd." *USA Today*, June 24, A1.

Black, Jason Edward. 2015. *American Indians and the Rhetoric of Removal and Allotment*. Jackson: University Press of Mississippi.

Black Power, White Backlash. 1966. Reported by Mike Wallace. 27 Sep. CBS.

Blackstone, William. (1765–70) 1915. *Commentaries on the Law of England*, edited by William Carey Jones. San Francisco: Bancroft Whitney.

Blomley, Nicholas. 2003. "Law, Property, and the Geography of Violence: The Frontier, the Survey, and the Grid." *Annals of the Association of American Geographers* 93 (1): 121–41.

———. 2005. "The Borrowed View: Privacy, Propriety, and the Entanglements of Property." *Law & Social Inquiry* 30 (4): 617–61.

Bloom, Joshua, and Waldo E. Martin. 2013. *Black against Empire: The History and Politics of the Black Panther Party*. Berkeley: University of California Press.

Blumin, Stuart M. 1989. *The Emergence of the Middle Class: Social Experience in the American City, 1760–1900*. Cambridge: Cambridge University Press.

Boaz, David. 2004. "Defining an Ownership Society." Cato Institute, 2004. www.cato.org/special/ownership_society/boaz.html.

Bobroff, Kenneth H. 2001. "Retelling Allotment: Indian Property Rights and the Myth of Common Ownership." *Vanderbilt Law Review* 54 (4): 1557–623.

Boggio, Jean. 2008. *Stolen Fields: A Story of Eminent Domain and the Death of the American Dream*. Belmont: Colerith Press.

Bolick, Clint. 1990. *Unfinished Business: A Civil Rights Strategy for America's Third Century*. San Francisco: Pacific Research Institute for Public Policy.

Bolick, Clint, and William Mellor. 1991. "The Quest for Justice: Natural Rights and the Future of Public Interest Law." Institute for Justice. http://www.ij.org/the-quest-for-justice.

Borchard, Gregory A. 2011. *Abraham Lincoln and Horace Greeley*. Carbondale: Southern Illinois University Press.

Bordewich, Fergus M. 2012. *America's Great Debate: Henry Clay, Stephen A. Douglas, and the Compromise that Preserved the Union*. New York: Simon & Schuster.

Botterill, Jacqueline. 2013. "Property Porn: An Analysis of Online Real Estate Advertising." In *The Routledge Companion to Advertising and Promotional Culture*, edited by Matthew P. McAllister and Emily West, 326–37. New York: Routledge.

Bravin, Jess. 2005. "Court Buttresses Eminent Domain; Local Governments Cleared to Take Private Property if Projects Promise Growth." *Wall Street Journal* (Eastern), June 24, A3.

Brenkert, George G. 1979. "Freedom and Private Property in Marx." *Philosophy & Public Affairs* 8 (2): 122–47.

Brenner, Elsa. 2005. "Homes Taken, Lives Rebuilt." *New York Times*, July 31, WC14.

Brilliant, Mark. 2010. *The Color of American Has Changed: How Racial Diversity Shaped Civil Rights Reform in California, 1941–1978*. New York: Oxford University Press.

Brimmer, Andrew. 1970. "Economic Integration and the Progress of the Negro Community." *Ebony*, August, 118–21.

Bronstein, Jamie L. 1999. *Land Reform and Working-Class Experience in Britain and the United States, 1800–1862*. Stanford: Stanford University Press.

Brooks, Corey M. 2016. *Liberty Power: Antislavery Third Parties and the Transformation of American Politics*. Chicago: Chicago University Press.

Brooks, Peter, and Paul Gewirtz, eds. 1996. *Law's Stories: Narrative and Rhetoric in the Law*. New Haven: Yale University Press.

Brooks, Richard, and Carol M. Rose. 2013. *Saving the Neighborhood: Racially Restrictive Covenants, Law, and Social Norms*. Cambridge, MA: Harvard University Press.

Brown, Adrienne R., and Valerie Smith, eds. 2015. *Race and Real Estate*. Oxford: Oxford University Press.

Brown, J. Larry, Robert Kuttner, and Thomas M. Shapiro. 2005. *Building a Real "Ownership Society"*. New York: Century Foundation.

Browne, Robert S. 1970a. "Barriers to Black Participation in the U.S. Economy." *The Review of Black Political Economy* 1 (2): 57–67.

———. 1970b. "Toward an Overall Assessment of Our Alternatives." *The Review of Black Political Economy* 1 (1): 18–26.

Brownson, Orestes Augustus. 1840. *The Laboring Classes: An Article from the Boston Quarterly Review*. Boston: B. H. Greene.

Bruun, Maja Hojer, Patrick J. L. Cockburn, Bjarke Skaelund Risager, and Mikkel Thorup, eds. 2017. *Contested Property Claims: What Disagreement Tells Us about Ownership*. London: Routledge.

Bryan, William Jennings. 1996. *The Cross of Gold: Speech Delivered before the National Democratic Convention at Chicago, July 9, 1896*. Lincoln: University of Nebraska Press.

Building and Loan Association of San Francisco. *Citizen's Report*. 12 May 1919. Box 461, USHC Real Estate Division, Record Group 3, National Archives, College Park, Maryland.

Bump, Philip. 2017. "What the Republican Tax Bill Actually Does." *Washington Post*, December 20. https://www.washingtonpost.com/news/politics/wp/2017/12/20/what-the-republican-tax-bill-actually-does/?utm_term=.91cf23594a18.

Bush, George W. 2003. "Remarks to Small Investors in Alexandria, Virginia, February 12, 2003." In *Public Papers of the Presidents of the United States: George W. Bush (2003, Book I)*, 156–61. Washington: G.P.O.

———. 2005a. "Address Before a Joint Session of the Congress on the State of the Union, February 2, 2005." In *Public Papers of the Presidents of the United States: George W. Bush (2005, Book I)*, 113–21. Washington: G.P.O.

———. 2005b. "Remarks to the National Summit on Retirement Savings, 28 February 2002." In *Public Papers of the Presidents of the United States: George W. Bush (2002, Book I)*, 308–11. Washington: G.P.O.

———. 2006a. "Executive Order 13406 of June 23, 2006, Protecting the Property Rights of the American People." *Federal Register* 71 FR 36973, June 28.

———. 2006b. "Remarks at a Bush-Cheney Reception in Dearborn, Michigan, July 24, 2003." In *Public Papers of the Presidents of the United States: George W. Bush (2003, Book II)*, 926–30. Washington: G.P.O.

———. 2006c. "Remarks in a Discussion on the National Economy in Bakersfield, California, March 4, 2004." In *Public Papers of the Presidents of the United States: George W. Bush (2004, Book I)*, 309–18. Washington: G.P.O.

———. 2007a. Inaugural Address, January 20, 2005. In *Public Papers of the Presidents of the United States: George W. Bush (2005, Book I)*, 66–69. Washington: G.P.O.

———. 2007b. "Remarks Accepting the Presidential Nomination at the Republican National Convention in New York City, September 2, 2004." In *Public Papers of the Presidents of the United States: George W. Bush (2004, Book II)*, 1855–63. Washington: G.P.O.

———. 2007c. "Remarks Following a Discussion with Small-Business Entrepreneurs, July 2, 2004." In *Public Papers of the Presidents of the United States: George W. Bush (2004, Book II)*, 1224–33. Washington: G.P.O.

———. 2007d. "Remarks in a Discussion in Lima, Ohio, August 28, 2004." In *Public Papers of the Presidents of the United States: George W. Bush (2004, Book II)*, 1775–94. Washington: G.P.O.

Calder, Lendol. 1999. *Financing the American Dream: A Cultural History of Consumer Credit*. Princeton: Princeton University Press.

Calhoun, John C. 1854. *Speeches of John C. Calhoun, Delivered in the House of Representatives and in the Senate of the United States. The Works of John C. Calhoun,* edited by Richard K. Crallé. 6 vols. New York: Appleton.

Canova, Timothy A. 2008. "Legacy of the Clinton Bubble." *Dissent* 55 (3): 41–50.

Canovan, Margaret. 1999. "Trust the People! Populism and the Two Faces of Democracy." *Political Studies* 47 (1): 2–16.

Carmichael, Stokely. (1971) 2007. *Stokely Speaks: Black Power Back to Pan-Africanism*. Chicago: Lawrence Hill Books.

Carmichael, Stokely, and Charles V. Hamilton. 1967. *Black Power: The Politics of Liberation in America*. New York: Random House.

Center on Budget and Policy Priorities. 2017. "Policy Basics: Where Do Our Federal Tax Dollars Go?" https://www.cbpp.org/research/federal-budget/policy-basics-where-do-our-federal-tax-dollars-go.

Chitty, Andrew. 2013. "Recognition and Property in Hegel and the Early Marx." *Ethical Theory and Moral Practice* 16 (4): 685–97.

Churchill, Ward, and Jim Vander Wall. 2002. *The COINTELPRO Papers: Documents from the FBI's Secret Wars against Dissent in the United States*. 2nd ed. Vol. 8. Cambridge, MA: South End Press.

Chused, Richard H. 1983. "Married Women's Property Law: 1800–1850." *Georgetown Law Journal* 71: 1359–425.

Clark, Christopher. 2012. "The Agrarian Context of American Capitalist Development." In *Capitalism Takes Command: The Social Transformation of Nineteenth-Century America*, edited by Michael Zakim and Gary John Kornblith, 13–37. Chicago: University of Chicago Press.

Clark, Emily. 1998. "Own Your Own Home: S. E. Gross, the Great Domestic Promoter." In *The American Home: Material Culture, Domestic Space, and Family Life*, edited by Eleanor McD Thompson, 135–53. Hanover, NH: University Press of New England.

Clark, Laurel A. 2010. "The Rights of a Florida Wife: Slavery, U.S. Expansion, and Married Women's Property Law." *Journal of Women's History* 22 (4): 39–63.

Clay, Henry. 1839. *Speech of Mr. Clay, of Kentucky, on the Subject of Abolition Petitions: Delivered in the Senate of the United States, February 7, 1839*. Washington: Gales and Seaton.

Clinton, William J. 1995. "Remarks on the National Homeownership Strategy, June 5, 1995." In *Public Papers of the Presidents of the United States: William J. Clinton (1995, Book I)*, 805–08. Washington: G.P.O.

Collins, William J. 2006. "The Political Economy of State Fair Housing Laws before 1968." *Social Science History* 30 (1): 15–49.

Condit, Celeste Michelle, and John Louis Lucaites. 1993. *Crafting Equality: America's Anglo-African Word*. Chicago: University of Chicago Press.

Congressional Budget Office. 2018. "Estimated Deficits and Debt Under the Conference Agreement of H.R. 1." Congressional Budget Office, January 2. https://www.cbo.gov/publication/53437.

Connolly, N. D. B. 2014. *A World More Concrete: Real Estate and the Remaking of Jim Crow South Florida*. Chicago: University of Chicago Press.

Coolidge, Calvin. 1922. "A Nation of Home-Owners." *The Delineator*, October, 16–17.

Coombe, Rosemary. 1998. "Contingent Articulations: A Critical Cultural Studies of the Law." In *Law in the Domains of Culture*, edited by Austin Sarat and Thomas R. Kearns, 21–64. Ann Arbor: University of Michigan Press.

Cooper, James Fenimore. 1845. *The Chainbearer; or The Littlepage Manuscripts*. New York: Lovell.

———. 1849. *The Redskins*. 2 vols. New York: Stringer and Townsend.

———. 1852. *Satanstoe*. 2 vols. New York: Stringer and Townsend.

Copeland, Roy W. 2013. "In the Beginning: Origins of African American Real Property Ownership in the United States." *Journal of Black Studies* 44 (6): 646–64.

Cott, Nancy F. 1997. *The Bonds of Womanhood: "Woman's sphere" in New England, 1780–1835*. 2nd ed. New Haven: Yale University Press.

Coyle, Dennis J. 1993. *Property Rights and the Constitution: Shaping Society through Land Use Regulation*. Albany: State University of New York Press.

Crane, Caroline Bartlett. 1925. *Everyman's House*. Garden City: Doubleday, Page and Co.

Croly, Herbert David. (1909) 1963. *The Promise of American Life*. Hamden: Archon Books.

Cuevas, Ofelia O. 2012. "Welcome to My Cell: Housing and Race in the Mirror of American Democracy." *American Quarterly* 64 (3): 605–24.

Curtis, Christopher M. 1997. "'Can These Be the Sons of Their Fathers?' The Defense of Slavery in Virginia, 1831–1832." MA Thesis, Virginia Polytechnic Institute and State University.

D'Antonio, Michael. 2016. *The Truth about Trump*. New York: St. Martin's.

Dauber, Michele Landis. 2003. "The War of 1812, September 11th, and the Politics of Compensation." *DePaul Law Review* 53 (2): 289–354.

Davenport, Coral. 2018. "E.P.A. Blocks Obama-Era Clean Water Rule." *New York Times*, January 31. https://www.nytimes.com/2018/01/31/climate/trump-water-wotus.html.

Davenport, Coral, and David E. Sanger. 2017. "'Learning Curve' as Rick Perry Pursues a Job He Initially Misunderstood." *New York Times*, January 18. https://www.nytimes.com/2017/01/18/us/politics/rick-perry-energy-secretary-donald-trump.html.

Davies, Margaret. 2007. *Property: Meanings, Histories, Theories*. Abingdon: Routledge-Cavendish.

Davies, Pearl Janet. 1958. *Real Estate in American History*. Washington: Public Affairs Press.

Davis, James Harvey. 1894. *A Political Revelation*. Dallas: The Advance Publishing Company.

Davis, Jefferson. 1848. *Speech of Jefferson Davis, of Mississippi, on the Oregon bill. Delivered in the Senate of the United States, July 12, 1848*. Washington.

———. 1850. *Speech of Mr. Davis, of Mississippi, on the Subject of Slavery in the Territories. Delivered in the Senate of the United States, February 13 & 14, 1850*. Washington: Towers.

Davis, John P. (1905) 1961. *Corporations: A Study of the Origin and Development of Great Business Combinations and of their Relation to the Authority of the State*. 2 vols. New York: Capricorn Books.

Debs, Eugene V. 1908. *Debs: His Life, Writings and Speeches, with a Department of Appreciations*. Girard, KS.: The Appeal to Reason.

Deloria, Vine. (1969) 1988. *Custer Died for Your Sins: An Indian Manifesto*. Norman: University of Oklahoma Press.

Demsetz, Harold. 1967. "Toward a Theory of Property Rights." *American Economic Review* 57 (2): 347–59.

Department of Defense and Environmental Protection Agency. 2020. "The Navigable Waters Protection Rule: Definition of 'Waters of the United States.'" *Federal Register* 85 (77): 22250–342.

Devyr, Thomas Ainge. 1842. *Our Natural Rights: A Pamphlet for the People*. Williamsburg.

Dew, Thomas R. 1832. *Review of the Debate [on the Abolition of Slavery] in the Virginia Legislature of 1831 and 1832*. Richmond: T. W. White.

Diamond, Michael. 2011. "Shared Equity Housing: Cultural Understanding and the Meaning of Ownership." In *The Public Nature of Private Property*, edited by Robin Paul Malloy and Michael Diamond, 37–64. Burlington, VT: Ashgate.

Dillon, John F. 1895. "Property—Its Rights and Duties in our Legal and Social Systems." *American Law Review* 29: 161.

Dimaggio, Anthony R. 2011. *The Rise of the Tea Party: Political Discontent and Corporate Media in the Age of Obama*. New York: Monthly Review Press.

Douglas, Ann. 1977. *The Feminization of American Culture*. New York: Knopf.

Douglass, Frederick. (1852) 2013. "What to the Slave Is the Fourth of July?" In *Great Speeches by Frederick Douglass*, edited by James Daley, 25–41. Mineola: Dover.

Downing, Andrew Jackson. 1848. "On the Moral Influence of Good Houses." *Horticulturalist* 2: 345–47.

Drucker, Jesse, and Alan Rappeport. 2017. "The Tax Bill's Winners and Losers." *New York Times*, December 16. https://www.nytimes.com/2017/12/16/business/the-winners-and-losers-in-the-tax-bill.html.

Dunn-Haley. 1995. "The House that Uncle Sam Built: The Political Culture of Federal Housing Policy, 1919–1932." Ph.D. Thesis, Stanford University.

Dyckman, Martin. 2005. "A Person's Home Is the Government's Parcel." *St. Petersburg Times* (State), July 3, 3P.

Dyer, Richard. 1997. *White*. New York: Routledge.

Eagle, Steven J. 2005. *The Birth of the Property Rights Movement. Policy Analysis* 558, December 15. Washington: Cato Institute.

Echeverria, John D., and Thekla Hansen-Young. 2008. "The Track Record on Takings Legislation: Lessons from Democracy's Laboratories." *Georgetown Environmental Law & Policy Institute Papers & Reports*.

"Editorial: The Forced Housing Issue." 1963. *California Real Estate Magazine*, December, 1.

Einhorn, Robin L. 2006. *American Taxation, American Slavery*. Chicago: University of Chicago Press.

Elkins, Caroline, and Susan Pedersen. 2005. "Introduction. Settler Colonialism: A Concept and Its Uses." In *Settler Colonialism in the Twentieth Century: Projects, Practices, Legacies*, edited by Caroline Elkins and Susan Pedersen, 1–20. London: Routledge.

Ely, James W. 2008. *The Guardian of Every Other Right: A Constitutional History of Property Rights*. 3rd ed. New York: Oxford University Press.

Engel, Kathleen C, and Patricia A. McCoy. 2001. "Tale of Three Markets: The Law and Economics of Predatory Lending." *Texas Law Review* 80 (6): 1255–381.

Engerman, Stanley L., and Kenneth L. Sokoloff. 2005. "The Evolution of Suffrage Institutions in the New World." *The Journal of Economic History* 65 (4): 891–921.

Epstein, Richard A. 2005. "Supreme Folly." *Wall Street Journal*, June 27: A14.

———. 2008. *Supreme Neglect: How to Revive Constitutional Protection for Private Property*. Oxford: Oxford University Press.

———. 2011. *Design for Liberty: Private Property, Public Administration, and the Rule of Law*. Cambridge, MA: Harvard University Press.

Ericson, David F. 2000. *The Debate over Slavery: Antislavery and Proslavery Liberalism in Antebellum America*. New York: New York University Press.

Face the Nation: Stokely Carmichael. 1966. Reported by John Hart, James S. Doyle, and Martin Agronsky. June 19. CBS.

Farrington, Joshua. 2012. "'Build, Baby, Build': Conservative Black Nationalists, Free Enterprise, and the Nixon Administration." In *The Right Side of the Sixties: Reexamining Conservatism's Decade of Transformation*, edited by Laura Jane Gifford and Daniel K. Williams, 61–80. New York: Palgrave Macmillan.

Fee, John. 2006. "Eminent Domain and the Sanctity of Home." *Notre Dame Law Review* 81 (3): 783–820.

Fergus, Devin. 2009. *Liberalism, Black Power, and the Making of American Politics, 1965–1980*. Athens: University of Georgia Press.

Fernández-Kelly, Patricia. 2015. "Land, Race, and Property Rights in American Development." In *Race and Real Estate*, edited by Adrienne R. Brown and Valerie Smith, 64–86. Oxford: Oxford University Press.

Finkelman, Paul. 2012a. "The Appeasement of 1850." In *Congress and the Crisis of the 1850s*, edited by Paul Finkelman and Donald R. Kennon, 36–79. Athens: Ohio University Press.

———. 2012b. "Introduction: A Disastrous Decade." In *Congress and the Crisis of the 1850s*, edited by Paul Finkelman and Donald R. Kennon, 1–17. Athens: Ohio University Press.

Finzsch, Norbert. 1999. "'Picking Up the Gun': Die Black Panther Party zwischen gewaltsamer Revolution und sozialer Reform, 1966–1984." *Amerikastudien/American Studies* 44 (2): 223–54.

Fishback, Price Van Meter, Jonathan Derek Rose, and Kenneth A. Snowden. 2013. *Well Worth Saving: How the New Deal Safeguarded Home Ownership*. Chicago: University of Chicago Press.

Fitch, John A. 1910. *The Steel Workers*. New York: Charities Publication Committee.

Fitzhugh, George. 1857. *Cannibals All! or, Slaves Without Masters*. Richmond: A. Morris.

Fitzmaurice, Andrew. 2014. *Sovereignty, Property and Empire, 1500–2000*. Cambridge: Cambridge University Press.

Fitzpatrick, Peter. 1992. *The Mythology of Modern Law*. London: Routledge.

Fogel, Robert William. 1989. *Without Consent or Contract: The Rise and Fall of American Slavery*. New York: Norton.
Foley, Elizabeth Price. 2012. *The Tea Party: Three Principles*. New York: Cambridge University Press.
Foner, Eric. 1984. "Why Is There No Socialism in the United States?" *History Workshop* 17: 57–80.
———. 1995. *Free Soil, Free Labor, Free Men: The Ideology of the Republican Party before the Civil War*. 2nd ed. Oxford: Oxford University Press.
Foner, Philip Sheldon. 1995. *The Black Panthers Speak*. New York: Da Capo Press.
Ford, James. 1931. "New Developments in the Better Homes in America Campaign." *Journal of Home Economics* (3): 223–28.
Forman, James. 1970. "The Black Manifesto." *The Review of Black Political Economy* 1 (1): 36–44.
Frazier, E. Franklin. 1971. "Negro Business: A Social Myth." In *Black Business Enterprise: Historical and Contemporary Perspectives*, edited by Ronald W. Bailey, 73–85. New York: Basic Books.
Freehling, Alison Goodyear. 1982. *Drift Toward Dissolution: The Virginia Slavery Debate of 1831–1832*. Baton Rouge: Louisiana State University Press.
Freehling, William W. 1990. *The Road to Disunion*. 2 vols. New York: Oxford University Press.
Freund, David M. P. 2007. *Colored Property: State Policy and White Racial Politics in Suburban America*. Chicago: University of Chicago Press.
Freyfogle, Eric T. 2007. *On Private Property: Finding Common Ground on the Ownership of Land*. Boston: Beacon Press.
Friedman, Lawrence M. 2005. *A History of American Law*. 3rd ed. New York: Simon and Schuster.
Friedman, Milton. 1962. *Capitalism and Freedom*. Chicago: University of Chicago Press.
Frymer, Paul. 2017. *Building and American Empire: The Era of Territorial and Political Expansion*. Princeton: Princeton University Press.
Gallagher, Victoria J. 2001. "Black Power in Berkeley: Postmodern Constructions in the Rhetoric of Stokely Carmichael." *Quarterly Journal of Speech* 87 (2): 144–157.
Garb, Margaret. 2005. *City of American Dreams: A History of Home Ownership and Housing Reform in Chicago, 1871–1919*. Chicago: University of Chicago Press.
Gates, Henry Louis. 1989. "TV's Black World Turns—But Stays Unreal." *New York Times*, November 12. http://www.nytimes.com/1989/11/12/arts/tv-s-black-world-turns-but-stays-unreal.html.
Gellman, David N. 2006. *Emancipating New York: The Politics of Slavery and Freedom, 1777–1827*. Baton Rouge: Louisiana University Press.
Genovese, Eugene D. 1965. *The Political Economy of Slavery: Studies in the Economy & Society of the Slave South*. New York: Pantheon Books.
Gilden, Bruce. 2008. *Fort Myers*. https://vimeo.com/46986021.
———. 2009. *Detroit: The Troubled City*. https://vimeo.com/44404424.
———. 2011. "No Place Like Home: Foreclosures in America." https://www.kickstarter.com/projects/1750079117/no-place-like-home-foreclosures-in-america/description.

Gillman, Howard. 1993. *The Constitution Besieged: The Rise and Demise of Lochner Era Police Powers Jurisprudence*. Durham: Duke University Press.

Glaeser, Edward L. 2011. "Rethinking the Federal Bias Toward Homeownership." *Cityscape* 13 (2): 5–37.

Glickman, Lawrence. 2020. "How White Backlash Controls American Progress." *The Atlantic*, May 21. https://www.theatlantic.com/ideas/archive/2020/05/white-backlash-nothing-new/611914/.

Glickstein, Jonathan A. 2002. *American Exceptionalism, American Anxiety: Wages, Competition, and Degraded Labor in the Antebellum United States*. Charlottesville: University of Virginia Press.

Greeley, Horace. 1850. *Hints Toward Reforms, in Lectures, Addresses, and Other Writings*. New York: Harper.

Greeley, Horace, and Henry J. Raymond. 1847. *Association Discussed: or, The Socialism of the Tribune Examined*. New York: Harper.

Greene, Jamal. 2009. "On the Origins of Originalism." *Texas Law Review* 88 (1): 1–89.

Greenhut, Steven. 2004. *Abuse of Power: How the Government Misuses Eminent Domain*. Santa Ana: Seven Locks Press.

Greer, Allan. 2017. *Property and Dispossession: Natives, Empires and Land in Early Modern North America*. Cambridge: Cambridge University Press.

Grey, Thomas C. 1980. "The Disintegration of Property." *Nomos* 22: 69–85.

Gross, Samuel Eberly. 1891. *Tenth Annual Illustrated Catalogue of Famous City Subdivisions and Suburban Towns*. Chicago: S.E. Gross.

Haar, Dan. 2005. "Plan Expertly Before Grabbing." *Hartford Courant* (Statewide), July 31, D1.

Haddad, William F., and G. Douglas Pugh. 1969. *Black Economic Development*. Englewood Cliffs: Prentice-Hall.

Hahn, Steven. 2009. *The Political Worlds of Slavery and Freedom*. Cambridge: Harvard University Press.

Halbert, Blanche. 1932. *The Better Homes Manual*. Chicago: University of Chicago Press.

Hamilton, Alexander, James Madison, and John Jay. (1788) 2009. *The Federalist Papers,* edited by Ian Shapiro. New Haven: Yale University Press.

Hansberry, Lorraine. (1959) 1994. *A Raisin in the Sun*. New York: Vintage.

Hardin, Garrett. 1968. "The Tragedy of the Commons." *Science* 162 (3859): 1243–48.

Harris, Cheryl I. 1993. "Whiteness as Property." *Harvard Law Review* 106: 1707–91.

Harris, Richard, and Robert Lewis. 1998. "Constructing a Fault(y) Zone: Misrepresentations of American Cities and Suburbs, 1900–1950." *Annals of the Association of American Geographers* 88 (4): 622–39.

Harrold, Stanley. 2019. *American Abolitionism: Its Direct Political Impact from Colonial Times into Reconstruction*. Charlottesville: University of Virginia Press.

Hartz, Louis. 1955. *The Liberal Tradition in America: An Interpretation of American Political Thought since the Revolution*. New York: Harcourt.

Harvey, David. 2005. *A Brief History of Neoliberalism*. Oxford: Oxford University Press.

Hawaii Housing Authority v. Midkiff. 467 U.S. 229 (1984).
Hayden, Dolores. 2003. *Building Suburbia: Green Fields and Urban Growth, 1820–2000*. New York: Vintage.
Hayek, Friedrich A. von. 1960. *The Constitution of Liberty*. Chicago: University of Chicago Press.
Hegel, Georg Wilhelm Friedrich. (1820) 1967. *Hegel's Philosophy of Right*, translated by T. M. Knox. London: Oxford University Press.
Hofstadter, Richard. 1948. *The American Political Tradition and the Men Who Made it*. New York: Knopf.
Hohfeld, Wesley N. 1913. "Some Fundamental Legal Conceptions as Applied in Judicial Reasoning." *Yale Law Journal* 23: 16–59.
———. 1917. "Fundamental Legal Conceptions as Applied in Judicial Reasoning." *Yale Law Journal* 26: 710–70.
Holt, Michael F. 1983. *The Political Crisis of the 1850s*. New York: Norton.
"The Homestead Bill." 1852. *National Intelligencer*, 22 April.
Hornstein, Jeffrey M. 2005. *A Nation of Realtors: A Cultural History of the Twentieth-Century American Middle Class*. Durham: Duke University Press.
Horwitz, Morton J. 1992a. *The Transformation of American Law, 1780–1860*. New York: Oxford University Press.
———. 1992b. *The Transformation of American Law, 1870–1960: The Crisis of Legal Orthodoxy*. New York: Oxford University Press.
HoSang, Daniel. 2010. *Racial Propositions: Ballot Initiatives and the Making of Postwar California*. Berkeley: University of California Press.
HoSang, Daniel, and Joseph E. Lowndes. 2019. *Producers, Parasites, Patriots: Race and the New Right-Wing Politics of Precarity*. Minneapolis: University of Minnesota Press.
"Housing Initiative Titled; Petitions Gathering Signatures for Public Vote." 1963. *California Real Estate Magazine*, December, 5.
Huffman, James. 2013. *Private Property and the Constitution: State Powers, Public Rights, and Economic Liberties*. New York: Palgrave Macmillan.
Huston, James L. 1998. *Securing the Fruits of Labor: The American Concept of Wealth Distribution, 1765–1900*. Baton Rouge: Louisiana State University Press.
———. 2003. *Calculating the Value of the Union: Slavery, Property Rights, and the Economic Origins of the Civil War*. Chapel Hill: University of North Carolina Press.
Huston, Reeve. 2000. *Land and Freedom: Rural Society, Popular Protest, and Party Politics in Antebellum New York*. New York: Oxford University Press.
Hutchison, Janet. 1989. "American Housing, Gender, and the Better Homes Movement, 1922–1935." Ph.D. Thesis, University of Delaware.
———. 1997. "Building for Babbitt: The State and the Suburban Home Ideal." *Journal of Policy History* 9 (2): 184–210.
Hyman, Louis. 2011a. *Debtor Nation: The History of America in Red Ink*. Princeton: Princeton University Press.
———. 2011b. "Ending Discrimination, Legitimating Debt: The Political Economy of Race, Gender, and Credit Access in the 1960s and 1970s." *Enterprise and Society* 12 (1): 200–32.

Institute for Justice. "About Us." 2002. The Castle Coalition: A Project of the Institute for Justice. http://castlecoalition.org/about.

Jacklin, Michele. 2005. "When Does Economic Benefit Trump Local Control?" *Hartford Courant* (Statewide), July 31, C3.

Jackson, Kenneth T. 1980. "Race, Ethnicity, and Real Estate Appraisal: The Home Owners Loan Corporation and the Federal Housing Administration." *Journal of Urban History* 6 (4): 419.

———. 1985. *Crabgrass Frontier: The Suburbanization of the United States*. New York: Oxford University Press.

Jacoby, Jeff. 2005. "Eminent Injustice in New London." *Boston Globe*, June 26, D11.

Jefferson, Thomas. (1785) 1982. *Notes on the State of Virginia*, edited by William Peden. Chapel Hill: University of North Carolina Press.

Johnson v. M'Intosh. 21 U.S. 543 (1823).

Johnson, Andrew. 1850. "The Homestead. Speech of Hon. A. Johnson, of Tennessee, in the House of Representatives, Thursday, July 25, 1850." *Congressional Globe*, 31st Cong. 1st Sess., App., 950–52.

Jones-Correa, Michael. 2000–2001. "The Origins and Diffusion of Racial Restrictive Covenants." *Political Science Quarterly* 115 (4): 541–68.

Judis, John B. 2016. *The Populist Explosion: How the Great Recession Transformed American and European Politics*. New York: Columbia Global Reports.

Julian, George Washington. 1872. *Speeches on Political Questions [1850–1871]*. New York: Hurd and Houghton.

Kades, Eric. 2002. "The End of the Hudson Valley's Peculiar Institution: The Anti-Rent Movement's Politics, Social Relations, and Economics." *Law & Social Inquiry* 27 (4): 941–65.

Katz, Stanley N. 1976. "Thomas Jefferson and the Right to Property in Revolutionary America." *The Journal of Law & Economics* 19 (3): 467–88.

Kazin, Michael. 1998. *The Populist Persuasion: An American History*. Rev. ed. Ithaca, NY: Cornell University Press.

Kelo v. City of New London. 545 U.S. 469 (2005).

Kent, James. 1832. *Commentaries on American Law*. 2nd ed. New York: O. Halsted.

Keyssar, Alexander. 2000. *The Right to Vote: The Contested History of Democracy in the United States*. New York: Basic Books.

Kim, Seung Min. 2020. "Trump's Conservative Imprint on the Federal Judiciary Gives Democrats a Playbook—If They Win." *Washington Post*, October 27. https://www.washingtonpost.com/politics/courts_law/court-barrett-senate-trump/2020/10/25/d9eed9c0-16bc-11eb-befb-8864259bd2d8_story.html.

Kim, Sung Bok. 1978. *Landlord and Tenant in Colonial New York: Manorial Society, 1664–1775*. Chapel Hill: University of North Carolina Press.

King, Martin Luther. 2010. *Where Do We Go from Here: Chaos or Community?* Boston: Beacon Press. 1968.

Klein, Naomi. 2008. "Disowned by the Ownership Society." *The Nation*, January 31. https://www.thenation.com/article/disowned-ownership-society/.

———. 2017. *No is Not Enough: Resisting Trump's Shock Politics and Winning the World We Need*. St. Ives: Allen Lane.

Knewitz, Simone. 2005. *Making Progress: Pragmatism and Utopia in the Works of Charlotte Perkins Gilman and John Dewey*. London: Turnshare.

———. 2018. "Creating an Ownership Society? Social Security Reform and the Temporalities of Libertarian Rhetoric." *Finance and Society* 4 (1): 60–75.

Kochhar, Rakesh, and Anthony Cilluffo. 2017. "How Wealth Inequality Has Changed in the U.S. since the Great Recession, by Race, Ethnicity and Income." *Pew Research Center*. http://www.pewresearch.org/fact-tank/2017/11/01/how-wealth-inequality-has-changed-in-the-u-s-since-the-great-recession-by-race-ethnicity-and-income/.

Kotlowski, Dean. 1998. "Black Power-Nixon Style: The Nixon Administration and Minority Business Enterprise." *The Business History Review* 72 (3): 409–45.

Krugman, Paul. 2005. "Confusions about Social Security." *The Economists' Voice* 2 (1): 1–9.

Kyllo v. United States. 533 U.S. 27 (2001).

Laclau, Ernesto. 2005. *On Populist Reason*. London: Verso.

———. 2014. *The Rhetorical Foundations of Society*. London: Verso.

Laclau, Ernesto, and Chantal Mouffe. (1985) 2014. *Hegemony and Socialist Strategy*. 2nd ed. London: Verso. 1985.

Lamb, Robert. 2010. "Liberty, Equality, and the Boundaries of Ownership: Thomas Paine's Theory of Property Rights." *The Review of Politics* 72 (3): 483–511.

Landry, Bart. 1987. *The New Black Middle Class*. Berkeley: University of California Press.

Lands, LeeAnn. 2008. "Be a Patriot, Buy a Home: Re-Imagining Home Owners and Home Ownership in Early 20th Century Atlanta." *Journal of Social History* 41 (4): 943–65.

———. 2009. *The Culture of Property: Race, Class, and Housing Landscapes in Atlanta, 1880–1950*. Athens: University of Georgia Press.

Lasch, Christopher. 1965. "Herbert Croly's America." *New York Review of Books*, July 1.

Lause, Mark A. 2005. *Young America: Land, Labor, and the Republican Community*. Urbana: University of Illinois Press.

Lazzarato, Maurizio. 2012. *The Making of the Indebted Man: An Essay on the Neoliberal Condition*. Los Angeles: Semiotext(e).

Leitch, Art S. 1964. "The Initiative—Its Purpose and Progress." *California Real Estate Magazine*, April 5.

Levinson, Mark. 2005. "Worse Than You Thought: Bush's Budget and the Gutting of Social Security." *Dissent* 52 (2): 30–34.

Levy, Collin. 2012. "Litigating for Liberty." *Wall Street Journal*, January 7–8. https://www.wsj.com/articles/SB10001424052970203513604577144902274972614.

Lewinnek, Elaine. 2014. *The Working Man's Reward: Chicago's Early Suburbs and the Roots of American Sprawl*. Oxford: Oxford University Press.

Lewis, John. (1888) 1900. *A Treatise on the Law of Eminent Domain in the United States*. 2nd ed. 2 vols. Chicago: Callaghan & Company.

Libby, Ronald T. 2014. *Purging the Republican Party: Tea Party Campaigns and Elections*. Lanham: Lexington Books.

Lipartito, Kenneth, and David B. Sicilia. 2004. *Constructing Corporate America: History, Politics, Culture*. Oxford: Oxford University Press.

Lippmann, Walter. [1914] 1917. *Drift and Mastery: An Attempt to Diagnose the Current Unrest*. New York: Henry Holt and Co.

Lipsitz, George. 1998. *The Possessive Investment in Whiteness: How White People Profit from Identity Politics*. Philadelphia: Temple University Press.

Little, Adrian. 1999. "The Politics of Compensation: Tom Paine's Agrarian Justice and Liberal Egalitarianism." *Contemporary Politics* 5 (1): 63.

Locke, John. (1689) 1988. *Two Treatises of Government*. Cambridge: Cambridge University Press.

Luck, Chad. 2014. *The Body of Property: Antebellum American Fiction and the Phenomenology of Possession*. New York: Fordham University Press.

Luken, Paul C., and Suzanne Vaughan. 2005. "'. . . Be a Genuine Homemaker in Your Own Home': Gender and Familial Relations in State Housing Practices, 1917–1922." *Social Forces* 83 (4): 1603–25.

MacKenzie, Scott R. 2013. *Be It Ever So Humble: Poverty, Fiction, and the Invention of the Middle-Class Home*. Charlottesville: University of Virginia Press.

Macpherson, C. B. 1962. *The Political Theory of Possessive Individualism: Hobbes to Locke*. Oxford: Clarendon Press.

———. 1978. *Property: Mainstream and Critical Positions*. Toronto: University of Toronto Press.

Madison, James. (1836) 1941. *Debates on the Adoption of the Federal Constitution in the Convention Held at Philadelphia in 1787, with a Diary of the Debates of the Congress of the Confederation as Reported by James Madison*, edited by Jonathan Elliot. Philadelphia: J. B. Lippincott.

Main, Carla T. 2007. *Bulldozed: "Kelo," Eminent Domain, and the American Lust for Land*. New York: Encounter Books.

Majewski, John. 2016. "Why Did Northerners Oppose the Expansion of Slavery? Economic Development and Education in the Limestone South." In *Slavery's Capitalism: A New History of American Economic Development*, edited by Sven Beckert and Seth Rockman, 277–98. Philadelphia: University of Pennsylvania Press.

Malcolm X. (1965) 1992. *The Autobiography of Malcolm X*, edited by Alex Haley. New York: Ballantine Books.

Mandel, Ernest. 1978. *Late Capitalism*. London: Verso.

Mann, Nick. 2012. "A Matter of Rights: Housing Referendums, California, and the Rise of the New Right." *Western Illinois Historical Review* 4: 52–68.

Marable, Manning. 1984. *Race, Reform, and Rebellion: The Second Reconstruction and Beyond in Black America, 1945–1982*. Jackson: University Press of Mississippi.

Marangos, John. 2008. "Thomas Paine (1737–1809) and Thomas Spence (1750–1814) on Land Ownership, Land Taxes and the Provision of Citizens' Dividend." *International Journal of Social Economics* 35 (5/6): 313–25.

Margo, Robert A. 2000. *Wages and Labor Markets in the United States, 1820–1860*. Chicago: University of Chicago Press.

Mark, Gregory A. 1987. "The Personification of the Business Corporation in American Law." *University of Chicago Law Review* 54: 1441–83.

Martin, Bonnie. 2010. "Slavery's Invisible Engine: Mortgaging Human Property." *The Journal of Southern History* 76 (4): 817–66.

Martin, Randy. 2002. *Financialization of Daily Life*. Philadelphia: Temple University Press.

Marx, Karl. (1844) 2005. *Economic and Philosophic Manuscripts of 1844. Karl Marx, Frederick Engels: Collected Works*, translated by Jack Cohen et al. Vol. 3. New York: International Publishers.

Mason, Paul. 2015. *PostCapitalism: A Guide to Our Future*. London: Allen Lane.

Massey, Douglas S., and Nancy A. Denton. 1993. *American Apartheid: Segregation and the Making of the Underclass*. Cambridge: Harvard University Press.

Matthews, Kristin L. 2008. "The Politics of 'Home' in Lorraine Hansberry's *A Raisin in the Sun*." *Modern Drama* 51 (4): 556–78.

McCabe, Brian J. 2013. "Are Homeowners Better Citizens? Homeownership and Community Participation in the United States." *Social Forces* 91 (3): 929–54.

McClanahan, Annie. 2017. *Dead Pledges: Debt, Crisis, and Twenty-First-Century Culture*. Stanford: Stanford University Press.

McCurdy, Charles W. 2001. *The Anti-Rent Era in New York Law and Politics, 1839–1865*. Chapel Hill: University of North Carolina Press.

McKissick, Floyd. 1969. *Three-Fifths of a Man*. New York: Macmillan.

———. 1970. "Black Business Development with Social Commitment to Black Communities." In *Black Nationalism in America*, edited by John H. Bracey, August Meier, and Elliott M. Rudwick, 492–503. Indianapolis: Bobbs-Merrill.

Mendenhall, Ed. 1964. "NAREB President Addresses CREA on Housing, Civil Rights." *California Real Estate Magazine*, April, 6.

Meyer, Stephen Grant. 2000. *As Long as They Don't Move Next Door: Segregation and Racial Conflict in American Neighborhoods*. Lanham: Rowman & Littlefield.

Mezey, Naomi. 2003. "Law as Culture." In *Cultural Analysis, Cultural Studies, and the Law*, edited by Austin Sarat and Jonathan Simon, 37–72. Durham: Duke University Press.

Mian, Atif, Amir Sufi, and Francesco Trebbi. 2008. "The Political Economy of the Subprime Mortgage Credit Expansion." *Quarterly Journal of Political Science* 8 (4): 373–408.

Miller, William Lee. 1996. *Arguing about Slavery: The Great Battle in the United States Congress*. New York: Knopf.

Mills, Charles W. 1997. *The Racial Contract*. Ithaca: Cornell University Press.

———. 2008. "Racial Liberalism." *PMLA* 123 (5): 1380–97.

Monroe, James. 1839. "First Annual Message, 3 December 1817." In *The Addresses and Messages of the Presidents of the United States*, 202–09. New York: McLean & Taylor.

Moreton-Robinson, Aileen. 2015. *White Possessive: Property, Power, and Indigenous Sovereignty*. Minneapolis: University of Minnesota Press.

Morris, Thomas D. 1996. *Southern Slavery and the Law, 1619–1860*. Chapel Hill: University of North Carolina Press.

Nadler, Janice, Shari Seidman Diamond, and Matthew M. Patton. 2008. "Government Takings of Private Property." In *Public Opinion and Constitutional Controversy*, edited by Nathaniel Persily, Jack Citrin, and Patrick J. Egan, 286–309. New York: Oxford University Press.

"NAREB President Hits Forced Housing Laws." 1963. *California Real Estate Magazine*, December, 5.

Nedelsky, Jennifer. 1990. *Private Property and the Limits of American Constitutionalism: The Madisonian Framework and Its Legacy*. Chicago: University of Chicago Press.

Newton, Huey P. 1969. "The Black Panthers." *Ebony*, August, 106–12.

———. 1972. *To Die for The People: The Writings of Huey P. Newton*, edited by Toni Morrison. New York: Random House.

New-York Daily Tribune. 1842–66. New York: Greeley and McElrath.

Nichols, Robert. 2020. *Theft Is Property! Dispossession and Critical Theory*. Durham: Duke University Press.

Nicolaides, Becky M. 1999. "'Where the Working Man Is Welcome': Working-Class Suburbs in Los Angeles, 1900–1940." *Pacific Historical Review* 68 (4): 517–59.

Nixon-Agnew Campaign Committee. 1968. "This Time, Vote Like Home Pitts' Whole World Depended on It." *Jet*, November 7, 8–9.

Nixon, Richard. 1968. "Bridges to Human Dignity." *Human Events*, May 25, 12–13.

Nozick, Robert. 1974. *Anarchy, State, and Utopia*. New York: Basic Books.

Ofari, Earl. 1970. *The Myth of Black Capitalism*. New York: Monthly Review Press.

Ogbar, Jeffrey. 2004. *Black Power: Radical Politics and African American Identity*. Baltimore: Johns Hopkins University Press.

O'Malley, Michael. 2012. *Face Value: The Entwined Histories of Money and Race in America*. Chicago: University of Chicago Press.

Oswald, Michael. 2019. "Jobs, Free Trade, and a Conspiracy: Trump's Use of Producerism." In *The Comeback of Populism: Transatlantic Perspectives*, edited by Heike Paul, Ursula Prutsch, and Jürgen Gebhardt, 109–25. Heidelberg: Winter.

O'Toole, Randal. 2012. *American Nightmare: How Government Undermines the Dream of Home Ownership*. Washington: Cato Institute.

Oubre, Claude F. 1978. *Forty Acres and a Mule: The Freedmen's Bureau and Black Landownership*. Baton Rouge: Louisiana State University Press.

Own Your Own Home Committee of Philadelphia. "The House That Bought Itself." USHC General Records, Own Your Own Home Campaign, Box 5, Record Group 3, National Archives, College Park, Maryland.

———. "How Glad I Am That I Agreed with John When He Proposed That We 'Own Our Home!'" USHC General Records, Own Your Own Home Campaign, Box 5, Record Group 3, National Archives, College Park, Maryland.

———. "The Man Who Owns His Home." USHC General Records, Own Your Own Home Campaign, Box 5, Record Group 3, National Archives, College Park, Maryland.

Pacific Legal Foundation. 2015. "PFL Lawsuit Challenges Obama Administration's New 'Waters of the United States' Power Grab." July 15. https://pacificlegal.org/

press-release/plf-lawsuit-challenges-obama-administrations-new-waters-of-united-states-power-grab/.

Paine, Thomas. 1795. *Dissertation on First Principles of Government*. Paris: English Press.

———. 1797. *Agrarian Justice, Opposed to Agrarian Law, and to Agrarian Monopoly: Being a Plan for Meliorating the Condition of Man, by Creating in Every Nation a National Fund*. Paris: W. Adlard.

Palmer, Tom G. 2004. "An Ownership Society Fosters Responsibility, Liberty, Prosperity." Cato Institute. http://www.cato.org/publications/commentary/ownership-society-fosters-responsibility-liberty-prosperity.

"Paul Ryan Reacts to Tax Reform Victory for GOP." 2017. *Good Morning, America*, December 20. https://abcnews.go.com/GMA/video/paul-ryan-reacts-tax-reform-victory-gop-51902702.

Peñalver, Eduardo M. 2006. "Property Metaphors and Kelo v. New London: Two Views of the Castle." *Fordham Law Review* 74 (6): 2971–76.

"People's Party Platform." 1892. *Omaha Morning World-Herald*, July 5. https://ww norton.com/college/history/archive/reader/trial/directory/1890_1914/12_ch22_04.htm.

Peters, John Francis. 2010. *Foreclosed, 2008–2010*. https://www.jfpetersphoto.com/archive/album/foreclosed-2008-2010.

Pew Research Center. 2019. "In a Politically Polarized Era, Sharp Divides in Both Partisan Coalitions." December 17. https://www.pewresearch.org/politics/2019/12/17/in-a-politically-polarized-era-sharp-divides-in-both-partisan-coalitions/.

Phalanx. 1843–45. New York: J. Winchester.

Phu, T. N. 2008. "Shooting the Movement: Black Panther Party Photography and African American Protest Traditions." *Canadian Review of American Studies* 38 (1): 165–89.

Pollack, Norman. 1987. *The Just Polity: Populism, Law, and Human Welfare*. Urbana: University of Illinois Press.

Postel, Charles. 2007. *The Populist Vision*. Oxford: Oxford University Press.

Powderly, T. V. 1890. "The Plea for Eight Hours." *The North American Review*, April, 464.

Priest, Claire. 2006. "Creating an American Property Law: Alienability and Its Limits in American History." *Harvard Law Review* 120 (2): 385–459.

"Proposition 14." 1964. *Time*, September 25, 23.

Quinn, Sarah. 2019. *American Bonds: How Credit Markets Shaped a Nation*. Princeton: Princeton University Press.

Radin, Margaret Jane. 1993. *Reinterpreting Property*. Chicago: University of Chicago Press.

Raiford, Leigh. 2011. *Imprisoned in a Luminous Glare: Photography and the African American Freedom Struggle*. Chapel Hill: University of North Carolina Press.

Ransom, Roger L. 1989. *Conflict and Compromise: The Political Economy of Slavery, Emancipation, and the American Civil War*. Cambridge: Cambridge University Press.

Reeves, Richard V. 2017. *Dream Hoarders: How the American Upper Middle Class is Leaving Everyone Else in the Dust, Why That Is a Problem, and What to Do about It*. Washington: Brookings Institution Press.

Reich, Charles A. 1964. "The New Property." *Yale Law Journal* 73 (5): 733–87.

Reitman v. Mulkey. 387 U.S. 369 (1967).

Remini, Robert Vincent. 2010. *At the Edge of the Precipice: Henry Clay and the Compromise that Saved the Union*. New York: Basic Books.

Reyes, Paul. 2010. "Picturing the Crisis." *New York Times*, October 12. https://opinionator.blogs.nytimes.com/2010/10/12/picturing-the-crisis/.

Rhodes, Jane. 1999. "Fanning the Flames of Racial Discord: The National Press and the Black Panther Party." *The Harvard International Journal of Press/Politics* 4 (4): 95–118.

Richards, Leonard L. 2000. *The Slave Power: The Free North and Southern Domination, 1780–1860*. Baton Rouge: Louisiana State University Press.

Richardson, Heather Cox. 2020. Letters from an American, October 27. https://heathercoxrichardson.substack.com/p/october-27-2020.

Rifkin, Jeremy. 2000. *The Age of Access: The New Culture of Hypercapitalism, Where All of Life Is a Paid-for Experience*. New York: Jeremy P. Tarcher / Putnam.

Rifkin, Mark. 2009. *Manifesting America: The Imperial Construction of U.S. National Space*. Oxford: Oxford University Press.

Rigueur, Leah Wright. 2015. *The Loneliness of the Black Republican: Pragmatic Politics and the Pursuit of Power*. Princeton: Princeton University Press.

Robertson, Lindsay G. 2005. *Conquest by Law: How the Discovery of America Dispossessed Indigenous Peoples of Their Lands*. Oxford: Oxford University Press.

Roediger, David R. 2007. *The Wages of Whiteness: Race and the Making of the American Working Class*. Rev. ed. London: Verso.

Root, Erik S. 2008. *All Honor to Jefferson? The Virginia Slavery Debates and the Positive Good Thesis*. Lanham: Lexington Books.

—, ed. 2010. *Sons of the Fathers: The Virginia Slavery Debates of 1831–1832*. Lanham: Lexington Books.

Rose, Carol M. 1994. *Property and Persuasion: Essays on the History, Theory, and Rhetoric of Ownership*. Boulder: Westview Press.

———. 1996. "Property as a Keystone Right?" *Notre Dame Law Review* 71 (3): 329–66.

Roy, William G. 1997. *Socializing Capital: The Rise of the Large Industrial Corporation in America*. Princeton: Princeton University Press.

Rucker, Philip, and Robert Costa. 2017. "Bannon Vows a Daily Fight for 'Deconstruction of the Administrative State.'" *Washington Post*, February 23. https://www.washingtonpost.com/politics/top-wh-strategist-vows-a-daily-fight-for-deconstruction-of-the-administrative-state/2017/02/23/03f6b8da-f9ea-11e6-bf01-d47f8cf9b643_story.html?utm_term=.17a1702bcb7a.

Rugh, Jacob S., and Douglas S. Massey. 2010. "Racial Segregation and the American Foreclosure Crisis." *American Sociological Review* 75 (5): 629–51.

Ryan, Mary P. 1981. *Cradle of the Middle Class: The Family in Oneida County, New York, 1790–1865*. Cambridge: Cambridge University Press.

Sahadi, Jeanne. 2018. "How High-Tax States May Try to Get Around the New SALT Deduction Cap." *CNN Money*, January 3. http://money.cnn.com/2018/01/03/pf/taxes/salt-deduction-high-tax-states/index.html?iid=EL.

"Saleet v. City of Lakewood: IJ Defeats Eminent Domain Abuse in Lakewood, Ohio." 2004. Institute for Justice. http://www.ij.org/saleet-v-city-of-lakewood.

Sandefur, Timothy. 2006. *Cornerstone of Liberty: Property Rights in 21st-Century America*. Washington: Cato Institute.

Sanders, Bernie. 2015. "Bernie Sanders Announces Bid for Democratic Presidential Nomination." https://berniesanders.com/bernies-announcement/.

Sarat, Austin, and Thomas R. Kearns. 1994. *The Rhetoric of Law*. Ann Arbor: University of Michigan Press.

—, eds. 2009. *Law's Violence*. Ann Arbor: University of Michigan Press.

Savage, Charlie. 2017. "Trump Is Rapidly Reshaping the Judiciary. Here's How." *New York Times*, November 11. https://www.nytimes.com/2017/11/11/us/politics/trump-judiciary-appeals-courts-conservatives.html.

Saxton, Alexander. 2003. *The Rise and Fall of the White Republic: Class Politics and Mass Culture in Nineteenth-Century America*. London: Verso.

Schachterle, Lance. 2009. "The Themes of Land and Leadership in 'The Littlepage Manuscripts.'" *Literature of the Early Republic: Annual Studies on Cooper and His Contemporaries* 1: 89–131.

Schermerhorn, Calvin. 2015. *The Business of Slavery and the Rise of American Capitalism, 1815–1860*. New Haven: Yale University Press.

Schiesl, Martin. 2013. *Residential Opportunity for All Californians: Governor Edmund G. 'Pat' Brown and the Struggle for Fair Housing Legislation, 1959–1963*. Los Angeles: The Edmund G. 'Pat' Brown Institute of Public Affairs, California State University.

Schmidt, Christopher W. 2011. "The Tea Party and the Constitution." *Hastings Constitutional Law Quarterly* 39 (1): 193–252.

———. 2013. "Defending the Right to Discriminate: The Libertarian Challenge to the Civil Rights Movement." In *Signposts: New Directions in Southern Legal History*, edited by Sally E. Hadden and Patricia H. Minter, 417–46. Athens: University of Georgia Press.

Schultz, David A. 1993. "Political Theory and Legal History: Conflicting Depictions of Property in the American Political Founding." *American Journal of Legal History* 37 (4): 464–95.

———. 2010a. "Courts Matter: The Supreme Court, Social Change, and the Mobilization of Property Rights Interests." In *Property Rights and Neoliberalism: Cultural Demands and Legal Action*, edited by Wayne V. McIntosh and Laura J. Hatcher, 11–27. Burlington: Ashgate.

———. 2010b. *Evicted! Property Rights and Eminent Domain in America*. Santa Barbara, CA: Praeger.

Sedgwick, A. G. 1882. "Constitutional Protection of Property Rights." *The North American Review* 135 (310): 253–65.

Self, Robert O. 2003. *American Babylon: Race and the Struggle for Postwar Oakland*. Princeton, NJ: Princeton University Press.

Seward, William Henry. 1884. *The Works of William H. Seward.* Vol. 2., edited by George E. Baker. Boston: Houghton, Mifflin and Company.

———. 1994. "Freedom in the New Territories. March 11, 1850 (In the Senate)." In *The Senate, 1789–1989: Classic Speeches, 1830–1993*, edited by Robert C. Byrd, 295–318. Washington: G.P.O.

Singer, Joseph William. 1982. "The Legal Rights Debate in Analytical Jurisprudence from Bentham to Hohfeld." *Wisconsin Law Review* 975: 986–1059.

———. 1991. "The Continuing Conquest: American Indian Nations, Property Law, and Gunsmoke." *Reconstruction* 1 (3): 97–103.

———. 2000. *Entitlement: The Paradoxes of Property.* New Haven: Yale University Press.

———. 2011. "Original Acquisition of Property: From Conquest & Possession to Democracy & Equal Opportunity." *Indiana Law Journal* 86 (3): 763–78.

———. 2014. *Property.* 4th ed. New York: Wolters Kluwer.

Sinha, Manisha. 2016. *The Slave's Cause: A History of Abolition.* New Haven: Yale University Press.

Sklansky, Jeffrey P. 2002. *The Soul's Economy: Market Society and Selfhood in American Thought, 1820–1920.* Chapel Hill: University of North Carolina Press.

Skocpol, Theda, and Vanessa Williamson. 2012. *The Tea Party and the Remaking of Republican Conservatism.* Oxford: Oxford University Press.

Smith, Adam. (1776) 1976. *An Inquiry into the Nature and Causes of the Wealth of Nations*, edited by R. H. Campbell and Andrew S. Skinner. Oxford: Oxford University Press.

Smith, Henry Nash. 1970. *Virgin Land: The American West as Symbol and Myth.* 2nd ed. Cambridge: Harvard University Press. 1950.

Smith, Paul. 2007. *Primitive America: The Ideology of Capitalist Democracy.* Minneapolis: University of Minnesota Press.

Snay, Mitchell. 2011. *Horace Greeley and the Politics of Reform in Nineteenth-Century America.* Lanham: Rowman & Littlefield.

Snowden, Kenneth A. 1995. "Mortgage Securitization in the United States: Twentieth Century Developments in Historical Perspective." In *Anglo-American Financial Systems: Institutions and Markets in the Twentieth Century*, edited by Michael D. Bordo and Richard Sylla, 261–98. Burr Ridge: Irwin Professional Publishing.

Society for the Abolition of All Slavery. 1842. *The Slavery of Poverty, with a Plan for its Abolition.* New York: Society for the Abolition of All Slavery.

Soederberg, Susanne. 2007. "Freedom, Ownership, and Social (In-)Security in the United States." *Cultural Critique* 65 (1): 92–114.

———. 2010. *Corporate Power and Ownership in Contemporary Capitalism: The Politics of Resistance and Domination.* London: Routledge.

Somin, Ilya. 2015. *The Grasping Hand: Kelo v. City of New London and the Limits of Eminent Domain.* Chicago: University of Chicago Press.

Sorkin, Andrew Ross. 2017. "Tax Cuts Benefit the Ultra Rich, but Not the Merely Rich." *New York Times*, December 18. https://www.nytimes.com/2017/12/18/business/dealbook/tax-bill-wealthy.html.

Spooner, Lysander. 1845. *The Unconstitutionality of Slavery*. Boston: Bela Marsh.
Stampp, Kenneth M. 1956. *The Peculiar Institution: Slavery in the Ante-bellum South*. New York: Knopf.
Stanley, Amy Dru. 1998. *From Bondage to Contract Wage Labor, Marriage, and the Market in the Age of Slave Emancipation*. Cambridge: Cambridge University Press.
"Statement of Policy." 1963. *California Real Estate Magazine*, October, 8–10.
Steinfeld, Robert J. 1991. *The Invention of Free Labor: The Employment Relation in English and American Law and Culture, 1350–1870*. Chapel Hill: University of North Carolina Press.
Stephenson, George M. 1917. *The Political History of the Public Lands, from 1840 to 1862: From Pre-Emption to Homestead*. Boston: R. G. Badger.
Stern, Sol. 1967. "The Call of the Black Panthers." *New York Times*, August 6, 186–87, 219–11.
Stern, Stephanie M. 2009. "Residential Protectionism and the Legal Mythology of Home." *Michigan Law Review* 107 (7): 1093–144.
Steward, Ira. 1868. *The Meaning of the Eight-Hour Movement.* Boston: I. Steward.
Stewart, Alvan. 1965. "A Constitutional Argument on the Subject of Slavery." 1837. In *Equal Under Law: The Antislavery Origin of the Fourteenth Amendment,* edited by Jacobus tenBroek, 281–95. New York: Collier.
"A Stucco House for $3600." 1910. *Ladies Home Journal*, April: 31.
Sugrue, Thomas J. 2005. *The Origins of the Urban Crisis: Race and Inequality in Postwar Detroit.* Princeton: Princeton University Press.
Tadman, Michael. 1989. *Speculators and Slaves: Masters, Traders, and Slaves in the Old South.* Madison: University of Wisconsin Press.
Taft, William Howard. 1894. "The Right to Private Property." *Michigan Law Journal* 3: 215–33.
Tait, Allison, and Luke Norris. 2011. "Narrative and the Origins of Law." *Law and Humanities* 5 (1): 11–22.
Tate, Charles. 1971. "Brimmer and Black Capitalism: An Analysis." In *Black Business Enterprise: Historical and Contemporary Perspectives*, edited by Ronald W. Bailey, 173–79. New York: Basic Books.
Teles, Steven M. 2008. *The Rise of the Conservative Legal Movement: The Battle for Control of the Law*. Princeton: Princeton University Press.
Thomas, Brook. 1984. "The Pioneers, or the Sources of American Legal History: A Critical Tale." *American Quarterly* 36 (1): 86–111.
Thrush, Glenn. 2020. "Full Transcript: President Trump's Republican National Convention Speech." *New York Times*, August 28. https://www.nytimes.com/2020/08/28/us/politics/trump-rnc-speech-transcript.html.
Tiedeman, Christopher G. 1890. *The Unwritten Constitution of the United States: A Philosophical Inquiry into the Fundamentals of American Constitutional Law.* New York: G.P. Putnam's Sons.
Tocqueville, Alexis de. (1835) 1969. *Democracy in America.* 2 vols. Garden City: Doubleday.
Toobin, Jeffrey. 2017. "Full-Court Press." *New Yorker*, April 17.

Torres, Sasha. 2003. *Black, White, and in Color: Television and Black Civil Rights*. Princeton: Princeton University Press.

Trigeaux, Robert. 2005. "Your Home Could Be Up for Grabs." *St. Petersburg Times* (South Pinellas), June 24, D1.

Trump, Donald. 2016. "Fighting the Establishment." Facebook, January 25. https://www.facebook.com/DonaldTrump/videos/10156563265515725/.

Tuchinsky, Adam. 2009. *Horace Greeley's New-York Tribune: Civil War-Era Socialism and the Crisis of Free Labor*. Ithaca: Cornell University Press.

Tully, James. 1994. "Rediscovering America: The Two Treatises and Aboriginal Rights." In *Locke's Philosophy: Content and Context*, edited by G. A. J. Rogers, 165–96. Oxford: Clarendon Press.

Underkuffler, Laura S. 2003. *The Idea of Property: Its Meaning and Power*. Oxford: Oxford University Press.

U.S. Census Bureau. 2020. *Quarterly Homeownership Rates by Race and Ethnicity of Householder: 1994 to Present*. https://www.census.gov/housing/hvs/data/histtab16.xlsx.

U.S. Census Office. 1832. *Abstract of the Returns of the Fifth Census*. 21 May. 23rd Cong., 1st sess., 1832. H. Doc. 269. Rpr. Duff Green, 1832.

U.S. Congress. 1826. House of Representatives. *Report of the Committee of Claims, in the Case of Marigny D'Auterive*. 30 January. 19th Cong., 1st sess., 1826. H. Rpt. 58, serial 141.

———. 1828. *Register of Debates*, 20th Congress, 2nd session.

———. 1848. *Legal Representatives of Antonio Pacheco*. 1848. 30th Cong., 1st sess., 9 February. H. Rep. 187, serial 524.

———. 1848. *Congressional Globe*, 30th Congress, 2nd session.

U.S. Constitution, art. 1, sec. 2, sec. 9.

———. art. 4, sec. 2.

———. amend. 5.

U.S. Government Accountability Office. 2006. HUD Homeownership Programs: Data Limitations Constrain Assessment of the American Dream Downpayment Initiative. https://www.gao.gov/products/GAO-06-677.

U.S. Supreme Court. 2004. Brief of Amici Curiae National Association for the Advancement of Colored People, AARP, Hispanic Alliance of Atlantic Country, Inc., Citizens in Action, Cramer Hill Resident Association, Inc., and the Southern Christian Leadership Conference in Support of Petitions, *Kelo v. City of New London*, 545 U.S. 469 (2005), No. 04-108.

Van Gelder, Sarah, ed. 2011. *This Changes Everything: Occupy Wall Street and the 99% Movement*. San Francisco: Berrett-Koehler.

Vance, J. D. 2016. *Hillbilly Elegy: A Memoir of a Family and Culture in Crisis*. New York: Harper.

Vandevelde, Kenneth J. 1980. "The New Property of the Nineteenth Century: The Development of the Modern Concept of Property." *Buffalo Law Review* 29 (2): 325–68.

Veblen, Thorstein. 1904. *The Theory of Business Enterprise*. New York: C. Scribner's Sons.

Veracini, Lorenzo. 2017. "Introduction: Settler Colonialism as a Distinct Mode of Domination." In *The Routledge Handbook of the History of Settler Colonialism*, edited by Edward Cavanagh and Lorenzo Veracini, 1–8. London: Routledge.

Vorenberg, Michael. 1993. "Abraham Lincoln and the Politics of Black Colonization." *Journal of the Abraham Lincoln Association* 14 (2): 22–45.

Waldron, Jeremy. 1988. *The Right to Private Property*. Oxford: Clarendon Press.

———. 2012. "Property and Ownership." *The Stanford Encyclopedia of Philosophy*. https://plato.stanford.edu/archives/win2016/entries/property/.

Warner, Sam Bass. 1962. *Streetcar Suburbs: The Process of Growth in Boston, 1870–1900*. Cambridge: Harvard University Press.

Washington, J. Charles. 1988. "*A Raisin in the Sun* Revisited." *Black American Literature Forum* 22 (1): 109–24.

Weber, Max. (1922)1978. *Economy and Society: An Outline of Interpretive Sociology*. 2 vols., edited by Guenther Roth and Claus Wittich. Berkeley: University of California Press.

Weems, Robert E. 2009. *Business in Black and White: American Presidents & Black Entrepreneurs in the Twentieth Century*. New York: New York University Press.

Weems, Robert E., and Lewis A. Randolph. 2001. "The National Response to Richard M. Nixon's Black Capitalism Initiative: The Success of Domestic Detente." *Journal of Black Studies* 32 (1): 66–83.

Wehner, Peter H. 2005. "Memo on Social Security." *Wall Street Journal*, January 5. https://www.wsj.com/articles/SB110496995612018199.

Weintraub, Jeff. 1997. "The Theory and Politics of the Private/Public Distinction." In *Private and Public in Thought and Practice: Perspectives on a Grand Dichotomy*, edited by Jeff Weintraub and Krishan Kumar, 1–42. Chicago: University of Chicago Press.

Weiss, Marc A. 1987. *The Rise of the Community Builders: The American Real Estate Industry and Urban Land Planning*. New York: Columbia University Press.

Weissmann, Jordan. 2012. "The Recession's Toll: How Middle Class Wealth Collapsed to a 40-Year Low." *The Atlantic*, December 4. https://www.theatlantic.com/business/archive/2012/12/the-recessions-toll-how-middle-class-wealth-collapsed-to-a-40-year-low/265743/.

Weld, Theodore Dwight. 1839. *American Slavery As It Is: Testimony of a Thousand Witnesses*. New York: American Anti-Slavery Society.

Wendt, Simon. 2007. *The Spirit and the Shotgun: Armed Resistance and the Struggle for Civil Rights*. Gainesville: University Press of Florida.

Weyl, Walter E. 1912. *The New Democracy: An Essay on Certain Political and Economic Tendencies in the United States*. New York: Macmillan.

"What Are Property Rights?. . .". 1964. *The Healdsburg Tribune*, May 14, 4.

"What Do the Negroes Want?". 1967. *New York Times*, November 19, 12 E.

Whitaker, Charles Harries. 1919. "Will the Kitchen Be Outside the Home?" *Ladies' Home Journal*, January, 66.

White, Eugene N. 2009. "Lessons from the Great American Real Estate Boom and Bust of the 1920s." Working Paper 15573. National Bureau of Economic Research. https://www.nber.org/papers/w15573.

Wiese, Andrew. 1999. "Black Housing, White Finance: African American Housing and Home Ownership in Evanston, Illinois, before 1940." *Journal of Social History* 33 (2): 429–60.

Wilkerson, William R. 2010. "Kelo v. New London, the Institute for Justice, and the Idea of Economic Development Takings." In *Property Rights and Neoliberalism: Cultural Demands and Legal Actions*, edited by Wayne V. McIntosh and Laura J. Hatcher, 59–74. Burlington: Ashgate.

Will, George F. 2004. "Despotism in New London." *Washington Post*, September 19, B07.

———. 2005. "Damaging 'Deference.'" *Washington Post*, June 24. http://www.washingtonpost.com/wp-dyn/content/article/2005/06/23/AR2005062301420.html.

Williams, Eric Eustace. 2005. *Capitalism & Slavery*. Kingston: Ian Randle Publishers.

Williams, Robert C. 2006. *Horace Greeley: Champion of American Freedom*. New York: New York University Press.

Wilson, L. H. 1964. "Editorial: Gettysburg–1964!" *California Real Estate Magazine*, July, 1.

Wirls, Daniel. 2007. "'The Only Mode of Avoiding Everlasting Debate': The Overlooked Senate Gag Rule for Antislavery Petitions." *Journal of the Early Republic* 27 (1): 115–38.

Wolf, Michael Allan. 2008a. "Hysteria versus History: Public Use in the Public Eye." In *Private Property, Community Development, and Eminent Domain*, edited by Robin Paul Malloy, 15–33. Burlington: Ashgate.

———. 2008b. *The Zoning of America: Euclid v. Ambler*. Lawrence: University Press of Kansas.

Wolfe, Patrick. 2006. "Settler Colonialism and the Elimination of the Native." *Journal of Genocide Research* 8 (4): 387–409.

Wolff, Edward N. 2013. "The Asset Price Meltdown, Rising Leverage, and the Wealth of the Middle Class." *Journal of Economic Issues* 47 (2): 333–42.

Wood, Gordon S. 1993. *Radicalism of the American Revolution*. New York: Vintage Books.

Woodmansee, Martha, and Mark Osteen. 1999. *The New Economic Criticism*. London: Routledge.

Workingman's Advocate. 1844. New York: John Windt and George Henry Evans.

Wray, L. Randall. 2005a. *Manufacturing a Crisis: The Neocon Attack on Social Security*. Policy Note 2005/2. Annandale-on-Hudson, NY: The Levy Economics Institute.

———. 2005b. *The Ownership Society: Social Security Is Only the Beginning . . .* Public Policy Brief No. 82. Jerome Levy Institute of Bard College.

Wright, Gavin. 2006. *Slavery and American Economic Development*. Baton Rouge: Louisiana State University Press.

Wright, Gwendolyn. 1983. *Building the Dream: A Social History of Housing in America*. Cambridge, MA: MIT Press.

Wright, Nathan. 1968. *Let's Work Together*. New York: Hawthorn Books.

Wyly, Elvin, C. S. Ponder, Pierson Nettling, Bosco Ho, Sophie Ellen Fung, Zachary Liebowitz, and Dan Hammel. 2012. "New Racial Meanings of Housing in America." *American Quarterly* 64 (3): 571–604.

Young America! 1845–49. New York: George Henry Evans.

Zahler, Helene Sara. 1941. *Eastern Workingmen and National Land Policy, 1829–1862*. New York: Columbia University Press.

Zakim, Michael, and Gary John Kornblith, eds. 2012. *Capitalism Takes Command: The Social Transformation of Nineteenth-Century America*. Chicago: University of Chicago Press.

Index

Page references for figures are italicized.

About the Author

Simone Knewitz is senior lecturer of North American Studies at the University of Bonn, Germany, where she also received her Ph.D. in 2010. She has also taught as deputy chair of American Studies at the University of Muenster and held research fellowships at George Mason University, George Washington University, and Harvard University. Simone Knewitz is the author of *Modernist Authenticities: The Material Body and the Poetics of Amy Lowell and William Carlos Williams* (Winter, 2014) as well as the coeditor, with Sabine Sielke and Christian Kloeckner, of the volumes *Beyond 9/11: Transdisciplinary Perspectives on Twenty-First Century U.S. American Culture* (Lang, 2013) and *Knowledge Landscapes North America* (Winter, 2016).

www.ingramcontent.com/pod-product-compliance
Ingram Content Group UK Ltd.
Pitfield, Milton Keynes, MK11 3LW, UK
UKHW020839290926
15470UKWH00004B/1444

9 781793 623751